About the author

Wilfred Cantwell Smith is Professor of the Comparative History of Religion and Chairman of the Committee on the Study of Religion at Harvard University. He has lived a fair part of his life in India and Pakistan and traveled widely throughout the Islamic world. He is the author of several important books, including *Islam in Modern History* (1957, 1977), *The Faith of Other Men* (1962, 1972); and *Faith and Belief* (1979). His writings have been translated into eight languages, including Arabic and Urdu. Professor Smith is an ordained minister of the United Church of Canada.

On Understanding Islam

Religion and Reason 19

Method and Theory
in the Study and Interpretation of Religion

MOUTON PUBLISHERS · THE HAGUE · PARIS · NEW YORK

On Understanding Islam

Selected Studies

WILFRED CANTWELL SMITH
Harvard University

MOUTON PUBLISHERS · THE HAGUE · PARIS · NEW YORK

Library of Congress Cataloguing in Publication Data

Smith, Wilfred Cantwell, 1916-
On understanding Islam

(Religion and reason ; 19)
Includes bibliographical references and index.
1. Islam—Collected works. I. Title. II. Series.
BP25.S6 297 81-871
ISBN 90-279-3448-7 AACR2

ISBN: 90-279-3448-7

Printed in the Netherlands

General Editor's Preface

At the present time a scholar of religion who lectures, reads papers and publishes will inevitably find his various products dispersed over a number of periodicals, *Festschriften* and other volumes, mostly published in different countries and often in different languages. This presents a problem which is especially pressing for those colleagues and students who want to follow the publications of a particular scholar over a number of years because of their scholarly standard and inner coherence of thought.

We are glad that Professor Wilfred Smith, an Islamicist of repute, has consented to bring together in one volume a selection of his contributions in the field of Islamic studies, papers and articles. Some of these have been published in non-Western journals, and others appear here for the first time. These contributions originated on different occasions, often in response to solicitations by colleagues and institutions. The record of their origin as contained in the various introductions shows an inter-human dimension of scholarly work which contrasts with those times when a scholar's findings were communicated mainly to his immediate pupils.

Professor Smith has never kept aloof from intellectual and moral engagement. Born in Toronto in 1916, he first studied Oriental Languages there, obtaining his B.A. in 1938. After two years of studying Theology and Oriental Languages at Cambridge, England, he went to Lahore where he taught Indian and Islamic History during the war, from 1941 to 1945. Here he published his *Modern Islām in India: A Social Analysis* in 1943. After the war he continued his study of Oriental Languages at Princeton University where he obtained his M.A. in 1947 and his Ph.D in 1948. After having spent another year in Lahore he was appointed Professor of Comparative Religion at McGill University, Montreal, in 1949, and in 1951 Director of the then just founded graduate Institute of

Islamic Studies at the same university. In 1957 his *Islam in Modern History* appeared. After a sabbatical year spent in India, Dr. Smith was appointed in 1964 Professor of World Religions at Harvard University, and Director of the Center for the Study of World Religions which was founded in 1957 and attached to the same university. In the meantime, in 1963, his *The Meaning and End of Religion: A New Approach to the Religious Traditions of Mankind* was published. After an interlude from 1973 until 1978, when he was Professor of Religion at Dalhousie University in Halifax, Canada, Dr. Smith returned to Harvard University in 1978 as Professor of the Comparative History of Religion, and Chairman, Committe on The Study of Religion. After some books published earlier, in 1979 his *Faith and Belief* appeared. In 1976 the anthology *Religious Diversity: Essays by Wilfred Cantwell Smith* had been published as a pocket book, edited and provided with a general introduction plus introductions to the different chapters by Dr. Willard G. Oxtoby. That book also contains a complete bibliography of Dr. Smith's publications up to 1975.

Anyone who is at all familiar with the main books of this author will recognize here problems and techniques of research which led to those books but which perhaps find a clearer formulation here. The great themes are the relations between different religious communities, the rise of particular religious orientations and movements, and specific problems with which Muslim communities have found themselves confronted in different historical and social situations both in the past and in recent times. The author's concern is the meaning that life and the universe have for Muslims in the light of the Islamic symbols, and the implications of a life lived within the particular symbol system of Islam. For him, Islam should be studied according to its historical and its non-mundane, 'transcendent', dimension which latter is mediated by revelation perceived by Muslims as the disclosure of a transcendent pattern of prescribed behavior. Moral responsibility linked to faith is recognized as a central fact of Islam over against which processes of reification and the rise of communalism are seen as degradations of faith and moral sense. Part IV, in particular, includes a penetrating reflection on how to interpret Muslim-Christian relations. Specific concepts and kinds of analysis are used to make the different religious traditions mutually intelligible. Dr. Smith stresses the existence of a joint Christian-Muslim history. Those readers familiar with the author's books on the modern period may find to their surprise essays here also dealing with what may be called classical Islam. With a keen analysis of basic concepts Professor Smith explores the dimension of faith and moral responsibility contained in early *kalām* texts.

It is not enough to say that Dr. Smith's work represents an effort of understanding on a level and a scale worth noting in Islamic studies and also beyond them. His particular, 'personalized' way of studying Islam itself deserves further attention. There is indeed, behind all the erudition and logical argumentation, an intricate relationship between the scholar's treatment of religion in terms of faith, tradition and truth perception, and his work on Islamic materials. Professor Smith reveals himself to be at the same time an Islamicist and a scholar of religious studies and also a thinker on religion, exploring the dimension of faith in Islam and in other traditions. This has led to several original interpretations of Islamic materials, to which the present volume testifies.

One of the current problems in Western scholarship concerned with religious data in non-Western cultures is that of grasping the meaning of those data for the people concerned, and the extent to which certain Western concepts may be helpful in grasping such meanings or, conversely, may create misunderstandings when applied indiscriminately. Throughout his work, Dr. Smith shows a self-critical attitude with regard to concepts and categories, and he wants to identify himself both as a historian and as an intellectual. He shows particular attention for the way in which religious matters have been conceptualized from within a given religious tradition and in particular religious schools and movements. It is perhaps precisely through his concern with the religious dimension of religious differences that he has become so strongly aware of the dangers of misunderstanding and has striven for improvement of the conceptual tools with which to study religious data. In Islamic studies this has meant that he has kept in mind, in his effort of understanding, that Muslims, too, would be potential critics.

It is hoped that this volume will find its way to scholars of Islam both Muslim and non-Muslim, as well as to a broader public whose interest for Islam 'beyond politics' has increased in recent years.

Utrecht, January 1980 JACQUES WAARDENBURG

Preface

In the course of my life I have been bold enough to write two substantial books on Islām, and have included substantial Islamic chapters in my two or three volumes on understanding the comparative history of religion more generally. In addition, on Islamic matters, I have written individual articles or given individual addresses, some published here and there in various journals, Festschriften, conference proceedings, and the like, some not previously published. Among these the most significant are here collected, and through the courtesy of the editor of the *Religion and Reason* series, made public.

The title that I have chosen, 'On Understanding Islām', has a double significance. First, in a quite straightforward way it enunciates a hope, I trust not too arrogantly, that these various pieces, arranged here as chapters constituting a more or less coherent book, may contribute to such understanding on the part of any who take the trouble to read this work. A sincere scholar naturally hopes that the studies on which he works and that he finally publishes will enable others to understand better the subject with which they deal. In the case where that subject is a religious tradition and its community and their faith, the matter becomes a mighty one; and understanding, a question delicate and profound. Misunderstanding is so easy and has been so common, of any religious position by outsiders, that one essays to overcome it, however partially, with some trepidation, and yet with stalwart courage. When in addition a modern writer on Islām has in view Muslim readers also, the enterprise is doubly venturesome; once again, trepidation and courage combine.

Secondly, however, the title suggests that in evidence here is a reflection on the very attempt towards understanding Islām; on what is involved in the endeavour of a scholar, himself a participant in another and often 'rival' religious process—the Christian—to understand. Accordingly, at the suggestion of the series editor, my friend and colleague Dr. Jacques Waardenburg, I have prefixed to each item in this collection a brief introductory note. Although each is minor, cumulatively they may illuminate the path along which one contemporary student of our religiously diverse world has travelled towards such understanding as he has been given the grace and has ferreted out the data to attain—of that world, and within it of the Muslim sector of our common humanity.

W.C.S

Contents

General Editor's Preface v
Preface ix
General Introduction xiii

PART ONE: GENERAL PRESENTATIONS
1. Islamic History as a Concept 3
2. The Shahādah, as Symbolic Representation of Muslims' Faith 26

PART TWO: SPECIFIC PRESENTATIONS
3. The Historical Development in Islām of the Concept of Islām as an Historical Development 41
   3.1 Introduction to the problem 42
   3.2 A study of the preliminary data 50
   3.3 The use of the word *islām* in Arabic book titles 64
4. Islamic Law: Its 'Sources' (*Uṣūl al-fiqh*) and *Ijtihād* 78
5. Islamic Law: *Sharīʿah* and *Sharʿ* 87
   5.1 The concept of *Sharīʿah* among some *mutakallallimūn* 88
6. Faith, in the Qur'ān; and its Relation to Belief 110
7. Faith, in Later Islamic History; the Meaning of *Taṣdīq* . 135
8. Faith, in Later Islamic History; the Meaning of *Arkān* .. 162

PART THREE: ISLĀM IN THE INDIAN CONTEXT; AND MUSLIM–HINDŪ RELATIONS
9. The Crystallization of Religious Communities in Mughul India 177
10. The '*Ulamā*' in Indian Politics 197
11. Aligarh and Religion: A Question 213
12. Religious Diversity: Muslim–Hindū Relations in India . 217

PART FOUR: MUSLIM–CHRISTIAN RELATIONS
13. Some Similarities and Some Differences Between Christianity and Islām 233
14. Muslim–Christian Interrelations Historically: An Interpretation 247
15. Muslim and Christian: Faith Convergence, Belief Divergence 265
16. Is the Qur'ān the Word of God? 282
Notes 301
Provenance 333
Publications of Wilfred Cantwell Smith 335
Selective Index 345

General Introduction

The first half of this volume deals with Islamics in and of itself, as it were internally; the second half (Parts III and IV) treats of Islamic involvement with the world around it. For any religious tradition, both are significant. The procedure in the former case (Parts I and II) is to consider specific concepts, with sufficient closeness to allow each to illuminate a way of perceiving the world, and what this entails. In Part I, the particular concepts are of a high order of generality in their import, so that these serve as introductory; in Part II, the items examined are more technical, although the implications are major, which is why they have been chosen. (To me it proves delightful, as well as rewarding, to find that the nuance of a particular grammatical form, for example, may serve as a clue to a profound human orientation to the cosmos.) Of the two sections on Islamic relations with others, Part III deals with India. The sector of the Islamic world that I know best, Pakistan and Muslim India, has for a thousand years been involved with the Hindū complex, and more recently with the British Rāj and Western-derived modernity. Part IV deals with Islamic relations with the Christian tradition—that of my own religious group—with which Islām has been involved throughout its time on earth, theologically, historically, and in many other ways—as well as being involved today through, for instance, scholarship such as this.

Eight (that is: half) of the chapters here have not previously been published in the Western world; one has not previously appeared in English; and three have not before been published at all.

PART ONE

General Presentations

1

Islamic History as a Concept

This piece, here published for the first time, was an address given to the annual meeting of the Middle East Studies Association of North America in 1975. The invitation to speak to the concluding plenary session of that gathering (held that year in Louisville, Kentucky) provided an opportunity to put together and to clarify certain thoughts that I had been developing on this highly general topic, in seeming contrast to the more meticulous work on detail that was also occupying me at about that time, such as the study of the meaning of the word arkān *(below, Part II of this present volume) which was published a few months later. To understand the life of Muslims involves an appreciation both of the comprehensive framework of the whole, and of specific items within it. It seems good to give careful consideration to both; we begin this collection with reflection on the over-all theme.*

The two-word phrase 'Islamic History' falls often from our lips quite glibly. Yet glibness here, I would suggest, is out of order. The monumental mightiness of the matters involved should give us pause. Each word is a mouthful, over which the sensitive might well choke; let alone, the two together. 'History' denotes a reality broader, deeper, more complex, more mysterious, than any human being can possibly understand. 'Islām', similarly. Not to be astonished, tremulous, diffident, dismayed, agog, in pronouncing either term would be obtuse; a phrase that links the two is well-nigh overwhelming.

At the very least it is worth our careful reflection together for a few moments.

I distinguish between historiography and history. By the word 'history' some mean an account of past events; but I mean those events themselves, and the dynamic process in which they are embedded: the course of human affairs, which we historians attempt, always inadequately, to discern, to understand, and as historiographers to make knowable to others, and intelligible. It is important that our concept of history formally and explicitly transcend our awareness of its content. Just as the world of nature is a reality to which scientific knowledge approximates, so too the reality of history is something to which our historiography only approximates, less or more closely.

Any of us from the outside who visit the Muslim world, especially if we stay in a city, are probably involved during the day in busyness and the hubbub of activity that distract or drown this out. In the early morning, on the other hand, if we are awake in time to listen, through the cool night air and against the still background of the first white streaks of dawn we may hear the *adhān* call to prayer as it floats melodiously: a splendid recitative, voiced from a nearby mosque, full of artistic beauty and—particularly, of course, for the Muslims themselves—full of rich meaning. I myself used to hear it so in Lahore. It is no small matter that the same call, at the same times of the day, in the same magnificent Arabic, is heard throughout the Muslim world: from Indonesia or the Philippines or China, through India and Central Asia and Iran, to the eastern and southern Mediterranean and down into Africa. It is a large world; its inhabitants form a large community; Islam is in every sense a *great* affair. The Muslim in Lahore, or in Samarqand or Kano, does not feel isolated, but is vividly conscious of belonging to a living community spread across the globe.

Not only does the call put him effectively in a setting that stretches far in space, from Java to Morocco. Also, it places him in an historical setting, stretching back in time, to a past glory of which he is both aware and proud. The same call to prayer, with its serene dignity, has been repeated five times each day over the centuries. By it, and the faith that it expresses, the Muslim is firmly related to a past that stands imposingly behind him, bequeathing him traditions and institutions that have stood the test of age, and are bound to patterns of life that made his ancestors great. A thousand years ago his civilization was the impressive world leader, along with China and Japan; the West was the third world, an under-developed area. Who knows how things will stand a thousand years hence?

In this call and in various other ways, the Islamic complex relates its participants to a present-day, world-wide community, and to an historical past. More important than either of these, however, it relates them to God. That call to prayer has profound secondary associations. Yet essentially, we must remember, it is a personal call, to each Muslim, to pray. It, and the many other symbols and rites and habits through which his faith is expressed and mediated, lift the individual out of his humdrum workaday world and place him in a setting that is theocentric, facing God. The morning call summons him in the name of Cosmic Truth to be up and doing. The faith that it intones is to permeate his life from dawn to nightfall, and from his inner chamber to his busy shop in the crowded market-place. Over the centuries, the Muslim has regulated the smallest detail of his life by the sacred law, and still to-day the memory of that suffusing spirit is alive.

Islam historically has changed the face of the world. Historically, it has also changed the heart of the Muslim. Space, time, and God are linked, not to say fused, at least ideally, in the Islamic moment. Space and time constitute the realm that we regularly designate as 'history'; that call to prayer exemplifies that insofar as history has been Islamic history, not merely space and time but also God are involved, are held in unity, *tawḥīd*. The *adhān* in particular, and Muslim history in general, pose the question of the significance of history, religiously—or: of faith, historically. To use one particular phrasing to designate the matter, they introduce us to the relation between time and eternity.

Western historians have tended at times to imagine, or to assume, that it is possible to deal with the historical without raising that portentous issue. A neat dichotomizing of the temporal and the eternal, of the secular and the spiritual, of the historical and the transcendent, is calculated to evade this problem. A study of Islamic history, if it be serious, will not let us off the hook so lightly. To study Islamic history is to study that relation, empirically manifested, historically operative.

I re-iterate, then, that we must remember with what a mighty category we have to do when we speak the category 'history'. The development of the concept of history in the nineteenth-century West was an enormous intellectual achievement—as great, one could contend, as the development of science. Indeed I am inclined to the view that an eventual fusion of these two, perhaps beginning now to emerge, will be requisite to our salvaging of our own Western civilization from disaster. I leave that aside for the moment, although we shall return to it finally. I myself am an historian, through and through. Yet (or therefore) I argue that our concept 'history' requires critical analysis. Great though it be as our inheritance, the category yet needs refining if it is to serve us adequately, for our apprehension of reality, specifically the reality of human affairs. One of the joys and responsibilities of studying a major civilization other than one's own, as we Western Islamicists are engaged in doing, is that it can help enormously towards enabling us all in the West to become intelligently self-critical of our own Western conceptual patterns. Our loyalty to a pursuit of truth enables us to move beyond a loyalty to our own predilections, and those of our society. We see the danger of subordinating the data that we study to the ideational patterns of our own always limited vision, and thus we are enabled to move significantly forward towards an improvement of our own windows on the world.

This is so particularly in the matter before us. The eighteenth and nineteenth centuries, in the West, understood humankind's religious life even less than do we, and thought it more negligible. To a considerable extent the concept of history that we have inherited tends to omit the religious, even the spiritual, altogether, and certainly the transcendent (this last, dogmatically?).

It would be idle to study Islamic history if this did not contribute to our better understanding of human history generically. We also are human; we also are historical. To enlarge one's apprehension of Islamic or of any other human history is to enhance one's self-awareness.

Let us see how this works in this specific case. In particular, we shall see that it disrupts any complacency in supposing that the historical and the transcendent are two separate categories.

Let us begin in the realm of art. My reason for this particular starting-point will become more fully evident later on. Yet right away one may recognize, in considering any work of art, that it is a synthesis of two elements, two that some have thought to call respectively historical and timeless. The word 'timeless' may or may not please you; I am not too happy with it—my own vocabulary tends to opt for 'transcendent'. Nor is the word 'historical' in this polarity felicitous; for it suggests that what it names is discrete from the other, whereas human history is especially characterized by their intertwining. Whatever one's phrasing to describe the situation, however, the fact is clear. Art has two dimensions. This fact sets our problem.

Each painting or sculpture, each piece of music, each poem that human beings produce has a context. In addition, each has also an intrinsic meaning; or shall we say, a human meaning. The former quality is never missing. No artistic creation but emerges out of and reflects its particular time-and-place setting (often called its historical setting). Nonetheless, if it not transcend that setting, then it is of little interest, and of little worth. The difference between great art and ephemeral lies here. Yet the difference between great art and ephemeral is not that great art has less of the historical, but rather that it has more of the timeless. In truly great art, the contextual is not negated; it is used, is subsumed, and is transcended.

Religious people are found saying that the eternal breaks through into time. This seems to imply that it was not there already. One's ability to see it is no doubt a breakthrough. Art, one might say, is an instance of something that breaks our ordinary obtuseness in such a way as to enable us to recognize a certain dimension as indeed there.

The literary critic Northrop Frye has remarked[1] about one of Shakespeare's great plays: 'You wouldn't go to *Macbeth* to learn about the history of Scotland—you go to it to learn what a man feels like after he's gained a kingdom and lost his soul'. Frye was thinking of eleventh-century Scotland; one cannot deny that *Macbeth* is an historical document of Shakespeare's own time, and students of the play may and should know something, or even much, of that early-seventeenth-century context. It would be rather pitiful, however, not to move beyond that. For reasons such as Frye gave, the play is as relevant to the twentieth century as it was to the seventeenth; though it had two links with the seventeenth, one of which no longer obtains. It has two links with the twentieth, too, but one of them is different, one the same. If you or I see or read *Macbeth*, that fact is then an event in our century; and if we are merely entertained by it, or merely 'interested' in it, then it remains at the level of mundane history. If, on the other hand, we are moved by it, are open to its transcendentally human quality, if what Frye calls our souls—I do not know what you call them; but whatever your vocabulary, I hope that you have not failed to notice that they are there—if our souls are changed, then from the experience there is a link of some sort not only with eleventh-century Scotland and seventeenth-century England and twentieth-century America or wherever, but also with that timeless or transcendent realm to which great artists help us to actualize our inherent potentiality to rise.

Similarly, The World of Islam Festival in London presently will bring together, one hears, many striking examples of the art of Muslims over the ages and around the world. These will illustrate Islamic history and culture, and those of us who can visit it bringing to it much historical-background awareness will be enabled the more adequately to appreciate the exhibition. Yet, unless also we can appreciate the art as art, as things of beauty, of intrinsic human significance, we shall have missed something. Art illuminates the world, and not merely illustrates its period. Unless the display helps to elucidate the human condition as such, and unless it can be appreciated by the non-specialist, the non-historian, then the exhibition will have failed.

If Beethoven were interesting only to musicologists, he would not really be interesting at all.

The optimum for approaching any work of art is, of course, to know both dimensions. It is possible, alas, to discern either alone. One can fail to appreciate any aesthetic quality in a given instance; alternatively, one may fail to appreciate any historical background. In the former case, there is erudition without sensitivity. The latter case, a seeing of the aesthetic dimension alone, can lead to a lowering even of that aesthetic appreciation—or eventually, especially in a later or radically different cultural situation, to a loss of it.

The academic task in such matters is delicate: to enhance historical awareness and historical criticism in such a way as to further accurate appreciation of the aesthetic, the transcendent—not to substitute for it.

To some degree, this type of consideration applies not only to art, but to all human matters. Certainly, to all humane matters. In this as in other ways, human life is like a work of art. Some might wish to insist that human life, individual and corporate, *is* a work of art, less or more effectively wrought; so that to study its affairs at any lower level is to distort, or to understand inadequately. This is perhaps to see things in too deliberate a fashion; better would be *vice versa*? Art is intrinsically human. It is not an addendum tacked on to human life, nor an ornament. It is not an extra frill that may be dispensed with in the apprehension of human affairs, of interest only to those who happen to be interested in it, as one among other aberrant extras. Rather, to fail to appreciate art is to fail to appreciate humankind.

The human is more than art, but includes art as an integral component.

Man is more than science, also; yet one understands neither humanity nor the scientific enterprise unless one sees science too as essentially, integrally, human—and man as essentially, integrally, a being that, as Aristotle said, desires to know, and to whom the rest of reality is in some degree intelligible. (To this scientific matter we shall be returning in a moment or two.)

Human life has a transcendent dimension, to use the vocabulary that I personally affect. The phrasing is certainly not important, but to see the aspect of human life that it connotes, is. Human life not only has, but from the beginning—from palæolithic times—has had, such a dimension. Accordingly, human history is paradoxical. Unlike the history of galaxies or seemingly of hippopotami, the history of men and women and children is that movement through time and space of persons for whom time and space constitute only part of the truth about their living, their being. Every work of art has a timeless dimension: it is the more compelling, the greater be the art. Every human life has a timeless dimension, the more salient the more truly human the person. Human history is the arena of the interplay between the temporal and the timeless—between the mundane and the eternal, the transcendent, or however one wish to call it. Human beings are self-transcending beings—a perplexing fact, admittedly; indeed, mysterious: yet an observational fact, nonetheless. One facet of this is that human beings are free: not fully, certainly, and yet not negligibly. We are conditioned—by our past and by our environment; that is, by mundane history. Yet we are not altogether determined by them, by it. The minority of thinkers who disagree with this do so out of dogmatic pre-conviction, not on the basis of evidence. To be a human being means to be partially open to sources of inspiration, aspiration, courage, loyalty, love, imagination, obligation, rationality, integrity, not given in one's mundane environment.

History is not a closed system.

All this is especially relevant, of course, for humanity's religious life. I am not suggesting that the non-historical dimension of human life is the religious dimension: that religion is concerned with the timeless. There have been certain other-worldly stances that have propounded some such view, perhaps; yet these are much rarer even among, for instance, Hindūs than is often supposed. Rather, what I am urging is that to live historically, as all human beings do, with a non-historical or a non-temporal, non-mundane dimension to their life, constitutes that life as human. The religious is what one does about this prior fact.

Human life is like a work of art; this is true of what it means to be human. Man is more than a link between causes; he and she are more than an item within a determined sequence. This is not a religious belief, but an empirical observation. Religious belief is an interpretation of it. The Islamic, for instance, to which we shall come in a moment, is one particular interpretation. The fact, however, is universal. If there be any who do not agree—do not understand what I am averring, do not see these facts, or whose own religious or irreligious beliefs stand in the way of seeing it, at least such will note that the overwhelming majority of intelligent people at most times and places throughout human history have seen the world so, and still do. *That* is a fact, certainly, which one must recognize, and must struggle to understand.

The work of art that Muslims produce is, becomes, Islamic art. The work of art that is the lives of Muslims, and in extension over a sequence of centuries the history that is constituted by the corporate human lives of Muslims, is similarly Islamic. In both cases, the artistic and the historical, the inspiration is in part Islamic, in part personal, in part contingent. The material in both cases is contingent, temporal. The result in both cases is in part contingent, in part timeless, transcendent. In the one case it is Islamic art, in the other case Islamic history.

Those who know anything about the history of the Jewish people know, of course, that for Jews, one day in seven is the Sabbath, holy unto the Lord; but will recognize that he or she would be a fatuously inept historian who imagined that a history of Judaism as a religion would be a history of life on those Sabbaths, while a secular history of the Jews would be a history of the other six days of each week. Rather, the symbolic sacred time of the Sabbath redeems and gives significance to, permeates, and largely shapes, the living of the entire week. Jewish history is a seamless whole, drastically different from what it would otherwise have been because every week throughout its course has been lived in the light of the Sabbath, and of what the Sabbath signifies. I am contending that no historian can understand the history of those other six days in Jewish life who does not understand what is happening on the Sabbath; that particular pattern that has served Jews for concentrating and symbolizing and giving pattern to their human involvement in transcendence. Theists have a vocabulary calculated to explicate what was happening; those who are not theists are challenged to hammer out some other interpretation of these centrally important matters, and are certainly not exonerated from wrestling with them, taking them very seriously.

Similarly, of course, with Christian history, but since that is my own, I shall not elaborate it, lest it be thought special pleading.

Similarly with Islamic history. It too has been not in two sectors, a religious and a secular. Rather, Islamic history in its totality has been what it has been because each day of that history has been lived by men and women whose lives have been enacted in a context that was mundane and, less or more richly, vividly, in a spirit that was transcendent. *Every* day began with that *adhān*, that call to prayer. And the history of every day has been in part (perhaps small part) shaped by it. More accurately, one should say that the everyday history of Muslims has been in part shaped by a bilateral truth: on the one hand, the *adhān*; on the other, the fact that we human beings are the kind of creature who know how to, and do, respond to such things: to realities in us and in our world that such things symbolize and reveal.

The business of the Islamic historian is to discern, to understand, and to make intelligible, the amalgam of mundane and divine without which the movement would not have been human, let alone Islamic. The Islamic has been that particular form of our generic human involvement in earth and heaven.

It is a mistake to think of the Islamic as one of the several ways of being religious. Rather, for fourteen centuries the Islamic has been one of the salient ways of being human.

Let me suggest three levels at which Islamic history offers itself for apprehension; three steps, if one will, that an outsider must take if he or she is to understand that history; three modes of this reality that we designate in our overly facile phrase, 'Islamic History'.

First, Islamic history is the framework within which Muslims have so lived. To live a human life is to live within a temporal context, a mundane framework, and to be conditioned, circumscribed, characterized, and yet not finally determined by it. Freedom, creativity, bungling, are individual or group responses of persons to situations that are historically given. In the case of Muslims—with the partial exception of those few who have lived as small minorities within others' cultures—the environment within which they have lived their personal lives, an environment in space and in time, has been what we as observers call Islamic history. So far it has gone through what may be termed three major periods. These may be called the classical, the mediaeval, the modern. These were a predominantly Arabic-speaking phase; there followed a predominantly Arabic-and-Persian cultural phase, presently giving way to a multilingual, with Arabic, Persian, Turkish, Urdū, Malay, and the like; these have been followed by a modern era about whose salient characteristics there is as yet no clear consensus. Geographically, the center of population, and perhaps of gravity, has shifted to the Indian Ocean area; linguistically, this is an era where all leaders of thought and society in the Muslim world have been and are, not merely bi-lingual, but linguistically bi-cultural, each knowing, and thinking in, at least one European language in addition to at least one Islamic language; and so on with economic, political, technological, and other involvements. Some analysts still affect a hoary polarity, to describe this era, between traditional and modern, as if that characterized what is happening; but that has been true ever since the beginning: all Muslims from the year one *hijrī*, like all human beings since the year one on any scale, have waked up every morning to live between what was then traditional and what was that day new. The establishment of an Umawī empire; al-Shāfiʿī's launching of a concept *Sunnat al-nabī*; the fall of Baghdād to Hulagu; the spread of the Ṣūfī orders: all were innovations presenting the Muslim world with a modernization problem much as have recent technological or economic involvements.

At this level, one's task is to apprehend the richness and variety, the dynamic and power, the depth, intricacy, beauty, and bathos of Islamic history: the range of human potentialities that were realized, and the changing pattern plus persisting continuity of their realizations. We all know a little of this. The more one knows, the better; but also the more one knows, the more vivid one's sense of how far this reality transcends our grasp. A life-time study is far too little, of course, to rise to this task, although even a little that some of us have done is enough to be entrancing and to let one begin to see the point. Our task at this moment, however, is neither that life-time's work, nor some small sector of it; but rather a reflection on seeing that history as a whole, and as a concept.

A basic point to be made here is that history still continues.

On November 8, 1980—a day not far off—the first fourteen centuries of Islamic history will come to a close. It is of the utmost importance, I suggest, that anyone considering Islamic history should realize with vivid sensitivity that *one* of the dramatic possibilities is that the most interesting, most creative, even most profoundly religious, sector of that history may lie in the future, not in the past. At the very least, one must recognize that Islamic history is still today very much in process. When I arrived in Harvard a decade and more ago, I found in the curriculum a course entitled 'Islamic History' which covered the period up to, in effect, the fall of Baghdād in 1258. There was another course listed in the university catalogue and entitled 'Near Eastern History', which continued the story from that point on. When I arrived in Lahore twenty-some years earlier, a course at the university there entitled 'Islamic History' was still more restricted, to the early centuries of Arab history; even the Muslim period of Indian history was omitted (was studied under another heading), and a great deal else. I predict that a time will come when both universities will recognize that this was wrong. The historical perception embedded in this tacit affirmation that Islamic History came to an end long since (an affirmation made casually in both cases, and on quite divergent grounds) is, I suggest, false—on at least two scores. For one thing, it fails to recognize the post-classical, or mediaeval, Islamic exuberance in the fourteenth to seventeenth centuries, of which among Western Islamicists for instance the late lamented Marshall Hodgson has striven mightily and marvellously to set us right. Islamic creativity—political, artistic, intellectual—in the Ottoman, Ṣafavī, and Mughul empires and elsewhere, not only, are involved but also expansion, in Africa and Indonesia and other far parts of the world. Secondly, the perception was false insofar as it postulated, at least in the Harvard case, once again that Western turn-of-the-century habit of thinking of Asia in general and of religion in general as *passées*: the ruthless insistence of modern secularism upon seeing current developments, self-triumphantly, as indisputably Westernizing secularist.

I do not know the future; nor do I feel that anyone is a good historian who imagines that he or she can know it, and especially not if one surreptitiously assumes that history, particularly the history of other peoples, is of course going in one's own direction. I certainly cannot predict that the next fourteen hundred years of Islamic history will be more spectacular than these last fourteen hundred; nor anyone else, that they will not be. I admit that a strong argument could be mounted that the signs of an Islamic renascence are less clear today than I thought that I discerned twenty years ago when I wrote *Islam in Modern History*. On the other hand, he or she would be a bold and venturesome prophet who was ready yet to opine that the increase in the price of oil will not prove of significancc primarily in the religious history of the Muslim peoples.[2]

Westerners have grown accustomed to treating economics as determinative. I have reservations, but we need not here quarrel about that, and one may go as far as one likes in regarding economic matters as major in Islamic history throughout its course, and until today, and yet it is still Islamic history in which it has played and no doubt continues to play its role.

My point is that economics also has been, and still is, a factor not alongside the Islamic, but within the Islamic complex. (This will be true even if, as may happen, the future religious history of our race subsumes, rather than preserves as separate, the various traditions.)

For it is a fallacy growing out of the particularities of the modern West to think of religion as one of the factors in human life, one among others. To impose this Western-cultural aberration on one's understanding of other civilizations is to distort. I would repeat my thesis that the Islamic has not been a particular way of being religious, but rather a particular way of being human. Economics is certainly important in human life, as are many other matters. Yet let none of them blind us to the fact that that life is human; and this means, in the Muslim case, that that history is Islamic.

It is this factorizing view, also, that was in part responsible in the Western case for calling only the classical period Islamic history. In this outlook, many factors in the development of the Near East from the seventh century A.D. to the thirteenth were at play, and during this particular era the Islamic factor appears to have been salient. Hence, to call this period 'Islamic history' can even be thought of as a kind of compliment to Islām in those days. As I have on more than one occasion stressed, however, Islām is not a factor in the life of Muslims. Rather (unless hypocritically idealized), it is the pattern that the various factors form. It is the meaning that the otherwise disparate elements have. It is the coherence and the quality of those otherwise diverse elements. It is the meaning that life in its variegated profusion has.

Islām is not the meaning that the Islamic symbols have for a Muslim; rather, it is the meaning that life and the universe have, in the light of those symbols.

Certain specific elements, themselves evolving dynamically in the course of history, have served to purvey this meaning, to foster the coherence, to enable the pattern to hold: elements such as the Qur'ān, the law, and the other overtly 'religious' items. These, however, mediate and express and nurture, but they do not constitute, the Islamic quality of Islamic living and Islamic history. The Qur'ān, the law, the mosques, the poetry of the Ṣūfīs, the *adhān*, and all the rest would have had but minor significance were it not that they enabled Muslims to deal with other matters, from medicine to military defeat, and from economics to ecology, in the particular ways that they did deal with them—ways that *are* Islamic history.

This brings us to my second level. The first was that Islamic history has constituted the framework within which Muslims have lived their human lives. The second is that it can be seen also as the goal of those lives. Islamic history has been Islamic in intention as well as in background.

Muslim men and women across the centuries have found themselves born into and surrounded by a world inherited from earlier generations of Muslims and stamped with an Islamic quality. The art by which their sensibilities were refined we call Islamic art (they did not know that it was that); the institutions by which their practices were moulded we call Islamic institutions; and generally, the context or framework for their living was that historical context or framework that we call Islamic. In every case, however, not only did they inherit this environment, willy-nilly; but in turn they also contributed to it, more often willy than nilly. They rejoiced to be Muslims; and the miniscule or large addendum that their living contributed to the on-going structure, and that they in turn bequeathed to generations following them, was not merely a mechanical reaction to that context but, they being human, was a small or large creative modification of it, fashioned in part by their choice, their will, their freedom. To some degree, like other human beings, they exercised that choice, that will, that freedom in mundane, selfish, petty, mean, or corrupt ways; but to some degree also, being human, they did so in visionary and inspired and lofty and transcending ways. Their vision, such inspiration as came their way, such loftiness as they attained, such transcendence as they were enabled to aspire to or to sense, took one or another Islamic form. The Islamic was the channel and the pattern through which was made visible their openness to transcendence, their human awareness of mystery and greatness, of beauty and truth and goodness.

One may or may not like their vision, their particular sense of mystery and greatness. Their awareness of beauty and truth and justice may or may not converge with one's own. Their response to being human may or may not jibe with the observer's response. That is the observer's problem. All that I am saying is that Islamic history has been what it has been, is what it is, and will be what it will be, because the Muslim response to being human has been, is, and quite possibly will continue to be, Islamic. Human beings are the creators, and not merely the victims, of history.

My second point, then, is that not only has Islamic history made Muslims, individually and corporately, what they have been; but also that those Muslims, *qua* Muslims, have made Islamic history what it has been. Islamic history has made Muslims Muslim. Muslims have made Islamic history Islamic.

The monumental significance of this fact must not escape us. For the Islamic relation to history has been quite special. In a sentence, certainly overly simplified and yet not absurd, the Muslim venture has been a vast endeavour to bend history to the will of God. Muslims have set out to *make* history Islamic—in a sense that we can understand only if we study the Qur'ān with drastic thoroughness, and then study and appreciate the elaborations and vicissitudes and innovations and diversities of the *tafāsīr* over the centuries; and the development of *fiqh*, and the machinations of the Macchiavellian politicians, and the poetry of the Ṣūfīs, and so on and on. We can understand, only if we listen with care to that *adhān* that summoned them to face each new day as it came along.

The Islamic ideal as apprehended by varying groups of Muslims has varied in time and space, and has persisted in diversified continuity through varying times and spaces. The ideal has elicited the effective response of Muslims in dramatically varying degree. Many another objective, conscious or unconscious, petty or grandiose, nasty or noble, has intertwined in its operation. Nonetheless, this ideal has seldom been totally absent, and perhaps never far away. For the entire Islamic movement has been a history-oriented enterprise—in a fashion that differentiates it, for instance, not only from Hindū but from Buddhist and even from Christian. Christian endeavours over the centuries to set up, for example, the Kingdom of God on Earth have been sporadic—intermittent with doctrines of a separation between Church and State. As a result Western history has seldom been Christian history; perhaps nowhere outside Byzantium. And Indian history has almost deliberately *not* been Hindū history. It has by no means been central to the Hindū genius to make history Hindū. Even the enormously energetic Buddhist missionary movement has cheerfully interpenetrated, and on principle accepted co-existence with, other movements in China, Japan, South-East Asia—so that there has not been, and it has not been intended that there be, a Buddhistic history comparable formally to Islamic history. In the Weltanschauung of Muslims, God has been seen as operating through the Muslim community to render history Islamic—that is, to have it rise to His will for it (*riḍā*'). Muslims have in varying degrees been well aware that the material through which He was working to this end was recalcitrant, as well as that His will was in part inscrutable; so that the actualities of Islamic history were recognized as approximating to that divine will in problematic (sometimes highly problematic) ways. At this *second* level, Islamic history has been and is today Islamic problematically, yes; but not negligibly. (Theoretically, the problem is the relation between *riḍā*', or *riḍwān*, and *mashī'ah*.)

(The Muslim reason for thinking at times of only the earliest period as Islamic History, has been the subsequent tendency to mythologize that period, omitting human foibles, contingency, and the mundane from a perception of that pristine era. The mixture may differ from time to time and from place to place, no doubt; at no time and at no place, however, is human history not a mixture of, an interaction between, the mundane and the transcendent. This is what it means to be human.)

We pass, finally, to our third level, where we must in fact move beyond the notion of Islām as an historical phenomènon. Of the various articles that I have published, the one whose title most titillates me is 'The Historical Development in Islām of the Concept of Islām as an Historical Development' [See below in this present collection, pp. 41-77]. As is well known, Muslims were almost from the beginning among the world's greatest historiographers. Yet for many centuries Islām was for them the name not of an historical movement but of a personal relationship to the ultimate truth of the universe, or of the personal act of self-dedication by which one responded to that truth and to its claims upon one. Only gradually did it become the name of the overt corporate results of that act, of the institutional complex of patterns resulting from the personal relationship, the name of a system. It was in the second half of Islamic history thus far that the term became at all widespread as the name of a religious system as an ideal; and only in very recent times that it has become the name of such a system empirically, in its historical and ever-changing development.

Specifically on the historical matter, not even in our own day, except peripherally, have Muslims, under Western ('modern') influence, de-transcendentalized their concept of Islamic history to the point of perceiving it, the way Westerners have been pushed by their own prejudices towards doing, as one subordinate sector among others within world history generally, under a ceiling posited by a this-worldly naturalism.

It is well known that Ṭabarī and others perceived world history as a whole and what we call Islamic history as taking its appointed place within this comprehensive drama; so that the point that I am now endeavouring to make is subtle. Let me see whether I can make it clear. For I feel that there is here a quite basic issue. It involves becoming critical of our own presuppositions about history, and indeed about humankind; but then, I need hardly belabour the point that if one is to understand a civilization other than one's own, one has to transcend one's own predilections, and to be self-critical of one's own assumptions. This last point that I would proffer is delicate and difficult, yet rewarding.

Again, to put the point in a nutshell, oversimplifying yet perhaps not absurdly, one must face the question as to whether Islām is a subsection of history, or *vice versa*. The former possibility we can see readily enough. What does the latter mean: history as a subsection of Islām?

Before approaching this, let me make a detour via that matter of science and history once again. At issue in these matters are questions as to which of one's categories are to be considered more basic than the others. There are some moderns for whom the category of 'science' is so ultimate that they would wish to make their understanding of history scientific; and even in some sense also, their understanding of humanity. For such minds, man is what science does or can or will adjudicate him and her as being. For me, on the other hand, history, and certainly humankind, are much more profound categories than is science. Science has arisen historically, is developing historically; its truths are just as historically relative as are any others, and in some ways conspicuously more so; and the role of science in culture will change historically in the future, quite possibly for the better. Certainly so far as humankind is concerned, I see science as a human achievement. It is one of the great things that we human beings have produced, certainly one of the most brilliant and most powerful; yet it is but one among others. I would take a humane view of science rather than a scientific view of man.

History is a wider, deeper, greater category than is science. Yet history, many have held, is not itself the final category. It is possible, and many would urge that it is right, to see the human as a category greater, wider, deeper, and more ultimate even than history. What does this mean? It is true that each of us is born at an historical time and place, and lives within an historical context, and dies. Yet it is not the case that the historical exhausts the human. At least, most intelligent persons have held this; and it is obtuse not to understand what they have been getting at: what the grounds for this judgement are, and what the meaning of it is. If it be true at all, it is true for every human life, presumably. Here, however, we are concerned only with the Islamic instance. The Islamic, I have urged, is the particular shape of the way in which Muslims have been human. What is meant, then, by saying that history is a facet of the Islamic, rather than *vice versa*?

It is not difficult to understand that Islamic art, for example, may be seen either as one sort of art, or as one aspect of Islām. Islamic art may be treated in the art department of a Western university, as one instance of the many kinds of art that have been produced by persons here and there throughout the world. Islamic art may be treated also within an Islamics programme in such a university, as one of the ways in which the Islamic spirit has expressed itself, one of the forms in which Islamic culture has been crystallized, one of the illustrative and then formative instances of Islamic life.

The same is true of, for example, Islamic theology. It may be considered as one form, among others, of theologizing. Alternatively, it may be considered as one way in which the Islamic enterprise has expressed itself: as an articulation in rationalistic prose of Islamic faith. That faith has found expression in many ways: in Ṣūfī forms and sensibilities, in ritual, in moral-legal patterns and procedures, in social institutions, in—as we have said—art (especially architecture and calligraphy and poetry), and also in theology. Among these many ways, the theological has been not the greatest or most central, and certainly not the primary, expression. Yet neither has this expression been negligible, and I personally continue to find it entrancing. Yet it is certainly seen truly if it be seen as a subordinate facet of the Islamic complex in its entirety. Islamic theology is one facet of Islām.

Similarly, Islamic history can be seen as one facet of Islamic life, of the Islamic spirit, of the Islamic pattern. That spirit has been expressed in many ways. The expression in the historical realm is one such way: central; immensely important; and yet ultimately, secondary.

To what? Perhaps I can illustrate what I mean with reference to the concepts of Heaven and Hell. It is possible to perceive these—and indeed, by using the word 'concepts' I have encouraged us to perceive them—as ideas in the minds of Muslims. In this fashion, as historians, we can see these ideas as subordinate aspects of a larger historical whole. We can trace their rise, as concepts, in a certain part of the globe at a certain era of time, and can trace their development and florescence, and perhaps their present-day decline. An historiographical study of the ideas of heaven and hell, ferreting out exact evidence, detecting development and influence, analysing processes, and all, could be a voluminous, precise, and impressive work. It would constitute, however, a monograph: concentrating on one subordinate item, of a quite specialized nature, within the broader spectrum of human history. In this vision, heaven and hell are particular items, and in the long run relatively minor ones, in the larger role of human history.

There is another way of looking at this matter, however; in some ways the reverse of this. It is the way that most Muslims have at most times looked at it. For them, Heaven and Hell are not ideas in their minds; rather, they are parts of the universe. In such a view, this world (*al-dunyā*) is also part of that universe, but it is a less major part, a less lasting part, a less ultimate. Human history, from this vantage point, is seen (and felt) as one facet of a larger whole; a rather transient aspect. God existed before, and will exist after, this world. You and I, also, shall remain, long after history is over. I have always been charmed that, unlike most Indo-European languages with a single word meaning 'eternal', Arabic has two terms, *azalī* and *abadī*, meaning, on the one hand, that which has always existed, had no beginning in time, and on the other hand that which will always exist, will have no ending. Only God, in Islamic thought, is both. You and I, as human beings, are *abadī*, in that once created we shall never pass away. The world, human history, is neither. It has a beginning; it will have an end.

It is in this sense that Islamic history is a subordinate part of Islām in general. Human history is one part of the Muslim's total vision.

This is not to belittle history. On the contrary, Muslims take history—human history—*very* seriously. It is for them the arena of ultimate concern, in the technical sense. Those who may have chanced to read my *Islam in Modern History* will remember my comparing there the Muslim attitude to history with the Hindū, the Christian, the Jewish, the Marxist, and the secularist. Just as, for Jews, the holiness of the Sabbath enhances the significance of the other six days of the week rather than degrading it—'If something is not ultimately significant, then ultimately nothing is significant at all; . . . for those for whom there is not something absolutely valuable, for them in the end nothing is valuable at all. If one day is not holy, then all days are boring . . .'[3]—so here the subordination of history to the divine makes history more important, not less. Modern secularism has, alas, demonstrated that those among us were wrong who thought that by getting rid of the 'bias' towards transcendence, humankind would find the secular more significant. This has turned out to be just not true: alienation, *anomie*, uncommittedness, nihilism have, rather, threatened to engulf our world. I am not asking anyone to assay whether the Muslims were right or wrong in perceiving the world as made by God. All that I am asking that one recognize is the empirical fact that, they having perceived it as created by God, they have taken the world very seriously.

It so happened that during a time when I was speculating along these lines in preparation for one of my Harvard classes, I saw one of Jean Genet's plays in which, with brilliant eloquence, that modern French critic portrayed the fatuity and meaninglessness of human affairs. It was perhaps from the sparkling contrast between that view of history and the standard Muslim view, that I was prodded into developing my present argument. And recently, while putting the finishing touches on this present address, I chanced to see another modern play, this time on the life of Billy the Kid, who had rather aimlessly killed fifteen people by the time he was twenty-one. If, on the other hand, one sees this world as the deliberate and important handiwork of the ultimate and transcendent God of all the universe, wrought with supreme Intelligence and Mercy, then this world is not absurd; not pointless; not to be trifled with.

Secondly, the world is taken seriously because history determines man's eternal destiny. The movement of thought here is in the reverse direction from that in the preceding point. The world with which one deals had been given its substance by God; in turn, the way that one deals with it as a person will give substance to one's own ultimate fate, infinite beatitude and infinite horror turning on how one plays one's role in history. History is ethically important; and ethics is cosmically important. Some things that one does are right; some are wrong; and it matters. The whole of this world from beginning to end—that is, human history; and specifically, Islamic history—is ultimately less important than a single human soul, yours or mine. Nonetheless, that world and that history hold a derivative importance because they are the arena of the determination of the fate of each human soul.

Every human life is lived within history. Yet ultimately, every human life is greater than history.

I conclude, then, by averring that Islamic history has been and continues to be the background and the goal of the human life lived by Muslims, and the transient but decisive determinant of that life's final significance; but is not itself that final significance, unless we see it transcendentally. To understand 'Islamic history' is to be seized of these issues that are at stake in it—are at stake in all human life.

Of course, I am not asking that one agree with the Muslim view on these matters. I myself am not a Musalmān, after all; and am not asking that anyone be. Neither do I believe in Heaven and Hell, except as metaphors. Nor do I ask that anyone believe. I *do* hold that it is demanded of us, as we contemplate that history, not that we agree with their view, but that we understand it.

It could be, moreover, that in understanding it we might find ourselves beginning to speculate as to whether perhaps in their own metaphorical way they may not have caught hold of certain aspects of being human that are, after all, pretty important.

2

The Shahādah as Symbolic Representation of Muslims' Faith

In 1961 I was asked by the Canadian Broadcasting Corporation to give a series of radio talks over the national network, on 'the religions of the world'. Although within my university (McGill) I had been giving a lecture course on the general field, this was virtually my first public appearance as something wider than an Islamicist. Rather than proffering as expected a brief outline of the various 'systems', I tried instead to convey a sense of what it might be like to be a human being living in the light of one or other of them. To do this I chose one small item from each complex (Hindū, Buddhist, Chinese . . .) and explored for the half-hour allotted to me in each case what this particular symbol would mean to a person of faith, a man or woman for whom it was religiously significant. This approach was in line with my general position that 'the study of religion is the study of persons', and that one should think not of an abstraction called 'Hinduism', 'Buddhism', or the like but of the way that the various elements constituting these are seen by participants. The various 'religions' as concepts are potentially misleading abstractions, I had come to feel, and the task of the student of religion is not to focus on them nor on their data except as a step towards understanding how those data are perceived by persons of faith; and even more, how the world is perceived, and life, in their light.

Accordingly, the title of the series I changed from 'The Religions of the World' to 'The Faith of Other Men'. (If I were doing it to-day, I would call it '. . . of Other Men and Women'.) In the subsequent Swedish translation this came out as, in effect, 'men of other faith'—a curious misunderstanding, since part of the point that I was hoping to elucidate was that while communities differ, their faith turns out, once one sees things from their angle, to be not so 'other' as at first appears.

The talks, prepared for popular presentation to a non-academic audience, were published at about the same time as my Meaning and End of Religion, *a much more hefty work with its careful scholarly documentation and elaborate argumentation. Despite the patent differences in style and size, I myself tended to see the latter as general theory with* The Faith of Other Men *as popularized application. The larger book had one chapter entitled 'The Special Case of Islam', examining in some depth the question of how far the Islamic instance diverges from or converges with the general non-reificationist understanding of religious life towards which (in and through my Islamic studies) I was moving.*

Presented here is the Islamics chapter from the series of radio talks. The Islamics chapter from the larger work is not included in this present collection; but one part of the detailed work on which it rested appears below, as our next entry. It studies the term Islām *and the process of its 'reification' historically. In the case of both books, the Islamics chapter, although perhaps the most competent, was nonetheless but one chapter among seven—the others dealing with Hindū, Buddhist, Chinese, Christian, and general considerations. For by this time—six years after my* Islam in Modern History *was published—my seeing Islām as an inherently and characteristically human involvement (rather than as 'a religion', unrelated to outsiders) had increasingly led me to see it as within the general pattern of humankind's religious and cultural life. The specific illuminated the general, and* vice versa. *Rather than as a 'we/they' matter, I had come to see religious diversity as a characteristic of 'us' as human. It was not fortuitous, accordingly, that the following year I left McGill and my specialization as an Islamicist, for Harvard, to work in the wider field of Comparative Religion. My interest in Islām did not cease; but I increasingly came to see it as one of the major ways of being human.*

Almost any visitor to India interested in the religious life of its people will note a striking difference architecturally between a

Hindū temple and a Muslim mosque. The temple is apt to be ornate, even florid. Its involute complexity suggests that truth is much more elaborate than one had supposed, and denies nothing, not even incongruity. Very different is the stark simplicity of the Muslim place of worship. The mighty Imperial Mosque in Delhi, for example, is a structure whose artistic impressiveness and power come from the use of straight lines and simple curves, splendidly graceful and yet austerely disciplined. Certainly it is brilliantly conceived and its impact is immediate: one grasps at once the balance and dignity, the spacious reverence, the serenity of its straightforward affirmation. Its architect's vision of the glory of God, and of man's service due to Him, is evidently an ordered vision.

Such a point is confirmed if one has the privilege of witnessing a service in such a mosque, especially at one of the great festival prayers, where perhaps a hundred thousand people array themselves in neat lines and bow in precise unison as token of their personal and corporate submission to the will of God, which is definite and sure.

A similar contrast can be seen in the realm of doctrine. For a Hindū, there are various systems of ideas, involute, elaborate, and always tentative, from among which he may choose. In contrast, the Muslim community symbolizes its belief in probably the simplest, tidiest creed in all the world. I am sure that you have all heard it: 'There is no god but God, and Muḥammad is God's apostle'. The Muslims themselves refer to this simply as 'the two words', or even 'the word'. And while this may be carrying compression just a trifle far, still its two pithy clauses are, certainly, as succinct and clean as one could hope to find.

Because of its centrality, and its neatness, this simple creed may well provide us with the item for our consideration of the Muslims. As with other religious communities, so with the Islamic, we choose here one element from out the formal pattern of their faith, in the hope that, exploring it, we may find that it can lead us, if not to the heart of their religious life, at least into its precincts, and can suggest something of the richness of what lies behind. What better emblem of the Muslim's faith, for our purposes, than this crystallized creed, which the Muslims themselves have chosen to sum up their belief? To repeat this creed is, formally, to become a Muslim; perhaps to understand it is to understand a Muslim. Or let me put the point more realistically: to begin to understand it may be to go some distance, at least, towards understanding the position of those whose faith it typifies.

In suggesting the coherence and simplicity of the Muslim confession of faith, I do not wish to suggest that it is limited or lacks profundity. A mosque may be very intricately decorated—fine interlacing arabesques and the endlessly delicate complexities of an elaborate calligraphy usually embroider the arches and the walls; yet these decorations, however ornate in themselves, are regularly held in strict subordination to an over-all pattern that is essentially simple, so that detail is organized into a coherent unity. Similarly in the realm of doctrine. The Muslim world has produced its philosophers and theologians, constructing elaborate systems of ideas—the names of Avicenna and Averroes are probably the best known in the West, but there are many others also who worked out in careful detail considerable structures of thought. And there were also meticulously elaborate systems of law, comprehensive and ramified. But again, these were subordinate to the higher truth, the simpler truth, of the creed.

As one gets closer to truth, one gets closer to God; and God is one. He is majestic, mighty, awesome, merciful, and many other things, but above all, for the Muslim, He is one. Every other sin, the theologians affirm, may be forgiven man, but not that of *shirk*, polytheism, the failure to recognize that the final truth and power of the universe is one.

Before we turn to questions of meaning, which are of course our chief concern, let us note a few points about the formula as a formula. I suppose that every effective religious symbol is not only inexhaustibly meaningful in what it stands for, but is also in some ways intrinsically interesting in itself. This one certainly is. We have already remarked that it is short. It is also pungent and crisp. In the original Arabic—the language in which it is always used, no matter what the actual language of the people concerned, from Indonesian to African Swahili; from South Indian Malayalam to Turkish—in Arabic it is resonant and rolling, packing quite a punch. It so happens that of the fifteen syllables, about half begin with an *l* sound, or end with it, or both. This liquid alliteration, added to the rhyme, and a very marked rhythm, is quite forceful. *Lā-'i-lā-ha-'il-lal-lāh*; *Mu-ḥam-ma-dur-ra-sū-lul-lāh.*

Then there is a calligraphic point. In the Arabic alphabet, which is anyway highly decorative, it so happens that this particular set of words when written out is strikingly patterned, and lends itself to very picturesque presentation.

The formula is certainly in constant service. For example, it is whispered in the ears of the newborn baby, so that its affirmation may be the first words that a Muslim shall hear on entering the world. And between then and its use at his funeral, he will hear it, and pronounce it, often and often and often. And apart from its ceremonial and—as it were—sacred use, it can be found in everyday affairs also. I remember a scene in India some years ago when my wife and I were one summer at a mountain resort in the Himalayas, and were out for a hike in the hills: we came upon a work-gang busy in the construction of a rude mountain road. It was, of course, all hand labour; they had crushed the stones with hammers, and were now rolling them with a large and very heavy roller. Rather in the fashion of sailors working to a sea shanty, they were rhythmically pulling this heavy roller in spurts of concerted effort: the foreman would sing out *Lā ilāha illā 'llāh*, and the rest of the gang, then, would put their shoulders to the ropes and with a heave would respond *Muḥammadur rasūlu 'llāh*. This went on and on, as they continued to work, with a will and with good strong heaves. *Lā ilāha illā 'llāh*, he would chant; *Muḥammadur rasūlu 'llāh*, would come the vigorous response. Such a scene represents, of course, a kind of living in which a split into religious and secular has not come—or has not yet come—to segment life. At a different level, of course, are the formal ceremonies in the weekly service of some of the Islamic Ṣūfī orders, in which the initiate devotees will induce a mystic ecstasy or trance by the solemn and rhythmic repetition or incantation of the formula.

Between these two comes a religious use such as that by the *mu'adhdhin* [the *adhān*-sayer, 'muezzin'] in his call to prayer five times a day, whose sonorous recitative from the minaret punctuates village or town life and summons the faithful to turn for a moment from their routine affairs to the life of the spirit.

I have called this creed a symbol; and in some ways it plays in Muslim life a role similar to that played, for instance, for Christians by the cross. Nonetheless it is not a pictorial sign but a verbal one, and this itself is significant and appropriate. The role of linguistic form, of words, in Islamic religious life is quite special. I have already spoken of the written word—calligraphy—as a typical Muslim art form. This community has carried the decorative use of writing probably further than has any other people. And take revelation itself. In the Christian case this takes the form of a person, whereas for the Muslim it too is verbal. In the Qur'ān, God makes Himself and His purpose known to man in the form of words. It is altogether appropriate, then, that the chief symbol of Islām should also be verbal.

So far, I have allowed myself to follow the usual Western practice of calling this two-phrase synopsis of the Muslim's faith a 'creed'. For to do this is not altogether misleading, though you will have seen that its place in Muslim life is only partly correlative with that of the creed for those of us who are Christians. It is time now, however, to modify this still further. We need to see more carefully ways in which the faith of other people is expressed in patterns that do not quite correspond to our own—or even to what we expect of them.

In some ways, then, the 'two words' of the Islamic assertion do constitute a creed, a statement of belief, but in other ways they do not; and the Muslims do not themselves call this formula a creed. They call it, rather, a 'witness'. Regularly the statement is preceded by the words 'I bear witness that' there is no god . . . and so on. And even when these actual terms are not employed, an idea of witnessing is involved, and can be quite basic. The Islamic has been one of the three great missionary communities in human history (along with the Buddhist and the Christian);[1] and the idea of bearing witness to his faith is quite central to a Muslim's attitudes. His assertion is not so much an affirmation of belief, as a proclamation—of conviction. And in a subtle fashion, there is involved here a point that I rather imagine is more basic in all religious life perhaps than is usually recognized. It is this: that it is not so much that the Muslim *believes* that God is one, and Muḥammad is His prophet, as it is that he takes this for granted. He presupposes it, and goes on from there.[2] From his own point of view, one might almost say that, so far as he is concerned, he *knows* that these things are so, and what he is doing is simply announcing them, bearing witness to them.

The same kind of thing is true, I think, of all religious life. One distorts one's perception of a Christian's faith, for example, by saying simply that he believes Jesus Christ to be divine, to be the son of God. He would rather say that he recognizes this—these are the facts, and he has been fortunate enough to see them. In the Christian case the matter has been somewhat complicated by the use in Western languages of a single verb, *credo*, 'I believe', and so on, both for intellectual belief (belief that) and for religious faith (belief in)—though men of faith have insisted that the two things are different. Anyway, I feel that true faith has already begun to crumble a bit, if it has not actually gone, as soon as people have reduced what used to be the data, the presuppositions, of their world-view to a set of true-or-false propositions—I mean, when what was once the presupposed context or intellectual background for a transcending religious faith becomes rather the foreground of intellectual belief. This is one of the fundamental problems arising from a recognition of religious diversity—that what used to be unconscious premises become, rather, scrutinized intellectualizations. At this new level the believer himself begins to wonder if he really 'believes', in this new sense (and often enough finds that he actually does not).

In the Islamic case, as in the Jewish, the word of God is, fundamentally, an imperative. And even the proclamation of God's oneness is in some ways more a command, to worship Him alone, than merely an invitation to believe that He is there alone. Faith differs from belief in many ways, and goes beyond it; one way is that faith in God's oneness is a recognition of His unique and exclusive authority, and an active giving of oneself to it. Like the Christian, the classical Muslim theologian has seen faith as a commitment. He would understand at once St. James in the New Testament writing, 'You believe that God is one? You do well: the devils also believe—and tremble'. To a truly religious man, the question is not one merely of belief, but of doing something about it.

Having said that, however, we on the outside may still ask what the presuppositions are; what belief is presumed, for those who do go on to commitment.

We find ourselves having come round, then, to the question that we earlier postponed, the question of the meaning of the 'two words'. What does it mean to say 'There is no god but God, and Muḥammad is His apostle'? What does it mean, that is, to a Muslim—to someone to whom these two clauses are not merely true, but profoundly and cosmically true, are the two most important and final truths in the world, and the most crucial for man and his destiny? Let us look at each in turn.

To say that there is one God, and that He alone is to be worshipped, means at its most immediate, as it meant in pagan Arabia when it was first proclaimed, a rejection of polytheism and idolatry. When Muḥammad captured Makkah in A.D. 630, and set up Islām in triumph, he gave a general amnesty to the human beings there who had resisted his cause and were now defeated, but he smashed without quarter the idols—three hundred and sixty of them, it is said—in the shrine of the Kaʿbah, the figures of the pagans' gods. From that day to this, Islām has been uncompromising in its doctrine of monotheism, and its insistence on transcendence: God the Creator and Judge is Lord of all the universe, is high above all his creatures and beyond them, and beyond all their imaginings—and certainly beyond all their representations. Other deities, it asserts, are but the figments of men's wayward imagination, are unadulterated fiction; they just do not exist. Man must not bow down to them nor worship them, or look to them for help, or think about them. God is God alone; on this point Islām is emphatic, positive, and clear.

Historically, as the Islamic movement has spread, across the centuries, from Arabia through the Near East and into Central Asia and has penetrated China, into India and South-East Asia, across Africa and still today is spreading down into Africa, it has met polytheism in many forms, has attacked it and replaced it. Like the Church in the Roman Empire and northern Europe, and later in the Americas, so Islām in large parts of the world has superseded polytheistic practice and thought with monotheistic.

At a subtler level, for those capable of seeing it, the doctrine has meant also at times, and certainly ought to mean, a rejection of human tyranny. God alone is to be worshipped, to be served. For the man for whom this faith is sufficiently vivid, this can mean that no earthly power, no human figure, deserves or can legitimately claim man's allegiance; and any attempt to impose a purely human yoke on man's neck is an infringement not only of human dignity but of cosmic order, and to submit to it would be sin. Admittedly there has been, especially in periods of decline, an alternative interpretation whereby God's governance of affairs is taken as determining not what ought to be but what is. This view has led to fatalism—a passive acceptance of whatever happens. Perhaps you will feel that I am intruding my own predilections here in siding with those Muslims who have taken rather the activist line, asserting God's will as something to be striven for, as was done more widely in Islām's earlier centuries, and is beginning to be done again in our own day. You will agree, in any case, that it is legitimate and proper, in interpreting other men's faith as in one's own, to try to see it at its best and highest. That at least is what I am trying to do throughout these talks.

There is still a third level of meaning, which was stressed particularly by the Ṣūfī mystics in the mediaeval period, and is beginning to get wide support today. According to this view, to worship God alone is to turn aside from false gods not only in the concrete sense of idols and religious polytheism, but also in the subtler sense of turning aside from a moral polytheism, from false values—the false gods of the heart. To pursue merely earthly goals, to value them, to give them one's allegiance and in a sense to worship them—goals such as wealth, prestige, sex, national aggrandizement, comfort, or all the other distractions and foibles of human life—this, says the sensitive Muslim conscience, like the sensitive Christian or Jewish one, is to infringe the principle of monotheism. Similarly, to look for help to purely mundane forces, to rely upon armies or clever stratagems, to trust anything that is not intrinsically good—this is to have more than one god. The affirmation that God alone is to be worshipped means, for the man of true piety and rigorous sincerity, that no other objective must claim man's effort or loyalty; he must fear no other power, honour no other prize, pursue no other goal.

I would mention, finally, one other interpretation of the 'no god but God' phrase, one that again has been put forward by some of the mystics. This one has not been widespread, even among these; yet I mention it because I personally find it attractive, and it shows the kind of thing that can be done. This particular view is in line with the general position taken by the mystics that the religious life is a process, a movement in faith. According to this interpretation, then, the statement that 'there is no god but God' is to be taken in stages. No man, this reading suggests, can legitimately and truly say 'God' who has not previously said, and meant, 'no god'. To arrive at true faith, one must first pass through a stage of unbelief. 'There is no god': this comes first, and must be lived through in all sincerity, and all terror. A person brought up in a religious tradition must have seen through that tradition, its forms and fancies, its shams and shibboleths; he must have learned the bleakness of atheism, and have experienced its meaninglessness and eventually its dread. Only such a person is able to go on, perhaps only years later, to a faith that is without superficiality and without merely cheap and second-hand glibness. If one has said 'there is no god' with the anguish of a genuine despair, one may then, with God's grace, go on to say '. . . but God', and say it with the ecstasy of genuine insight.

Let us turn, next, to the second proposition: 'Muḥammad is the apostle of God'. The first thing to grasp here is that this is a statement not about Muḥammad's status but about his function. The Islamic concept of apostle, or prophet, is quite special; and one is misled if one too readily assumes that this corresponds to ideas familiar to us in the West. The underlying notion here, and it is tacitly presupposed by the formulation, is that God has something to say to mankind, and has from time to time chosen certain persons in various communities through whom to say it; the assertion here is that Muḥammad was one of those persons. It too, then, is in significant degree, and even primarily, a statement about God. As the theologians worked it out, it involves the conviction that God is not essentially passive, inscrutable, content to remain transcendent; rather, that from all eternity, and as part of His very nature, He is the kind of God who has something to say to mankind. What He has to say is what some would call the moral law. When He created the universe and when He created man, He did not exactly create the moral law, for this comes closer to being, rather, a part of Himself—but anyway He ordained it, or set it forth, and He created man to receive it, free and responsible to carry it out.

This is the first affirmation. The second is that He communicated this moral law to mankind. He did not leave man to grope about in the dark, to discover for himself, by his own efforts, what he could. No; God Himself acted, and spoke—spoke through the mouth of the prophets and apostles, beginning with Adam; that is, from the very beginning of history. Religion is nowadays sometimes spoken of as man's search for God. On this, the Islamic position is like the Jewish and the Christian, rejecting such a view emphatically, and asserting rather that God takes the initiative. As Micah put it, in our Judaeo-Christian tradition, 'He hath *shown* thee, O man, what is good . . .'. Man's business in the religious life is not a quest but a response.

Thirdly, in the message that God communicated is to be found, in the Muslim view, not what is true so much, though of course they do hold this, but what is *right*. The position differs from the Christian in that it is a revelation *from* God, more than *of* God.

The apostle or prophet is one who conveys to men the message that God wants them to know; namely, how they should live. Accordingly, out of the message, theoreticians and systematizers have extracted and constructed a law, finally elaborated in all detail and ultimately turned into a static system.

One last point, and with this I close. I said a moment ago that the phrase 'Muḥammad is the apostle of God' is a statement not about Muḥammad's status so much as about his function. Let me elaborate this just a little. The position stands over against the quite different Christian orientation, which sees the person of Christ as central and ultimate, pre-existent and divine. Muslims also posit a central and ultimate truth, pre-existent and divine, namely the Qur'ān—not a person but a book; or better, what the book says. Muḥammad plays in the Islamic scheme the role played in the Christian system by St. Paul or St. Peter; namely, that of an apostle who proclaims among men God's gift to them, which in the Islamic case is the scripture. In contrast to the Christian conviction, you might almost say that the Muslims' affirmation about their prophet is not a statement about Muḥammad's person at all, but about the Qur'ān and 'what Muḥammad brought'. To say that he is an apostle, sent by God, is to affirm these things that we have noted, about God, and about the kind of universe that we live in, and about the human situation, and morality; and then within that framework it is to assert further that the message purveyed by Muḥammad is authentic. If you belive this, then you are accepting as incumbent upon you in an ultimate moral sense the practical duties that flow from this tradition. For you are recognizing the obligation to perform them as not of human origin but of divine. Those of us for whom the content of morality is not defined in this historical source should nonetheless not allow this to obscure from us the cosmic things that those inspired from this source are saying about morality, about man, and about God.

PART TWO

Specific Presentations

3

The Historical Development in Islām of the Concept of Islām as an Historical Development

This study was presented to a conference on Muslim historiography held in 1958 at the School of Oriental and African Studies at the University of London. The invitation to participate set me to wrestling with Islamic conceptions of history, and this, I found, involved me in turn in thinking about historical (and historicist) conceptions of Islām. This paper, written a couple of years after I had completed Islam in Modern History, *proved highly significant in the further development of my own thinking: about Islām itself, and how I should understand it, and therein also about the general problem of the conceptualizing of religious matters from within a given religious position and from the outside; and about the divergence between these two; and as a dynamic of modern times, their growing interrelatedness. The problem that I articulated specifically in certain paragraphs here (p. 59) continued to haunt me until I solved it in my chief theoretical work of that decade,* The Meaning and End of Religion, *published five years later.*

The directions of my work were influenced by the discovery, in probing detailed data, that the attempt genuinely to understand one religious movement involves one in a requirement to understand all, and to understand religious diversity as a fact of human life, and the long-term shift in categories as a fact of human thinking.

3.1 INTRODUCTION TO THE PROBLEM

When human beings think or talk about religion in general or any one particular religion, they do so under three main heads. The first is personal; the second and third are systematic and institutional, are objectified. The first, the personal, considers the life of the spirit, the quality of faith, for a specific individual. It is immediate, concrete, and existential. My faith is my own, in a highly personal and private sense, and is different from my brother's and indeed even different from what it was ten years ago. Any man's or woman's religious life is a dynamic reality. To conceptualize it is precarious and doubtless always inadequate, though sometimes important.

The second and third considerations are more impersonal, are community possessions: the religious systems to which whole bodies of people 'belong'. The system may be conceptualized in two ways: as ideal, or as historical reality. Between ideal and actuality, essence and existence, there is always a well-known gap. Probably in the case of religion that gap yawns at its widest, since here by the very nature of religious aspiration the ideal tends to be at its loftiest and purest, whereas the actuality (apparently by the very nature of man and his and her society) has sometimes proven highly corruptible and almost always immensely involved, subject to the influence and even domination and distortion of a great variety of other factors.

In addition, then, to my Christian faith which is utterly my own and no one else's, a quality of my personal life and of my eternal destiny, not directly observable by others, there is 'Christianity' in general, an abstract system which in some sense I share with millions of others. Or rather, there are two Christianities: 'true Christianity' or the ideal which the theologian tries to formulate but which he knows transcends him, on the one hand; and on the other, the Christianity of history, which the sociologist or other observer notes as a human, sometimes all too human, complex.

The relation of John Doe's Christianness (the fact or quality of his being or becoming a Christian) to Christianity in general, or to true Christianity, is a serious and difficult question—for him, for a philosopher or an historian observing him, and for a student of *Religionswissenschaft*.

The same sort of consideration applies in the case of Islām. To put the matter in other terms, the word 'Islām' is used in at least three distinct ways, to refer to three related yet different things. First, there is the Islām, the self-commitment, the *taslīm kardan*, of an individual Muslim: his own personal submission to God, the act of dedication wherein he as a specific and live person in his concrete situation is deliberately and numinously related to a transcendent divine reality which he recognizes, and to a cosmic imperative which he accepts. Secondly and thirdly there are the Platonic ideal and the empirical actuality of the total system of Islām as an institutionalized entity. This is a generalized pattern, of the religion in the one case as it ideally is, at its conceivable best, and in the other case as tangible reality, a mundane phenomenon, historical and sociological.

I may designate these three as Islām the active personal faith, Islām the religious system as transcendent ideal, and Islām the religious system as historical phenomenon. In the first case, the Arabic term *Islām* is a *maṣdar*, a verbal noun, the name of an action rather than of an institution. It is the response of a particular person to a challenge. That person's whole being is involved, in a transaction, as it were, between his soul and the universe; and, according to his conviction, his eternal destiny is at stake. It involves a decision, private and inalienable. His personal submittingness—if we may use such a term—is, of course, quite distinct from any other person's. Between this action (*islām*) and the fact of his personal faith (*īmān*) the relation is not altogether straightforward and has been much discussed; yet in general the two are of the same order of ideas. 'Islām' here may not mean exactly what 'faith' means (and no one, Muslim, Christian, or philosopher, has ever been able satisfactorily to translate religious faith into words); but it means something comparable.

In the second and third cases, 'Islām' is the name of a religion. On the whole, there is a tendency here for believing Muslims to use the term in the second sense, as an ideal, and for outside observers to use it in the third sense, as an historical-sociological actuality. This is because men generally tend to talk about other people's religions as they are and about their own as it ought to be. If they have no faith of their own they usually think of all religion as observably practised. As a result, insiders and outsiders may use the same words but be talking of different things.

However, this distribution of meanings is not absolute. Believers also recognize that their religion has in fact had a history, a mundane application, an objectively institutionalized development; and although they may regard this as perhaps but a sorry reflection of the transcendent ideal, yet they may still call it Islām, in its earthly version as it were. Similarly non-believers, although they cannot share with the faithful the notion that ideal Islām is eternal and universal, a pre-existent idea in the mind of God, a final truth, yet may and often do postulate an ideal entity, Islām, which transcends the practice of the community and transcends perhaps even the concepts of individual Muslims.

Accordingly, one may stress the point that the word 'Islām' has three kinds of meaning, without postulating what that meaning in any case is. There is room for wide divergence as to what constitutes the personal piety of the individual Muslim; as to what the ideal of 'true' Islām essentially is; as to what has been the actual quality of the Islām that has observably existed over now many centuries in time and over increasingly many areas in geographic space and with many, not yet always clearly elucidated, ramifications in human society. One also leaves open the difficult and subtle question of the relations among the three things, which are obviously connected at the same time as obviously different. One would certainly not aspire to closing the discussion as to what Islām is, in any of these realms. Rather my suggestion is that the threefold discrimination here put forward may help to let that discussion be carried forward more fruitfully.

In particular, my purpose in the present paper is to give an historical dimension to such discussion. The concern is with the history of ideas. Understanding is furthered not only if we clarify the concepts that we are using, as a first step towards refining them so that they may serve with more adequate justice to represent in our minds that to which they refer. Understanding is also furthered if we may appreciate more clearly the historical process by which the concepts now available to us have come to be used with the content with which today we are using them.

My long-range ambition, I may confess, is to come closer to an understanding of what Islām (and, ultimately, religion) really is. In the meantime, however, I content myself with the veriest prolegomenon to this: namely, a preliminary concern with certain instances of what various people at different times and places have thought it to be.

In particular, it has seemed to me on investigation that although today thc word 'Islām' is used in the three senses mentioned, this was not always so. At least, the relative proportion of usage was in the past greatly different. Indeed I am somewhat impelled to the conclusion that the concept of Islām as a religious system, and especially as an historical system, is increasingly dominant but relatively modern.

I have found that a similar historical development is in evidence in other religions also.

Through the centuries of man's religiousness in general, and particularly within the development of each of the individual world religions, there seems discernible a long-term trend towards self-conscious systematization. What begins as active practice and faith gradually becomes, or is thought to become, definable pattern. The personal experience, behaviour, or belief of individual or group is abstracted and generalized, is conceptualized as an independent entity. Religion in general, and particularly the great religions, have been undergoing an historical process of reification.

In an as yet unpublished address,[1] I have tentatively examined this process for the concept of religion in general and for the religions other than Islām. I have also touched on the Islamic instance, stressing the similarities and the differences in its conception. My conclusion was that the Islamic religion, for various reasons which are susceptible of study, has been in some ways from the beginning the most reified of all the world's religions; and yet that like others it began (was proclaimed in the Qur'ān) as a ringing personal summons to individual men and women to have faith in God and to commit themselves wholeheartedly to His commands; with the institutions and a conceptualized system of what we now call Islām the result of that faith and commitment. I suggest that the result has come into historical existence and (then?) into conceptual thought more gradually and indeed in its modern form much more recently than is usually recognized. Such a process of tardy reification is readily demonstrable for 'Christianity', 'Hinduism', and the rest. I have come to believe that Islamic history evinces something comparable, and the present study is an attempt to investigate this.

The fundamentally rewarding task would be to make a study of the history of the world 'Islām': to discover the evolution of its usage and meaning over the centuries and the variety of connotations that it has evinced in the course of its historical development. We have been recently reminded that 'the history of Muslim religion has yet to be written'.[2] One preliminary approach to that historical study of the religion might be the historical study of the word. Clearly it would be a formidable task, perhaps the work of a lifetime. What I am attempting here is very considerably less ambitious, a first step towards that preliminary approach. Yet despite the quite limited scope, already the results seem suggestive. That they have significance is made more probable in that this verbal study confirms the development suggested independently by other considerations.[3]

The term *islām* in the Qur'ān itself has been the object of considerable study, both by Muslims and recently by Western scholars.[4] The two groups differ in that the latter, regarding the text as expressive of the mind of Muḥammad, aim at reconstructing the historical meaning of the seventh century A.D., whereas Muslims, regarding it as expressive, if we may say so, of the mind of God, may legitimately interpret it in the light of a continuingly contemporary understanding of its timeless validity. For our purposes, of the study of the historical development of the concept 'Islām' in the minds of men, in all its senses, a rewarding and manageable study would be an investigation of the history of *tafsīr* relating to this word.[5] Muslims and outsiders may disagree as to what Islām really is (and in the nature of the case a Muslim must equate what it really is and what the word means in the Qur'ān). Yet they may come together in discussing how specific persons at certain times and places have understood it. In the matter of the Qur'ān text, historical consideration may well be focused on what it probably meant to the seventh-century Arabs who first heard it. This can be supplemented, of course, with internal textual considerations of what in the light of their own context the words most probably mean.

In the case of the term *islām* in the Qur'ān I have two observations to put forward. The first is that the word is relatively little used. It occurs eight times in all, *īmān* forty-five times. Similarly *mu'min* in its various forms is more than five times as frequent as *muslim*.[6]

Secondly, where it is used, it in some cases inevitably carries our first sense of the word, as an act of personal faith. That is, it is indisputably a *maṣdar*.[7] In other cases it may do so. I myself do not necessarily find a systematic, institutionalized sense even in the classic verses where it is customary nowadays to see the religion as being named. *Inna al-dīna ʿinda-llāhi-l-islām* (3: 19) may be read as stating the essential religious truth that 'the proper way to worship God is to obey Him'. I will not, however, repeat here my reasons supporting this and similar interpretations. One may assert, however, that there is no instance in the Qur'ān where (as often happens later) the dynamic sense of the term as personal faith is patently absurd or grammatically intolerable.

For subsequent centuries one cannot, as I have said, at this stage investigate the whole history of the word *islām*. What I have done is to take a highly restricted but not insignificant body of material: namely, the titles of books in Arabic. Even this I have further restricted by considering (except for the modern period) only those titles entered by Brockelmann. His *Geschichte der arabischen Lit-*

teratur lists in the index (in alphabetical order) some twenty-five thousand titles, of works written over the entire course of Islamic history from the beginning until about 1938. I have gone through this list, culled out all instances where the word *islām* appears,[8] and rearranged these in chronological order. For the modern period (from A.H. 1300) I have supplemented Brockelmann from other sources, though not extensively. The detailed results of this project are offered as appendices (part 3) of this present paper. The conclusions that seemed to me to arise from an examination of these data will constitute the body of my study, part 2.

Before concluding this introductory section I may make certain general observations on my method and on the actual construction of my lists. In some ways these constitute the most significant part of the study: the presentation of data. The interpretation that I have been induced to give to those data may prove controversial or unpersuasive; but for those who might wish to query it it remains important that there be available the facts on which it rests.

My list of titles is unquestionably imperfect. To begin with, I myself have doubtless missed the odd entry in the Brockelmann index that may have escaped my hurrying eye. Moreover Brockelmann, I find, and it is hardly surprising, has made occasional slips, both in his index and elsewhere. Further, there are such possibilities as that what appear in such a listing to be distinct works may sometimes prove on examination to be rather divergent titles from various manuscripts of the same treatise. The next step in this investigation, and unfortunately I have not yet been able to take it except for modern works, would be to check these titles against the works to which they refer. The process of doing this, though lengthy, would be useful and would undoubtedly modify the material here presented in some of its details. I have, with apologies, taken the liberty of presenting my results at this interim stage because of the time limit imposed by the Conference [in London to which this presentation was submitted] and because I see no reason to suppose that the conclusions to be inferred from the results would be seriously modified in principle. It is the general trends that seem to emerge, rather than the details, that are of interest.

A large-scale question is that the massive work of the new Institute for Manuscripts of the Arab League in Cairo is in process of superseding Brockelmann, or anyway of revealing his catalogue as limited. His listing, however, remains a very sizeable sampling, not inadequate for the discerning of trends.

Another objection that might be made is that classical and mediaeval Arabic book titles were often highly stylized and not always informative of the subject-matter of the work. For one thing, however, I have found on examination that this is not as extensively true as is sometimes thought, and in any case there is no forceful reason for questioning the validity on this basis of such generalizations as are induced from such occurrences of our terms as are found; this practice perhaps reduces the number of occurrences, but not the relative distribution or the meanings when the terms are used. Besides, the use or the lack of use of a term in a title, whatever may be the cultural-conventional reasons for it, does I feel bear some relation to the fixing or lack of fixing of that idea in currency.

I have arranged the material in three lists. The first (List A) is of all Arabic titles that I have found up to the year 1300 *hijrī* containing the word *islām*. It is based squarely on Brockelmann, not only for entries but in general for dates and references. I have added one item (A 34) not in his list, of an early work published recently in Cairo; this happened to come to my notice, and perhaps does not disrupt the objectivity of the study. The items are listed chronologically according to the date of death of author, so far as feasible.

The second list, B, is for titles more recent than 1300 *hijrī*. Its items are arranged so far as feasible according to the date of first publication. All Brockelmann entries are included, and in addition such works as happen to be in my personal collection and those that came to my attention in the two libraries in which I did most of the detailed work for this study. It lists works in Arabic in which the term *islām* figures, whether translations or originals; in general, pamphlets are excluded. A fair number of entries from Brockelmann have been checked in this list against the original works. The desideratum that remains is to make this survey more nearly complete—a task of not too great proportions.

The third list, C, enumerates a handful of titles proffered to me by persons in Cairo as the result of my discussions. I have separated them from List B because they occur as illustrations of a point already made, materials serving a thesis rather than *vice versa*: I felt that it would distort the objective and inductive nature of the study to base it on a list constructed in part *ad hoc*. Some of these titles are such striking exemplifications of certain usages, however, that it seemed worthwhile to append them.

Let us turn, then, to consider the lists, to see what inferences arise.

3.2 A STUDY OF THE PRELIMINARY DATA

To begin with, the number of entries in my lists is significant. For list A it is rather small, but not negligible. In classical and mediaeval Muslim times religious books were numerous, yet titles on 'Islām', although they do occur, are considerably less common than today. (In classical and mediaeval Christendom, so far as I have been able to discover, no one ever wrote a book on religion or on Christianity.) In all, I have found in Brockelmann to the year 1300 *hijrī* eighty-four titles. The proportion of this to the total number of titles listed is tiny.[9]

The proportion to titles in which the word *īmān* occurs is also interesting. From a comparable study of Brockelmann's index, not here listed,[10] I have found *īmān* used in fifty-six titles until 1300 *hijrī*. In other words, during these centuries, *islām* slightly outnumbers *īmān* in titles, in a ratio of three to two.[11] We have already seen that in the Qur'ān the ratio was one to five, in favour of *īmān*. In modern times, this ratio changes to over thirteen to one.[12] That is, *islām* gets much less attention than *īmān* in the Qur'ān, gradually comes to get slightly more attention as Islamic history proceeds, and today is vastly more considered.[13]

Let us turn, next, to the meanings that attach to the term 'Islām' in the various instances. The context often makes reasonably clear that the author is using the word in one sense or another.

To begin with, one finds several cases in which the work evidently is referring to *islām* in the personal sense—of commitment, *taslīm*, the act of faith. In these cases, a substitution of the word *taslīm* for *islām*, though it might change the significance slightly, is meaningful and not absurd. This is fairly clear in such works as al-Sullamī's *al-Farq bayna al-īmān wa-al-islām* (number A 18 in the list), which explore the distinction between having faith and submitting to God. I would add al-Ghazzālī's *Fayṣal al-tafriqah bayna al-islām wa-al-zandaqah* (A 7), or the mystic Ibn al-ʿArabī's *al-iʿlām fī-mā buniya ʿalayhi al-islām* (A 16); and Ibn Taymīyah's *Risālah fī al-islām wa-al-īmān* (A 23).

In two striking instances (A 6, 54) the usage is not only specifically personal but indeed individual: al-Wāʿiẓ al-Bakrī al-Baṣrī's *Islām al-Ṭufayl b. ʿĀmir al-Dawsī* and al-Marṣafī's *Tanzīh al-kawn ʿan iʿtiqād islām Firʿawn*, where it is exclusively a question of the *islām*, the commitment, of one man.

Even if one thinks, as a non-Muslim or a non-religious Muslim is likely to do, of *islām* in these last two cases as a technical term, with an institutional rather than a divine reference, it is still obvious that it would mean 'becoming a Muslim' (and one may draw attention to the verb, 'becoming'). And even so I would feel that in a case where the author or reader is pious, he would be thinking of the content of the becoming-a-Muslim concept, which is a religious content; that is, an act of surrender to God.

Again, in the case (A 34) of Ibn Rajab al-Ḥanbalī's *Ghurbat al-islām* (The Strangeness of Islām) (8th/14th century), recently published by a *shaykh* of the Azhar, the title of the work is perhaps not in itself at once lucid, and indeed the modern editor writes a sixty-page introduction largely concerned with explicating terms to show why Islām in its true sense is indeed 'strange' or rare. In the course of this he remarks that the word *islām* has two meanings, self-surrender to God without an understanding faith, and with it.[14] (It may also be mentioned that the title-page carries the legend *wa-yusammā kashf al-kurbah bi-wasf ḥāl ahl al-*

ghurbah. Whether this means that the title *Ghurbat al-islām* is not actually original, or not as old as the text, is not clear to me.) In any case the allusion is to a *ḥadīth* affirming that *islām*, presumably in its 'true' sense of genuine surrender to God, is rare.

Somewhat similar considerations would doubtless apply to the mystic 'Alī al-Idrīsī's *Bayān ghurbat al-islām* (A 51), and to al-Ghazzālī's *Risālah fī manbaʿ al-islām* (A 8).

Titles with the doublet phrase *al-īmān wa-al-islām* (8 times so, 6 times *vice versa*: A 18, 44, 46, 50, 53, 59, 60, 80; and 23, 24, 62, 63 79, 81) begin about the 8th/14th century. Other works that have been considered thus far in this group are also late, the only earlier ones being the Ibn al-ʿArabī one mentioned (7th/13th century) and the two of al-Ghazzālī (d. 505/1111). To this group should possibly be added, I would feel, two works (A 74, 73) from the end of our period, in the 13th/19th century: both by an Indian Shīʿī author, Dildār: *Huṣām al-islām fī naqḍ mā dhakarahu ʿAbd al-ʿAzīz fī bāb al-nubūwah*, and *ʿImād al-islām fī ʿilm al-kalām*; the latter being alternatively entitled *Mir'āt al-ʿuqūl fī ʿilm al-uṣūl*.

There is a further group of titles, beginning as early as the 3rd/9th century and continuing without serious interruption to the 13th/19th, with our term in the form *sharā'iʿ al-islām* (5 times, and twice in the singular: A 2, 3, 21, 52, 75, and 12, 25—in the latter case with *sharʿ*), *qawāʿid al-islām* (3 times, and once in the singular: A 9, 19, 29, and 26), *arkān al-islām* (3 times: A 22, 66, 67), *qawāṭiʿ al-islām* (A 56), and so on (cf. A 4, 5, 69, 81). In this case it does not seem to me possible to say clearly at first glance in what sense the word *islām* is being used. It could mean the action of submitting to God, or it could be the name of a religion as a systematic ideal in the sense that we are exploring. There are some indications that suggest the former. For example, Hilāl al-Maqdisī's *Lawāzim al-islām wa-al-īmān* (MS., A 81; uncertain date) is again of that class that correlates *islām* with faith, making it in my judgement unambiguously personal, as in the other instances of that pairing that we have been considering. (It may be mentioned in passing that I have found no title of any work of the present century mentioning *islām* and *īmān* in the same breath.)

Again, as late as the 12th/18th century, in the case of an Indian author writing in Arabic, two manuscripts of his work (A 69) have survived, one bearing the title *Farā'iḍ al-islām* and the other *Farā'iḍ al-īmān.* Again, a slightly more recent author has left a work entitled *Farā'iḍ al-din wa-wājibāt al-islām* (A 72), where the *farā'iḍ* could logically be either *farḍ kifāyah* or *farḍ ʿāmm.* To me it somewhat seems that the use of *wājib* here, with its implication of moral responsibility, rather strengthens the suggestion that the author had in mind the individual person, who, after all, is alone able to take on that responsibility. The question here, and with *farā'iḍ* and *lawāzim*, turns on one's attitude to duty.

In all the cases being considered in this group, properly to determine the meaning that the word had for the author in each instance, one would of course have to read the book with imaginative care; and I have not been able to do this as yet. Sometimes it is not even an available resource: for example, al-Ṭabarī in his Chronicle refers to a work that he has written entitled *Basīṭ al-qawl fī aḥkām sharā'iʿ al-islām* (A 2), and in his Commentary refers to *al-Laṭīf min al-bayān ʿan aḥkām sharā'iʿ al-islām* (A 3), which are quite possibly alternative titles to the same treatise, but in any case no manuscript has survived; or at least, up to 1938 or so, none had been discovered.

In any case, a question as to what was in the author's mind is not the whole story. For, whatever a writer may intend, his words (as all of us who write, learn sometimes to our sorrow) have to stand in their own right, and people who hear or read them may read into them meanings of their own. Once a book exists, if its words can mean or appear to mean a certain thing, then whether or not the author intended them to mean that, they may nonetheless contribute to the currency of that idea. In the matter that we are discussing, it is not impossible that phrases like *sharā'iʿ al-islām* may have been launched with 'Islām' meaning religion or piety in our first sense, as personal reverence and morality, but may have contributed to the ambiguity by which it eventually came to mean the religion in our second sense, the institutional system. The puritanical founder of the Wahhābī movement has a book listed as *Faḍl al-islām* (A 71). This is reminiscent of late nineteenth- and early twentieth-century writings in the field of apologetics bearing such titles as *Faḍā'il al-Islām*. Yet, though I do not have access to Ibn 'Abd al-Wahhāb's work, which so far as I know has not been published, yet knowing what one does of his general point of view and his *daʿwah*, I should be surprised if he meant by *islām* here what the apologists now mean by it. To him it was a moral imperative to be obeyed rather than an idealization to be admired or defended. This is one of the many points where I must do more research.

In somewhat similar case are the six titles (beginning 7th/13th century) bearing the words *ahl al-islām* (A 20, 41, 57, 62, 63, 64) and one with *millat al-islām* (A 30). Perhaps *jamharat al-islām* (A 15) should also be added here.[15] Here again in two instances the full phrase is *ahl al-islām wa-al-īmān*—which again suggests the personal response to a challenge. Nonetheless it would seem to me that there is a certain ambiguity here, and phrases such as this and those of the preceding group doubtless helped to ease a transition from *islām* as personal commitment to Islām as a systematized ideal.

This transition is illustrated further in the phrase *shaykh al-islām* (A 10, 28, 31, 35, 42, 43, 45, 77, 82, 84), applied three times to Ibn Taymīyah, twice to Ibn Ḥajar, once each to various others. One should also add *ḥujjat al-islām* for al-Ghazzālī (A 83: MS. of uncertain date) and presumably the Shīʿī *rūḥ al-islām* (A 76: 13th/19th century) for Salmān. The usage *shaykh al-islām* begins from the first half of the 6th/12th century, very considerably earlier than Süleyman the Magnificent's or the Ṣafavīs' first establishing of a formal, official post with that name.

Another difficulty that arises here, and indeed besets one throughout this work, is the problem of not being sure whether the titles as given in Brockelmann are in fact as ancient as the works that they describe, or whether they may not have been added under the pressure of later style. An example of this process is the work of al-Wāqidī, entitled when it was written in the second century presumably *Futūḥ bilād al-ʿajam wa-Khurāsān* or the like but published in a modern edition with the new title *Futūḥ al-islām bi-bilād al-ʿajam wa-Khurāsān* (B 6).[16] For example, the work *Tarjamat shaykh al-islām al-Bulqīnī* (A 45) is listed as found in two manuscripts, one in Istanbul and one in the Escorial—but the latter omits the words *shaykh al-islām* from the title, which leaves one wondering whether this usage is indeed as old as the fall of central Spain after all. Again, Ibn Qudāmah's tribute (A 31) to his mentor is variously listed as *Tarjamat Taqī al-Dīn ibn Taymīyah* or as *Manāqib shaykh al-islām ibn Taymīyah.*[17]

However, until more meticulous and thorough research is feasible in this rather virgin field, one must presumably accept the titles given and the dates of the authors to whom the works are ascribed; the latter as in any case indicating a minimum date for the introduction of a new connotation or usage, even if there be a serious possibility of its being misleadingly early.

Finally within this category we turn to consider a work of Ibn Taymīyah himself called *al-Ḥisbah fī al-islām* (A 27). We must note that this is the first time, and apparently the only time until the present century, that the phrase *fī al-islām* is used. This is a most interesting wording, and it has developed far in our own day, as we shall presently be noting. The use of *fī* makes quite clear that Islām is an entity, something with parts, something that things can be inside of or outside of—not in the Ṣūfī sense of *bāṭin* and *ẓāhir* but in the concrete sense of an organized observable pattern. This is the modern sense to many people. Yet it is obvious when one reflects on it that the terminology *kadhā wa-kadhā fī al-islām* would not readily be used by persons for whom the term *islām* signified in its Qur'ān sense a personal relationship between the soul and God. (It is notable that Ibn Taymīyah appears in our list with more entries than any other classical or mediaeval author.)

We have now surveyed all but seventeen of the titles in which the word *islām* occurs during the first thirteen centuries of Islamic history. We have discovered that so far the term is either correlative with *īmān*, actually or potentially, as the designation of a man's personal acceptance of responsibility before God, or else is used in such a context as to be ambiguously either this or the idealized ideal; except for the Ibn Taymīyah work just noted, where the ideal is perhaps clearly indicated. Chronologically, with only a handful of exceptions, these titles begin with al-Ghazzālī.

We turn finally to examine these remaining seventeen. Two of them are by non-Muslims. One is the recent (12th/18th century) work, rather curious, of a Christian entitled *Taḥīyāt al-islām fī mā warada bi-al-salām wa-al muṣāfaḥah wa-al-qiyām* (A 65). The other is early and in fact is the first recorded work altogether by anyone in whose title the word *islām* appears. It has not survived, but the name is reported as given in a passing reference in the sceptical and rather ribald circle of Bashshār b. Burd at the court of al-Mahdī. I venture to call him a non-Muslim because of his associations and because he reputedly dedicated to the Byzantine emperor this treatise with the title *Mathālib al-ʿarab wa-ʿuyūb al-islām* (A 1).

This relates to the point on which I have remarked above, which I have elaborated in my previously mentioned papers,[18] and to which I shall return for the modern period: namely, the significance of the use by outsiders of a name to designate a religious system in which they do not themselves believe.

There remain then fifteen titles. I have set them aside for separate consideration, because in them we seem to see a transition towards the development of a new and more mundane meaning of Islām, where this term designates not the religion or piety of the Muslims but the Muslims themselves, the community or its historical culture.[19] In some cases the transition is only partial, in some cases perhaps complete. The complete list is as follows:[20] A 11, 13, 15, 17, 32, 33, 36, 37, 39, 40, 47, 49, 55, 58, 61.

If these cases are carefully considered, reflection seems to lead one to conclude that the word *islām* has become the name not even of a religion but of a culture or a community. It apparently signifies not the relationship of obedience and submission of the individual before his Creator, nor even the ideal pattern of such relationships systematically organized into a group order to which the life of the community ought to conform. It signifies rather the life of the community as it actually is and has been, without consideration as to what it ought to be.

The use of the phrase *mulūk al-islām* is worth attention. Parenthetically one may note that it follows by three centuries and more the introduction, not in literature but in politics, of a title such as *Sulṭān-i islām* for an actual ruling prince. The Seljüq Sulṭān Sanjar in the early part of the 6th/12th century is referred to by this title in a Persian *sawgand-nāmah* and is called *malik-i islām* by al-Ghazzālī himself in a Persian letter; and the Īl-Khānī and Ṣafavī rulers later are repeatedly called *pādishāh-i islām*.[21] We may discern in such cases that *islām* has not altogether lost its transcendent reference: the idea is not only that the ruler is a ruler of Muslims, but that he has the moral responsibilities and spiritual prerogatives and authoritative legitimacy of ruling them *ad dei gloriam*, as it were. The point of giving him such a title was to affirm that his being ruler, despite his not being *khalīfah*, was part of the proper, the Islamic, the divinely prescribed order of things.

Similarly in some of the book titles that we are considering. The full titles of two of the more recent (9th and 10th/15th and 16th centuries) suggest this, considering some of their specifically Islamic duties as rulers: *Nuṣḥ mulūk al-islām bi-al-taʿrīf bi-mā yajibu ʿalayhim min ḥuqūq ilá bayt al-kirām* [sic] (A 37) and *Taḥdhīr a'immat al-islām ʿan taghyīr binā' al-bayt al-ḥarām* (A 58). In earlier cases, however, there seems little to suggest this. Al-Maqrīzī's *mulūk al-islām* in Ethiopia (A 40) means perhaps little or nothing more than Muslim kings, or perhaps more accurately Muslim kings of a Muslim community. And in *ḥukamā' al-islām* (A 11) (and perhaps *jamharat al-islām* [A 15]) does *islām* mean anything more than the Muslim community? Similarly al-Bayyāsī's modern-sounding reference to *ṣadr al-islām* (A 17) presumably has in mind the appearance of Islām as an historical phenomenon. If one thinks of Islām in its stricly theological sense, according to Muslim conviction, it appeared with Adam and has re-appeared at least with each of the prophets.

This secularizing tendency, if we may call it that, culminates in the small group of history works that form virtually a series—A 32, 33, 36, 38, 39, 49—stemming from the seminal study of Shams al-Dīn al-Dhahabī (8th/14th century). This monumental and influential political and intellectual historiographical work from the time of the Prophet Muḥammad to the author's own day was widely copied, imitated, abridged, revised. Let us consider its title, *Ta'rīkh al-islām*. This phrase can have two possible meanings, so far as I can see. It cannot mean the history of a personal commitment, of an individual attitude to God's command: that would conceivably be *ta'rīkh islāmī* or *ta'rīkh islāmikum* or *ta'rīkh islām fulān*, but this would be rare—a sort of spiritual biography. What *ta'rīkh al-islām* could mean would be, first, the history of the religion, as an organized system; and secondly, the history of the Muslim community.

The former has never been written. It is a fascinating subject, and one that I myself have occasionally dreamed of attempting: a history of the religion of Islām, its development as a religious Weltanschauung across the centuries, the changes that it has undergone as it has been adopted by different peoples, in different conditions, and at different times. Muslims, on the whole, not only have not written such an account but to some extent theoretically preclude themselves from writing it—for to a believing Muslim in the modern mood Islām if conceived as a religious system tends to be conceived as fixed, as given by God: it does not change from one place or one generation to another; it has no history. The inappropriateness or at least the radical nature of this suggestion becomes perhaps clear if one translates 'history of Islām' by the revealing phrase *taṭawwur al-islām* or *taṭawwur dīn al-islām*. It is perhaps not rash to predict that such a book will first be written by a non-Muslim (though one would like to hope that this prediction will be proved wrong).[22]

The other meaning that the words *ta'rīkh al-islām* could have, and actually the one that they have had, is the history of the Muslim community. The concept that the community has a history is straightforward enough and is theologically quite acceptable. What is curious in this case is the meaning that the word *islām* then takes on. Does it not, as I have remarked, designate then not an ideal but an actuality; not what God asks of men but what men choose to give Him?

This concludes our survey of the classical and mediaeval periods; but before turning to the present century we should note that this last way of looking at Islām is the normal one for outsiders. This is the accepted meaning of the term 'Islām' for non-believers. For example, the standard Western orientalist has tended to look at Islām as a mundane phenomenon, an historical actuality that he objectively studies. For him it is not an idea in the mind of God, but a purely human construction on the stage of history. I personally do not share this; and indeed part of my present study in trying to wrestle with the problem of an outsider attempting to understand a religion not his own is pushing me to the conclusion that such understanding requires a fairly serious revision of many of our terms and concepts. At the very least one must learn to view Islām not only as an objective historical phenomenon but also as the ideal that lies behind it; not the overt behaviour of the Muslim but the inner aspiration of his heart. Even this, I feel, will eventually have to be refined, if not superseded. It would seem to me highly possible that we shall come to recognize that a religion, and therefore religious history, and therefore human history, cannot be properly understood without an effective awareness of its transcendent dimension.[23]

In the meantime, however, it is not surprising, and perhaps was inevitable, that outsiders in the first instance have approached Islām in this unidealist fashion, have seen it as something totally within the empirical world. The result is that this is the meaning that the term 'Islām' has come to have in European languages.

The importance of this point for our present study is that one seems to find in this matter as in others a powerful impact recently of the modern West on the Muslim community itself, or at least on those sections of it that read, and often think, in one of the European languages.

Turning, then, to my list B, and studying the usages that it displays, one finds oneself asking whether there has not been during fairly recent times in the Muslim world an increasing and now widespread tendency to use the word 'Islām' in the sense of the tangible historical reality that has actually existed.

In list B one finds a small number of works that continue the older tradition from the mediaeval period (e.g., B 1, 2, 16, 22, 27, 65, 67, and the subtitle though not the title of B 28). Such usages are very soon greatly outnumbered, and for modern-type books replaced, by the newer and more mundane meaning. The tendency is again illustrated by the many modern books being published and widely read in our century entitled *Ta'rīkh al-islām*. Examples of this are: B 30, 32, 56, 59; and one may add the extremely popular series of Aḥmad Amin, *Fajr al-islām, Ḍuḥā al-islām, Ẓuhr al-islām, Yawm al-islām* (B 41, 53, 74, 80).

One finds also titles such as *Ta'rīkh ṣadr al-islām* (B 77; cf. 31), and if one considers the title *Mabādi' al-islām* (B 47), one realizes that this phrase might mean 'the principles of Islām' as a systematic ideal, but instead the author means 'the beginnings of Islām' as a concrete actuality.

Similarly when a person writes a book called *Ashhar mashāhīr al-islām fī al-ḥarb wa-al-siyāsah* (B 18) or *al-Mustashriqūn wa-al-islām* (B 64) one may, of course, be quite sure that by 'Islām' he is not thinking of *taslīm kardan*. May one not also surmise as in the former case certain, and in the latter case probable, that he is not even thinking of the ideal religious system but more likely of the historical civilization? Similarly a title such as *al-Islām fī al-ḥabashah* (B 62). In this case, the word *islām* must designate the historical religious situation as it exists. The ideal pattern of Islām, in its systematic sense, is presumably the same in Ethiopia as anywhere else. If one writes, or for that matter reads, a book *al-Islām fī al-ḥabashah* obviously one has in mind not the transcendent pattern of Islām, but one of its actual historical expressions.

This point is further clarified if we go back to the phrase of Ibn Taymīyah, *al-Ḥisbah fī al-islām* (A 27). Presumably Ibn Taymīyah's work is at a theoretical level, a treatise on *ḥisbah* as it ought to be, according to ideal Islamic prescription. One can imagine a quite different work by, let us say, a Western economic historian; his study might well have the same title, but it would discuss *ḥisbah* and the *muḥtasib* not as they ought to be but as they actually were in the history of a given time and place. For instance, such a study would include any corruption that may have taken place. By comparing these two concepts one can forcefully see the difference in the two meanings of *islām*.

This is illustrated precisely when de Boer's work entitled *The History of Philosophy in Islam* is considered. This was translated also into Arabic as *Ta'rīkh al-falsafah fī al-islām* (B 69). It is clear that the phrase *fī al-islām* here means something different from what it means in Ibn Taymīyah's *al-Ḥisbah fī al-islām*.

The same difference occurs in the phrase *fī al-islām* between *al-Mujaddidūn fī al-islām, 100 h.-1370 h.* (B 79) and *Ḥuqūq al-Nisā' fī al-islām* (B 4 and 49). With this latter, compare *al-Riqq fī al-islām, al-zawāj fī al-islām*, etc. (B 5, 68, 70); and with the former, *Ta'rīkh al-qaḍā' fī al-islām* (B 55) and a few other *fī al-islāms* that we shall consider presently. Attention may be drawn to the point that the first title here incorporates boundary dates, illustrating almost explicitly that an historical rather than a timeless Islām is in mind. Our hypothetical Western economist's work fancied above might well be entitled (and strictly would have to be entitled, at least implicitly) 'The *Ḥisbah* in Islām from Year A to Year B'; whereas Ibn Taymīyah's work on the *ḥisbah* in Islām could not accept dates.

The de Boer translation brings us to what I am beginning to believe was perhaps crucial in this matter: the question of an impact from the West, from non-Muslims. That this has been operative is suggested, apart from its inherent plausibility, by a careful scrutiny of some of the works published. For example, the only two books of Shaykh Muḥammad 'Abduh in whose title the word *islām* appears (B 15, 26) were both written in explicit reply to outside attacks on Islām—that is, attacks on what non-believers thought Islām to be. The earlier work was in answer to a European article; the latter, *al-Islām wa-al-radd ʿalá muntaqidīhi*, 1902, is an answer to the non-Muslim Arab, Faraḥ Anṭūn. It is perhaps of interest to note that the word *islām* in the earlier article reproduces the same word used in the Arabic translation of Hanotaux's originally French article, a translation that was published in the Cairo journal *al-Mu'ayyad* and provoked ʿAbduh's response.[24]

Again, the first work, very influential and often revised and republished, of perhaps the most energetic, most prolific, and most characteristic of the writers introducing the new attitude, Farīd Wajdī, was, from its second edition, entitled *al-Madanīyah wa-al-islām* (B 19). It was not only an apologetic for Islām in dispute with two Frenchmen, B. Constans and J. Simon, but was actually first written in French and then translated into Arabic.[25] Another of the modern works in which *islām* appears in the title in the historical sense was *al-Islām, khawāṭir wa-sawāniḥ*, which is a translation from the French of H. de Castries. The very fact that the word *islām* can be translated from a non-believer's language into Arabic by a Muslim without discomfort is significant.[26]

Besides the translations, there is the writing of books in Arabic by non-Muslims. One of the first, and most influential, was *Ḥadārat al-islām fī Dār al-Salām* (B 3), by a Christian Arab (Cairo, 1888 and in later editions); a work that is said[27] to have been a forerunner of the still more popular and effective Christian writer, Jurjī Zaydān.[28]

To come to a later period, one may note such a work as B 44: *Ta'rīkh al-ḥarakāt al-fikrīyah fī al-islām—al-ḥarakāt al-ijtimāʿīyah* (Jerusalem, 1928), which is a Marxist history, in which *islām* means an historical phenomenon, as the phrase *fī al-islām* once more suggests.

In fact, during the formative period of the first three decades of the present century *hijrī* (roughly, from the 1880s to the First World War), I have found that works that are either translations from the French, or are by non-Muslim Arabs, form a quite substantial proportion of the titles in which the term *islām* appears; and that they use this term chiefly in its objective-historical sense. If one adds also those instances where Muslim writers are explicitly answering outsiders' attacks on Islām, then during this period approximately one-half of the usages are in this sense non-indigenous.[29] Since that period, however, Muslims themselves have adopted this usage, and nowadays it considerably exceeds any other meaning for the term in Arabic titles.

Indeed, I have come to believe that these years should be examined to see whether they do not constitute a critical point in the development of the thinking of Arab intellectuals about Islām; and whether during this time the transition did not take place, and take place quite largely under Western impact, to this non-transcendent reference.[30]

Similarly later, in 1927 in Cairo there appeared *Ta'rīkh falsafat al-islām* by Muḥammad Luṭfī Jumʿah (B 39). This title does not mean a history of the philosophy of the religion of Islām, nor even a history of Muslim philosophy of religion; but simply a history of such general philosophy as has occurred within Muslim civilization. It is instructive, therefore, to learn that this book was criticized in an article by Maḥmūd al-Khuḍarī in Cairo as being but a plagiarism from the work of the German orientalist Munk.[31]

In these various ways, then, through books in European languages read by Muslims, through books in Arabic and other Muslim languages written by non-Muslims, through the translations, as well as perhaps through the waning of a lively personal faith among some members of the Muslim community themselves, the word 'Islām' in an outsiders' meaning would seem to have established itself in the languages and perhaps even the thinking of the modernized Muslim world.

In the 1930s, a writer in a sense protests against this development, and in a sense acquiesces in it, by publishing a book entitled *al-Islām al-ṣaḥīḥ* (B 61). By this time one hardly noticed it; whereas a thousand or perhaps fifty years earlier it would not have occurred to him or to his readers that there was any other kind of Islām to write about.

The secularizing tendency culminates perhaps in a work (B 73) published in Cairo a few years ago which included in its title the astonishing phrase *al-ilḥād fī al-islām*. To reflect on these words is to realize how profoundly the meaning of *islām* has changed!

My attention has been called, in line with this last phrase, to certain other titles in which the usage of *fī al-islām* betrays a similarly novel conception (list C).

To sum up, then, one may say that to an outsider it would seem that there has been a tendency over the centuries and especially in modern times for the connotation of the word 'Islām' gradually to lose its relationship with God, first by shifting from a personal piety to an ideal religious system, a transcendent pattern, then to an external, mundane religious system, and finally by shifting still further from that religious system to the civilization that was its historical expression.

ISLĀM

3.3 THE USE OF THE WORD *ISLĀM* IN ARABIC BOOK TITLES CHRONOLOGICALLY ARRANGED.

List A. Listed here are the eighty-four instances during the first thirteen centuries of Islamic history in which the word *islām* occurs in one of the titles given in Brockelmann, *Geschichte der arabischen Litteratur*. Entries are, so far as feasible, arranged chronologically, according to the date of death of the author. Information not from Brockelmann is in square brackets. References are to Brockelmann, volume and page.

1. *Mathālib al-ʿarab wa-ʿuyūb al-islām*, Yūnus ibn Farwah. 2nd/8th century. S(upplement) I, 109.
2. *Basīṭ al-qawl fī aḥkām sharāʾiʿ al-islām*, al-Ṭabarī. 224–5/839–. S I, 218.
3. *al-Laṭīf min al-bayān ʿan aḥkām sharāʾiʿ al-islām*, al-Ṭabarī. S I, 218.
4. *Daʿāʾim al-islām*, Qāḍī al-Nuʿmān. –363/–974. S I, 325.
5. *al-Ishrāf fī ʿilm farāʾiḍ al-islām*, al-Mufīd ibn al-Muʿallim. –413/–1022. S I, 322 and S III, 1201 ad 323.
6. *Islām al-Ṭufayl b. ʿĀmir al-Dawsī*, al-Wāʿiẓ al-Bakrī al-Baṣrī. 5th–6th or 7th/11th–12th or 13th century. S I, 616, S III, 1220.
7. *Fayṣal al-tafriqah bayna al-islām wa-al-zandaqah*, al-Ghazzālī. –505/–1111. G(rundwerk) I, 421, no. 13; S I, 747.
8. *Risālah fī manbaʿ al-islām*, al-Ghazzālī. S I, 747, no. 23b.

9. *al-Iʿlām bi-ḥudūd qawāʿid al-islām*, Abū al-Faḍl ʿIyāḍ. −544/−1149. S I, 632. no. 6.
10. *Durar al-kalām fī faḍl al-ʿilm wa-manāqib shaykh al-islām*. ʿAbd al-Karīm al-Khalīfatī. 1st half 6th/12th century. S II, 525.
11. *Ta'rīkh ḥukamā' al-islām*, Ẓahīr al-Dīn al-Bayhaqī. 499–565/1105–1169. G I, 324; S I, 557.
12. *Sharīʿat* (or: *Shirʿat*) *al-islām ilá Dār al-Salām*, Sadīd al-Dīn Imāmzādah al-Sharghī (Jarghī?/Jūghī?). 491–573/1098–1177. G I, 375; S I, 642.
13. *Ādāb al-islām*, al-Balawī (ibn al-Shaykh). 526–604/1132–1207. Attributed to Abū ʿUbayd, –ca. 223/–ca. 837. S I, 167 (cf. S I, 543).
14. *Iʿtiqadāt (firaq) al-muslimīn* (or: *al-islām*) *wa-al-mushrikīn*, Fakhr al-Dīn al-Rāzī, 543–606/[c. 1148]–1209. G I, 507; S III, 1245. [The term *Islām* in this title would appear to be a twentieth-century innovation of Brockelmann himself (S III, 1245) and is evidently simply an error. The alternative *Muslimīn* is given in G I, 507, no. 25 (in the 1898 edition); G I, 668, no. 25 in the 1943 reprint; in the Nashshār edition (Cairo, 1356/1938); and in the citations of the manuscripts (Leiden, Cairo) to which Nashshār refers (preface, pp. 3–4). It is omitted at S I, 923. Further, the reference on which Brockelmann's entry in S III, 1245 is ostensibly based—namely, the catalogue of the ʿAq[ā'id] section of the Taymūr Library, Cairo, item 178—while not available to me in the form that Brockelmann presumably consulted (G I, 1943 ed., p. 934), is given in the subsequently published edition of that catalogue (*Dār al-Kutub al-Miṣrīyah—Fihris al-khazānah al-Taymūrīyah*, *al-juz' al-rābiʿ*, 1369/1950, p. 103) as *al-Firaq al-islāmīyah wa-ghayruhā*. My search through almost a dozen other references to al-Rāzī's works (Katip Celebi, Shawkānī, Kantūrī, etc.) has not uncovered any form other than *muslimīn*.]
15. *Jamharat al-islām*, al-Shayzarī. −626/1229. G I, 259; S I, 374.

16. *al-Iʿlām fī mā buniya ʿalayhi al-islām*, Muḥyī al-Dīn ibn al-ʿArabī. 560–638/1165-1240. G I, 444 (new ed. G I, 576).
17. *Kitāb al-iʿlām bi-al-ḥurūb fī ṣadr al-islām*, Jamāl al-Dīn al-Bayyāsī. –654/–1255. G I, 346; S I, 589.
18. *al-Farq bayna al-īmān wa-al-islām*, ʿAbd al-ʿAzīz al-Sulamī. 577–660/1181–1262. G I, 431; S I, 767, no. 23.
19. *Qawāʿid al-islām*, ʿAbd al-ʿAzīz al-Sulamī. S I, 767, no. 2a.
20. *Targhīb ahl al-islām fī sukná al-Sha'm*, ʿAbd al-ʿAzīz al-Sulamī. G I, 431; S I, 767, no. 20k.
21. *Sharā'iʿ al-islām*, Najm al-Dīn Jaʿfar al-Ḥillī al-Muḥaqqiq al-Awwal. 602–676/1205–1277. G I, 406; S I, 711, no. 1.
22. *Arkān al-islām fī al-tawḥīd wa-al-aḥkām*, ʿIzz al-Dīn al-Dīrīnī al-Damīrī. 612–697/1215–1297. G I, 452, no. 7.
23. *Risālah fī al-islām wa-al-īmān*, Ibn Taymīyah. [661–728]/[1263–1328]. S II, 121, no. 30.
24. *al-Kalām ʿalá ḥaqīqat al-islām wa-al-īmān*, Ibn Taymīyah. G II, 104; S II, 121, no. 30 (#23, 24 are the same work?—Brockelmann, *loc. cit.*).
25. *al-Qiyās bi-sharʿ al-islām*, Ibn Taymīyah. S II, 125, no. 117.
26. *Qāʿidat al-islām*, Ibn Taymīyah. S II, 122, no. 62.
27. *al-Ḥisbah fī al-islām*, Ibn Taymīyah. S II, 125, no. 131.
28. *Arbaʿūn ḥadīth, riwāyat shaykh al-islām Ibn Taymīyah* [title is modern?]. Anon., but after 728/1328. S II, 121, no. 14.
29. *Qawāʿid al-islām, ʿAqīdah*, Abū Ṭāhir Ismāʿīl al-Jayṭālī. –730 or –750/–1329 or –1349. S II, 349/2, no. 2.
30. *Taḥrīr al-aḥkām fī tadbīr millat al-islām*, Ibn Jamāʿah. 639–733/1241–1333. S II, 81, no. 4.
31. *Manāqib shaykh al-islām Ibn Taymīyah*, Muḥammad ibn Aḥmad ibn Qudāmah al-Maqdisī. 705–744/1306–1344. S II, 119, last line; 128/4b, no. 2.
32. *Ta'rīkh al-islām*, Shams al-Dīn al-Dhahabī, 673–748/1274–1348. G II, 46; S II, 45 (G II [rev.], 57 ff.)
33. *Nukhbat al-iʿlām bi-ta'rīkh dawlat al-islām*, al-Dhahabī? S II, 45.

[34. *Ghurbat al-islām, wa-yusammā Kashf al-kurbah bi-waṣf ḥāl ahl al-ghurbah*, al-Ḥāfiẓ al-Imām Shaykh al-Islām ibn Rajab al-Ḥanbalī, Taḥqīq Aḥmad al-Sharbāṣī, Cairo: Dār al-Kutub al-ʿArabīyah bi-Miṣr, 1373/1954. Source: Library of American University at Cairo, School of Oriental Studies. The author's dates (from pp. 53, 60 of Introd.): 706 (736?)–793/ca. 1306 (1336?)–ca. 1393. (Cf. S II 130, no. 13; evidently the title with *Islām* is modern?)]

35. *al-Aʿlām al-ʿalīyah fī manāqib shaykh al-islām Ibn Taymīyah*, Sirāj al-Dīn al-Bazzāz. –804?/–1401? S II, 120.

36. *Dhayl Ta'rīkh al-islām*, ʿAbd al-Raḥīm al-ʿIrāqī. –806/–1404. S II, 70, no. 22.

37. *Nuṣḥ mulūk al-islām bi-al-taʿrīf bi-mā yajibu ʿalayhim min ḥuqūq ilá al-Bayt al-Kirām* [*sic*], al-Miknāsī ibn al-Sakkāk. Between 807/1404 and 914/1508 (MS date). S II, 362/9, no. 2.

38. *Nuzhat al-anām fī ta'rīkh al-islām*, Ibn Duqmāq. –809/–1407. G II, 50; S II, 49.

39. *Mulakhkhaṣ ta'rīkh al-islām*, Muḥammad ibn Muḥammad al-Jazarī. –833/–1429. SN II, 45 (= S III, 1250).

40. *al-Ilmām bi-akhbār man fī/bi arḍ al-ḥabashah min mulūk al-islām*, al-Maqrīzī. –845/–1442. G II, 40; S II, 37, no. 1.

41. *al-Iʿlām bi-ta'rīkh ahl al-islām*, Ibn Qāḍī Shuhbah. –851/–1448. S II, 50.

42. *Muṣannafāt shaykh al-islām Ibn Ḥajar*, Aḥmad b. Khalīl al-Lubūdī. Died between 748/1348 and 953/1546—Brockelmann [presumably died between 852/1449 and 953/1546, since Ibn Ḥajar died 852]. S II, 73; 85.

43. *al-Jawāhir wa-al-durar fī tarjamat shaykh al-islām Ibn Ḥajar*, Shams al-Dīn al-Sakhāwī. No date, but Ibn Ḥajar died 852/1449. G II, 68; S II, 73.

44. *Shurūṭ al-iʿlām fī-bayān* (or: *mabānī*) *al-īmān wa-al-islām*, ʿUmar ibn Mūsá al-Ḥimṣī Sirāj al-Dīn. 777–861/1376–1457. G II, 117; S II, 144.

45. *Tarjamat shaykh al-islām al-Bulqīnī*, Ṣāliḥ ibn ʿUmar al-Bulqīnī. 791–868/1389–1464. S II, 115.

46. *al-Iḥkām fī maʿrifat al-īmān wa-al-islām* (or: *al-aḥkām*), Muḥammad ibn Sulaymān al-Muḥyawī al-Kāfīyajī. 788–879/1386–1474. G II, 115. [Note: *islām* only in the index, S III 910; presumably Brockelmann's mistake.]
47. *Duwal al-islām al-sharīfah al-bahīyah*, Muḥammad al-Qudsī. –881/[–ca. 1476]. S II, 52.
48. *Mafākhir al-islām fī faḍl al-ṣalāt ʿalá al-nabī ʿalayhi al-ṣalāt wa-al-salām*, Muḥammad ibn Aḥmad al-Tilimsānī. –901/–1495. S II, 362/6 a (not in title index).
49. (*Wajīz al-kalām bi-*) *Dhayl Duwal al-islām*, Shams al-Dīn al-Sakhāwī. –902/–1497. S II, 32, no. 3; G II, 34 (rev. ed., G II, 43/9, no. 3).
50. *Sharḥ al-īmān wa-al-islām*, al-Suyūṭī. –911/–1505. G I, 180; S II, 189, no. 169 pp. [Note: There is confusion here (Brockelmann index, S III 1093) with another work of the same title by the 4th/10th cent. writer Abū ʿAbd Allāh al-Zubayr.]
51. *Bayān ghurbat al-islām bi-wāsiṭat ṣinfay al-mutafaqqihah wa-al-mutafaqqirah min ahl Miṣr wa-al-Sha'm wa-mā yalīhā min bilād al-aʿjām*, Abū al-Ḥasan ʿAlī al-Idrīsī. –917/–1511. S II, 153.
52. *Masālik al-afhām ilá tanqīḥ sharā'iʿ al-islām*, Zayn al-Dīn ibn ʿAlī al-ʿĀmilī al-Shahīd al-Thānī. (Written 964/1557.) 911–966/1505–1558. G I, 406; S I, 711–12, no. la.
53. *al-Īmān wa-al-islām wa-bayān ḥaqā'iqihimā wa-ajzā'ihimā wa-shurūṭihimā*, Zayn al-Dīn ibn ʿAlī al-ʿĀmilī al-Shahīd al-Thānī. SN II, 450 (= S III, 1286).
54. *Tanzīh al-kawn ʿan iʿtiqād islām Firʿawn*, al-Ghumrī Sibṭ al-Marṣafī. –970/–1562. S II, 463.
55. *Ḥuqūq ikhwat al-islām*, al-Shaʿrānī, Abū al-Mawāhib. –973/–1565. G II, 338, no. 30; S II, 466.
56. *al-Iʿlām bi-qawāṭiʿ al-islām*, Ibn Ḥajar al-Makkī. 911-973?/1505–1565? G II, 388; S II, 527.
57. *Itḥāf ahl al-islām*, Ibn Ḥajar al-Makkī. G II, 388; S II, 528, no. 18.

58. *Taḥdhīr a'immat al-islām ʿan taghyīr binā' al-bayt al-ḥarām*, Ibn Ziyād al-Ghaythī [al-Ghayṭī?]. 900–975/1495–1568. G II, 404 (new ed. G II, 532/2, no. 10).
59. *Risālah fī al-īmān wa-al-islām*, Najm al-Dīn al-Ghayṭī. –981/ –1573. S III, 1288; SN II, 468, no. 23.
60. *Risālah fī ḥaqīqat al-īmān wa-al-islām*, Aḥmad al-ʿIbādī (ʿAbbādī). –994/–1586. S II, 441.
61. *Ta'rīkh al-islām bi-Dimashq wa-al-Sha'm*, Muḥammad al-Baṣrāwī. Before 1005/1596 (date of MS). 10th/16th century? S II, 406.
62. *ʿAqīdat ahl al-islām wa-al-īmān*, ʿAlī al-Qāri' al-Harawī. –1014/–1605. S II, 543, no. 155.
63. *Taʿrīf ahl al-islām wa-al-īmān bi-anna Muḥammadan ṣlʿm lā yakhlū minhu makān wa-lā zamān*, Nūr al-Dīn ʿAlī al-Ḥalabī. –1044/–1634. G II, 329 (=2nd ed. G II, 432, no. 4a); SN II, 457 (=S III, 1287).
64. *Saʿādat ahl al-islām*, Abū al-Ikhlāṣ al-Shurunbulālī. –1069/ –1658. G II, 313; S II, 431, no. 7.
65. *Taḥīyat al-islām fī-mā warada bi-al-salām wa-al-muṣāfaḥah wa-al-qiyām*, Dhū al-Nūn b. Jirjīs al-Mawṣilī. 12th/18th century. S II, 506; 980.
66. *Jāmiʿ arkān al-islām*, Sayf ibn Nāṣir al-Ḥarūṣī. (Pub: Cairo, 1346; no date: written after 520/1126.) SN I, 692 (=S III 1226).
67. *Kifāyat al-ghulām fī jumlat arkān al-islām*, ʿAbd al-Ghanī al-Nābulusī. –1143/–1731. G II, 347; S II, 474, no. 35.
68. *Ḥujjat al-islām fī rasm al-khaṭṭ al-muwāfiq li-rasm al-imām*, Muḥammad Badr al-Islām. Written 1157/1744. S II, 606.
69. *Farā'iḍ al-islām/al-īmān*, Muḥammad Hāshim al-Sindī al-Tattawī. –1174/–1760. S II, 612/13, no. 3.
70. *Uṣūl al-īmān/al-islām*, Muḥammad b. ʿAbd al-Wahhāb. 1115–1206/1703–1791. S II, 531, no. 7.
71. *Faḍl al-islām*, Muḥammad b. ʿAbd al-Wahhāb. S II, 531, no. 14.
72. *Farā'iḍ al-dīn wa-wājibāt al-islām*, Mīrghanī. –1207/–1792. S II, 523.

73. *ʿImād al-islām fī ʿilm al-kalām* or *Mir'āt al-ʿuqūl fī ʿilm al-uṣūl*, Dildār al-Laknawī. 1166–1235/1753–1820. S II, 852/8, no. 2.
74. *Ḥusām al-islām fī naqḍ mā dhakarahu ʿAbd al-ʿAzīz al-Dihlawī fī bāb al-nubūwah*, Dildār al-Laknawī. S II, 852/8.
75. *Jawāhir al-kalām fī sharḥ Sharā'iʿ al-islām*, Muḥammad Ḥasan b. Muḥammad Bāqir al-Najafī al-Iṣfahānī. –1268/–1851. Published Tehran, 1271, 1273–78, 1286–87, 1301. S I, 712, no. i.
76. *Nafas al-Raḥmān fī manāqib/faḍā'il rūḥ al-islām sayyidinā Salmān*, Ḥusayn b. Muḥammad Taqī al-Nūrī. Published Tehran 1285/1866. S II, 832/47, no. 1.
77. *Ḥāshiyah ʿalá sharḥ shaykh al-islām ʿalá al-Īsāghūjī*, ʿUllaysh al-Mālikī. –1299/–1881. S II, 738.
78. *Ḍaw' al-shams fī sharḥ qawlihi buniya al-islām ʿalá khams*, Abū al-Hudá al-Ṣayyādī. Published Istanbul 1300 (1883). 1266–1327/1850–1909. S II, 869, no. 22.

The following are not dated:

79. *Fatḥ al-Raḥmān fī mā yaḥṣulu bi-hi al-islām wa-al-īmān*, Muḥammad b. Ziyād al-Waḍḍāḥī. (n.d.) S II, 994.
80. *Muqaddimah fī al-īmān wa-al-islām*, Abū Isḥāq al-Tūnisī, (n.d.) S II, 992, no. 28.
81. *Lawāzim al-islām wa-al-īmān*, Hilāl b. Muḥammad al-Maqdisī. (n.d.) S II, 991/21a.
82. *Sharḥ risālat shaykh al-islām*, Ismāʿīl al-Nābulusī. (n.d.) S II, 1005, no. 82.
83. *Sharḥ ʿalá qawl ḥujjat al-islām al-Ghazzālī laysa fī al-imkān . . .*, Muḥammad al-Nashshārī. (n.d.) SN I, "746" (sc. 747), no. 23h (=S III, 1230).
84. *Kayfa kāna ẓuhūr shaykh al-islām Muḥammad ibn ʿAbd al-Wahhāb*, 13th/19th century? S II, 531.

List B. Listed here are eighty-one instances in the modern period (14th century *hijrī*) of Arabic book titles containing the word *islām*. Unless otherwise designated, the references are to Brockelmann; but this has been supplemented by a few items culled from the catalogue of the Majlis Library, Tehran; from the library of the School of Oriental Studies of the American University at Cairo; from the personal collection of the present writer (designated here w.c.s.); and in one or two instances from the library of the Institute of Islamic Studies, McGill University, Montreal (designated here McG). The libraries mentioned have not, however, been systematically searched. Brockelmann entries stop in the later 1930s.

The works are designated by place and date of publication, and are arranged approximately in chronological order of publication except for items 1 and 2. These two titles are included here rather than in List A for the purely formal reason that our rule has been to arrange entries by date of author's death where date of publication is not known. Certainly in every other respect (and perhaps even in this, if date of composition or publication were available) there two resemble, or continue, the classical mediaeval tradition rather than inaugurating the modern (B 1 is in fact, like A 52, a commentary on A 21).

1. *Hidāyat al-anām (fī sharḥ Sharā'iʿ al-islām bi-ṭarīq al-istidlāl ʿalá wajh al-basṭ al-tāmm)*, Muḥammad Ḥusayn al-Kāẓimī. 1230–1308/1815–1890. S I, 712, no. m.; S II, 796/22.
2. *Dharā'iʿ al-islām*, Muḥammad Ḥasan al-Māmaqānī. 1238–1325/1822–1905. Several vols., S II, 798/33.
3. *Ḥaḍārat al-Islām fī Dār al-Salām*, Jamīl Nakhlah ibn Mudawwar. Cairo, 1888, 1905, 1932/[ca. 1306], 1323, [ca. 1351]. S III, 184.
4. *Bākūrat al-kalām ʿalá ḥuqūq al-nisā' fī al-Islām*, Ḥamzah Fatḥ Allāh. 1266–1336/1850–1918. Būlāq, 1308 [ca. 1890]. S II, 724.
5. *al-Riqq fī al-Islām*, Aḥmad Bak Shafīq. French original; annotated Arabic translation by Aḥmad Zakī Bak. Būlāq, 1309 [ca. 1891]. S III, 282/w.c.s.

6. *Futūḥ al-Islām bi-bilād al-ʿajam wa-khurāsān*, al-Wāqidī. Cairo, 1309/1891. S I, 208.
7. *al-Mustaqbal li-al-Islām*, Tawfīq al-Bakrī. 1287–1351/1870–1932. Cairo, 1310 [ca. 1892] S III, 82.
8. *Ijmāl al-kalām fī al-ʿArab wa-al-Islām*, Muṣṭafá al-Dimyāṭī. Cairo, 1313/[ca. 1895]. G II, 483; S II, 734/9, no. g.
9. *al-Islām khawāṭir wa-sawāniḥ*, Arabic trans. by Aḥmad Fatḥī Zaghlūl, from French original by H. de Castries. Cairo, 1315, 1329 [ca. 1897] [ca. 1911]. S III, 326.
10. *Khulāṣat al-kalām fī tarjīḥ dīn al-Islām*, Abū al-Maḥāsin Yūsuf al-Nabhānī. 1266–/1849–. Cairo, 1317 [ca. 1899]. S II, 765, no. 50.
11. *Saʿādat al-anām fī ittibāʿ dīn al-Islām*, Abū al-Maḥāsin Yūsuf al-Nabhānī. Cairo, n.d. [ca. 1318/1900]. S II, 764, no. 5.
12. *Tanbīh al-afhām ilá maṭālib al-ḥayāh al-ijtimāʿīyah fī al-Islām*, Rafīq Bak b. al-ʿAẓm, 1282–1343/1865–1925. Cairo, 1318 [ca. 1900]. S II, 755/4, no. 2; III, 388.
13. *Ḥumāt al-Islām*, Muṣṭafá Bak Najīb. Cairo [1319], 1901. S III, 308.
14. *al-Islām fī ʿaṣr al-ʿilm*, Farīd Wajdī. Cairo, 2 vols., 1320 [ca. 1902]. S III, 325; 2nd ed. 1350 [ca. 1931]—from catalogue of Majlis Library, Tehran.
15. *al-Islām wa-al-Naṣrānīyah maʿa al-ʿilm wa-al-madanīyah*, Muḥammad ʿAbduh. Cairo, 1320, 1323, 1341, [ca. 1342] 1902 [ca. 1905], 1922, 1923. S III, 320.
16. *Kitāb al-bayʿ min sharāʾiʿ al-Islām*, Muḥammad Hādī al-Ṭihrānī. Tehran, 1320/1902. S II, 797/30, no. 3.
17. *al-Niẓām wa-al-Islām*. Ṭanṭāwī Jawharī. 1287–/1870–. Cairo, 1321, 1331 [ca. 1903] [ca. 1912]. S III, 327.
18. *Ashhar mashāhīr al-Islām fī al-ḥarb wa-al-siyāsah*, Rafīq Bak b. al-ʿAẓm. 1282–1343/1865–1925. 4 vols., Cairo [ca. 1321], [ca. 1326], 1903, 1908.
19. *al-Madanīyah wa-al-Islām*, Farīd Wajdī. Cairo, 1322, 1331, 1345/1904, [ca. 1913], 1927. S III, 324.

20. *Kashf shubahāt al-Naṣārá wa-ḥujaj al-Islām*, Rashīd Riḍā. Cairo, 1322 [ca. 1904]. S III, 323.
21. *al-Islām dīn al-fiṭrah*, ʿAbd al-ʿAzīz Jāwīsh. ca. 1323?/1905? Cairo, n.d. [before 1359/1940], w.c.s., 2nd ed.
22. *al-Inṣāf fī (taḥqīq) masā'il al-khilāf min kitāb Jawāhir al-kalām fī sharḥ Sharā'iʿ al-Islām*, Muḥammad Ṭāhā al-Ṭabarsī. Tehran, 1324 [ca. 1906]. S II, 798/32.
23. *Ta'rīkh duwal al-Islām*, Rizq Allāh Maqaryūs al-Ṣidqī. Cairo, 1325–6, 1343/1907–8, 1923. S III, 423.
24. *al-ʿArab qabla al-Islām*, Jirjī Zaydān. Cairo [ca. 1327], 1908. S III, 189, no. 13.
25. *Tanwīr al-afhām fī maṣādir al-Islām*, St. Clair Tisdall. Cairo? between 1318/1900 and 1328/1910? Library of S.O.S., Am. Univ. at Cairo.
26. *al-Islām wa-al-radd ʿalá muntaqidīh*, Muḥammad ʿAbduh. Cairo, 1327, 1343, [1344]/1909, 1924, 1925. S III, 320.
27. *Dhikrá dhawī al-faḍl fī muṭābaqat arkān al-Islām*, Muḥammad Bāshā al-Jazā'irī. Cairo, 1327/[ca. 1909]. S II, 887.
28. *al-Hay'ah wa-al-Islām: fī istikhrāj muktashafāt al-hay'ah al-jadīdah min ẓawāhir sharīʿat al-Islām*, Muḥammad ʿAlī Hibat al-Dīn al-Shahrastānī. Baghdad? 1328 [ca. 1910]. 1301– /1883–. S II, 807.
29. *al-Dīn wa-al-Islām*, Muḥammad Ḥusayn al-Najafī. 2 vols., Sidon, 1370–71 (? lege 1330?) [ca. 1911]. S II, 802.
30. *Mukhtaṣar ta'rīkh al-Islām*, Ṣadr ad-Dīn al-Ṣadr. Baghdad, 1330 [ca. 1911]. S III, 495.
31. *al-Qaṣīdah al-ʿalawīyah aw Ta'rīkh shiʿrī li-ṣadr al-Islām*, ʿAbd al-Masīḥ al-Anṭākī. 1874–1920. Cairo, 1338/1920. S III, 179, 344.
32. *Tuḥfat al-anām, mukhtaṣar ta'rīkh al-Islām*, ʿAbd al-Basīṭ al-Fakhūrī. Beirut [ca. 1338]/1920. S III, 423.
33. *Tarjamat al-Qur'ān wa-mā fī-hā min mafāsid wa-munāfāt al-Islām*, Rashīd Riḍā. Cairo, 1340/[ca. 1922]. S III, 323.
34. *al-Islām wa-uṣūl al-ḥukm*, ʿAlī ʿAbd al-Rāziq. Cairo, 1344/1925. S III, 329.

35. *al-Islām wa-uṣūl al-ḥukm wa-al-radd ʿalayh*, Yūsuf al-Dijwī. Cairo, n.d. [ca. 1345/1926?]. w.c.s.
36. *Ḥaqīqat al-Islām wa-uṣūl al-ḥukm*, Muḥammad Bakhīt. Cairo [1345]/[1926]. S III, 329 [gives the date as 1343, but this precedes that of the work that it answers].
37. *Naqd kitāb al-Islām wa-uṣūl al-ḥukm*, Muḥammad al-Khiḍr Ḥusayn. Cairo, 1345/[1926]. S III, 330.
38. *Ta'rīkh al-Islām wa-al-khulafā' al-rāshidīn*, ʿAbd al-Wahhāb al-Najjār. Cairo, 1345/[1926]. S III, 309 f.
39. *Ta'rīkh falsafat al-Islām fī al-mashriq wa-al-maghrib*, Muḥammad Luṭfī Jumʿah. Cairo, 1345/1927. S III, 276.
40. *Al-Islām wa-Āsiyā amāma al-maṭāmiʿ al-ūrubīyah*. Cairo, [ca. 1347]/1928. McG.; trans. from French of Eugène Jung.
41. *Fajr al-Islām*, Aḥmad Amīn/Ṭāhā Ḥusayn/ʿAbd al-Ḥamīd al-ʿIbādī. Cairo, [ca. 1347] 1928. S III, 305.
42. *Mawāqif ḥāsimah fī ta'rīkh al-Islām*, Muḥammad ʿAbd Allāh ʿInān. Cairo, [ca. 1347] 1928. S III, 212.
43. *Yusr al-Islām wa-uṣūl al-tashrīʿ al-ʿāmm*, Rashīd Riḍā. Cairo, 1347 [ca. 1928]. S III, 323.
44. *Ta'rīkh al-ḥarakāt al-fikrīyah fī al-Islām—al-ḥarakāt al-ijtimāʿīyāh*, Bandalī Jawzī. Jerusalem, ca. 1347/1928. S III, 423.
45. *Madanīyat al-ʿArab fī al-jāhilīyah wa-al-Islām*, Muḥammad Rushdī al-Jarkashī. Cairo, [ca. 1348] 1929. S III, 310.
46. *Al-Islām wa-al-mar'ah*. Baghdad, 1348 [ca. 1929]. Catalogue of Majlis Library, Tehran.
47. *Mabādi' al-Islām*, ʿAbd al-Ḥaqq Manṣūr. Beirut, 1349/1930. S III, 423.
48. *Al-Islām, kitāb yahdī al-khalq ilá al-ḥaqq wa-yadʿū al-anām ilá al-Islām . . . dīnī, akhlāqī, adabī, ijtimāʿī*, Asʿad Luṭfī Ḥasan. Cairo, 1350/1932. w.c.s.
49. *Nidā' li-al-jins al-laṭīf fī ḥuqūq al-nisā' fī al-Islām*, Rashīd Riḍā. Cairo, 1351 [ca. 1932]. S III, 323, no. 14.
50. *Shuyūkh al-Azhar wa-al-ziyādah fī al-Islām*, ʿAbd Allāh b. ʿAlī al-Najdī al-Qasīmī. Cairo, 1351 [ca. 1932]. S III, 209.

51. *Duwal al-ʿArab wa-ʿuẓamāʾ al-Islām*, Aḥmad Shawqī. 1868–1932. Cairo, [ca. 1352] 1933. S III, 40.
52. *al-ʿĀlam al-Islāmī wa-al-ʿArab qabla al-Islām*, Muʿammar Riḍā Kaḥḥālah. Damascus, [ca. 1352] 1933. S III, 424–425.
53. *Ḍuḥā al-Islām*, Aḥmad Amīn. Cairo, 2 vols., 1351–53/1933-35. S III, 305.
54. *Kitāb al-Islām māḍīyihi wa-ḥāḍirih*, ʿAbd al-Bāqī Surūr Naʿīm. Cairo. 1352/1934. w.c.s.
55. *Taʾrīkh al-qaḍāʾ fī al-Islām*, Maḥmūd b. Muḥammad b. ʿArnūs. Cairo, 1352/1934. Library of S.O.S., Am. Univ. at Cairo.
56. *Taʾrīkh al-Islām al-siyāsī*, Amīn Saʿīd. Cairo, 1353 [ca. 1934]. Catalogue of Majlis Library, Tehran.
57. *al-Islām wa-al-Shīʿah al-imāmīyah*, Hādī ibn Ḥusayn al-Ashkūrī. Sidon, 1353 [ca. 1934]. S II, 805/69.
58. *al-Islām wa-al-tajdīd fī Miṣr*. Arabic trans. by Maḥmūd ʿAbbās al-ʿAqqād from English of C.C. Adams. Cairo, 1353/1935. S III, 310 (supplemented).
59. *Taʾrīkh al-Islām al-siyāsī wa-al-dīnī wa-al-thaqāfī wa-al-ijtimāʿī*, Ḥasan Ibrāhim Ḥasan. Cairo, 4 vols., 1353/1934. w.c.s.
60. *Niẓām al-nasīʾ ʿinda al-ʿArab qabla al-Islām*, Ibn Fāṭimah. Cairo, 1354/1935. Catalogue of S.O.S. Library, Am. Univ. at Cairo.
61. *al-Islām al-ṣaḥīḥ, baḥth wa-taḥqīq*, Muḥammad Isʿāf al-Nashāshībī. Jerusalem, 1354/1935. S III, 394.
62. *al-Islām fī al-Ḥabashah*, Yūsuf Aḥmad. Cairo, 1354 [ca. 1935]. Catalogue of Majlis Library, Tehran.
63. *al-Islām wa-al-ḥaḍārah al-ʿarabīyah*, Muḥammad Kurd ʿAlī. Cairo, [1352], 1354/[1934], 1936. S III, 434. (Earlier date from Catalogue of Majlis Library, Tehran.)
64. *al-Mustashriqūn wa-al-Islām*, Ḥusayn Harrāwī. Cairo, 1355/1936. Catalogue of S.O.S. Library, Am. Univ. at Cairo; w.c.s.
65. *Khulāṣat al-kalām fī arkān al-Islām*, ʿAlī Fikrī. Cairo, 1355/1936. w.c.s.

66. *al-Ṣirāʿ bayna al-Islām wa-al-wathanīyīn*, ʿAbd Allāh b. ʿAlī al-Najdī al-Qasīmī. Cairo, 1356 [ca. 1937]. S III, 209.
67. *Ghāyat al-marām fī ʿaqā'id ahl al-Islām*, al-Ḥājj Ḥamdī al-Aʿẓamī. Baghdad, [1356?], 1367/[1937?], 1948. w.c.s.
68. *al-Zawāj fī al-Islām*, Asʿad Luṭfī Ḥasan. Cairo, 1357/1938. w.c.s.
69. *Ta'rīkh al-falsafah fī al-Islām*. Arabic trans. by Muḥammad ʿAbd al-Hādī Abū Rīdah. Cairo, 1357, 1367, 1374, 1377/1938, 1948, 1954, 1957. w.c.s.
70. *Ādāb al-ḥarb fī al-Islām*, Muḥammad al-Khiḍr Ḥusayn. [Cairo], n.d. (before 1359/1940). w.c.s.
71. *Rasā'il al-salām wa-rusul al-Islām alladhī waḍaʿahu li-ahl Amrīkā*, Yūsuf al-Dijwī. Cairo, n.d. [before 1359/1940]. w.c.s.
72. *al-Islām wa-al-ṭibb al-ḥadīth*, ʿAbd al-ʿAzīz Ismāʿīl. Cairo, before 1363/1944.
73. *Min ta'rīkh al-ilḥād fī al-Islām*, ʿAbd al-Raḥmān Badawī. Cairo, [ca. 1364] 1945. w.c.s.
74. *Ẓuhr al-Islām*, Aḥmad Amīn. 4 vols., Cairo, 1364–[ca. 1374]/1945–55. w.c.s.
75. *al-Islām dīn al-insānīyah*, Arabic trans. by Ḥabībah Shaʿbān Yakun of English original by Mawlānā Muḥammad ʿAlī. Beirut, 1365/1946. w.c.s.
76. *al-Islām ʿalá muftaraq al-ṭuruq*, Arabic trans. by ʿUmar Farrukh from English of Asad Weiss. Beirut, [ca. 1365], [ca. 1367], [ca. 1370]/1946, 1948, 1951. McG.
77. *Muqaddimah fī ta'rīkh ṣadr al-Islām*, ʿAbd al-ʿAzīz al-Dūrī. Baghdad, [1368] 1949. w.c.s.
78. *Hādhā huwa al-Islām*, Muḥammad ʿAbd al-Qādir al-ʿAmmāwī. [Cairo], n.d. [shortly before 1371/1952]. w.c.s.
79. *al-Mujaddidūn fī al-Islām, 100 hijrī–1370 hijrī*, ʿAbd al-Mutaʿāl al-Ṣaʿīdī. Cairo, n.d.; after 1370 [ca. 1951].
80. *Yawm al-Islām*, Aḥmad Amīn. Cairo, [ca. 1371] 1952. w.c.s.
81. *Mustaqbal al-Islām*, Muḥammad ʿAbd al-Qādir al-ʿAmmāwī. Cairo, 1371/1952. w.c.s.

List C. Four titles supplied by a friend in Cairo to illustrate certain extreme instances of the phrase 'Fī al-islām'; but the works themselves were not available to the present writer, nor a written reference source.

1. *al-Naẓarīyah al-siyāsīyah al-yūnānīyah fī al-Islām*, ʿAbd al-Raḥmān Badawī. Cairo.
2. *al-Rūm al-malikīyūn fī al-Islām*, Ḥabīb Zayyāt. Beirut.
3. *al-Ṣalīb fī al-Islām*, Ḥabīb Zayyāt. Beirut (Harisah).
4. *al-Dayyārāt al-naṣrānīyah fī al-Islām*, Ḥabīb Zayyāt. Beirut.

4

Islamic Law: Its 'Sources' (*Uṣūl al-fiqh*) and *Ijtihād*

This paper represents my first published venture into the question of Islamic Law. It is also my first public statement on an Islamic issue proffered to a predominantly Muslim audience on formal Muslim invitation. I was one of several Western students of Islamics invited to participate along with Muslim scholars in an 'International Islamic Colloquium' held at the University of the Panjab, Lahore, Pakistan, at the end of 1957 and the beginning of 1958. The venture of the outsider/insider mixture of speakers worked none too smoothly, but the experiment was a bold one and we may reflect that the Christian Church, for instance, has hardly as yet begun to invite knowledgeable members of other communities to share in its discussions of internal Christian issues. I have always felt that to write about Islām is a sensitive and deeply responsible undertaking: for one human being to participate intellectually in the spiritual life of another group is always venturesome. My own contribution was indeed a bold one, although it was also, of course, fundamentally simple, as was appropriate given that my probing of the sharīʿah *side of the Islamic complex was incipient only. Since it was a Muslim conference it seemed appropriate to deal with a topic currently exercising Muslim minds. The interpretation may seem unduly Platonic, for a proposed presentation of a Semitic world-view. The germ of the idea, however, had been lodged in my mind a dozen years earlier when I had read a brief homily on* ijtihād *in the Azhar Journal. A few years after this conference, I developed further my inquiry into the Law, and produced the study on the historical development of the concept* sharīʿah, *which constitutes the next entry of this present collection. The two papers may be seen as linked through a recognition of the characteristic role of the grammatical form* maṣdar *in Arabic, and therefore in Islamic thought—as I remark in my introduction to that next essay.*

It has often been stated that in the religion of Islām the sources of the Law are four. These are listed usually as the Qur'ān, the Sunnah, *ijmāʿ*, and *qiyās*; though there has been discussion as to whether there are not, or should not be, rather three sources, or five. In any case, many have held that there are various sources, and consideration has been given, and it was felt, rightly given, to the matter of designating what precisely those sources are or have been or ought to be.

With this view has gone the further idea that *ijtihād* is or has been or may (again) become a source of law, a method of determining what Islamic Law shall be. The point is of not only academic interest. A major question in modern Muslim life in many countries, a question of social and political and economic and even psychological significance, is whether and how far and by whom *ijtihād* may be exercised in changing the Law or modifying it or adapting it to new conditions.

The purpose of the present essay is to suggest tentatively that the intellectual handling of these matters might be advanced if the basic presuppositions were further clarified. I do not wish to plunge into any discussion on the actual content of the Law, either past or present, nor on the techniques of any process of adaptation or conservation for the future. Rather, I would venture to raise a question as to the framework within which all such discussion proceeds.

First, is it not true that in any just interpretation of Islām the Law has only one source: God. It is God who determines what man should and should not do; how society should and should not operate. The Qur'ān, the Sunnah, and the rest are not sources of the Law; they are rather sources of human knowledge of the Law. It is through the Qur'ān, Muslims have believed, and through the behaviour of the Prophet, and in various other ways, that the transcendent pattern of prescribed behaviour has been disclosed. This is revelation: a procedure for letting man know, in whole or in part, what God's will[1] is. Had there been no revelation, there would still be a Law. The only difference would then be that humanity would have been left in the dark as to what it is. (At least so the standard view. The Muʿtazilah, who were repudiated by the community in earlier centuries, in part held that even without revelation man, through the exercise of his reason, might, perhaps, at his best, attain to an awareness of what the Law is, though revelation simplifies and confirms and makes graphic and cogent.)

It is a question, then, of apprehending something that independently exists. Our apprehending of it, and even God's revealing of it, do not alter the nature of the commands. They alter only our relation to them. God, and God alone, is *al-Ḥākim*. The Qur'ān and the rest are *uṣūl al-fiqh*, roots of *fiqh*, discernment. *Fiqh* is, fundamentally, not the system of *aḥkām*, but the science of finding out what that system is. Similarly, the *ʿulamā'* are persons who allegedly 'know' (root *ʿ-l-m*) what the *aḥkām* are.

The Law, then, is divine. *Fiqh*, *'ilm*, jurisprudence, are human. The Law is eternal; knowledge of it is temporal, historical. The human element is not *merely* human, since guidance has been vouchsafed to man by God in this matter. This is what, in many ways, Islām is all about. Nonetheless, it remains human, of this world.

If we turn next to *ijtihād*, the same principles help to illuminate. The *mujtahid* is one who exerts himself to ascertain what the Law is. His *ijtihād* does not modify the Law; it simply is successful or otherwise in discovering it. To say that the gate of *ijtihād* has been closed is to affirm that men in the past have discovered all that there is to know about the Law. The theory asserts that a considerable effort and a considerable lapse of time were necessary to reach this stage. For the Muslim community obviously and admittedly did not begin in complete possession of a full knowledge of the Law; the whole Law was not yet fully known at the time of the Prophet's death, even though revelation was by then completed. On the contrary, the community is held to have rounded out this knowledge only a couple of centuries later. Those centuries' understanding of revelation is the point at issue.

One of the questions that Muslims are asking themselves and each other now that they are confronted with a world conspicuously in transition, now that they are facing unprecedented problems and responsibilities and opportunities, is whether or not the Law changes. We must recognize that in the first instance this is a problem not for the *mujtahid* but for God. Today's conditions are new. Tomorrow's, it seems probable, will be still newer, stranger. Does God require of man in these changed conditions, and changing ones, the same behaviour as he required previously; or has He new commands? The view that His requirements are modified, has been incorporated into the formulation *tataghayyaru al-aḥkām bi-taghayyur al-azmān*. God, presumably, remains *al-Ḥākim*; so that this principle asserts that God—who presumably knows very well that the twentieth century is what it is and that the twenty-first will be something else again, and indeed is ultimately responsible for this newness; it is He who makes the world anew—God lays upon mankind an evolving imperative, just as He surrounds mankind with an evolving environment. This is a logically tenable position, though one not widely held.

We must recognize, however, that this principle is not the same as the principle of *ijtihād*. It is possible to reject this doctrine; it is possible to believe that the Law is not only eternal but immutable, the same yesterday, today, and forever, and nonetheless to be persuaded that the early Muslims' grasp of that Law was incomplete. One may hold that those early interpreters were simply inadequate, that they missed certain basic truths in their human apprehension of the transcendent pattern, or interpreted some parts of it well yet conceivably, being human, misinterpreted other parts. Or, alternatively, one may hold that inevitably and in the nature of the case they interpreted the eternal Law in terms of their own relativities, their own needs and conditions; and that this, though not eternally valid, was quite inevitable and indeed for them quite right and proper. For, one may even postulate as a general principle that human understanding of divine truth is inevitably human, partial, relative, and more or less *ad hoc*; that the Law is perfect and fixed, but man's apprehension of that Law is, and always must be, imperfect and destined to be superseded.

In the former of these two cases the task of the *mujtahid* is to set the old interpretations right. Man today must correct the mistakes of his predecessors. In the latter case the task of the *mujtahid* is to do for our day what they did for theirs. One honours and applauds the great and, for a time, superbly serviceable achievement of their interpretation for their time, and presses on in the endeavour to do as much for ours. Yet one recognizes that modern man, too, is a man, is fallible. One may say humbly that although their classic version of what the Law means for human life is no longer relevant or fully relevant to us, yet modern man in working out his own version of what it means for human life today may be less successful than they were in their time. With luck, with devoted effort, with divine guidance, the new interpretation may be as good; or it may be not so good. In any case, it must be done. Even the prospect of executing the task less adequately than they executed theirs, does not absolve one from the task. The Muslim community's twentieth-century apprehension of the Law may be more or equally or less adequate for the twentieth century than its ninth-century apprehension was for the ninth; but it would still be more adequate for the twentieth century than the ninth-century version is for the twentieth century. So runs the argument.

A belief in an unchanging Law in its transcendent, ultimate sense is not incompatible, therefore, with a profound conviction that *ijtihād* in our day is not only legitimate but necessary—and necessary not only because of social and legal exigencies, but morally; necessary in the sense that God Himself requires of man that we always anew strive to discern His meaning. He does not require, or expect, that we will discern it totally and ultimately, for that is, perhaps, beyond both our capacity and our need; but that we strive to discern it insofar as it applies to the actual situations in which we find ourselves. There is even a *ḥadīth* that asserts that He is pleased with man's striving even when it is ineptly done, let alone His being doubly pleased when the endeavour breaks through to some true understanding. *Man ijtahada wa akhṭa'a, fa-lahu ajr; wa-man ijtahada wa aṣāba, fa-lahu ajrān.*

If even an unchanging Law may require an evolving interpretation, then how much more, one might suppose, a Law that is itself developing. Yet even here, on more careful analysis, it becomes apparent that, as we urged in the beginning, *ijtihād* and a change in the Law are two quite separate things. For, oddly enough, it is logically possible to believe that the *aḥkām* change without there being need for a radical re-interpretation. This indeed is roughly the actual position of many of the *ʿulamā'* class, the men who are custodians of the established traditional interpretation. For, they can point out, the traditional exposition of *fiqh* itself included provisions for progressive modification of its own dicta. These provisions have of late centuries not been much used, perhaps, but they are there. Within the structure of classical jurisprudence certain principles of flexibility and adaptation are enunciated and carefully defined. Even the society of those who framed that jurisprudence, though more stable than ours (and different from it), was not, of course, entirely static. They, too, had to contend with some novelty, with some unprecedented cases. Life has never been inanimate! It is possible to argue, therefore, and it has been argued, that the regulations already laid down within the corpus of received Islamic legal scholarship prescribe and define, with precision, the freedom that is available to the community or its leaders in dealing with novel situations; and that these prescriptions are binding. The interpretation of the injunctions may change, but the degree and process and technique of that change are defined from within the extant interpretation. No other re-interpretation is either desirable or permissible.

Others may contend that the situation today is so novel, that not only is what is required of us new but that new ways of ascertaining it are also requisite: that loyalty to God's continuing purpose demands that the whole structure of traditional discernment (Arabic, *fiqh*), whatever its past validity, be superseded now by a new apparatus for translating His transcendent demands into human legalities.

To sum up, then: We would suggest that the modern Muslim faces in theory four possibilities: (1) that the Law is fixed, and that the community's understanding of that Law is fixed; (2) that the Law is fixed, but the understanding of it develops; (3) that the Law develops, but the community's understanding of it and of its development is fixed, is available in the ancient books; (4) that the Law develops, and that the understanding of it is also subject to development.

In no one of the four cases does man determine or change the Law. We conclude as we began: it is God who pronounces on good and evil. Man's task is to learn those pronouncements and to declare them. The practical question is, whether this task has already been completely discharged or, if not, whether the traditional custodians of the classical interpretation alone may discharge it (or alone have the right to state who is qualified to discharge it and under what conditions); or whether the task devolves upon any section of the community able and willing and qualified to take it up, and consists not in modifying yesterday's law but in attaining insight into today's.

Two final considerations. One is that if a Muslim (or a Muslim group) genuinely and reverently believes that God's requirements for modern life are different from what the classical *ʿulamāʾ* set forth, there really is not much that anyone disagreeing can do about it. A *mujtahid* is a man of faith who endeavours, we have argued, to discern what God's will (*amr* or *marḍī*) for today is. An exponent of the traditional view may argue that according to that traditional view this man has no right to be a *mujtahid*. Yet this man may answer that it is precisely the authority of that traditional view rightly to interpret God's mind, that he is questioning or that for him has broken down. It is ultimately a matter of conscience. And in matters of conscience authority cannot be imposed, it must win one's inner allegiance by its own persuasiveness. *Lā ikrāha fī al-din*. In the last analysis (on the Day of Judgement, as the older metaphor phrased it), man stands alone before his Maker to answer for his choices and his convictions. A Muslim is not Muslim if he refuses to acknowledge God's imperative. But no one on earth has the right to say that he is not Muslim if he honestly disagrees with others as to what that imperative is.[2]

The author of the present paper is not himself a member of the Muslim community, but he is a human being living like members of that community in the perplexing and fluid modern world, which he believes, like them, God has made and for which he believes, like them, God has some purpose. As to what that purpose is in its over-all generality he, like them, has a faith; but what it is in concrete particularities, in precise answer to specific issues as they arise, he feels needs to be discerned. And even on the question as to how one should go about discerning it, and by what procedure one should move from the data of revelation to the technicalities of decisions, he feels that there can be honest differences of opinion that deserve respect. As an observer of the Muslim community it is, perhaps, not illegitimate for him to note that that community appears to an outsider to be in somewhat the same case. Our discernings may, and doubtless will, differ. The need to discern, men seem to hold in common.

My second concluding point has to do with the fact that we have throughout referred to Law with a capital L, the Law that God ordains (*sharaʿa*). The Western counterpart of this concept, I have elsewhere suggested, is Justice, which also transcends, but only partially eludes, man's comprehension. Apart from this ultimate Law or Justice there is the Western concept of law as administered, to which Muslim countries have of course also their counterpart in the law with a small 'l' that is applied in their courts. The relation between the law that is in force and Islamic Law as a final principle is precisely the question that Pakistan, for instance, concretely faces. Canada, too, faces a somewhat comparable problem in that a judge, on assuming office, takes an oath not that he will administer the law but that he will administer justice according to the law; and the Canadian legislature is presumed to modify and to advance the justiciable law in the light of changing circumstances on the one hand and in the light of persistent (transcendent) Justice on the other. The techniques, both theoretical and practical, for effecting this, and their success or failure, as well as the conception of what justice is, are, of course, different in Canada and Pakistan, in Western civilization and in Islām. But that the law of the courts, by which man is judged on earth, bears some relation to the higher Law by which he is judged by a higher authority, and that this relation is the continuing responsibility of the community, seem common to us all.

5

Islamic Law: *Sharīʿah* and *Sharʿ*

My preliminary treatment of this topic was read to the Islamics section of the International Congress of Orientalists' quadrennial meeting held in Moscow in 1960 (my first visit to the Soviet Union). My teacher Sir Hamilton Gibb was not at that meeting, but I reported to him privately later some of my surprising conclusions; he seemed to find the data and the ideas entrancing, as did I, and he encouraged me to push ahead with the investigation. Accordingly, when I was invited a little later to contribute to a Festschrift in his honour, I developed the inquiry into this present study, and it was published in that volume in 1965. The work constituted for me an important step in my discernment of the transcendent element in the conceptualizing by Muslims of their world, of the dynamic historical element in the process of that gradual conceptualizing, and of the intellectual task of an outsider's representing to himself and to his fellows the Islamic, and by extrapolation any religious or human, movement.

If, however, the discoveries involved in this inquiry were markedly illuminating for the observer attempting to understand Islām, they seemed potentially even more significant, if not drastically revisionist, for Muslims themselves. The historical data, once become visible, impinge in principle on Muslim consciousness, not only on outsiders'. As in the preceding presentation here (on ijtihād*), modern scholarly awareness constitutes 'knowledge about', for the observer; but also for the religious spirit contributes to self-consciousness. This is a recognition that now, some twenty years later, is pushing me towards forging a synthesis between the comparative history of religion and Christian (or Islamic, or global) theology.*

In my introductory comment to the preceding article in this collection (p. 79 above), I remark on the significance of the maṣdar*, and its recognition as linking these two studies. (To fẹel the verbal* *force of that grammatical form is often rewarding in one's careful reading of Arabic, I have found.) Of these two papers one might say that their basic point has to do with my coming to see the significance of the fact that both* fiqh *and* sharʿ *are originally verbal nouns, with the subject of the verb being in the former case man (previous chapter, above) and in the latter case God (this chapter).*

5.1 THE CONCEPT OF SHARĪʿAH AMONG SOME MUTAKALLIMŪN

The idea of *sharīʿah* has come to play an important and indeed central role in Islamic religious life. Also, although more recently, it has become the fashion in Islamics scholarship in the West to recognize the law as fundamental, and to insist that those who would understand Muslims' faith must understand this law and its religious significance, its centrality. Professor Gibb himself wrote in 1949, in a chapter that he entitled 'The Sharīʿa' in his *Mohammedanism*: 'It [that is, the *sharīʿah*] permeated almost every side of social life and every branch of Islamic literature, and it is no exaggeration to see in it, in the words of one of the most penetrating of modern students of the subject, "the epitome of the true Islamic spirit, the most decisive expression of Islamic thought, the essential kernel of Islam" '.[1] The quotation here is from Bergsträsser (1935), whose actual words were: '*Das islamische Recht, in seinem weiteren, die Regelung des Kultes mit umfassenden Sinn, ist der Inbegriff des echt islamischen Geistes, die entscheidendste Ausprägung islamischen Denkens, der Wesenskern des Islam überhaupt*'.[2]

On the Musim side, this new understanding has, I believe, met no criticism but rather has been welcomed, as an advance towards better understanding. I myself as a student have taken these suggestions to heart. I have increasingly come to feel, and to assert,[3] that in order better to understand the Islamic tradition and the faith of Muslims one must come to grips with this notion. Certainly I have found that I could understand phenomena of Islamic history, and establish rapport with many currents in contemporary Islamic society, much more effectively since learning to view the tradition and the faith from this angle.

The present paper, accordingly, is offered not as in any way dissenting from the views set forth above; but rather as possibly carrying them further, with the suggestion of certain possible refinements. My inquiry will be seen to suggest that, at least for the earlier centuries, a closer understanding may involve a more personalized and moralized conception than 'law'.

For if this matter plays an important and central role in the total Islamic position, it would seem reasonable to imagine that we should find it profitable and illuminating to ascertain how the role of the (or a) *sharīʿah* has been formulated by those whose business it was to formulate, to conceptualize the Islamic scheme: namely, the men of *kalām*.

I am primarily concerned with the religious aspect of the inquiry. Of course, the historian of Islamic civilization is also involved. Since the law clearly has finally become quite central in Islamic society and thought, the historian can ask few more significant questions than how that law came into being, both actual and conceptual. Considerable work has been done of late, most notably by Schacht, on the historical evolution of the law from the inside, as it were: the development, step-by-step, of its content and to some degree also of its form. My attention here is turned rather to a view of the *sharīʿah* from, as it were, the outside: the development of the *sharīʿah* as a concept, its rise among a salient class of Muslim religious thinkers into consciousness, and then self-consciousness. There is a process of its gradually becoming explicit.

Obviously, a thorough inquiry in this field would be a large undertaking. To deal adequately with the topic, even when restricting inquiry to *kalām*[4] writing, would require a comprehensive survey that could well involve producing another book on the scale of Wensinck's *Muslim Creed*. I leave that task to better qualified scholars, or to some later and more leisured time. Meanwhile, it is perhaps legitimate to use an opportunity such as the present to report in interim fashion on preliminary results, if only because these are surprising, and raise questions that I am happy to submit for criticism and comment.

My initial idea was to collect a few major instances of how the *mutakallimūn* thought about the *sharīʿah*, and to study and analyse such passages, as a first step. On preliminary investigation, however, it turned out that the problem is different. For apparently the *mutakallimūn* did not think about it. The evidence that I have collected strongly suggests that a *sharīʿah* is not a major concept for classical Islamic thinkers.

My observations so far are based on the following materials (in chronological order):

From the second century of the *hijrah*:
al-Fiqh al-akbar I[5]

From the third century of the *hijrah*:
the Muʿtazilah[6]
the *Waṣīyah* attributed to Abū Ḥanīfah[7]

From the fourth century of the *hijrah*:
al-Ashʿarī[8]
al-Fiqh al-akbar II[9]
the Ḥanbalī, Ibn Baṭṭah[10]
al-Bāqillānī (*Kitāb al-tamhīd*)[11]
[the Shīʿī Ibn Bābawayh, but this was available to me only in translation[12]]

From the fifth century of the *hijrah*:
al-Baghdādī (*Kitāb uṣūl al-dīn*)[13]
al-Juwaynī (*Kitāb al-irshād*)[14]
al-Ghazzālī (the *ʿAqīdat ahl al-sunnah fī kalimatay al-shahādah*, in the *Iḥyā*,[15] bk. ii, sect. 1; and *al-Iqtiṣād fī-al-iʿtiqād*)[16]

From the sixth century of the *hijrah*:
al-Nasafī[17]
al-Shahrastānī[18]

From the seventh century of the *hijrah*:
the obscure poet Ibn al-Ḥanẓalah[19]

From the eighth century of the *hijrah*:
al-Taftāzānī on the *Aqāʿid Nasafīyah*, with super-commentaries thereon from later centuries by al-Khayālī, al-Siyālkūtī, and al-Isfarāʾīnī.[20]

It is evident that the material surveyed is not complete, and I am the first to recognize that more work is required. Yet perhaps it will be agreed that neither is it unrepresentative, so that this interim report on results is perhaps not unjustified. I hope to follow up my investigations with fuller study, finding the avenues that have been opened up quite exciting; but also, I am hopeful that others may be stimulated to turning their attention to the problems raised.

My first observation is that to a considerable degree these thinkers do not use a concept *sharīʿah* at all. In the later centuries, they use the idea in passing, incidentally; or use other forms from the root *sh-r-ʿ*. Yet I see no escaping from the main conclusion: that the *sharīʿah* is a concept with which Islamic thinkers in the formative and classical periods were not concerned.

I do not mean that the idea does not occur. The word is used now and then—though extremely seldom before the fifth century, and even from that time a great deal less frequently than one might suppose, and certainly, at all times, vastly less than other basic terms such as *Allah*, *kitāb*, *nabī*, *sunnah*, *ʿaql*, *bidʿah*, etc. (including also, in the realm with which we are concerned, *aḥkām*, *amr*, *wājib*, *taklīf*). The word *sharīʿah* occurs, but it is not an important concept in the sense that writers are found discussing it or analysing it, or are concerned to get their readers to give attention to it. It is not treated as one of the Islamic issues.

Let us look at the matter more precisely. First of all, we note that in the following cases the root *sh-r-ʿ* does not even appear:
(i) *al-Fiqh al-akbar I* of (reputedly) Abū Ḥanīfah.
(ii) al-Ashʿarī's synopsis, in *al-Maqālāt al-islāmīyīn*, of the position of *Ahl al-ḥadīth wa-al-sunnah*. He calls this, *Jumlat mā ʿalayhi ahl al-ḥadīth wa-al-sunnah; . . . fa-hādhihi jumlat mā yaʾmurūna bihi wa-yastaʿmilūnah*; he ends by subscribing to it

himself, saying, *Wa-yarawnah, wa-bi-kull mā dhakarnā min qawlihim, naqūl, wa-ilayhi nadhhab.*[21] The synopsis takes the form of sixty-three articles as enumerated by McCarthy;[22] a *sharīʿah* is not mentioned.

(iii) *Waṣīyat Abī Ḥanīfah.*

(iv) The tables of contents, or headings, or section names, of any of the works appearing up to the middle of the fifth century.[23]

Personally I cannot but find this paucity of reference significant. It might be objected that the concept does not have space devoted to it in these largely controversial works not because it was peripheral, but, quite on the contrary, because it was so central that everyone took it for granted without argument. This sounds plausible, perhaps, until one reflects that the same by no means applies to concepts such as God, prophethood, and so on, which were surely no less central. And a scrutiny of the rather elaborate and full list of headings of al-Ashʿarī's *Maqālāt*[24] shows that he considers and names 401 topics, some of which are admittedly the various sects, the Bayyānīyah, the Kaysānīyah, and so on, but others include matters such as the following:

ikhtilāfuhum fī-al-Qur'ān[25]
ikhtilāfuhum fī-al-insān, mā huwa.[26]

If the Muslims of those times disputed in ways worth al-Ashʿarī's noting, on what is man, I hardly see how one can argue that the existence of a *sharīʿah* was so taken for granted that it did not get discussed. On God there were explicit questions of great subtlety: not only *al-qawl fī kalām Allāh, mā huwa*,[27] but also different sides taken on issues such as whether God knows things before they exist;[28] whether in addition to saying about Him, *lam yazal samīʿan*, one may also say *lam yazal sāmiʿan*;[29] whether He is powerful over what He knows will not exist;[30] whether the arrangement of the Qur'ān, as well as its content, is a miracle;[31] and so on.

The only conclusion to which I am able to come is that within the range of al-Ashʿarī's knowledge or interest (which were wide), a *sharīʿah*, as such, was not a topic of discussion or concern in the Islamic community of the first three centuries.[32]

In the fourth century one begins to find the concept coming into play. Al-Ashʿarī himself, though not in this work, does make use of it in two others. Before we turn, however, to consider these and other instances that will help us to form a positive judgement as to the evolution of the concept and to elucidate its significance, let us go on to consider a few cases that show not only that it was possible, but that it continued to be possible, to state to oneself or to one's fellows the Islamic faith without making much of a *sharīʿah* concept, or resorting to it only incidentally.

In the Shīʿī statement by Ibn Bābawayh al-Qummī (died 381/991), which Fayẓī has translated, it is not stated that one should believe in, or conform to, the or a *sharīʿah*, although indirectly the term is introduced, in the plural, under the heading of the prophets, of whom it is affirmed that there have been 124,000, 'And verily the leaders of the prophets are five in number round whom the heavens revolve, and they are *aṣḥāb al-sharāʾiʿ*, namely . . . Noah, Abraham, Moses, Jesus and Muḥammad, on all of whom be peace'.[33] In this case, one may infer that the *sharīʿah* concept is taken for granted, though it is not altogether clear from this passage itself whether the singular of *aṣḥāb al-sharāʾiʿ* might not be *ṣāḥib al-sharāʾiʿ* for each prophet, as admissibly as *ṣāḥib sharīʿah*; nor whether the word might not mean 'path' or 'way', as a still non-technical term, which is indeed how Fayẓī, himself both a Muslim and a lawyer, translates it.[34] However that may be, this is the only occurrence of the word in this creed of over a hundred pages.[35]

Our next theologian is Ibn Baṭṭah al-ʿUkbarī, whose *profession de foi* has recently been published.[36] He died in 387 h., a few years after Ibn Bābawayh; and was a Ḥanbalī, so that his concern with the law might be presumed to be striking. But not so. In approximately 25,000 words of text, derivatives of *sh-r-ʿ* occur but twice; and in neither case is it 'the' *sharīʿah* of Islām. In the opening doxology, God is praised for many mercies, and also: *al-ḥamdu li-Allāh ʿalá al-sharāʾiʿ al-ṭāhirah wa-al-sunan al-zākiyah wa-al-akhlāq al-fāḍilah.*[37] Clearly here, as the correlatives show, and the plural number, *sharāʾiʿ* are, as in the Qurʾān, 'ways', not codes of law—a series of activities, not yet a patterned system of incumbencies. The only[38] other use of the root, this time in the singular, is in a passage to explain the repugnant aberrations of the Zarathushtrians:

wa-qīla innahu kāna li-al-Majūs dīn wa-kitāb. fa-waqaʿ malik minhum ʿalá ukhtihi . . . ḥattá baqiya fī al-Majūs nikāḥ al-akhawāt wa-al-ummahāt; wa-baṭalat sharīʿatuhum al-ūlá.[39]

Next we may turn to the most successful formulator of them all, Abū Ḥafṣ ʿUmar Najm al-Dīn al-Nasafī (died 537 h.), whose statement of the faith was quickly welcomed and remained accepted and virtually standard till almost yesterday. 'Yes', said the community, 'this is indeed what we believe'. Now al-Nasafī does not, in fact, manage to explicate his faith without calling in the concept *sharīʿah* at all; but he comes very close to doing this. In his *ʿAqīdah*, I find the term once: not in his saying positively how, or even that, a good Muslim is involved with it, but in his objecting to the non-believer's jeering at it:

wa-istiḥāl al-maʿṣīyah, kufr. wa-al-istihānah bi-hā, kufr. wa-al-istihzā' ʿalá al-sharīʿah, kufr.[40]

This illustrates clearly enough that by this time (sixth century) the concept was established and accepted, 'taken for granted' if one likes—but it was still not felt necessary as such to the Muslim's conceptualizing of his faith.

Another instance of a somewhat comparable kind, going farther than al-Nasafī in incorporating the notion into a statement of faith, making it quite clear that the concept was accepted and obvious, but still not quite either defining or explicating it, and certainly not emphasizing it, is al-Ghazzālī. In his summary of Muslim beliefs, *Qawāʿid al-ʿAqā'id*, that he puts into Book Two of his great *Iḥyā'*, he again does not affirm it directly, but assumes it and asserts that to be a believing Muslim requires that one recognize that Muḥammad's *sharīʿah* has abrogated the other ones:

'Maʿná al-kalimah al-thāniyah', wa-hiya al-shahādah li-al-rusul bi-al-risālah: wa-annahu baʿatha al-nabī al-ummī al-Qurashī Muḥammad . . . fa-nasakha bi-sharīʿatihi al-sharā'iʿ, illā mā qarrarahu minhā.[41]

Enough then, on the negative side. It is time to turn to a constructive interpretation. I think that we have done enough to show that the *sharīʿah*, however important it may have been in fact, was not basic or central or emphasized as a concept in Islamic thought in these centuries. We have also seen, however, that while at the end of the third century it was apparently not a major idea at all, a few hundred years later it had become current as background in Islamic thinking, even if still not in the forefront of it.

This, then, is my first conclusion; a negative one.

There are, however, numerous passages, especially in the writings of the fifth and sixth centuries, on which it is, I think, possible to base positive conclusions that will lead us out of the impasse into which my investigations thus far reported seem to have led us. Altogether I have collected about two hundred passages in which the root *sh-r-ʿ* occurs. Of these, the chief are in al-Baghdādī (d. 429 h.),[42] Imām al-Ḥaramayn (d. 478 h.), and al-Shahrastānī (d. 548 h.). I may say also that I have learned perhaps at least as much from the passages where the root does *not* occur. For the clue to much of the whole problem lies in considering those passages where modern authors speak of the law, whereas the classic Muslim ones, it turns out, did not.[43]

It would take too long to present here the detailed evidence on which my constructive conclusions are reached. Besides, my study is not yet complete; not nearly full enough. What I can do at this stage is, first, to give my count of distribution of the occurrences of the root in the sources that I have surveyed. Next, I will state summarily the most important observations to which I have come; these I propound here as hypotheses, formulated on the basis of careful study of empirical instances, but still waiting to be more widely tested, to be inductively proven or refined. Finally, I will consider a particular passage of al-Shahrastānī, deliberately chosen as one of the most difficult passages from the point of view that my other evidence has induced me to develop: this would seem one instance where, if anywhere, my thesis might be disproven, so that if this passage can be interpreted in the new way, then my thesis will have been at least elucidated, if not corroborated. And contrariwise, those unpersuaded will have their evidence ready to hand.

First, then, to supplement the instances already noted, up through the third century, where the root does not occur at all, the following table shows the usage where it does:

TABLE OF DISTRIBUTION
Concept *sh-r-ᶜ* among the *Mutakallimūn*

date of death	writer	*sharīᶜah* i. The Islamic *sharīᶜah*	*sharīᶜah* ii. other	*sharᶜ* & *sharᶜī*	*shirᶜah*
324 h.	al-Ashᶜari	3	3	2	
381 h.	Ibn Bābawayh		1		
387 h.	Ibn Baṭṭah		2		
403 h.	al-Bāqillāni	4	14	6	
429 h.	al-Baghdādi	3	1	12	
478 h.	al-Juwayni, Imām al-Ḥaramayn	1	4	79	
505 h.	al-Ghazzāli	1	1	12	
537 h.	al-Nasafi	1			
548 h.	al-Shahrastāni	1	4	14	2
626 h.	Ibn al-Ḥanẓalah		1		
791 h.	al-Taftāzāni	1	4	2	
later centuries	al-Taftāzāni's commentators	3	ca. 6	ca. 9	
		18	41	136	2

Total occurrences studied: 197

From this table, two matters deserve comment. First, insofar as the term *sharīᶜah* is concerned, it is used to refer to what we today (both Muslims and outside students) call 'the' *sharīᶜah* of Islām less than one-third of the time; the concept is primarily used for other purposes. Secondly, in any case this term is used considerably less than *sharᶜ* in its various forms. Much of our problem, therefore, turns on eliciting the meaning of this latter term where it occurs.

The distribution would seem to be in itself significant. Further study will, of course, uncover further usages, and new and possibly crucial passages will certainly turn up. It will be interesting to see whether the general ratio among the different forms is significantly modified by including a larger total number of instances. One weakness of the count that I have done is that I have included the adjectival form *sharʿī* along with *sharʿ*; after I had made the count, especially of al-Juwaynī, I wished that I had discriminated between these two. Some will perhaps wish to argue that *sharʿī* is, or is used as if it were, an adjectival form from *sharīʿah*, rather than, or as well as, from *sharʿ*. I would hardly wish to base my rebuttal of this argument on purely grammatical grounds; the matter is rather one of contextual usage, where at least in the earlier part of the period covered and to some significant degree throughout it, the meaning of the term in at least a majority of cases relates more naturally, as I read the texts, to *sharʿ*. To establish this point, however, or even to examine it, a separate grouping of adjectival instances would have been helpful, and in a more thorough study will be necessary. However, we shall return to it below.

In any case, I shall now simply state, in summary form, the positive conclusions to which I have tentatively come. As previously remarked, I propound them as hypotheses. I begin the enumeration with number 2, counting as number 1 the negative conclusion already set forth, that the *sharīʿah* was not a central concept.

I suggest, then:

2. That the term *sharīʿah* is used primarily in somewhat negative contexts: in reference to people who do not accept it, to situations in which the (or a) *sharīʿah* is rejected or abrogated or neglected or absent. This observation is an objective one, based on the inductive statistical study of the term in the passages where I have found it. It holds not in every case, but in a considerable majority. It may be correlated, moreover, with a general tendency in religious life, and the history of religious life, for reification to begin with that which one rejects, or which one defends when others have re-

jected.[44] It may be correlated also with the readiness of Western scholars to use the term (or 'law') where, on turning up the references that they give, one finds that the original Muslims used rather terms that signify something more immediate, personal, and theistic.[45] I shall return to this point in conclusion 6 below.

3. That *Sharīʿah* and *sharʿ* are not interchangeable, in virtually any of the writing that I have studied, which means beyond the eighth century. *Sharīʿah* is a concrete noun, specific; it can be particularized, and commonly is so, in phrases such as *sharīʿatunā, sharīʿatuhu, al-sharīʿah al-nabawīyah, hādhihi al-sharīʿah, sharīʿat Mūsá*, and once, *sharīʿat al-islām. Sharʿ*, on the other hand, has a distinctive and fundamental meaning of its own. In contrast to the particularity of *sharīʿah*, so far as I could discern, *sharʿ* is always absolute.[46] In many of the instances where it occurs, it is used adverbially, *sharʿan*—especially as correlative with (contrasted to) *ʿaqlan*. In others, it appears in the form *al-sharʿ*. As is known, it does not have a plural; which is another aspect of its being absolute, not particular.

My submission is that it is always a maṣdar.

Schacht, in the article *Sharīʿa* in the *Encyclopaedia of Islam*,[47] remarks that it is originally a *maṣdar* but implies that it became synonymous with *sharīʿah*. This observation is obviously correct, in both its parts. The question that concerns us is the process by which it moved from the first meaning to the second. So far as *kalām* writing is concerned, the transition had not yet taken place during the period covered here. The materials that I have investigated, I have come to feel, cannot be adequately understood unless this is grasped.

Sharʿ is a *maṣdar*, referring not to a system, a law, but to a process; not to an entity, but to an activity. *Its subject is always God.* It refers to the process or act of His assigning moral quality and moral responsibility to human life.

This point is quite crucial; I shall attempt to elaborate it in our consideration of the Shahrastānī passage with which we shall conclude below.

4. That *al-ʿaql* is a noun, the translation of the Greek *νους*, for

the rationalists, the Muʿtazilah, and such groups; but that it is not a noun, but also a *maṣdar* for their opponents, who became the orthodox Muslims. This, I think, is the difference between the two groups. That is, for the latter it meant not 'reason' (certainly not 'Reason' with a capital 'R') but 'reasoning'. The subject of its verbalness is man. Therefore whereas for the Greek tradition, and its Muslim adherents, *al-ʿaql* is a transcendent ideal, for the others it is a human activity, an empirical (and very unideal) actuality.

In the dispute between those who were for and those who were against *al-ʿaql*, therefore, the word designated radically different things to the two sides. This is, indeed, the difference between them: that the former did, and the latter did not, see *al-ʿaql* as an hypostasized or universal, self-subsisting entity.

The constant correlation *ʿaqlan/sharʿan* is important, and can be adequately understood, I submit, only adverbially, dynamically.

5. That *sharʿī* means, primarily, not 'legal', but 'moral'. Similarly *taklīf* means not 'legal responsibility', as it has been often translated (for example, by Elder for Taftāzānī), but moral responsibility. The implication is that the concept of law is not prior to the concept of responsibility, but *vice versa*. That this is chronologically so can be proved from my documentation. That it is logically so is of extreme importance for the entire structure of Islamic faith.

I am suggesting, accordingly, that the adjective *sharʿī* relates primarily to *sharʿ*, not primarily to *sharīʿah*. Particularly in such phrases as *al-aḥkām al-sharʿīyah*, the original significance—maintained for quite a good while—is that the *aḥkām* are each a divine command morally incumbent and immediately personal, for which men will be answerable on the Day of Judgement. Only later does this phrase become depersonalized and eventually de-transcendentalized to the point where it is equivalent to *aḥkām al-sharīʿah*.

6. That what has lately, both by modern Muslims and more recently by Western scholars, been conceived as obedience to, or transgression of, a law, was conceived *and felt* by the Muslim writers under survey as obedience or disobedience to God.[48] The

difference, I submit, is altogether profound and crucial: no proper understanding of religious life is possible unless this difference is apprehended, and deeply felt. In the Islamic tradition, so far as its history now seems apparent, the idea of a law is the result, not the cause; and on the whole a rather late, and some would be prepared to argue a slightly dubious result. At least, it would not be impossible to contend that historically the rise of a concept law as religiously absolute may be correlated with a decline, if not of Islamic civilization, anyway of the vigour of its intellectual and religious life. However this may be, less controversial is the point on which we have already lightly touched: that a concept *sharīʿah* as law is appropriate primarily in those cases where one's sense of God and His immediate intervention, and one's sense of *engagement*, of one's own immediate cosmic moral involvement, are weak or absent. Hence the uninvolved Western scholar's over-readiness to use the term in the Islamic case, the classical Muslim's use of it primarily for other people's *sharāʾiʿ*, and the use by modern Muslims whose sense of the nearness of God and of their personal relation to Him is markedly less than was that of their ancestors.

An opportunity to check the above formulations (based on observation of other works) presents itself in the case of al-Shahrastānī's *Nihāyat al-iqdām*.[49] This treatise was not included in the survey reported above. It contains passages where the terms *sharīʿah*, *sharʿ*, and other forms of the root occur rather frequently. Of particular significance, it would seem that some of these passages can be taken, as indeed they have been taken by the editor and translator Guillaume, in a way that contradicts my understanding, particularly the idea that 'law' is not primary in Islamic ethics, but derivative. I conclude deliberately by presenting and considering the most crucial passages, since they are by far the most salient instances of any *kalām* writing that I have met that could be used *against* my suggested interpretations.

If Guillaume's interpretation of these passages is correct, or is the only correct one, it does not follow that my thesis falls to the ground. I admit readily enough that eventually there did obtain in the Islamic world the reified notion of 'law' that modern Muslims and Western scholars have put forth. If that is the notion to be discerned here, then the process of reification among the *mutakallimūn* began earlier and more clearly than I have above suggested. Besides, I admit also, of course, that transitions were gradual, that some usages are ambiguous, and that traces of later modes of thought, or tendencies towards them, can in fact be detected in earlier writings. Certainly these particular paragraphs gave me pause, after other passages had surprised me by pushing me to the unexpected hypotheses that I have propounded. All in all, however, my understanding of the issues will be shown weak if it does not seem to contribute at least something to illuminating also these critical discussions.

First, let us consider the following passage:[50]

al-Qāʿidah al-sābiʿat-ʿashar
fī al-taḥsīn wa-al-taqbīḥ
wa-bayān an lā yajibu ʿalá Allāh taʿālá shay' min qabīl al-ʿaql, wa-lā yajibu ʿalá al-ʿibād shay' qabla wurūd al-sharʿ.

Madhhab ahl al-ḥaqq anna al-ʿaql lā yadullu ʿalá ḥusn al-shay' wa-qubḥihi fī ḥukm al-taklīf min Allāh sharʿan, ʿalá maʿná anna afʿāl al-ʿibād laysat ʿalá ṣifāt nafsīyah ḥusnan wa-qubḥan, bi-ḥaythu law aqdama ʿalayhā muqdim, aw aḥjama ʿanhā muḥjim, istawjaba ʿalá Allāh thawāban aw ʿiqāban. wa-qad yaḥsunu al-shay' sharʿan wa-yaqbuḥu mithluhu al-musāwī lahu fī jamīʿ al-ṣifāt al-nafsīyah. Fa-maʿná al-ḥasan mā warada al-sharʿ bi-al-thanā' ʿalá fāʿilih; wa maʿná al-qabīḥ mā warada al-sharʿ bi-dhamm fāʿilih. wa idhā warada al-sharʿ bi-ḥusn wa-qubḥ, lam yaqtaḍi qawlahu ṣifatan li-l-fiʿl. Wa-laysa al-fiʿl ʿalá ṣifah yukhbiru al-sharʿ ʿanhu bi-ḥusn wa-qubḥ; wa-lā idhā ḥakama bihi albasahu ṣifatan fa-yūṣafu bi-hi ḥaqīqatan. Wa-ka-mā anna al-ʿilm lā yuksibu al-maʿlūm ṣifatan, wa-lā yaktasibu ʿanhu ṣifatan, ka-dhālik al-qawl al-sharʿī wa-al-amr al-ḥukmī lā yuksibuhu ṣifatan wa-lā yaktasibu ʿanhu ṣifatan; wa-laysa li-mutaʿalliq al-qawl min al-qawl ṣifah, ka-mā laysa li-mutaʿalliq al-ʿilm min al-ʿilm ṣifah.

At issue here is the fundamental divergence of ethical world-view between Greek and Semitic. Perhaps it is not too drastic an oversimplification to aphorize that the former tends to think in terms basically of good and bad, the latter in terms basically of right and wrong: axiology over against deontology. For the one, morality derives from ontology, from (metaphysical) indicatives; for the other, from imperatives. A subsidiary (or corollary? or concomitant?) distinction is that the epistemology of the one is through reasoning, of the other through revelation. Yet for neither is an epistemology primary. On the one hand, reason preceded reasoning (ὁ λογος is eternal, man is adjectively λογικος—by participating, though imperfectly, in that pre-existing absolute). On the other hand, God speaks to man because He has something (imperative) to say (apart from the fact that God's speaking to man presupposes God, the utterly primary).

It is the dispute between these two primary views that is reflected in Shahrastānī's paragraph before us. As is typical, when two seriously, radically, divergent positions meet, each side tends to neglect or to underplay the presuppositions of the other, each arguing against the corollaries of the opponent's position, while retaining the premises of its own. Each side can readily prove to its own satisfaction that the other's corollaries are illogical, because of its own passionate—or simply, quiet—conviction about its own primary vision.

Crucial, it would seem to me, in this passage is Shahrastānī's word *fāʿilih.* As Sir W. David Ross has remarked, at a much lower level of divergence from the Greek view: 'The essential defect of the . . . theory [of G. E. Moore, that duty is to act productively of good] is that it ignores, or at least does not do full justice to, the highly personal character of duty'.[51] Shahrastānī is concerned to insist that morality is an attribute not of things but of persons. I must do A not because A is good, not because of any quality inherent in A, but because I, a human being, have been commanded to do it by the living and imperious God. *Sharʿ* here, then, is a *maṣdar*, is God's imposing of obligations on mankind. Things are lifeless, are beneath us, are morally indifferent; duty comes not from them but from above us, from God. *Laysa al-fiʿl ʿalá ṣifah yukhbiru al-sharʿ ʿanhu bi-ḥusn wa-qubḥ*: the deed is not characterized by some priorly given quality of its own that it is God's business to go about and discern, and once He has discovered it then to fashion injunctions to mankind in accord with it. No; rather, it is His assigning of injunctions directly to us that constitutes our moral obligation—that, and nothing more (nor less).

It may be noted that he has not fully understood the position that he is rejecting (just as his opponents, and their modern sympathizers like Guillaume, did not fully understand *his* position here). For he still seems to feel that even if deeds *did* have inherent qualities of vice and virtue, still man's duty to *do* them would be a function of God's enjoining that upon him, with rewards and punishments. This is a nice illustration of our general position that he was refuting the conclusions, but ignoring the premises, of his adversaries; and of Professor Gibb's remark that the Muslims 'never appreciated the fundamental idea of justice in Greek philosophy'.[52] Similarly when on the next page he presents his opponents' view (*al-afʿāl ʿalá ṣifah nafsīyah min al-ḥusn wa-al-qubḥ, wa-idhā warada al-sharʿ bi-hā kāna mukhbiran ʿanhā, la muthbitan lahā*), I would translate: 'Deeds have an inherent quality of virtue and vice, and when there is an ordaining of moral obligation on men with regard to them this indicates what that quality is rather than establishing it'—and again I would imagine that the author here does not *feel* (as his opponents do) that man would have a personal sense of moral obligation directly to a mere mundane act, whatever its inherent characteristic of beauty or ugliness; that he merely feels that God, to Whom and to Whose activity of assigning incumbencies he *does* feel moral obligation, is here being reduced to serving simply as an agent making incumbent upon man what the universe has somehow made incumbent (*yajibu*—371, lines 5-6) upon Him to vitalize moralistically. Of course, Shahrastānī resents such a reduction. He still sees in this a universe in which God enjoins (*sharaʿa*) on man the doing of this and that, with concomitant rewards and punishments; but one in which the initiative lies not with God, but with His creation.

It will be noted that, thus far in this discussion, I have not discussed revelation. So far as I can see, this is not relevant to the debate and is not mentioned. Revelation, of course, *does* give news about, rather than establishing, what is right and wrong; and no one feels this more strongly than a devout revelationist—for whom God determines what is right and wrong, and God alone.[53] This is irrelevant to the discussion, however, because it could play a role indifferently in either case. If good and bad were inherent as pre-existent qualities of things (or deeds), they could still be made known to man by revelation. And if right and wrong were the free ordaining of a living God, it would still be logically possible that they not be known to man by revelation. There could still conceivably be a *sharʿ* of God but no *sharīʿah* of Muḥammad (a divine assigning of moral obligation, but no making known of its content, in explicit pattern). Contrariwise, there could conceivably be a *sharīʿah* of Muḥammad with no *sharʿ* of God, if God did not determine right and wrong, yet did in His mercy send the prophets to mankind to make known to them the good and evil that were determined for them by the nature of things. (This last, indeed, is what orthodox Muslims tended to think that the Muʿtazilah believed.)

Nothing is incumbent on man, I see Shahrastānī here as maintaining, until God imposes moral obligation upon him. In fact, this is how I would translate the final clause of his heading to this chapter: *lā yajibu ʿalá al-ʿibād shay' qabla wurūd al-sharʿ*. Guillaume, however, taking *sharʿ* as not different from *sharīʿah*, translates: 'nothing was [sic] incumbent on men before the coming of the Sacred Law' (his p. 119). (He translates the same phrase *qabla wurūd al-sharʿ*, of p. 374, lines 3-4, as 'before Islām', his p. 120—presumably he intends, before the seventh century A.D.). Similarly he gives 'The good is what the code approves',[54] which is certainly wrong insofar as it omits the personalistic emphasis (*fāʿilihi*) and which, anyway, might more truly be seen as: 'the meaning of "good" is that of which the divine enjoining of duty commends the doer'.

Similarly, on p. 372, our author contends that a false sentence is not intrinsically better or worse, morally, than a true one. Some truths, he says, are not very pretty.[55] There are some who would agree with this, holding that it is not lies themselves, but the telling of lies, that is wrong. Our author goes further: for him, the telling of lies, even, is not intrinsically moral or immoral. What is wrong, hellishly so, is for *me* to tell a lie—or for you to do so. And the reason for this is that God has created us and commanded us not to lie. The fact that God has enjoined certain things and prohibited certain things (for mankind) is what is called *sharʿ*.

Al-sharʿ is something that takes place in heaven, while *al-sharīʿah* is something that (does not take place since it is not an activity, but) exists (as a thing) on earth. *Al-sharʿ* is God's ordaining that man shall act thus-and-so; *al-sharīʿah* is the systematic formulation of the ordinances into an explicit (revealed) pattern or statement. *Al-sharʿ* is that by which man becomes morally obligated to act thus-and-so; *al-sharīʿah* is that by which man knows that he is obligated. *Al-sharʿ* is something that God does; *al-sharīʿah* is something that man hears (that a prophet brings).

To the mind of a Muslim whose sense of the divine revelation is vivid, the distinction between these two, although significant, may not be clarified markedly. For the outside student, however, for whom the two are by no means interchangeable, and indeed have no inherent connection, to confuse the two can prove seriously misleading. Unlike the Muslim, he does not see (and feel) *al-sharīʿah* as divine; so that it becomes an intellectual blunder to conceive *al-sharʿ* as positive.[56]

Once again, the *Nihāyah* provides the most searching test of this analysis of these two terms. I may cite passages that would serve most readily to challenge the distinction proposed, or as the earliest refutations of it for those inclined to reject. Above I stated that, unlike *sharīʿah*, I had not found *sharʿ* particularized: its usage was always absolute (*al-sharʿ*), never indefinite (*sharʿun*) nor specific (like *sharīʿatuhu*, *hādhihi al-sharīʿah*, etc.). This was true of the material there surveyed, but I found two sets of exceptions in this present work, to which it is proper (and instructive) to call attention now. One is towards the end of the Shahrastānī chapter already considered, where the phrases *fī sharʿ abīnā Adam* and *fī sharʿ nabīyinā Muḥammad* occur (more fully *al-ḥukm . . . fī sharʿ . . .*).[57] Guillaume translates: 'The law (of marriage) in the code of our father Adam' and 'the law . . . of our Prophet Muḥammad'. Again, towards the end of the book, in the discussion on abrogation, one finds *fī sharʿihim*[58] (*hum* here refers to the prophets prior to Moses), which Guillaume renders as 'theirs [namely, their law]'. His translations are natural enough (at least, at first blush); and undoubtedly if we do not have here instances where the eventual synonymity of *sharʿ* and *sharīʿah* begins to appear, at least one must confess that such usage as this must have facilitated the later transition. Nonetheless, after careful reflection I have concluded that even these passages may be seen as illustrating, rather than refuting, my thesis. I should feel less sanguine in urging this, were it not that the total contexts where these usages occur read, to my mind, much more cogently and illumined, if they are read with the contrasting sense of the two words in mind. This is particularly true of the final section (Arabic, 499–503; trans., pp. 158 f.).

We leave aside for the moment the one occasion where *sharʿuhum* occurs, for later discussion. Otherwise, I think there can be no doubt but that *sharīʿah* (used eleven times, ten of them either indefinite or particularized, plus three further times in a particularized plural) designates the overt 'code' of law, existent on earth, that both Guillaume and I see in it, while *ḥukm* (used almost twice that often) is not a system of law, but a concrete moral injunction, and *sharʿ* (used only four times: twice adverbially, and twice absolutely) designates God's activity of assigning moral colour(s) to human life. The respective meanings come out well in the evolutionary claim, *takhtimu al-sharīʿah bi-kamāl ḥāl al-sharʿ al-awwal* (p. 503, lines 8–9), meaning that the ostensible Islamic law code perfectly represents on earth the full pristine moral commands of God in heaven.

One may with confidence maintain that the adverbial *sharʿan*, in both cases typically parallel to *ʿaqlan*, means 'morally'. In the following: *Al-aḥkām rājiʿah ilá aqwāl al-shāriʿ, wa-tūṣafu al-afʿāl bi-hā qawlan lā fiʿlan, sharʿan lā ʿaqlan* (p. 502, lines 2–3), I would see the author as contending that moral injunctions derive from the decrees of Him who assigns obligations, and deeds are characterized by them through decree, not factually; morally, not rationally.

There remains, then, one question: whether the *sharʿ* of particular persons is anything other than their *sharīʿah*. In the three instances of this that I have found, all in Shahrastānī (enumerated above),[59] certainly this is a feasible way to take it. Nonetheless, it is meaningful even here to see the term, rather, as a *maṣdar*, with God as the subject of its verb and the pronoun as its object.[60] Thus:[61] *A-laysa al-ḥukm fī nikāḥ al-ukht li-al-ab wa-al-umm fī sharʿ abīnā Adam* [sc. *Ādam*], *ʿalayhi al-salām, bi-khilāf al-ḥukm fī al-jamʿ bayna al-ukhtayn al-mutabāʿidatayn fī sharʿ nabīyinā Muḥammad, ṣallá Allāh ʿalayhi wa-sallam?* This might be taken as signifying the ordinance to marry a sister that was decided upon (that God decided upon) for Adam and imposed on him [and his children] over against the different injunction that was among those decreed as morally incumbent upon Muḥammad [and his successors]. Thus, *sharʿ fulān* would signify 'the moral dispensation laid upon' so-and-so. I certainly feel that Guillaume's translation ('The law of marriage in the code of our father Adam is in opposition to the law of marriage of our Prophet Muḥammad'), apart from missing the immediate force of *ḥukm*, impinging directly on one's conscience, also suffers from seeing the Islamic *sharīʿah* as too Muḥammadan, as if he were its author. The transcendence is left out, while my apprehension of *sharʿ* retains it: my proposal amounts simply to the suggestion that there was something of it in the author's mind, prompting him to use this particular term here.

In the one remaining instance, the point is similar, though perhaps clearer. And indeed the verbal force of *sharʿ* is explicitly corroborated here, in that other forms of the verb occur freely: not only *shāriʿ*, which we have already noted once (it occurs again, p. 502, line 1, in a clause right along with *sharʿ*, certainly helping to verbalize, to *maṣdar*-ize, the latter), but also *mashrūʿ* (five times, esp. p. 500, lines 17 ff.), which is found in a sentence with both *sharīʿah* (indefinite singular and particularized plural) and the *sharʿuhum* that we must now examine. In all this, my analysis of these terms may be seen to be confirmed rather than rebutted.

In discussing *naskh*, Shahrastānī asks whether the pre-Mosaic prophets had been under some different moral obligations from Moses:[62] *fa-naqūlu: lā shakk anna Mūsá, ʿalayhi al-salām, ta'akhkhara wujūdan ʿan Adam* [*sc. Ādam*] *wa-Nūḥ wa-Ḥūd wa-Ṣāliḥ wa-Ibrāhīm wa-Ismāʿīl wa-Yaʿqūb wa-jamāʿah min al-anbiyā' wa-al-asbāṭ, ʿalayhim al-salām. a-hal kāna jamīʿ mā warada bihi Mūsá mashrūʿan lahum; aw minhā mā kāna mashrūʿan wa-minhā mā lam yakun mashrūʿan? fa-in kāna kulluhu mashrūʿan lahum, fa-lam yarid Mūsá bi-sharīʿah aṣlan; bal, qarrara al-sharā'iʿ al-māḍīyah. wa-in warada bi-ḥukm wāḥid ghayr mā thabata fī sharʿihim, fa-qad taḥaqqaqa anna al-ḥukm al-awwal marfūʿ bi-dhālik al-ḥukm; aw qad intahá muddat al-ḥukm al-awwal; wa-tajaddada hādhā al-ḥukm. fa-thabata al-naskh.* This means: If all the injunctions of which Moses brought the revelation had been made morally incumbent already on his predecessors (had been laid upon them), then Moses did not 'come with' a *sharīʿah*, a public statement of injunctions and of their obligatoriness—he was not the bringer of a revelation, but rather the confirmer of previous revelations. If, on the other hand, he 'came with' (brought to mankind a statement of) a single imperative that had not been established in (God's) ordaining of moral injunctions on them (again, *maṣdar* with objective genitive), then it is proven that the first injunction has been lifted by that one . . . .

A new *sharʿ* involves, as a corollary (not as a synonym), a new *sharīʿah*.

I would conclude, then, with two final hypotheses:

7. That for *kalām* writers, during the centuries surveyed, the (or a) law does not determine right and wrong. Only God can, and only God does, do that.[63]

8. That the dictum that the central fact of Islām as a religion is the idea of law[64] should perhaps be modified in the direction of saying that the central Islamic fact religiously has been the idea of

moral responsibility. The law is the result of that responsibility, not its cause; the sociological or mundane product, not its cosmic basis.

6

Faith, in the Qur'ān; and its Relation to Belief

The next three studies are of the Islamic concept of faith, as represented in the word īmān; *first, in the Qur'ān, and then as explicated in subsequent centuries by intellectuals in the Muslim community. All three are relatively recent, and signify my growing awareness of the matter of faith in Islamic life and indeed in human life. Dramatic for me was my discovery that I was wrong—most of us were wrong—in linking faith too tightly with believing, or confusing the two. Linked they have been, no doubt: faith and belief are not the same, and in earlier times no one thought that they were, I discovered, and yet historically they have intertwined. Many years and much study intervened between my first becoming aware that the two were not synonymous in traditional Islamic thought, and my eventually clarifying what the link between them has been, and what the (radical) difference. At stake in this venture were not only an outsider's understanding of Muslim religious life and of the Islamic vision, but also the very foundations of Christian theology, and the central question of philosophy, the meaning and form of truth.*

It is of course not surprising, although some scholarship makes but little provision for this, that an endeavour to understand a major religious orientation and its civilization should entail a confronting of the ultimate questions of both life and intellect. Even at a less deep level, to study another age and culture is, if one be alert, to become aware of the idiosyncracies and foibles, not to say the aberrations, of one's own. I had grown up supposing, as many another modern Westerner, that being a Christian is a question of believing certain things, and being a Muslim, of believing certain things; it was with some excitement therefore that through a study of the Qur'ān I came to question in a focussed way whether belief is indeed religiously central, or was classically seen as being so. The first draft of the paper that here follows accordingly bore the title 'Believing as a religious category; with special reference to the Qur'ān'. A few years later I rephrased this to become, 'Is believing what religious people do?'. The present version herewith is the text of a lecture delivered in Lahore in 1974, one of a series of two under the title 'Faith and Belief'; this first presentation bore the subtitle 'some considerations from the Islamic instance', while the second (of which more below) carried the same title but its subtitle was 'some considerations from the Christian instance'. For by this time I was agog at finding that the new understanding powerfully illuminated not only Islamic matters but also both Christian thought and the comparative question as to the relation between Christian and Islamic. Five years later (after twelve years of elaborate work) I am publishing my second substantial comparativist volume, also with the title Faith and Belief. *Still another version of this present essay constitutes its Islamics chapter, other chapters being on Buddhist, Hindū, Christian, and Western-secular, involvements in this issue, with then some philosophic inferences. (Part of the Christian material is included in this present collection below, in our section on Muslim–Christian relations: pp. 265-281.)*

The occasion for the Lahore pair of lectures was the great honour that was done me in my being invited to give the Iqbal Memorial Lectures at the University of the Punjab, where I had taught thirty years before. The introduction here accordingly touches on that.

It is virtually a standard formality for a lecturer to begin by saying that it is an honour, and a pleasure, for him to have been asked to give that lecture. I could wish that this were not so, for I wish none of you to imagine that in my case this is a mere formality, or anything remotely 'standard'. On the contrary: when the invitation came, I was deeply moved. Far from a formal matter, it was for me something personal and gripping.

For one thing, it has provided the opportunity for me to return to this city, in which I spent what were in certain ways the very best years of my life; and to renew old friendships which have been for me of major importance and delight. My affection for Lahore has been intense: I owe to this exciting city and to its inhabitants who befriended me here years ago a large part of both my heart and my mind. Moreover, apart from the lively pleasure that this return visit to my old home brings me, there is the signal honour that is involved in my being allowed to participate in this distinguished series of the University of the Punjab's most prestigious lectures, the Iqbal Memorial. I understand that I am the first foreigner on whom this honour has been conferred. Not that when I lived here thirty-some years ago anyone ever made me feel 'a foreigner'. This was my home. Certainly I was made to feel at home here; and at that time I fully expected to spend my life in these parts. In the end, this was not to be: destiny was otherwise, and my life has gone forward in other parts of the world. I have, then, left you, and have lived and developed elsewhere—always, it is true, with a piece of my heart left here behind in your keeping: in trust, or perhaps you may say, as a hostage. That being so, your having searched me out and invited me to return, not merely as a visitor but in the altogether special role of Iqbal Memorial Lecturer, have touched me profoundly. Of course, it is an honour that I do not deserve, but that I certainly cherish. Allow me, then, in all humility and sincerity, to thank your Vice-Chancellor and all those who have had anything to do with the conferring of this momentous dignity. You can little guess how much this has meant to me.

Formidable though the assignment be, therefore, I could not say 'no' to the invitation when it came. Nonetheless, neither did I feel competent to rise to the task of delivering a lecture to a company such as this about Iqbāl. There are, however, two ways in which honour can be done to the memory of a great figure. One is to analyse and to interpret his life, his writings, his thought. The other is to receive his inspiration, to apply our minds to those issues and topics with which he was himself concerned: to look not towards him, but towards those things at which he looked before us, acknowledging our debt. The Vice-Chancellor's invitation specified that the lecture might be about Iqbāl, or 'on any theme in which [he] evinced direct or indirect interest'. I have chosen the latter: have chosen to invite you to consider with me these two days a matter in which I feel sure that Iqbāl would have been interested—namely, faith and belief, the relation between them and the distinction between them, as a generic human issue but partly as illustrated in Islamic and in Christian instances.

This is a matter on which I have been working explicitly for the past few years and implicitly for the past many decades: in a sense, ever since I became seriously engaged with Islamic life and the attempt to appreciate and to understand it, and in the light of it to understand also my own Christian heritage. The connection with Iqbāl is close. For it was in part his thought and work that contributed to enabling me to apprehend, insofar as I could apprehend them, the Islamic vision and the faith of Muslims underlying the beliefs and patterns of the overt Islamic tradition.

Iqbāl had died two years before I reached Lahore. I do not exactly remember when I first read his Six Lectures;[1] perhaps before I arrived in these parts, although it was here that I learned to take them very seriously. I do remember clearly, vividly, when I was in process of learning Urdū here, my first introduction to his poetry. I began with *Bang-i Darā*. My heart and my mind were stirred, my imagination was enriched, my vision of the world and certainly of Muslim culture was deepened and enlarged, by the encounter with Iqbāl then begun. For thirty and more years that vivifying experience has developed in my thought and feeling; and any understanding of life and of faith—not only of Muslim life and faith, but of human life and faith—that I may have since attained, owes something indelible to him. Besides, as I have said, the questions to which I have addressed myself, and that I address in these talks, are questions with which his own concern was deep.

Accordingly, I have deemed it not inappropriate to proffer before you, for your consideration, two lectures on Faith and Belief, as my small tribute to the memory of that great figure whose work has inspired us all. I have, of course, no pretension that what I have to say will be adequate to the occasion; nor to the topic. Both are beyond my capacity. Yet you may be sure that my views on these mighty matters would be still less adequate than they are, had it not been for the inspiration and stimulation of Iqbāl.

There is still a further reason why I have thought to use this occasion to lay before you, for criticism, some ideas on the issue of faith and belief, Islamic and Christian. It is this. As I have indicated, for some while now I have been working on the problem of the relation of religious faith to intellectual belief, to conceptual formulation, to theology: in the Christian case and throughout the world, investigating Buddhist and Hindū and other areas as well as Western. I am hoping soon to complete this study and to submit it for publication. It has been my custom to publish things having to do with Islām only after first submitting them, if feasible, for critique and comment to Muslim friends, so as to have their reaction. The particular matters of faith and belief are so central, so deep, so ultimate, that it is especially important that I have the advantage of your response before I make final, in printed form,[2] the ideas that I have formulated.

Some might think it unduly bold of me to come to Lahore and to propose to lecture on so delicate and personal and yet so mighty a matter as faith and religious belief, even though the point of my presentation be comparative: an attempt to speak not simply on Islamic faith and Islamic belief, which would indeed be presumptuous of me, but of the similarities and differences as I see them that may by suggested, as an hypothesis, between the Islamic and the Christian. The interrelation between these two is a matter on which, as such, no one is an authority; and therefore my groping endeavour to propose a possible understanding of it may perhaps be allowed. In this case, however, you may be sure that I am grateful for this opportunity to discover your reaction to the ideas that I shall put forth. Although it would be awkward for me actually to write the entire lecture in this form, nonetheless, especially this evening with the Islamic material, I am quite genuinely, and firmly, in effect prefacing every sentence of my talk, and certainly the total presentation of it, with the question: 'Is it the case that . . . ?' I hope that each of you will accept this question as directed to him; and will be kind enough to let me know your answer. I sincerely hope that you will tell me how far I have understood, and how far I have misunderstood, Islamic positions.

As I have said, under the very special circumstances pertaining to me personally and to my own life and involvements, it was altogether unthinkable for me to decline the honour of the invitation to deliver these lectures. Nonetheless, fundamentally I have come to Lahore not to speak but to listen; not to affirm but to question; certainly, not to teach but to learn. Let us turn, then, to the substance of my presentation.

My topic, as you have heard, is 'faith and belief'. Now you might imagine that if I am to speak on those two matters, I might begin by indicating what I mean by the two terms. This is not quite so straightforward as it might seem, however. Maybe, if my presentation be at all persuasive, we may end up by being better able to clarify the two notions. At the beginning, on the other hand, I wish to stress ambiguities rather than clear definitions. I shall argue against the view that the two are the same: that to have faith is to believe, although this is often said. I shall argue that, however similar the two may appear to be, if we think about them carefully we shall realize that they are quite different. Believing, I shall contend, is not what religious people basically do; in either the Islamic, or the Christian, instance. Believing is not a classical religious category.

If faith is *not* belief, however, what is it? That is a tricky question, I hold. It is easier to say what believing is, although it is much more important to know what faith is. Both, anyway, are worth exploring. This much I may say at the outset: by 'faith', the English word, I mean *īmān*. For 'belief', as an English word, what the proper Arabic or Urdū equivalence may be, will emerge as we proceed. Part of my argument will be that it is a mistranslation (it has become a mistranslation) to render *īmān* in English as 'believing'. Let us see whether you will be persuaded to agree.

Believing, I shall suggest, is not of ultimate significance. Faith, on the other hand, is.

According to both the Islamic and the Christian traditions, faith is man's most decisive quality. The Day of Judgement, that mighty metaphor to which both groups have resorted, is envisaged primarily as a determining of who has had faith and who not. Heaven and Hell are felt to be not too stupendous characterizations of the cosmic significance for man of the question involved. It is, indeed, many have averred both within and without these two communities, the ultimate human question.

Small wonder, then, that the subordinate question, 'What is faith?' has itself been a matter both of importance and of debate. It is a question of great fascination: one on which I hope perhaps to write a book before I die. These days I have in press two separate articles on particular parts of the answer that was given in the Islamic case by the classical and mediaeval scholars. [*I referred here to the studies on* taṣdīq *and* arkān, *which are reproduced next in this present collection.*] As a Christian and as a comparativist, as well as a student of Islamics, I find the *kalām* definitions of faith exciting; and of universal, not simply Islamic, significance. At the moment, however, I wish to answer the question 'What is faith (*īmān*)?' only in the negative manner of arguing that it is not belief. In my second lecture, later this week [*reproduced towards the end of this present collection: pp. 265–281*], I will demonstrate that there was a time when the English word 'believe' did mean 'to have faith'; but that was a long time ago, and the confusion has arisen because of an historical change in meaning of the English concept. There are a few Western Christians who still use 'believe' in its older sense; but they are a dwindling group. Here, in any case, I shall deal not with the classical conception of believing, but with the modern. Let me begin with a few observations on this, in an attempt to clarify what it involves.

To elucidate the notion of belief one turns first, I suppose, to the counterpart concept of knowledge. Others of you will be more sophisticated than I in the matter of analysis of knowledge as a concept. Notoriously, it is tricky. Yet for our purposes here, of clarification, it is ordinary language that concerns us, not philosophical or technical analysis. For the man in the street, may we not say that knowledge involves two things: (i) certitude, and (ii) correctness, in what one knows. To use very unsophisticated terms indeed, in ordinary parlance one knows whatever one knows when there is a close positive relation of that knowledge both to inner conviction and to outward, objective facts.

At this same level of casual yet prevalent usage, uncritical and unanalytic yet by the same token both widely and deeply held, there is the common-sense notion of believing. This differs from knowing precisely in that it involves perhaps one, or perhaps both, of again two things: (i) a lack of certitude; or (ii) an openness as to the correctness or otherwise of what is believed.

Thus one may say that so-and-so knows that Ankara is the capital of Turkey. Alternatively, one may say that someone else believes that Istanbul is the capital of Turkey. Further, onc may say that a third person believes that Ankara is the capital of Turkey; in this case we happen to know that he is right, yet by our phrasing the point that he believes it, we communicate the notion that he himself is not sure. His opinion happens to be right, yet it is not knowledge because he himself holds it with a certain tentativeness. On the other hand, the view of our second man, who is under the impression that Istanbul is the capital, is also not knowledge, no matter how strongly he may hold it. The intensity of his own assurance may rise however high, but will not turn his belief into knowledge so long as his view is mistaken (or in a different case, even *might* be mistaken). Similarly in his neighbour's case: the actual accuracy of his position may be total, yet this will not turn his belief into knowledge so long as he himself harbours misgivings.

Accordingly, the overtones of our use of 'believing' may be striking, or subtle. When we say 'they believe', this may be disdainful; when we say 'I believe', this may be modest.

In ordinary parlance, then, 'believing' is the concept by which we convey the fact that a view is held, without a decision as to its validity—explicitly without that decision.

This being so, small wonder that believing has become then the characterization *par excellence* for religious positions, in the modern world. For when we turn from ordinary (secular) usage to the specifically religious domain, the situation is nowadays not strikingly different.

On the one hand, so far as inner conviction is concerned, this notion of believing correlates beautifully with the lack of confidence that in our day characterizes a large, and growing, number of believers. They believe something, perhaps hesitantly or perhaps deliberately even to the point of being willing to stake their life upon it; yet in either case they are not quite sure. Not quietly sure, with that unruffled awareness of intellectual perspicuity. Secondly, with regard to the question of objective validity, of some kind of external factual correctness of the positions held, the very notion of 'believing' makes room nicely, and indeed necessarily, for the wide variety of religious positions with which modern men and women are inescapably familiar. Both the believer and the non-believer have come to recognize that any position that they may or may not hold is one among many. Jews believe X, Muslims believe Y, Christians believe Z—even among Christians, Mennonites believe one thing, Roman Catholics another, Presbyterians still another. And all of them recognize that this is so. This makes for a very different sort of situation from what obtained in an earlier day, or may obtain in less pluralist societies, where a particular stand is not recognized as a *particular* stand, but is 'the' religious position. There, one may take it or leave it, but one does not choose it as one from among many. 'Do you believe X or don't you', is a different question from, 'Do you believe X, or Y?'.

'True or False' may serve formally for a test of knowledge; but belief is more complicated than that, and the modern pluralistic world confronts the religious man or woman more subtly with an essay-type examination question.

Before I go on, then, to challenge the currently accepted assumption about believing as a finally adequate religious category, let me first of all stress my recognition of its apparent appropriateness to the modern scene. My emphasis on this point is, in fact, part of my argument. Having affirmed that what modern persons in the modern world do religiously is 'of course' interpreted in terms of believing, I will not then go on to suggest that 'nonetheless' at other times and places things have been different. On the contrary, my thesis comes closer to being rather that believing has become an apparently appropriate category for the modern world and *therefore* is not appropriate for other times and places.

Let me emphasize, then, the very simple point that I make first: namely, that 'believing' is the straightforward and almost innocent interpretation of what religious people have been doing in the modern world when they have taken a position. For they are seen, rather naturally, as taking it as some sort of venture; and, as one possible venture among others. Some believe one thing, others another; neither they nor the rest of us are quite sure that they are right (nor, anymore, even that they are wrong), even though many be confident that even so, the venture is well worth taking.

Both the participant and the observer seem able to agree that in taking the stance, they are doing something to which 'believe' happily applies. Where one cannot know, let's believe, say some; where one cannot know, let's not believe, say others; where no one knows, many believe, say several. 'What do they believe?', has become a standard question about other religious people; what do we, or what shall I, believe, a standard question about oneself.

At least, this was the case, at an unsophisticated level, until fairly recently. On more careful scrutiny, it turns out that the concept has been serviceable at a critical level only with reservations. The popular notion, though understandable as rough-and-ready conceptualization, has had to be interpreted, sometimes uneasily, by more reflective thinkers. Both the theologian, in attempting precise formulations for the Church from the inside, and the anthropologist, in attempting to describe the believing of primitive tribes, have found themselves having to operate with more refined notions of belief than the man-in-the-street has been content to use. This, too, is significant; both in itself and for the course of our argument here. Believing, as a religious category, has for the modern world been an easy, and natural, and apparently cogent, over-simplification.

Some try to wriggle out of the difficulties that arise by taking refuge in the more refined, more precious, more traditional notions that can be and usually are smuggled into the concept of believing by believers when they are pressed. At these we shall look in our next lecture. Meanwhile, when I speak of believing as a religious category, I intend believing in the modern prevalent sense of that term, as signifying that an opinion is held about which the person who holds it, or the society that gives or receives information about his or her holding it, or both, leave theoretically unresolved the question of its objective intellectual validity.

Believing so conceived is the religious category *par excellence* of the recent Western world, I submit. Let us now turn to the second part of my paper, and allow me to submit further that such a category is altogether foreign to the Qur'ān. At least, I propose this and look forward to receiving your comments on the thesis, once I have developed it. As you will hear in my second lecture, I also hold that it is foreign also to the Bible, and to classical Christian thought.

The general position to which I am in process of coming is that believing as a religious category is inept, is illegitimate, and even for the modern world has become unserviceable. I mention that general position, however, only to leave it aside. For the moment, my thesis is much more limited; and for it my evidence, I aspire to show you, more complete and compelling. The thesis is simple: that in the Qur'ān, the concept 'believe' (as a religious activity) does not occur (and does not occur for very good reasons).

Now the facts are that any English translation of the Qur'ān that you may pick up, whether by Muslim or by Westerner, is replete with the terms 'belief', 'believing', 'believer', 'non-believer', and the like, and that these are pivotal. Yet I am suggesting that to render in this way any word in the Qur'ān, or in the classical Islamic world-view based upon it, is a mistranslation. My thesis, then, has at least the perhaps dubious virtue of novelty, and might seem to be rather absurdly bold. It is not quite so radical as this might make it seem, however; for the reasons for these translations, or mistranslations, are complex, though in some cases fairly obvious. For one thing, the renderings have been made in the nineteenth and twentieth centuries; for another, the influence of earlier Biblical language has been immediate, and strong. It is not difficult to see why the notion of believing has got into the renderings, even if the contention be valid that I now put forward. Let me endeavour to expound to you my interpretation.

To show that a religious concept 'believe' does not occur in the Qur'ān, then, I begin by calling attention to the fact that words for 'knowing' are frequent and emphatic (*ʿarafa*, and especially *ʿalima*). The notion of knowledge is re-iterated and vivid. In fact, in the Royal Egyptian edition of the Qur'ān text, now standard, I calculate that the more frequent of these two terms for knowing (let alone, both together) occurs on the average more than once per page.

Secondly, the standard word presumably for 'believing' in later Islamic theology (*iʿtaqada* etc.) does not occur in the Qur'ān. The root *ʿaqada*, originally 'to tie a knot', either literally or in the figurative sense of binding a person by a legal or moral commitment, to make a binding engagement, occurs seven times in the Qur'ān: twice as a verb—

ʿaqadat aymānukum (4:33)
ʿaqqadtumu-l-aymāna (5:89)

and five times as a noun; illustratively:

al-naffāthāt fi-l-ʿuqad (113:4)
ʿuqdat al-nikāḥ (2:235)
awfū bi-l-ʿuqūd. (5:1)

Furthermore, the work that I have done on mediaeval *kalām* texts shows, I have found, that the VIIIth form *iʿtaqada*, which does not occur in the Qur'ān but is introduced later along with *ʿaqīdah* and *ʿaqā'id* in the sense of 'creed', begins by meaning not 'to believe' something but rather to bind oneself, to commit or pledge oneself to, to take on the engagement of living in accord with a given position; and that only gradually across the centuries does it take on the more neutral meaning of 'to believe' something intellectually. We shall return to this idea in our second lecture.

Of the various terms that do occur in the Qur'ān and that might be, and indeed have been, translated as 'believe', there are two that constitute the crux of our inquiry. They are drastically different from each other; the fact that nonetheless in relatively modern times both have regularly been translated, or I would say mistranslated, into English as 'believing' illuminates our whole matter. They are, first, *āmana* (with *īmān* 'faith', as the verbal noun) and secondly, *ẓanna*, *yaẓunnu*—in modern Arabic 'to think', 'to opine', 'to hold an opinion'.

Without any question, I feel sure that you will allow me to say, the fundamental concept in the Qur'ān, overwhelmingly vivid, is that of God, presented as Creator, Sovereign, and Judge, powerful, demanding, succouring, majestic, laying upon humankind inescapable imperatives and offering us inexhaustible rewards. The fundamental category on the manward side is that of faith: the positive recognition and acceptance of the divine summons, the committing of oneself to the demands, and thus being led to the ultimate succour. The term for faith, *īmān*, is itself a verbal noun, *maṣdar*; and the more strictly verbal forms quite predominate—so that it is more just to speak not of faith, simply, but rather of the act of faith. Faith is something that people do more than it is something that people have; although one may primarily say that it pertains to something that people are, or become. The Qur'ān presents, in reverberatingly engaging fashion, a dramatic challenge wherein God's terror and mercy, simultaneously, are proclaimed to humankind, whereby we are offered the option of accepting or rejecting His self-disclosure of the terms on which He, as Creator and Ruler of the world and of us, has set our lives. 'What the Qur'ān presents is a great drama of decision: God has spoken His command, and men thereupon are divided, or, rather, divide themselves, into two groups—those who accept and those who spurn; those who obey, and those who rebel'.[3] This, it is averred, is the way the universe was originally set up, and man's life within it: that this is so is now made known, with resonant clarity and force; and men, now that they have this knowledge, must act accordingly.

Two or three terms are used for the act of rejecting the invitation. One is *jaḥada*; the most strident is *k-f-r*, from which *kāfir* (usually translated 'infidel') is derived, with its radically pejorative sense of 'spurner'. Even in modern Arabic, let alone mediaeval, classical, and Qur'ānic, and in Persian, Urdū, and Turkish, this word never comes to mean simply not to believe (it would be ludicrous, would it not, to translate with any form of this root the notion that so-and-so does not believe that Istanbul is the capital of Turkey or that the Middle East peace talks will be successful). Indeed, there are verses that explicitly indicate that the mind accepts but the will repudiates. A clear example is sūrah 27, verse 14: 'They rejected them [the signs of God] although they knew very well in their hearts that they were true' (*jaḥadū bi-hā wa-stayqanat-hā anfusuhum*). These various verbs, moreover, are regularly found embellished with adverbs indicating that man's rejection of God's bounty and authority is out of haughtiness, arrogance, stubborn wilfulness, *ẓulman wa-ʿulūwan* (27:14). Similarly with *kafara*, *kufr*. It is a choice, actively made. To speak at a mundane level, one might be tempted to say that the whole matter was to the Prophet himself so vivid, so overwhelmingly convincing, so startlingly clear, so *mubīn*, so divinely authentic, that it never really crossed his mind that one would not *believe* it. How could anyone not believe God? *Kufr* (so-called 'infidelity'), the heinous sin, the incomprehensibly stupid and perverse obduracy, is not unbelief but 'refusal'. It is almost a spitting in God's face when He speaks out of His infinite authority and vast compassion. It is man's dramatic negative response to this spectacular divine initiative.

The positive response, equally dynamic, is called 'faith', *īmān*. The *kāfir*, the ingrate, is he who says 'no' to God; and the *mu'min*, 'the man of faith', is he who accepts, who says 'yes'. As the theologians subsequently explain, *īmān*, faith, is self-commitment: it means, and is said to mean, almost precisely, *s'engager*. I was very interested to discover Najm al-Dīn al-Taftāzānī, perhaps my favorite *mutakallim*, while writing in Arabic, resorting to the Persian word *giravīdan* to explain faith, just as modern existentialists writing in English resort to the

French words *s'engager, engagement*. And the French word *gage* is exactly equivalent with the Persian word *girav*.

Another interpretation that I have heard is that just as the word 'amen' in English, from this same root via Hebrew, or *āmīn* in Arabic, is used at the end of a congregational prayer or worship service as an act whereby the congregation participates, in its turn, in what the leader has done or said, accepting it then for themselves or incorporating themselves into his act, saying 'yes' to it, so the *mu'min*, the man of faith, the yes-sayer, the amen-sayer, is he who volunteers, who says 'I, too'. By it, he identifies himself with the communal and cosmic activity. *Āmana*, the act of faith, names the positive response to the divine and dramatic challenge.

I do not wish to overstress the component of the will in the act of faith; for Muslim writers have differed on this point, and the analysis is tricky. The element of intellectual recognition should not be excluded. Yet here also the concept is to be accurately rendered by 'recognize' rather than 'believe'. We shall be returning to this point presently, and again in our next lecture.

Meanwhile, the Qur'ān provides another example from which we may illustrate the orientation quite sharply. Let us consider the concept *mushrik*. This term is usually translated 'polytheist'. It is taken as designating what would be rendered in our modern terminology as a man who, if you like, believes in many gods. Now in a sense the term does indeed mean polytheist, but with a difference that, though at first it may seem subtle, is in fact radical. The root *sh-r-k*, as you know, means 'to associate'; and the concept *shirk*, which again is basically a verbal noun, a *maṣdar*, and again is translated 'polytheism', means, more literally, associating other beings with God—which in the Islamic scheme is the unforgivable sin. It means, one soon enough realizes on reflection, treating as divine what is in fact not so. God is seen as being one, alone; He only is to be worshipped. This overwhelming affirmation is, of course, fundamental to the Qur'ān's whole presentation; so that to associate any second being with Him (I hope that you can hear the capital H there) is stupid, wicked, and wrong. The *mushrik*, accordingly, is not that man who simply believes in many gods;

but, if one is to use the term 'believe' at all, it is the man who *perversely* believes in many gods. Or, more precisely, one may note that at this level the Arabic means, almost literally, 'to believe in more gods than there are'. Built into the word as a word, and into the concept as a concept, is the fallacy of what it names. It is, therefore, a vehement pejorative, an inherently derogatory term. The repellent quality is not merely connotation, but denotation.

Therefore, no man could use this term *mushrik* of himself—except that penitent Muslim who was repudiating his former sin and blindness, or later that mystic Muslim who confessed in tears imperfection in his sincerity, pleading that his intellectual recognition of God's oneness was not matched in full purity by a total singleness of heart in his devotion. Otherwise the phrase 'I am a *mushrik*' is at the intellectual level a logical self-contradiction; since if one actually did believe that there are more gods than one, then this term would not describe one's belief. It describes and analyses such a belief from the point of view of those who reject it. It is a monotheist concept for a polytheist.

Indeed, once again a notion of 'believe' is not quite appropriate anyway; since in a sense Muḥammad or any convinced Muslim did not doubt that the idols of the pagans existed; but simply affirmed that they were not gods, were merely sticks and stones. It was not their existence that was in question, but the absurdity of worshipping them, of treating them as if they were divine. Similarly today: those who worship money, or devote themselves to the advancement of their own career, or pander to self-gratification, are *mushrik* not in the sense that they recognize the existence of these distractions—we all know that they exist—but in that they are associating them with God in, we might phrase it, their scheme of values, are consecrating their life in part to them rather than consecrating it solely to the only reality that is worthwhile, worshipful, worthy our pursuit: namely, God.

The atheist, the monotheist, the polytheist, then, to use our modern neutralist terms, form a series that in the Qur'ān and in classical Islamic consciousness is seen, and felt, and designated, as all within the monotheistic framework. All three are conceptualized from the point of view of *al-Ḥaqq*, the Truth. Accordingly, the series is set forth as, respectively, the *kāfir* (translated as 'infidel'), that cantankerous ingrate who rejects, the *mu'min* ('person of faith'), that blessed one who, by divine grace, recognizes the situation as it is and commits himself to acting accordingly, and the *mushrik* ('the associator'), who distorts the situation by elevating, in his perverse imagination or perverse behaviour, to the level where only God the Creator sits, some of God's creatures, treating *them* as if they too were divine.

In much the same fashion the so-called 'creed' of you Muslims is not a creed at all, if by creed one means an affirmation of belief. It is, rather, explicitly a *shahādah*, a bearing witness. The Muslim does *not* say, I believe that there is no god but God, and I believe that Muḥammad is the apostle of God. Rather, he asserts: 'I bear witness to' these facts. His regarding them as facts, not theories, as realities in the universe not beliefs in his mind, is, as I have elsewhere suggested,[4] of more basic significance than is usually recognized. The witness formula affirms that he is relating himself in a certain way—of obedience, recognition, service—to a situation that already, and independently, and objectively, exists. He is corroborating it, not postulating it. Monotheism, for him, is the status quo, cosmically; in the formula it is not in process of being believed but is assumed, is presupposed, and is in process only of being proclaimed.

The concept of witnessing in Islamic life is a profound one. It, indeed, is a major category. It is a religious category worthy of the name.

Now you may protest that this is all very well, but does it not presuppose that there is, indeed, a God, that He has indeed spoken and all the rest? My answer is that this is precisely the point: that these notions are not believed, they are presupposed. One may note, even, that they are presupposed equally in both the 'yes' and the 'no' cases: the concepts not only of faith but of infidelity, *īmān* and *kufr*, both presuppose the whole outlook. The one does not imply belief, the other, lack of it; rather, both equally imply a preceding conceptual framework within which the one designates active acceptance, the other, active rejection. We have already seen that the concept translated 'polytheism' presupposes monotheism.

The difference between believing something, and presupposing something, is crucial. The concept 'belief' does not occur in the Qur'ān: and it would be self-contradictory to ask that what is presupposed should be explicated.

Perhaps the following illustration will seem too homely; although I trust, not too irreverent. I hope that you will forgive me if it seems too utterly petty. I should perhaps also explain that I myself do not own a car, although almost everyone in America seems to have one, including the students. Anyway, I have sometimes told my students that the case of a Muslim may perhaps be formally compared, on a radically lower plane (but of course not substantially), to the driver of a car looking for a place to park and confronted with a 'No Parking' sign. In such a situation, there are various possible reactions. He may, for instance, on the one hand simply obey the sign and go off to look elsewhere. Or, he may park anyway, thinking 'Oh, well, the police are not very vigilant in these parts, and I will try my luck—maybe I will get away with it'. Or, he may feel that even if caught, he can trust the lenience or friendly indulgence of the authorities. Or he may think that it is worth paying the fine, even if it does eventuate, so urgently does he wish to park. Or he may simply lack the self-discipline to submit to regulations, even though he have some sort of haunting sense that he ought to do so. On the other side of the matter, if he does obey the regulation, he may do so out of fear of punishment, or out of respect for the law, out of a sense of good citizenship, or whatever. Now all these reactions, whether positive or negative, all presuppose his acceptance of the validity of the sign. A new situation arises when some sceptic comes along and suggests that the sign is in fact not authentic, that it has been put up not by the police, but by some pranksters who are simply making mock of outsiders to their neighbourhood.

A quite new dimension is introduced into the whole situation if our driver is now asked, or asks himself, whether he believes the sign. Previously he took for granted that it was authoritative; the only question was whether or not he should obey it. Former questions about his character, about his relation to the law, to the community, to his own self-discipline, about his being able or willing to afford a fine, and the like—these become transformed once one makes possible for him, and especially once one makes necessary or central for him, the new question of whether he *believes* it. On the tacit assumption that the 'No Parking' sign was authoritative, a whole spectrum of possible actions was involved, a whole series of questions, a whole range of significance; and—I tell my students— if an entire community made this tacit assumption, a whole community life (with every degree within a full gamut of loyalty and disobedience, cohesion and dissent). Once that prior assumption is called into question, however, the matter assumes a radically new aspect. The issue of its authenticity raises a quite new series of questions, and shifts the range of significance—for both the individual and the community—on to quite new, and different, ground. I am not yet saying that whether he believes the sign's authenticity is an illegitimate question: I am merely saying that it is a different question.

I then go on to make the same sort of point about the Christian use. The Muslims among you may more easily understand the point that I am making if you think about it in the Christian instance, to which we shall turn in the second lecture—or in relation to any cultural theory that you do not believe, but of which you see the historical results and within which you can observe that there are some persons who are faithful and some who are not. No doubt it is important to believe what is right. Yet the Qur'ān itself affirms that such theoretical believing, even recognizing, is not enough—as when it refers to those who recognize the truth intellectually as clearly as they recognize their own children, and yet still do not respond with faith:

ʿarafū-hu ka-mā yaʿrifūna abnāʾahum (2:146).

The whole matter is further illuminated if we turn, finally, to the other Qur'ān concept that has been translated in modern times into modern English as 'believe': namely, *ẓanna*, *yaẓunnu*, *ẓan-*

nan. So far as the mundane world is concerned, this is pretty much what this term does, indeed, signify. It means to think something, to form in the imagination an idea or opinion or assessment, to adjudge, to conceive. And for immediate day-to-day matters, it leaves fairly well open the question of the validity or correctness of the conception; or is used in cases both good and bad. It occurs here and there in the Qur'ān in this relatively neutral sense. It occurs also, however, and more often, in another sense, functioning more closely as a specifically religious category, and here it takes on a different and rather special meaning; and to look at this, I suggest, can be educative.

This root occurs in various forms 70 times in the Qur'ān. Thus it is reasonably common; although *āmana*, to have faith or to make the act of faith, and *ʿalima*, to know, each occur more than ten times as often. I must not overstate my case: of the 70 occurrences, perhaps as many as 20, certainly some 15, have various other connotations than the one to which I wish to draw attention. Many of you will think right away of these. They include half a dozen or so where the usage implies a pondering, reflecting upon, entertaining in the mind, even occasionally of religious realities (falling into The Fire; the Resurrection; the encounter with the Lord), as well as a few that are ambiguous, and some casually neutral, plus three or four where the judgement being reported is clearly seen as correct. I have here references for the chief verses for this group; but will not enumerate them—as I say, several of you will have them in mind.[5]

In the great majority of cases, however, some forty-nine or fifty (roughly seventy percent), the term is used for men's having an opinion about God or His doings, but one that is woefully and manifestly awry. It designates in these instances a religious belief, no doubt; but a belief of a particular kind: namely, a wrong one. Far from being neutral as to the validity of the position held, the term is used in contexts where the idea is to convey the absurdity or perversity of that view. It is the full, clear opposite of 'knowledge', and designates human whimsy and foolish fancy—in a clear polarity. I find it interesting that similarly certain traditional

Christian thinkers, such as the Protestant Reformer John Calvin, later set up a dichotomy between God's revelation, on the one hand, and the arrant absurdities of depraved human imagination on the other. If this be religious belief, it is yet radically different from faith. Indeed, between what is designated by this *ẓanna*, to conjure up imaginative fancies, and *āmana*, to respond positively to God's clear summons, the contrast is stark.

It is not, however, always direct: it comes out in the differing relation of each to knowledge. Faith in the Qur'ān is closely correlated with knowledge: the two refer to the same matters, so that man accepts that which he knows. *Ẓanna*, on the other hand, so far as this religious level is concerned, comes into sharp collision with it; the connotations of *ẓanna* as a religious category are fixed in terms of its clear opposition to knowledge.

(Both relationships, one might remark in passing, diverge from the classical Greek distinction between *doxa* and *epistēmē* or *gnōsis*, where opinion may be a first step on the path to eventual knowledge. In the Qur'ān case, rather, knowledge comes first—given by God; faith is the positive response to it, *ẓanna* is the pitiful and puny alternative to it.)

In the Qur'ān, then, in these half-a-hundred usages *ẓanna* is roundly derided. The form of the statements is usually something like this: they *ẓanna* x, but in fact y. You may see that 'believe' here does make a possible translation; yet one misses the flavour of the presentations if one omits from the rendering the recognition that *ẓanna* is in fact a derogatory term, a pejorative. Let us recall some illustrative verses:

'They *ẓanna* about God other than the Truth, the *ẓann* of the times of ignorance' (3:153; and 'Truth' here deserves a capital T!): *yaẓunnūna bi-llāhi ghayra-l-ḥaqqi ẓanna-l-jāhilīyah.*

'About it they have no knowledge; rather, a following of *ẓann*!' (4:157): *mā la-hum bi-hi min ʿilmin illā-ttibāʿal-l-ẓann.*

'The majority of them do not follow anything but *ẓann*. Verily, *ẓann* is no substitute for Truth!' (10:36). This last phrase is repeated more than once; as usual, the English translation seems sadly feeble in comparison with the forceful and pungent rhetoric of the original: *inna-l-ẓanna lā yughnī mina-l-ḥaqqi shay'an.*

'You *ẓanna* that God was not aware of much of what you were doing' (41:22): *Wa-lākin ẓanantum anna-llāha lā yaʿlamu kathīran mimmā taʿmalūn.* Again, I tell my students that the ridicule implicit in this denunciation will be appreciated only by those who have some sense of the vividness of the Qur'ānic imagery and the almost devastating presentation of God's awareness of all that men do. 'He is all-observant . . .': *huwa baṣīrun ʿalīm.*

'Verily they *ẓanna*, as you *ẓanna*, that God would not resurrect anyone' (72:7): *wa-'annahum ẓannū ka-mā ẓanantum 'an lan yabʿatha-llāhu 'aḥadan.* Again, the total and almost vehement assurance that God will resurrect, that the Day of Judgement is indeed coming, in explosive fury, is to be remembered here.

'That is your *ẓann* which you *ẓanna* about your Lord—and it has ruined you' (41:23). . . . *ardākum.*

Often, the word appears in verses along with radically pejorative terms (*al-sū'*, *kādhib*, *kāfir*, etc.) There are, it is true, some cases where the *ẓann* of men about God is simply wrong, while there is little or no disdain: for example, in 12:110, where 'they *ẓanna* that all is lost, but We (God) rescued them'. And there is actually one verse (34:20) where this root converges with *ṣ-d-q*, truth—but it is Iblīs here, the Devil, about whom the Qur'ān is speaking. The passage might be taken in different ways; one could suggest, 'And Satan verily made come true against them his *ẓann* [we might translate it here 'his machinations'] for they follow him, all but a few of those who have faith'. One may note again the polarity over against *mu'minīn.*

Most of these instances, then, refer to man's *ẓann* as wicked or pitiable or ridiculous; and in any case wrong. The term is used to characterize with disdain the opinions of men that lead them astray.

In the Qur'ān, then, my submission is, *ẓanna* does not mean simply to believe, but to believe wrongly. Insofar as the other term, *āmana*, faith, means 'to believe' at all, it means, even those who would like to press that interpretation would have to admit, to believe rightly. More accurately: insofar as there is an intellectual component in *āmana*, it means, not 'to believe', but 'to recognize': to become aware of the situation as it in fact is. All this iṣ because, of course, implicit in the Qur'ān, and also explicit in it, is the view that the truth is given, is clear, is known. If the truth is known, then men's ideas may be categorized in terms of it—but this is precisely, as we have seen, what the modern Western concept of believing explicitly does *not* mean. On the contrary, modern 'believing' as a concept inherently postulates that truth, in the religious field, is not known.

The difference, of course, is that modern 'believing' is an anthropocentric concept; whereas the whole Qur'anic world-view is theocentric. It is theocentric not only as a whole, but in all its parts. The concepts with which it operates are concepts whose meaning, implication, and presupposition are saturatedly theocentric. And of course, I insist with my students that as soon as they reflect upon it they must recognize that this is all very natural, very much to be expected. You will not have failed to notice, I am sure, that I remarked above that an outsider might be found saying that to the Prophet Muḥammad the whole vision was so vivid, and it became so vivid to his community, that in a sense one might be tempted to say that it never occurred to him or them that people would not believe it, unless somehow their hearts had been hardened and their capacities sealed by God Himself. At least, the question that it might or might not be true was not an intellectual issue for them. Yet even to speak of Muḥammad here, or of the community, is to betray one's own anthropocentric scepticism. It is the way of speaking of the outsider who thinks of the Qur'ān in relation to Muḥammad, or to the Muslims. Within its own terms, however, and as it is read by Muslims, of course, the Qurān is the word not of Muḥammad but of God. It is not your scripture, but His. And since it is God who is speaking, after all, He knows what is true and what is false. It is entirely logical, and indeed natural, entirely legitimate and indeed inescapable, that when God is speaking, men's opinions are assessed and interpreted in the light of His truth. Since God knows what is right and what is wrong, the terms in which He addresses humankind leave no room for our human epistemological bewilderments. It was in order to salvage us from these that in this scripture He mercifully came to our rescue.

The Qur'ān view is theocentric, then, in sharp contrast to the anthropocentrism of the modern Western view. 'Believing' as a religious category has become an anthropocentric concept. No wonder, then, that it characterizes our modern age; but no wonder, also, that within it faith is feeble. To believe is not only different from faith; one may wonder whether the two are not alternatives.

At least, conceding the point, as you will remember that I earlier was quite willing to do, that presuppositions are indeed inescapably important, might we not toss out the aphorism that if faith, classically, presupposed belief, then belief, modernly, presupposes scepticism.

With this we conclude. Presuppositions are indeed of massive importance. The history of religion is primarily the history of faith. And so far as the intellectual or conceptual level is concerned, the history of religion is the history of presuppositions as much as it is of the ideas that men and women have explicitly held. It is only in terms of the presuppositions that the overt ideas reveal their true import. Moreover, in addition to the tacit context within which expressed ideas have been held, there is also an important history of the mode in which they were held. Classical Muslims were hardly conscious of believing anything, in the modern sense. In my next lecture I shall argue that the same holds true also for classical Christians—although it be the modern West, and the English language, that have generated our modern problem. Next time we not only shall consider Western developments, which I find fairly parallel, but also shall try a little to see what inferences perhaps may be drawn, for the modern intellect, and what some implications may be, for the modern religious crisis—and also for Muslim–Christian relations, which in a sense are my fundamental interests in these lectures.

For both of us, I am suggesting, faith and belief, far from being one and the same thing, are in fact two quite disparate matters. In belief, we differ from each other; and—given the condition of the modern world and the modern intellect—both of us from our forefathers. In faith, on the other hand, conceivably we differ less than one might imagine.

7

Faith, in Later Islamic History; the Meaning of *Taṣdīq*

Shortly after taking up my work in Islamics at McGill University I was asked to review a modern English translation of an Arabic fourteenth-century theological commentary on a twelfth-century Islamic statement of faith.[1] *Until that time I had been concerned primarily rather with present-day Islamic movements, and contemporary problems faced by modern Muslims, many of them my friends. To them, mediaeval theology had not been seen as particularly relevant. (It does not much figure in my first two books,* Modern Islām in India *and* Islam in Modern History.*) This commentary, however, proved fascinating. Its author (Taftāzānī) presently also came to be numbered among my friends; and recently, when* The Christian Century *in Chicago twenty-five years later asked various others and me to name 'the ten books that have changed your life', I included this Arabic text in my list.*

What struck me most forcefully, perhaps, was the curious, even tantalizing, quality of studying a theology that one does not 'believe' but that is nonetheless fascinating, and that within its own terms—if only one can truly apprehend these—is important, insightful, and even 'true': humanly true.

Over the years since, at both McGill and Harvard, I have read this and related texts with students, Muslim and other, and have conducted lively seminars on kalām. *(The rich distinctiveness of the Islamics Institute at McGill was well illustrated when one year a course on Islamic theology was taught jointly by the Dean of Theology of the Muslim University, Aligarh, and myself, with a joint student body. Theologies are not usually studied or taught so.)*

The long-term result of this (very long-term indeed: two or three decades were involved in wrestling intermittently with and reflecting on the issues raised) was a new apprehension of what theology, mediaeval or whenever, Islamic or Christian or whatever, at heart consists in: what theology as such, what human theologizing, has fundamentally been (and may yet become)—and indeed, human conceptualizing. In the meantime I was struck by how easy it is for an outsider to misapprehend what the texts are saying—just because he does not 'believe' them; and easy perhaps also for an insider, just because he does (or thinks he ought to).

An instance of this arose in that very first encounter with the Taftāzānī text. The translator had rendered the term īmān *by 'belief', which was standard enough and might have seemed reasonable in itself but did not in fact make genuine sense of the contexts in which the word occurred. It did not finally cohere with what Taftāzānī was saying about it: the argument in his text almost seemed to be affirming at times that* īmān, *as he and other mediaeval Muslims understood it, is not belief. From this observation eventually grew twenty-five years later my two recent volumes,* Belief & History *and* Faith & Belief. *The 'belief' translation, although troublesome otherwise, seemed however to be corroborated by the mediaeval author's explication that* īmān *is* taṣdīq *(rendered as 'assent'—an English word of whose history only later did I come to be critically aware). It was a good while before I sorted out carefully what writers had in mind when they used this Arabic word—by dint of studying the matter much more comprehensively and closely, and especially of examining the latter term's use in a wide range of contexts.*

This present paper, setting forth my answer to this specific problem, was written in response to an invitation to participate in a conference being organized by my Harvard colleague Professor Muḥsin Mahdī in honour of Professor Emeritus there Harry A. Wolfson (who also had written on the term taṣdīq, *as is noted below). I was absent on sabbatical at the time, which gave me the leisure to get my notes together and to put in order a presentation; I returned to Harvard to attend the conference and to read this piece (1971). It is being published here probably for the first time.*

It and certain others of the papers presented to that conference were in process of publication with the Arabic portions being composed in Beirut, when it became a minor casualty of the heart-rending Lebanese civil war. Subsequently publication was taken in hand by the State University of New York at Albany, where it is due perhaps to appear presently—hence my word 'probably' just now. The Albany version and this present one are in press simultaneously.

Faith (*al-īmān*), some Muslims held, is overtly doing something; some, that it is saying something; most, that it is an inner act. Various combinations of the three were also canvassed. In the rhyming formulation that came to prevail:

al-īmān taṣdīqun bi-al-janān, wa [*aw*] *iqrārun bi-al-lisān, wa*[*aw*] *ʿamalun bi-al-arkān.*

Our purpose in this present paper is to explore the point made concerning the inner dimension, and specifically the language used in setting it forth. *Al-īmān huwa al-taṣdīq* (or, more fully: . . . *al-taṣdīq bi-al-qalb*). If faith is indeed this movement of the heart, as the majority of Muslims came to hold, we would go on to ask: What, then, is *taṣdīq*?

This has seemed to many a simple matter. The present investigation would suggest that, on the contrary, the question is subtle, complex, and important. The meaning of the word is not so evident as most have assumed.

I leave here quite untouched the question as to what else faith might or might not be. Muslim thinkers deliberated on the relation among the three dimensions noted above; and the development of their positions has been studied by some Western scholars. That too I leave aside.[2] Into the meaning of the notion of *taṣdīq* as here engaged, however, few in modern times seem to have inquired.

In a careful and persuasive paper, Professor Wolfson several years ago showed that the word *taṣdīq* was used in classical Arabic logic in the sense of the mind's making a judgement,[3] in continuance of a similar notion in late Greek thinking. It is the purpose of this present paper to submit that in addition to that *falsafah* usage,[4] the term served also in *kalām* in another sense. I shall suggest that especially in the major formula *al-īmān huwa al-taṣdīq* the additional considerations have an important, even decisive, bearing. Indeed they are remarkably revealing for understanding not only Islamic but general human concerns.

In this issue I have been interested for some time, both philosophically and technically. In presenting for consideration now certain observations, I hope to illuminate the problem, or at least to show that it is more elaborate than has often been recognized. If the solutions here propounded are not themselves accepted, at least some of the ramifications will, it is hoped, have been brought to attention, and over-simplification discouraged.

Before the matter is tackled in specific detail, two general reflections are in order. The first is major. It is this: that religious faith as a virtually universal human quality or characteristic is, surely, a delicate and problematic affair. Many a profound and careful theologian in many a community has averred that this quality transcends verbal description, and rational apprehension. Many a modern student, whether in the social sciences or in history or in the humanities, recognizes that the religious faith of persons and groups eludes his or her easy grasp. What is this human involvement, which has inspired so much of the world's greatest art and heroism and brutality; has underlain very decisively so much of humanity's civilizations and humdrum life? If at the turn of our century the sophisticated intellectual could dismiss religious faith on one or another secular score, nowadays such an intellectual recognizes rather that we have not yet understood it. If the believer could accept it as relatively straightforward, he too now more openly senses mystery. The more that light is thrown upon it from various modern investigations and increasing historical awareness, the more complex and elusive it is seen to become.

Clearly, faith has taken many different forms. There has been variety: both of gross forms, of which 'the Islamic' form is one, overtly different from Christian or Buddhist or Hindū; and a variety of subtle forms, of which there have been many within, for instance, the over-all Islamic pattern, forms of which the Sunnī and the Shīʿī, or the Ṣūfī and the legalist and the philosophic, or the urban and the village, or one century's and another's, or one man's and his brother's, are variations. Along with such endless variety seems to go also, in human history, an impressive persistence.

We should be cautious, therefore, in imagining that we have understood or defined faith, either in general or in any particular case. Also, by the same token we do well to give careful heed to any major instance in human history where a significant and intelligent group has proffered a thesis of what it considers faith, or anyway its own faith, to be.

Our second general consideration, at the introductory level, is that the concepts available to us for an understanding or interpretation of faith, and especially faith of another people or age or religious system, are themselves particular. They are both limited and specific. This is true of the concept 'faith' itself, which in modern Western usage has connotations deriving from two main traditions. One is the Christian, developed basically in the New Testament but incorporating through the Old the tradition of ancient Israel, and in the course of its history incorporating also much of the tradition of Greek thought, and in recent times enlarged to the Judaeo–Christian. The second is the objective-critical, the academic: especially since the Enlightenment, the tradition that considers faith from the outside, and more recently that observes it, generically but passively, in a wide variety of forms across the world. It is clear that the Islamic concept of faith, classically, is and must be formally and in principle different from both of these.[5]

Despite considerations such as these, I propose in the present article to translate *īmān* by 'faith' (and this despite certain more technical and yet fundamentally important considerations also, such as that in Arabic this term is a *maṣdar*, is verbal, is the name of an act before it is the name of a quality). I do so because to do otherwise would distract us too radically from our primary subject matter here, the meaning of *īmān*'s predicate, *taṣdīq*. My procedure is to postulate that none of us adequately understands 'faith', either in general or in the particular Islamic case.[6] Accordingly, we can explicitly mean by 'faith' something somewhat beyond our intellectual apprehension, something towards a partial clarification of which we can hope to move. If this openness for 'faith' can be maintained, then we can go on towards elucidating, if not what it is or was, at least something that Muslims classically held it to be: namely, *taṣdīq*.

Yet here too our elucidatory predicates are also particular. The English term 'believe', for example, is redolent of both ambiguity and particularity. Like French *croire* and German *glauben*, the word comes into modern usage saturated with its classical Christian past and its Western intellectualist-neutralist-scepticist currency. To say that *ṣaddaqa* means 'to believe' (as has regularly been said) can be therefore (and regularly has been?) misleading or ambiguous or both. Even *fürwahrhalten*, an explicatory predication of *glauben*, leaves open, of course, the notoriously problematic question of truth (*Wahrheit*)—to which is relevant the important Arabic distinction between *ḥaqq* and *ṣidq*, as we shall presently observe. And *credo*, I believe it can be shown, has changed its meaning over the centuries.[7]

Part of the present thesis is that the concept *taṣdīq* means that for Muslims faith was discerned and interpreted in ways significantly differing from those current in the modern West.

The *object* of faith in the Islamic case has of course been explicitly different—conceptually—from its object among other communities. This is manifest enough, and many have thereupon contented themselves with specifying that difference of object, leaving then unexplored and even unasked a question as to the form of the faith that is oriented to that object. Christian faith is faith in God and Christ . . . ; Muslim faith is faith in God and the Qur'ān and Muḥammad . . . . My concern here is to supplement this obvious point, suggesting that the pluralism of faith around the world is not merely that faith is (and/or is conceived to be) a relationship to *x*, to *y*, to *z*, in various cases. I would focus rather on the more subtle matter of attempting to ascertain the human side of those relationships in each case. On more careful consideration it turns out that, in the various religious patterns that variegate human history, faith is a P-relationship to *x*, a Q-relationship to *y*, an R-relationship to *z*, and so on. (It might even then turn out that P, Q, R, are as different from each other as are *x*, *y*, *z*.)

A neglect of this personalist, or formal, quality of faith, as distinct from its object, or substantial 'content', has support within many traditions, where in each case the particularity tends to be taken for granted. In the Islamic instance, for example, faith was at times explicated merely in terms of its object: faith is faith in *x*, Muslims said with formal tautology (along with substantive force). In the words of the classic *ḥadīth: al-īmān an tu'mina bi-Allāh wa bi-malā'ikih wa bi* . . . .[8] This tells us nothing, and assumes that we need to be told nothing, as to what faith itself is; only, where it is directed.

At other times, however, and that constitutes our interest here, Muslims did ask what faith inherently is; and their standard answer often was: it is *taṣdīq*.[9] What did they mean when they said that?

It is not surprising that Christians, and Western ex-Christians, have tended to suppose that they meant, 'faith is belief'. This is not surprising, given their own background and presuppositions in these matters; given their own relation to Islamic data (which, as outsiders, they themselves do not 'believe' but suppose that Muslims do); and given the superficial plausibility of the translation. This last is enhanced by the fact with which we began, that the logicians in classical Arabic, as distinct from the theologians, did, as Wolfson has demonstrated, employ *taṣdīq* to mean the making of an intellectual judgement, following the Greeks. A closer examination of the texts, however, shows that for *kalām* the 'believing' notion is inadequate. It is the argument of the present inquiry, at least, that this is a mistranslation. To suppose that for Muslims faith is belief, or that they themselves thought so, is, I suggest, to misunderstand.

To explore this, we must clarify certain understandings of truth. Those who interpret *taṣdīq* as 'believing' arrive at that position by rendering it first as 'holding to be true'. Truth, however, in itself, and man's relations to it, are intricate and subtle matters, which repay rather careful consideration.

The present thesis is that more critical awareness of what sorts of issue are at stake in this concept is needed if we are to apprehend the *taṣdīq* notion adequately, as it bears on religious life. Our proposal, accordingly, is to develop first a rather general interpretation of this term (*taṣdīq*) in the context of a comprehensive Islamic view of truth; and then with this orientation to confront specific passages of *kalām* writing that, it is submitted, illustrate and confirm the suggested rendering. The actual working method, of course, was in fact the other way around. Over the course of some years a wrestling with particular passages which did not seem to make sense with the standard renderings, pushed me to modify these, and finally to attain a new understanding of what was being said and within what framework of ideas.

What is truth? We may begin our presentation by recalling simply that there are three roots in the Arabic language around which crystallized Muslims' concepts on this mighty question. These three are *ḥaqqa*, *ṣadaqa*, and *ṣaḥḥa*. All three have something to do with truth. Yet the three are, of course, quite distinct—which fact in itself can serve us instructively. If I might over-simplify in order to introduce a major point, I would suggest that the first has to do with the truth of things, the second with the truth of persons, and the third with the truth of statements. But let me elaborate.

First, *ḥaqqa*. When a Western student first learns Arabic, he is taught that *ḥaqq* sometimes means 'true', sometimes means 'real'. He may perhaps remember that the same remark actually had been made to him also about the Latin term *verus*, which can mean 'real', 'genuine', 'authentic', and also 'true', 'valid'. If he goes on to learn Sanskrit, he will meet the same point again with regard to that language's (and civilization's) term *satyam*: it too denotes both reality and truth. Eventually he may come to realize that what is happening here is not necessarily that all these peoples are somehow odd folk who have confused or converged two matters, or used one word indiscriminately for two different notions; but that it is perhaps rather the modern West that is odd, is off the track, in having somehow dichotomized a single truth-reality, in having allowed its conception of truth to diverge from its conception of reality. At least, an important case can be made for such a view.

Even the West today harbours remnants of this ealier usage. For Western civilization, decidedly, was built upon concepts of this type. Westerners still at times can speak of true courage, or false modesty; of true marriage or a true university; even of a true note in music. I mentioned this once, however, to a professional philosopher only to have him dismiss it as metaphorical, and not really legitimate or even significant. Only propositions, he said, are *really* true or false. And even for non-analysts among us, whatever our residual vocabulary, there has come to be widespread today a certain discomfort, most will probably agree, with any but a very imprecise position that things, qualities, actions, can be true or false. Things are just there, somehow, many feel, and it is only what one says about them that is subject to this discriminating judgement.

However that may be, in Arabic *ḥaqq* like *satyam* and *veritas* refers to what is real, genuine, authentic, what is true in and of itself by dint of metaphysical or cosmic status. Accordingly, it is a term *par excellence* of God. In fact, it refers absolutely to Him, and indeed *al-Ḥaqq* is a name of God not merely in the sense of an attribute but of a denotation. *Huwa al-Ḥaqq*: He is reality as such. Yet every other thing that is genuine is also *ḥaqq*—and some of the mystics went on to say, is therefore divine. We leave this issue, however, simply noting that *ḥaqq* is truth in the sense of the real, with or without a capital R.

Secondly, *ṣadaqa*. Our excursus about *ḥaqq* was in order to make sense of the remark now that this term *ṣadaqa* refers to a truth of persons. It matches to some extent Western notions of honesty, integrity, and trustworthiness; yet it goes beyond them. It involves being true both (i) to oneself and to other persons, and (ii) to the objective situation with which one is dealing. Propositional truth is by no means irrelevant here. It is not ruled out or even set aside. Rather, it is subordinated, being incorporated as an element within a personalist context. For indeed the term is of course used predominantly, although not exclusively, for 'telling the truth'. This is often the simplest way to translate it; yet there is something more. What that something more involves, at the pesonalist level, becomes apparent when one considers, in both Arabic and English, the contrasting concept of telling a lie. *Ṣadaqa* is the precise opposite of *kadhiba*, 'to be a liar'. This latter, as is its translation in English, is a highly revealing usage. For it denotes the saying of something that not only is untrue, but that also the speaker knows to be untrue, and says with an intent to deceive. The Arabs do not normally use *kadhiba*, as English does not use 'liar', in the case where a person says something inaccurate but in good faith.

It is curious, as we shall develop later, that English has the concept 'lie' and 'liar' corresponding more or less exactly to the Islamic concept of *kadhiba*, a personal falsity, untruth at the level of human intent and practice, and of interpersonal relations, but does not have an exact equivalent to, has not formulated a special concept for, the counterpart notion of *ṣidq*: truth of strictly personalist focus.

This concept, then, has been a central one for Muslims, not least in their religious life, and is central too for the thesis that is being advanced in this paper. We will return to pursue it further, therefore, presently. I set it aside for a moment to consider briefly the third term, *ṣaḥḥa*.

This verb, and its adjective *ṣaḥīḥ*, although expressing important notions, have been much less spectacular in Islamic life, and especially in the realm that concerns us here. The words mean, more or less, 'sound', and refer to quite a variety of matters, such as being healthy or being appropriate. One would hardly think of it right off as a term for 'truth' at all, except that its usage does, indeed, overlap in part with that of that English word (especially as used in modern logic) in that it may be used in Arabic of propositions when they are what we would call true or correct. (*Hādhā ṣaḥīḥ*, *hādhā ghalaṭ*—or, *khaṭa'*, or simply *ghayr saḥīḥ*.)

Of these three Arabic concepts, it is to be noted that the first two have strongly polarized contraries. *Ḥaqq* stands in stark and even awesome contrast to *bāṭil*, as the true and the false, or the real and the 'phony'. Behind the one is metaphysical power, while the other in strident dichotomy from it is ludicrously vain and vacuous. To distinguish between the two is one of man's most decisive tasks or prerogatives. Again, there is the resonant pair of *ṣidq* and *kadhib*, or to use the more personalist terms, *ṣādiq* and *kādhib*: the honest man of truth stands squarely over against the despicable and wretched liar. At play here is the Islamic vision of man's dramatic freedom and moral choice, in a world where decisions matter.

Ṣaḥīḥ, on the other hand, has no clear opposite. One of its applications is to a person being in sound health; possible alternatives are that he or she may be weak, or sick, or old, or not old enough, or missing a limb, or what not; but there is no clear other pole.[10] The only opposite of 'sound' is a wide range of unsoundness, of unspecified imperfections; although as we have already noted, in the particular case of a sentence, if it is not *ṣaḥīḥ*, true, then one may perhaps call it mistaken, *ghalaṭ* or *khaṭa'*. A railway timetable that is no longer in force, or an argument that is not cogent, various sorts of things that do not come off or are not in good working order, may be characterized as not *ṣaḥīḥ*; but this designates a quality that is not a category, or at least not a cosmic one. In other Islamic languages too—Persian, Urdū, and others, as well as Arabic, those familiar with these languages will readily agree—this third notion, used for, among other things, propositional truth, has by far the feeblest moral connotations of the three.[11]

Indeed, the first and the second are saturatedly, bristlingly, moral; they, and their respective pejorative contraries, are highly moralistic. Human destiny is at stake with them, and human quality. And, appropriately enough, it turns out on inquiry that the third root, *ṣaḥḥa*, does not even occur in the Qur'ān. The other two reverberate in it, mightily.

It would hardly be an exaggeration to see the Qur'ān as a vibrant affirmation that the loci of significant truth are two: the world around us, and persons. The reality of the former is divine. The inner integrity of the latter, and our conformity to, and commitment to, the real, are crucial. Indeed, this is what human life is all about.[12]

Let us return, then, specifically to *ṣadaqa*, *yaṣduqu*, *ṣidqan*. Being a resonant term in the Qur'ān, for Muslims it formulates a cosmic category, constituting one of the basic points of reference in relation to which human life and society take on meaning in the Islamic complex.

If we consult the Arabic dictionaries, we find illuminating presentations and analyses of this word. In virtually all cases these are given in conjunction with the correlative *kadhiba*. And in virtually all cases, given first, or made quite basic, is the link with speech. Since the dictionary entries under *ṣadaqa* converge substantially in their understandings of the term, at least insofar as our concerns here are at issue, it is representative enough for our purposes to cite illustratively from *Lisān al-ʿArab* and *Tāj al-ʿArūs*.[13] First, we note that although *ṣadaqa* and *kadhiba* are considered in their relation to speech, they are viewed as applied there not only to what in modern logic would be called statements or propositions, but to all sorts of things that man may say—including questions and much else. Explicitly indicated is that the speech may be about the past or about the future, in the latter case whether by way of promise or otherwise; and it may be indicative, but also either interrogative, or imperative, and even supplicative. Thus a question may be not *ṣidq*, truthful, if it involves something of the 'Have you stopped beating your wife?' sort. Similarly a command, such as 'Give me back my book', or an entreaty, 'Would you please give me back my book?', may be *ṣidq* or *kadhib*, truthful or lying, depending upon whether the person addressed has the book, and the one speaking genuinely wishes it back.

In general, these and other dictionaries clearly make the point that *ṣidq* applies to that sort of speech in which there is conformity of what is said simultaneously with two things: (i) what is in the speaker's mind; and (ii) what is actually the case.[14]

Particular discussion is given to an assertion that 'Muḥammad is the Apostle of God' when it is made by someone who says it insincerely. This is the Muslim's paradigm of a true statement; and clearly there were qualms about asserting that it could ever become not right—yet without sincerity it cannot be called valid. One view is that any utterance may be half *ṣidq*, in reference either to the speaker's sincerity or to the objective facts; but there is full *ṣidq* only when both are satisfied. Similarly, when there is reference to the future, then *ṣidq* demands congruity both between inner conviction and a man's words, and between the latter and his subsequent deeds.

The verb may take a direct object of the person addressed, inasmuch as telling the truth, in this sense, and lying, are matters of personal interrelations. *Ṣadaqahu* or *kadhibahum* indicate that the truth and falsity under consideration here are attributes of a statement in its role of establishing or constituting communication between or among human beings. Here again, it may be noted that the modern West maintains in its conceptualization of lying an implication that one can hardly tell a lie alone on a desert island, yet has tended to relinquish this interpersonal dimension from its conception of speaking truth.

Comparable considerations operate when the Arabic verb is used of human actions other than speaking. Transitional is a phrase such as *ṣadaqahu al-naṣīḥah*: 'He was true in the advice that he gave him', or 'He spoke the truth to him in his advice', or 'He advised him with *ṣidq*'. This implies that the counsel was both sincere, and effectively wise. Non-verbally: *ṣadaqahu al-ikhā'*, 'He was true towards him in brotherliness', or '. . . behaved towards him with true brotherhood'. Again: *ṣadaqūhum al-qitāl*, 'They fought them with *ṣidq*', or 'They were true against them in battle'. This means that they fought against them both with genuine zeal and with good effect.

Throughout, *ṣidq* is that quality by which a person speaks or acts with a combination of inner integrity and objective overt appropriateness. It involves saying or doing the right thing, out of a genuine personal recognition of its rightness, an inner alignment with it.

In modern English, negative concepts like lying and cheating conceptualize overt performance in terms of the performers and their moral quality, inwardly, as well as in terms of the objective outward facts or rules. On the other hand, English conceptually has not developed carefully, or formulated strongly, counterpart positive concepts to assess and to interpret behaviour in these trilateral terms.[15] This is what the notion *ṣadaqa* precisely does.

Human behaviour, in a word or deed, is the nexus between man's inner life and the surrounding world. Truth at the personalist level is that quality by which both halves of that relationship are chaste and appropriate—are true.

The Muslims were no fools when they regarded this as an important human category. Modern Western logic has done a radical disservice, symptomatic perhaps of a serious disruption in human life, by championing the position, nurtured by impersonalist objective science, that the locus of truth and falsity is propositions, rather than the persons who use them. At least, so I have attempted to argue in a recent philosophical paper.[16] In that study I explore a little some of the differences and their ramifications between the orientation implicit in the concept *ṣidq* and the orientation increasingly current in Western or 'modern' intellectual and social life in its notion of truth—differences that seem crucial and ramifications that seem profound.

Next let us consider the second form: *ṣaddaqa*, *yuṣaddiqu*, *taṣdīqan*. Like other *tafʿīl* forms, it constitutes an intricate causative or double transitive of wide potentiality. If *ṣadaqa* means to say (or to do) something that is at the same time both inwardly honest and outwardly correct, what then does the reactivated form *taṣdīq* signify? I may enumerate four meanings.

First, of course, it can mean 'to regard as true'. Its primary object may be either a person, or—less usually—a sentence; so that *ṣaddaqahu* means, 'He held him to be a speaker of the truth', or may mean, 'He held it to be spoken truly'. These might be rendered, if one liked, as 'He believed him' (or 'it'); yet there are two caveats. One is that in both cases, it is because he trusted the speaker. It can indicate that he held him to be *ṣādiq*, a speaker sincerely of truth on a particular occasion, or held him to be *ṣiddīq*, an habitual teller of the truth by moral character. Secondly, a rendition by 'believe' is inadequate also because it omits the reference to objective validity, since 'believe' in English has become so openly neutral a term. One can believe what is false. I have not checked enough passages to be able to affirm flatly that *taṣdīq* applies only to believing what is in fact true; and yet I think that there can be no question but that, even if there are some exceptions, the standard implication still is strongly one of objective truth as well as of sincerity. This is a cosmic human quality, with little room for sheer gullibility. Accordingly, one should translate, at this level, not by 'believe' but by 'recognize the truth of'. The difference is deep.

Even this, however, takes care of only one side of the double reference: that to the correctness of what is so regarded. There is still the other side, the personal sincerity involved. This operates at least as strongly in this second form as in the first. And the personalism is of both the primary subject and the secondary: to recognize a truth as personal for others, and as personal for oneself. Thus, if I give *taṣdīq* to some statement, I not merely recognize its truth in the world outside me, and subscribe to it, but also incorporate it into my own moral integrity as a person.

A second standard usage of this form is that it means, not 'He held him to be a speaker of the truth', but rather 'He *found* him to be so'. One may hear a man's statement, and only subsequently find reason or experience to know that that man was no liar.

Thirdly, it may indicate this sort of notion but with a more active, resolute type of finding: that is, 'He *proved* him to be a speaker of truth,' or confirmed or verified the matter. Thus the common phrase, *ṣaddaqa al-khabara al-khubru*: 'The experience verified the report'. Accordingly, *taṣdīq* has become the term for scientific experimental verification, proving something true by test, although the notion of vindicating the experimenter as well as the experiment is never far distant. A stricter translation of the phrase just quoted would be, 'The experiment verified the report and the reporter'.

Fourthly, still more deliberately, *taṣdīq* may mean to render true, to take steps to make come true. One instance of this is one's own promise: a radically important matter. Thus, one of the meanings of *ṣiddīq* is *alladhī yuṣaddiqu qawlahu bi-al-ʿamal,*[17] 'He who validates what he says in what he does'; and another, *man ṣadaqa bi-qawlihi wa-iʿtiqādihi wa ḥaqqaqa ṣidqahu bi-fiʿlihi,*[18] 'He who is truthful in his speech and in his inner conviction, and who actualizes his truthfulness in his behaviour'.

Furthermore, *muṣaddiq* is given as equivalent to *ṣiddīq*[19] (and, conversely, *ṣiddīq* as equivalent to *dhū taṣdīq*[20] or *dāʾim al-taṣdīq*[21])—presumably in any or all of the senses of this adjective, including that simply of an intensive: *al-kathīr al-ṣidq*[22] and *man kathura minhu al-ṣidq.*[23]

On the other hand, when *ṣiddīq* is said[24] to signify, rather, one who is outstanding (*mubāligh*) in both *al-ṣidq* and *al-taṣdīq*, the meaning of the latter is presumably activist: *ṣidq* refers to this person's sincerely speaking the truth, and *taṣdīq* to his or her sincerely acting it. *Taṣdīq* in all these references clearly has nothing to do with 'believing'. It is not being said that the Virgin Mary[25] and other *ṣiddīqūn* excel in being credulous or in gullibility!

To summarize: *Taṣdīq* is to recognize a truth, to appropriate it, to affirm it, to confirm it, to actualize it. And the truth, in each case, is personalist and sincere.

All of this is in general; what has been said thus far is on the basis of the mediaeval Arabic dictionaries. And there is legitimacy in having begun so, with ordinary language, before we turn to the specifically theological intepretations; since those men of *kalām* who promoted the thesis that faith is *taṣdīq* would habitually begin by stressing the straightforward linguistic grounds for this. *Al-īmān fī-al-lughah al-taṣdīq,*[26] they were wont to stay, referring to traditional usage. This is over against the logician's use of the latter term,[27] behind which, as Wolfson has shown, lies a Greek rather than an Arab tradition.

When classical Muslim thinkers, then, on being asked what faith is, affirmed that it is *taṣdīq*, what did they have in mind? The historian of religion is interested in various conceptions of faith around the world, and this one not least. If we ponder this formula a little, and correlate it with the several versions that we have just noted of *taṣdīq*, we can see that it makes good sense. We can appreciate what the men of religion meant when they said that faith is doing or making or activating truth: doing personal truth, or making truth personal.

In a quite general and preliminary way, we may list some linguistic implications. To begin with, faith is then the *recognition* of divine truth at the personal level. Faith is the ability to recognize truth as true for oneself, and to trust it. Especially in the Islamic case, with its primarily moral orientation, this includes, or makes primary, the recognition of the authenticity, and moral authority, of the divine commands. Thus there is a recognition of the obligatoriness of moral obligations; and the acceptance of their obligatoriness as applying to oneself, with the personal commitment then to carrying them out.

Again: it is the personal making of what is cosmically true come true on earth—the *actualization* of truth (the truth about man).

More mystically, it is the *discovery* of truth (the personal truth) of the Islamic injunctions: the process of personal verification of them, whereby, by living them out, one proves them and finds that they do indeed become true, both for oneself and for the society and world in which one lives.

Taṣdīq is the inner appropriation and outward implementation of truth. It is the process of making or finding true in actual human life, in one's own personal spirit and overt behaviour, what God—or Reality—intends for man.

And with many a passage strongly insisting that faith is more than knowledge, that it is a question of how one responds to the truth, one may also render the proposition 'faith is *taṣdīq*' as 'Faith is the ability to trust, and to act in terms of, what one knows to be true'.

All these are not bad definitions of faith, one will perhaps agree.

They are not, and are not meant to be, definitions of Islamic faith. Rather, they are Islamic definitions of human faith. At issue here is not the content of faith but its form, not its object but its nature; in question is not what is true, but what one does about what is true.

Of course, the Islamic epistemological point that Muslims learn what the final truth is about man's duty and destiny through the divine disclosure of it (in their case, in the Qur'ān) was of course taken for granted in the theological treatises, and eventually colours the further discussion of faith a little—although surprisingly little. As my presentation will perhaps make clear, and as a book on which I am working will more explicitly document, a sizeable portion of many passages in Islamic theology about faith could be introduced word for word into Christian discussions of the matter almost without modification, and with considerable profit. And the same might be true, to some degree, in humanist discussions.

We are concerned, it will be recalled, with the human quality of faith, not with its object. In the past, concern with object has distracted students from discerning *either* the similarities *or* the differences among conceptions of faith's form, both of which on inquiry turn out to be striking.

For of course (still apart from any question as to the object of faith), in addition to correspondences of form, there are also divergencies. Between the Islamic and the Christian religious orientations, there have been certain fundamental differences of tone; and of course even more pronounced are the differences between the classical Islamic and the modern semi-sceptical Western. These have implications for the respective notions of faith, considered as a human phenomenon. I will note two.

One has to do with an Islamic sense of clarity. Mystery, although of course for Muslims by no means absent, yet has been something that—especially outside Ṣūfī circles—they have played up deliberately and conceptually much less than have Christians. For Muslims, God's revelation is clear, *mubīn*. (This word occurs on an average more than once per *sūrah* in the Qur'ān.[28])

A second difference has to do with the fact that the Islamic orientation is in general more moralist, more practical (more 'legalistic', as Christians have tended to say of it and of the comparable Jewish orientation, but this can be seriously misleading[29]). It is more dynamic, with its revelation primarily of God's will (as distinct from the Christian case, with its revelation primarily of God's person), and derivatively then with its primary stress on *fiqh* more than on theology. For Muslims, 'the eternal Word of God is an imperative'.[30]

The radical inadequacy of the standard Western understanding of Islamic notions of faith (especially as 'believing') appears at at least two levels, relating to these two matters. One is a divergence in relation to knowlege; the other in relation to moral action.

For the Muslim, God's revelation being clear (*mubīn*), it leads at once to knowledge. The concept of knowledge is vividly communicated by the Qur'ān. The verb *ʿarafa* is less common, occurring about 70 times; but *ʿalima* much more so, 856 times which, for instance, in the now standard Royal Egyptian edition, means on an average of more than once per page. The concept is lavishly imprinted in Muslim consciousness, and is central to the Islamic drama: God has acted to make quite manifest to men and women what He would have them know. Faith is humankind's positive response.

In relation to knowledge, then, a major difference at once appears between faith in its typically Islamic form and in some of its Christian forms. For many Westerners, including Christians, faith has come to be thought of as having to do with something less than knowing, so that that to which it is oriented is 'taken of faith' or is 'believed' (and will be *known*, perhaps, only beyond the grave); hence also, 'the leap of faith'. To have faith is to believe, not yet to know.[31] For Muslims, on the other hand, faith is on the other side of knowledge; not on this side of it.

Actually, there was an early stage in the course of Muslim reflection on these matters when faith was equated with knowledge (*maʿrifah*); while others equated it rather with acting in accord with what is known. The latter position does not concern us here; besides, its inadequacy was quickly made apparent, in the Khārijī excesses at the practical level, and theoretically in its failure to make room either for the hypocrite, *munāfiq*, who had *ʿamal* without *īmān*, or for the sinner, who has *īmān* without (full) *ʿamal*. The other equation, faith is knowledge, proved equally unsatisfying, and was also soon discarded; yet by deprecation, it was negatively kept alive in that later writers kept recurring to it to explain how much it leaves out. It was criticized, however, on the grounds that in fact faith is *more* than knowldge. Faith is not knowledge, it was agreed; yet it has to do with what is known. In Christian scholastic thought, opinion, faith, and knowledge form a series in that order;[32] in *kalām*, the order is, rather, opinion, knowledge, faith.

Al-īmān wājib fī mā ʿulima, as Taftāzānī explicitly says: man is required to have faith in those things that are known.[33] *Al-taṣdīq*, others said, 'means a binding of one's heart *ʿala mā ʿulima*'.[34] Again, it is a submitting *li-mā ʿulima*.[35]

Just as faith for Muslims has to do not with believing but with knowing, so *kufr*, rejection, is not a lack of belief, not an intellectual position that holds that something is otherwise than is the case, and certainly it is not mere ignorance. Rather it, too, like its correlative *īmān*, presupposes knowledge; for it is an active repudiation of what one knows to be true. This is why it is a sin, and indeed a (the) monstrous sin. It is the one final, cosmic (or some would say, the one final human) wrong: the deliberate saying of 'no' to what one knows to be right. This, too, is set forth in the Qur'ān; for instance, in two passages repeatedly cited by the *mutakallimūn* in their discussions of the relation between faith and knowledge. One (colouring the perception of Christians by many Muslims to this day) sets forth the point that some to whom the Book was sent 'know it as they know their own sons'[36] and yet do not respond with faith. The other speaks of men who rejected the signs of God 'even though within themselves they knew full well' that they were true.[37] Cited also, if less frequently, is the reference to those who rejected after they had accepted.[38]

The Islamic scheme, then, envisages God's acting, and thereby man's knowing; so that the important question becomes man's response: the response to what is now known. Ideally, there are two basic reactions possible: to accept, or to reject (*īmān*, or *kufr*).[39] The object of faith being thought of as pellucid and incontrovertible, the issue is, what does one do about that which one knows?

Faith, then, is the positive response to God's initiative. It is not merely knowledge: it includes knowledge, but is something else as well. That something additional, the men of *kalām* came to agree, is *taṣdīq*. *Huwa* (that is, *al-taṣdīq*) *amr zā'id ʿalá al-ʿilm*.[40]

We turn, then, from faith to *taṣdīq*; for we are now in a position to address ourselves to the question with which we began, as to what this term means in *kalām*. We can now see that it designates not belief, but knowledge; and not merely knowledge, but knowledge of the truth plus something else. (Neither of these two components—neither that of knowing the truth, nor that of the something additional—is found in the current Western translations; nor, quite, in the logicians' *taṣdīq*.[41]) 'There is no getting away from it', says al-Taftāzānī, 'that the difference is manifest between knowing, being quite sure about, on the one hand, . . . and, on the other hand, *taṣdīq* and *iʿtiqād*'[42]—in that the latter include the former and add to them. Again: 'There were some Qadarīs who took up the position that faith is knowledge; but our scholars are agreed that that position is wrong—since there are the People of the Book who used to know that Muḥammad . . . was a prophet "as surely as they knew their own sons", and yet there is no question but that they were *kāfir*s because of the absence of *taṣdīq*; and since among the *kuffār* are some who know the truth in full certainty, but simply reject it, out of "stubbornness and haughtiness" ' (and he then quotes Qur'ān 27:14 as I have done).[43] Again, the ninth-century (*hijrī*) commentator al-Kastalī writes: '*Taṣdīq* does not mean knowing that something said or the one who says it is true (*ṣidq*): otherwise, it would have to be the case that everyone who knows the truthfulness of the prophet . . . would have *īmān* in him (be *mu'min* of him), and this is just not so—indeed, there were many among the *kuffār* who knew that [the Prophet] was telling the truth . . . ,' and he goes on to quote the same Qur'ān passages.[44]

What, then, is *taṣdīq*? Clearly, it lies in the realm of activist sincerity. *Ṣidq*, as we have seen, designates truth at the personalist level, of recognition and integrity: the second form of the verb designates an activating of this.

Fundamental for understanding one of the prime meanings of *taṣdīq* in this connection is a remark such as the following of al-Ṭabarī:

al-qawm kānū ṣadaqū bi-alsinatihim wa-lam yuṣaddiqū qawlahum bi-fiʿlihim.[45]

Obviously this is not 'to believe' but rather to confirm, to actualize the truth. They '. . . spoke the truth with their tongues, but did not corroborate what they were saying with their deeds'. Or one might use such verbs as 'authenticate' or 'validate'. An older usage in English would legitimately appear here if one translated by: '. . . they were not faithful to what they were saying, in their deeds'.

This actualizing aspect of *taṣdīq* is illuminated, again, in the oft-cited statement, *al-īmān mā waqara fī al-qalb, wa-ṣaddaqahu al-ʿamal.*[46] 'Faith is that about which the heart is firm, and that deeds validate (authenticate, corroborate)'.

Again, and more theologically, the fact that God Himself is called *mu'min* is also explained, for instance by al-Baghdādī, as His being activatingly faithful in this sense:

wa-Allāh mu'min li-annahu yuṣaddiqu waʿdahu bi-al-taḥqīq.[47]

'God is "faithful" because He gives *taṣdīq* to His promise, carrying it out in effective realization (or actualization)'.

(It would be ludicrous to translate either *īmān* or *taṣdīq* as 'believing' in any of these cases—and I feel, in any cases at all.)

The difference, then, between knowledge and *taṣdīq* lies in the sincerity and in the operationalist addenda denoted by the latter term. Knowledge is the perception of a truth outside onself; *taṣdīq* is the personal appropriation of that perception. It is the inner reordering of oneself so as to act in terms of it; the interiorization and implementation of the truth in dynamic sincerity. *Taṣdīq* means not 'to believe' a proposition but rather to recognize a truth and to existentialize it.

The existentializing is basic; and I have come across one instance where the parallel to modern existentialist phrasing, even, is both curious and entrancing. There are many passages, for instance in Taftāzānī's commentary on Nasafī's *ʿAqāʾid*, where the activating force of *taṣdīq* is conspicuous. In one such, he explicitly rejects in so many words the notion that this term means to believe, and even to recognize as true. He rejects it as altogether inadequate, and goes on to make the matter more interesting in his endeavour to set forth the notion of self-commitment that is at issue. For, just as in English modern existentialists in order to express this notion turn to French and borrow thence the terms *engagé* and *engagement*, so this mediaeval writer, in struggling to express the existentialist involvement that 'faith' connotes, turns to Persian and introduces into his Arabic a Persian term, *giravīdan*—which indeed is virtually the precise counterpart of *s'engager*, since *girav* is the Persian for that for which *gage* is the French: namely, the stake or pawn or pledge that is put up as a warranty by a participant in an affair. 'The true nature of *taṣdīq* is not that there should take place in the mind the attribute (or the attributing) of veracity to what is said, or to the person who says it, unaccompanied by a yielding to it and an accepting of it for oneself. On the contrary, it is rather a yielding to and accepting of that, such that the term "surrender" applies to it as Imām Ghazzālī has made clear. All in all, it is the meaning that is expressed in Persian by *girawīdan—s'engager*.'[48]

All this is especially relevant to, and leads to a consideration of, the second of the two fundamental orientations that we averred to be characteristic of Islamic life and significant for its faith—namely, the moral. For the truth to which the Muslim must respond is largely a moral truth. The knowledge conferred by revelation is largely a knowledge of moral requirements, of commands, of duties: *awāmir*, *aḥkām*, *farāʾiḍ*. In the moral life especially, as all of us recognize, knowledge is not yet virtue. The recognition that something ought to be done is not yet the recognition that I ought to do it, not yet the resolve to do it, not yet my personal decision so to act. Involved in the moral life is a particular quality or act, more than and other than knowledge and its awareness of objective truth, a quality that brings one to the point of committing oneself to act in terms of what one has recognized as right. This is *taṣdīq*, and to have it is to have faith.

This notion of 'reaching a certain point' is brought out sharply in the following:

> *annahu* [*sc. anna al-īmān*] *al-taṣdīq al-qalbī alladhī balagha ḥadd al-jazm wa-al-idhʿān.*[49]

This is in a discussion of the position that faith is a yes-or-no matter, rather than a more-or-less one. One either decides to act, or one does not. Hence *ḥadd*, the dividing line or boundary between two realms; here, that of deliberation and that of decision. *Al-jazm*, also, communicates this same idea. The basic meaning of *jazama, yajzimu, jazman* is 'to cut off', 'to cut short', 'to come to an end' (thus it means to pronounce the final consonant of a word without a vowel); and the derived and standard meaning then is 'to decide', 'to judge', 'to resolve', 'to be positive or certain about something', 'to make up one's mind'. The notion seems to be that of terminating that period of deliberation and pondering wherein one is mulling a thing over. More or less literally, then: 'faith is that appropriation of truth by the heart that comes to the point of decision and compliance'. With it, one crosses over from awareness to engagement.

One of the compelling expositions of the matter comes in the fuller elaboration of a statement by the late writer al-Kastalī that we have already quoted in part: '*Al-taṣdīq* does not mean knowing the truth . . . ;[50] no, it is rather a yielding to what is known and a letting oneself be led by it, and the soul's being quiet and at peace with it and its accepting it, setting aside recalcitrance and stubbornness, and constructing one's actions in accordance with it.'[51] (This is a beautiful example of a passage that Christian theology could be happy and proud to take over word for word . . . .)

Another explication, again completing a passage already introduced in part:[52] 'The distinction is inescapably clear between, on the one hand, knowing the moral injunctions, being quite sure about them, and on the other hand appropriating their truth actively to oneself and binding oneself to them.'[53]

The moralist orientation of faith comes out in many passages such as this, where traditional Western translations appear as altogether inept. Phrases such as *al-īmān bi-al-farḍ,*[54] *al-taṣdīq bi-al-aḥkām,*[55] and *taṣdīq al-ḥukm*[56] are standard. Their significance is clear when our existentialist self-committing understanding is recognized, of *āmana* as 'to acept' and *ṣaddaqa* as 'actively to personalize for oneself the truth of'. 'Believe' will not do, however. One 'believes' a doctrine, or 'believes in' a person (as Christians have it); but when the revelation is a command, the appropriate category is other. With injunctions the object of faith, the nature of faith is a moral stance.

It may be noted that both *ṣidq* and *taṣdīq* are regularly used with *khabar* (also *mukhbir*, etc.)[57], but it must be remembered that these latter terms refer not to reports or statements in the indicative mood necessarily or even especially, but to anything that is said, including imperatives. As an illustration:

mā akhbarahu bihi min awāmirihi wa-nawāhīhi.[58]

It may further be remembered that the *mukhbir* here is God (not Muḥammad).[59] In the Islamic orientation, faith is primarily a personal acceptance of the divine imperatives for oneself.

Turning to a statement of al-Nasafī, in his widely accepted *ʿAqā'id*, wc find the following:

al-īmān huwa al-taṣdīq bi-mā jā'a min ʿind Allāh taʿālá.[60]

The impulse of a Westerner is to take the last six words here as a paraphrase, or even as a technical term, for the Qur'ān. Strictly, however, it is neither; and to neglect what is actually being said can be misleading, omitting the subtleties. For at issue here is not a *taṣdīq* of the Qur'ān (outsiders are of course conscious of this 'object' of faith, since it is what manifestly separates Muslims from themselves). It is, rather, a *taṣdīq* of what is from God: in principle, whatever it be. (It is true that Muslims regard the Qur'ān as this; but that is assumed here, not said.) The difference is fundamental. Faith is not to recognize something as divine revelation; it is to recognize divine revelation as authoritative—authoritative for onseself, personally. To be a person of faith is not to accept something as from God; rather, if something is from God, then to be a person of faith is to incorporate that into your life and to act accordingly.

Some would be tempted to suspect that I am forcing the interpretation here, and reading too much into the text. Let us turn to the commentators, then. The most widely accepted of them, Taftāzānī, says that the above phrase means:[61]

> *ay, taṣdīq al-nabī, ʿalayhi al-salām, bi-al-qalb fī jamīʿ mā ʿulima bi-al-ḍarūrah majī'uhu bihi min ʿind Allāh taʿālá, ijmālan.*[62]

'To give *taṣdīq* in one's heart to the Prophet, on him be peace, in all that he is indubitably known as having brought from God, in general.'[63] 'Believing' and 'regarding as true' are ruled out here. For, explicitly it is a matter of what one already knows to be from God. Faith is a response to what one indisputably knows to be of divine origin.[64] And indeed the word *ijmālan* confirms that at issue here is the principle of *taṣdīq* of whatever is transcendent. The author implicitly goes on to say that faith is not infringed by lack of knowledge as to what precisely *was* revealed. For the next sentence in his text reads:

> *wa-innahu kāfin fī-al-khurūj ʿan ʿuhdat al-īmān wa-lā tanḥaṭṭu darajatuhu ʿan al-īmān al-tafṣīlī.*[65]

By *hu* here he understands *al-īmān al-ijmālī* (more exactly, *al-īmān ijmālan*). Faith in principle (faith in general) 'is sufficient to enable a person to discharge his obligation to have faith; and it does not rank lower than detailed faith'.

Faith, then, was understood by classical Muslims not in terms alien to modern men, nor in terms parallel to but never converging with other communities' involvements, but rather in ways deeply discerning and universally human. Admittedly, the Muslim world did, to use an infidel's term, 'believe' (Muslims would say, rather, 'recognize') that the Qur'ān is the Word of God; within that framework of ideas they set forth their analysis of the human condition. *Kalām* is a statement within, not about, their Weltanschauung; and to that statement the concept of *taṣdīq* could and did make an impressive and significant contribution.

It may seem to the patient reader that in my exposition of this term I have overly belaboured my point, elaborately commentating upon passages whose meaning is self-evident, being at pains to defend interpretations that hardly require elucidation, and piling up evidence that reiterates the obvious. I have been pushed to this, I suppose, in order to render it unlikely that in the future anyone will ever again translate *īmān* as 'belief', or *kāfir* as 'unbeliever'. The question is not what one believes, but what one does about what one believes or recognizes as true. At issue, in the matter of faith, is what kind of person one is.

8

Faith, in Later Islamic History; the Meaning of *Arkān*

One of my happy memories is of a delightful dinner party in the luxurious Beirut flat of a former student of mine, by then a prominent figure in that city's Muslim circles. This was a few years before Lebanon had fallen prey to the lacerating civil war that has since devastated that unfortunate land. After dinner we adjourned to the open verandah to enjoy the peaceful moonlit summer evening. As has often been the case, I was the only non-Muslim in the gathering. I forget whether we were eleven in all, with the Muslims dividing five-to-five on the issue under discussion, or whether there were eleven besides myself, in which case the divergence was not quite so exactly symmetrical but still a fairly even six-to-five. I had raised a question that had been teasing me for some time in my study of the history of Muslim understanding of faith: namely, whether the word arkān *in the mediaeval formulae defining it referred to the 'pillars of Islām', or meant the limbs of the human body. I knew from experience in my classes with Muslim participants, reading Taftāzānī's* Sharḥ al-ʿAqā'id *together, that both readings seemed plausible and that those that adopted either interpretation tended to feel quite sure that it was the right one, and tended to be surprised that anyone had thought of the other as a serious possibility. The discussion raged that evening for a couple of hours, all of us much engaged by the issue, but it was quite indecisive. The group included some considerable scholars.*

On my return to North America, I resolved to solve the problem, and this present article presents my solution. As often happens, the implications turn out to be much larger than one imagines at the start. The occasion for putting in order the data that I unearthed in the course of my fairly elaborate investigation, and for marshalling the arguments that in the end convinced me as to which interpretation is right, was the publishing of a Festschrift in honour of my former colleague and close friend at the Islamics Institute at McGill University, the Turkish sociologist Niyazi Berkes. He and I had never discussed this particular point, but I felt that he would be interested in the problem—especially as I have come to see that it ramifies far more widely than at first appears.

Faith is man's most decisive quality, according to various of the world's cultural traditions, including the Islamic. The Day of Judgement, for those who resort to that mighty metaphor, is envisaged primarily as a determining of who has had it and who not. Heaven and Hell are felt to be not too stupendous characterizations of the cosmic significance for man of the question involved. It is, indeed, many have averred, the ultimate human question.

Small wonder, then, that the subordinate question, how to conceive faith, has itself been a matter of debate. Muslims and Christians, for example, agree that faith is the final criterion for man's destiny, and the human shape of the right relationship between the Divine and man. Yet they disagree as to the divine shape of that relationship; disagree, some would say, as to faith's 'object' (or 'content'). Internally, also, within the Muslim community and within the Christian community men have understood faith in varying ways and formulated their understandings variously. Even their multiple formulations can then be diversely understood; and especially is the understanding by one group of the formulations of another a delicate matter. Some say that faith is *x*, some that it is *y*; what *x* means, and what *y* means, may then still be canvassed. (This is particularly true for outsiders if *x* and *y* are Arabic words!)

For some years I have developed an interest in Muslim conceptions of faith, and have recently begun a formal study of the matter. Relatively few modern scholars have given heed to this question. I have discovered also that the issue is more elaborate than it heedlessly appears. For example: among Muslim expositions, a chief formula has been that faith is *taṣdīq* (*al-īmān huwa al-taṣdīq*). I have of late devoted some time to an endeavour to elucidate what that word should be understood as meaning;[1] arguing that its implications are highly interesting and have not seldom, I contend, been misinterpreted. In the present instance I attend to another wording, suggesting that it too raises some significant ambiguities. If what faith is be controversial, even what Muslims have affirmed it to be is not so clear as one might have imagined.

Some Muslims, it is well known, have held that faith (*al-īmān*) is something internal; some, that it is saying something; and some, that it is overtly doing something. Roughly: that faith is an act of the heart, that it is public confession, that it is works. Faith is thought, and/or word, and/or deed.

The third view—that faith is works (*sc.* good works) tended to become the position adopted particularly by the Khārijī movement. The second view became that adopted in the majority community for all practical purposes in mundane and social life, and in law: he is a *mu'min* who recites the *shahādah*. (The point here is not merely verbal: it is a matter, rather, of publicly taking on a commitment to live as a member of a given community, with its rights and responsibilities.) The first view, that faith is an inner matter (usually: *al-taṣdīq bi-al-qalb*), tended to become dominant in theory among the most recognized theological schools. Yet, no simple position but was felt to be vulnerable alone. Various refinements were in order; and various combinations and correlations of any two, or of all three.

A neat wording established itself as summing up the all-three position: that faith is

taṣdīq bi-al-janān
wa-iqrār bi-al-lisān
wa-ʿamal bi-al-arkān

—a formula that was characterized standardly in later centuries as 'the position of the generality' of scholars.[2] My purpose in this present study is to inquire into the meaning of the last word here. What are the *arkān* in this formula?

Several, among both Muslims and outside students of Islamics, take it as signifying ('obviously'?) 'the pillars', *sc.* of Islām: the well-known five chief duties of a Muslim, for which *al-arkān* has become, as everyone knows, the technical term. Before adducing arguments against a simple adoption of this view, I must acknowledge that it seems to have the support (perhaps not deliberated, however, and not quite unambiguous) of such major Arabists as Wensinck,[3] Laoust,[4] Izutsu,[5] usually Jeffery[6] and perhaps Gardet and Qanawātī,[7] as well as a certain percentage among my Muslim friends, Arab and other, to whom I have on occasion put the matter. It would seem, clearly, a possible reading.

The alternative view, for which I shall argue that there is more persuasive logical, contextual, and empirical support, is that *arkān* in this phrase signified the limbs of the human body.

A still further question emerges, however, as to what is meant by deciding between two possible interpretations of the meaning of a given word in a given phrase. The implications of this turn out to be slightly formidable. What does it mean to say that a given text means some specific thing? In other words: the religious or human question, What is Faith? leads to the historical question, What have Muslims affirmed faith to be? This in turn raises the linguistic question, What have they meant when they affirmed (in Arabic) that it is such-and-such? and finally the quasi-hermeneutic question, What do we mean when we say that in affirming it to be *x* they have meant *a*?

Let us consider the word *rukn*. The basic notion of the root *r-k-n-* (used with *ilá*) is to incline towards, to lean upon, to rest upon, to be supported by. The noun *rukn*, plural *arkān* (also, *arkun*) , signifies that upon which something rests, by which it is supported; according to the classical dictionaries it denotes the strongest side of a thing and, generally, strength, resource.[8] It is that on which something or someone rests or relies; what gives something or someone strength. It has come to mean the corner of a building, or the pole of a tent. In philosophic discourse, it designates an essential condition. The meaning 'human arms and legs' ('limbs', 'members'), while not common,[9] is found. According to this last, the phrase *ʿamal bi-al-arkān* here would be precisely equivalent to *ʿamal bi-al-jawāriḥ*.

The arguments in favour of understanding the term in the 'faith' context as signifying (the five) 'pillars' are essentially two. The first is the general prevalence of this meaning for *arkān*, especially in religious usage. The second is the number of modern Western scholars of repute, as well as of several Muslims whom I have questioned on the matter, that so understand it. These two points may be thought of, perhaps, as basically one, with the second deriving from the first. We shall return to this. In any case, the fact is that in most instances the phrase would appear to be satisfyingly rendered in either way. How, then, is one to decide between them? My thesis is that although at first glance in any one instance both seem possible, careful reflection and a critical scrutiny of many instances push one inescapably in the direction of *jawāriḥ*.

To develop this, I will present arguments at several successive levels; noting first matters that make the 'limbs' interpretation plausible, and moving on to ones that make it, I suggest, conclusive.

Let us begin with some general considerations, of grammar, logic, and symmetry. For one thing, if *al-arkān* were the five pillars of Islām, one might have expected rather *al-ʿamal* than the reiterated indefinite *ʿamalun*; and most translators have in fact surreptitiously introduced a definite article into their renderings. Faith, they report, these Muslims see as assent of the heart, confession, and 'the practice of Islām's chief duties'; whereas the formula is asserting rather that faith is an inner orientation[10] (*taṣdīqun*; not *al-taṣdīq*), a verbal profession, and a [sic] matter of external, physical behaviour. Similarly not decisive at all, yet suggestive, are two further points. One is that the use of *bi-* here with *ʿamal* might perhaps be seen as just a whit awkward, if *al-arkān* are 'the pillars' and therefore the object of the verb. (Would *li-* or an accusative or objective genitive not be smoother?)[11] The second point is that the parallel with the other phrases, both in grammatical structure involving *bi-* in all three instances and in general meaning, favours *arkān* as 'limbs' (in a construction comparable to 'heart' and 'tongue'), and militates against the altogether asymmetrical 'five pillars'.

At this level of argument, there is also the point that one of the five pillars—and indeed the most important of them, it could be said—is the *shahādah*, which has already been canvassed in the second phrase of the formula: *iqrār bi-al-lisān*. One might expect, then, something like 'the remaining four pillars'.[12] If it be retorted that similarly the tongue is one of the bodily members or limbs, the answer is that, indeed, Ibn Ḥajar al-Haythamī does follow *iqrār bi-al-lisān* with the wording *wa-ʿamal bi-sā'ir al-jawāriḥ.*[13]

These formal considerations, however, are less weighty perhaps than more substantial questions as to what is under consideration. The fact is that the point at issue was the general problem as to the relation between faith and works. On this matter, the Islamic world developed, as did the Christian world, continuing debate; and the controversy was pitched in the widest possible terms: not whether faith involves doing this or that specific thing, but more fundamentally, does it involve *doing*, as such. As Gardet nicely, and rightly, puts it: '*Aʿmāl* désigne le domaine de l'agir humain'; and he adduces the philosophic usage of the adjective *ʿamalī* to refer to the practical or the ethical.[14] For some centuries, in *kalām* and elsewhere, the discussion ranged on the question of acts in general—bodily acts, as it was sometimes said. The Khārijī movement split the community on this point; the Muʿtazilah in particular, and the theological enterprise in general, arose fundamentally out of an attempt to deal with it. The standard terminology is *al-ʿamal, al-fiʿl, al-aʿmāl, al-afʿāl*, often elaborated into *ʿamal bi-al-jawāriḥ*, as we have seen, *aʿmāl al-jawāriḥ, afʿāl al-jawāriḥ.* Other expressions are *fiʿl al-wājibāt, ʿamal al-ṭāʿāt, adā' al-farā'iḍ*, etc.—all exceedingly general. In other words, the stage was set for the debate in quite general terms, or occasionally in terms of *al-jawāriḥ*; it was then continued, in quite general terms, or with reference to *al-jawāriḥ*, or with reference to *al-arkān.* There is utterly no suggestion anywhere of a shift's being involved in the changes of phrasing. On the contrary, as we shall presently see: certain writers make the shift from one word to the other on the same page.

Although I have not actually counted usages, probably it is safe to say not merely that the word *jawāriḥ* is fairly standard in these contexts, but also that it occurs several times more often on the whole than does *arkān*, throughout the various texts taken altogether—and especially in the earlier ones, a point to which we shall return. It is never superseded, however, but continues alongside the other. Illustrative is the fifth/eleventh century Qur'ān commentator Ṭūsī, who mentions that he and the Muʿtazilah differ on whether *afʿāl al-jawāriḥ* are part of faith; he, holding that they are not, distinguishes them from *afʿāl al-qulūb*, which he says are.[15] This seems to be exactly the same discussion as that between *ʿamal bi-al-arkān* and *taṣdīq bi-al-qalb*.

Still more substantially, one may raise the point that the works of faith, for a Muslim, involve a good deal more than just 'the pillars'. There is a well-known *ḥadīth* according to which faith has seventy-some parts, the highest of which is proclaiming the *shahādah* and the meanest of which is, not one of the pillars, but merely removing an obstruction from a path. This *ḥadīth* gets quoted in the course of discussions about faith and works—faith, confession, and works—and indeed even in discussions where the last of these is worded *ʿamal bi-al-arkān*.[16] If works are part of faith, more than five (or four) are involved![17] More concretely, the debates include a discussion as to whether the supererogatory works (*al-nawāfil*) are part of faith.[18] Even among those who included works within faith, on this point some said 'yes',[19] some 'no'.[20] No one ever seems to have said, or to have been rebutted for saying, that the pillars were, while other *aʿmāl ṣāliḥah* or *ṭāʿāt* were not, *min al-īmān*. The discussions as to faith's increasing and decreasing, with works, spoke quite freely and casually of non-pillar works.

Furthermore, in the discussions, writers moved quite easily from the positive to the negative: some of the overt, external acts that might or might not constitute faith, according to the issue under debate, were obligations to be carried out, but others were prohibitions to be avoided.[21] In particular, the question of *not* committing adultery came into consideration,[22] a very important matter in connection with the question of faith, but it has nothing to do with the five pillars. Or the discussion could revolve about *al-kabā'ir* generally. It would hardly be wrong to affirm that it would appear that for several writers to commit an overt behavioural sin is to act *bi-al-arkān*; that is, with the members of one's body.

We turn next to the chronological question, of historical development. We have already mentioned that the use of *ʿamal bi-al-jawāriḥ* seems to have been prevalent earlier than *ʿamal bi-al-arkān*,[23] and seems gradually to have given way to the latter. My suggestion is that the reason for this change of vocabulary to express the same idea is really quite simple: namely, rhyme. The gradual adoption among the various writers, whether pro or con, of the formula with *al-arkān* came about, one may suppose, because of its neatness and the sheer attractiveness of its rhyming.

This hypothesis may be advanced not simply as plausible, as a hunch; rather, there is concrete evidence to favour it. In the first place, the introduction of the word *janān* to replace *qalb* in the first phrase of our tripartite formula is clearly late. Equally clearly, it does not change the meaning. It is a rare synonym: one of the commentators presumes that it will not be familiar to his readers, and explains how to pronounce it.[24] Once incorporated, however, this word is retained in the phrasing (not exclusively); presumably for no other reason than that it rounds out the rhyme. In general, there is demonstrably an historical development towards rhyming. In later centuries, the tripartite formula with the three rhyming phrases became, as we have seen, established; the historically earliest wordings tend to have no rhyme (. . . *qalb*, . . . *lisān*, . . . *jawāriḥ*); in between, come instances where *qalb* remains but the other two phrases rhyme: . . . *qalb*, . . . *lisān*, . . . *arkān*.[25]

Secondly, this point is manifested in the usage of particular writers. Some of these use *qalb* and *jawāriḥ*, in sentences where the specific points are being discussed individually, but a few sentences or paragraphs later choose *janān* and *arkān* when one or both of these run together with *lisān*, so that the rhyme appears. Although I should not wish to affirm that it does not occur, I may report that I have myself not noticed *janān* used as the word to designate the locus of *al-taṣdīq* except in a rhyming context. (Otherwise the discussion is worded rather with *qalb*.) On a less elaborate scale, the same applies to the use of *arkān*. It too I have not found without rhyme. (*Janān* seems always to occur only with both *lisān* and *arkān*; *arkān* only with at least *lisān* in the immediate neighbourhood.)

Bāqillānī, for instance, at one place writes *jawāriḥ* with *ʿamal* three times, in discussing the role of works in faith; but then later on on the same page and in the course of the same argument he switches to *arkān* when it becomes a matter of the tripartite formula, and a matter of relating works to confession and to sincerity. He now uses *arkān* three times, but each time in rhyme.[26]

Still more telling is the case of Ghazzālī's wording in his discussion in the *Iḥyā'* of the relation between *īmān* and *islām*.[27] At first blush it would seem that he uses the phrases *ʿamal bi-al-jawāriḥ* and *ʿamal bi-al-arkān* interchangeably, the two occurring within a few lines of each other. On more careful reading, however, it appears that his own predilection is for *jawāriḥ*, and that *arkān* occurs only when he is quoting others; and specifically, is quoting the tripartite formula[28] (in which he still uses *qalb*; *janān* does not appear). He presents the position of those who hold that faith is not only an inner adherence of the heart and the verbal confession but also *al-ʿamal bi-al-arkān*; and he then discusses it. Within the course of a few lines, after having adduced this phrase, he considers the case of the man who has all three, then that of him who has the first two and some only of the third, but with major sins, and finally the case of the person who has the first two without *al-aʿmāl bi-al-jawāriḥ*.[29]

That is, he uses *arkān* when quoting others' words, citing an established rhyming pattern, but reverts to the more common term when making his own case, setting forth what naturally comes to his own mind. Patently he is not conscious of changing the subject (just as Bāqillānī was not, in shifting in the other direction).

Pehaps, then, we have arrived at an answer to our question, of whether it is possible actually to determine which of the two potential meanings of this word is here in use. It would seem incontrovertible that Ghazzālī understood others to mean by *ʿamal bi-al-arkān* what he himself meant by *ʿamal bi-al-jawāriḥ*. When he read *arkān*, he understood 'limbs'. Similarly it seems fairly evident that other classical writers used the two interchangeably.

Finally, however, a still more decisive instance may be presented. We have already remarked that Bāqillānī writes of a man's action *bi-al-jawāriḥ*, and then within a rhyming context switches to *arkān*. After citing the formula in the established form (*ʿamalun bi-al-arkān*), however, he elaborates his point in his own wording and moves to a verbal form, where he writes, tellingly: *aqarra bi-lisānihi . . . wa-ʿamala bi-arkānihi.*[30]

This would seem to clinch the matter. One might have argued that *al-arkān* could be the pillars of Islam; but is it not inescapable that *arkānuhu* are 'his bodily members'?[31]

To sum up, then. It is our submission that in classical and mediaeval Islamic texts the word *arkān* as part of a definition of faith designated the limbs of the human body, and was a synonym of *jawāriḥ*; and was so understood.

We do not wish to leave the matter there, however, lest we fall victim to the error, against which I have urged on other occasions, of supposing facilely that the meaning of any text or sentence is simply its original meaning. This is a fallacy of historicism. Human language is an enormously complicated and delicate matter, as are indeed all interrelations among human beings. Language is a form of communication; and the meaning of a sentence is in part what the person intends who speaks or writes it, and in part what those persons understand who hear or read it. I am an historian, and am interested in the history of meanings. Important words, phrases, doctrines, especially in the religious field, demonstrably and significantly have a history of meanings.

I observe that there seems to have taken place over the centuries a certain historical development in the meaning of the theological phrase *ʿamal bi-al-arkān*. It began by meaning '. . . limbs', I contend; and for many, I have ascertained, it has continued to mean that. For others, on the other hand, the meaning has become (and I stress that word) the five pillars (or: four, omitting the *shahādah*, consciously or unconsciously). This is so not only for Western scholars and non-Muslim Arabs, as we have seen; but for some Muslims, including even some serious and learned scholars among my acquaintance, and quite possibly including a fair number of *al-ʿawāmm*; for instance, one may guess, in the villages. I have not ascertained the situation with regard to villagers; I have, however, with some learned persons, including even one Azharī. The word has come to be interpreted by some as the pillars; this also is an historical fact.

I have not seen an historical study of the rise of the term *al-arkān* to designate the five pillars of Islām.[32] At first, they were not called that;[33] eventually, they standardly were. In other words, during the early centuries of Islamic history there was a process whereby the word *arkān* came to be used in definitions of faith, as we have been noting; and there was a process by which the word *arkān* came to be used in the designating of the five chief overt duties of a Muslim. Whether there may have been some inter-involvement between the growth of the usage in the two contexts is perhaps allowable speculation. In any case, the *fiqh* usage came to predominate over the *kalām* one, as is perhaps not surprising; so much so that, as we have seen, some at least have arrived at a point of forgetting the latter. An historical study might usefully look into the question as to whether conceivably, when *arkān* began to be used in 'faith' contexts, the word had not yet acquired the 'five pillars' meaning, but that as it began to be more and more widely adopted in religious literature and parlance in the latter sense it gradually came in men's minds to designate that primarily, and eventually for some few, at least, exclusively.

The very plausibility of the 'pillars' meaning even in the faith formula, however superficial it appear on closer analysis—the plausibility with which we began our study here—has surely contributed something to its prevalence. The five pillars are handy and in some sense obvious illustrations of what is meant by pious behaviour, by religious bodily actions.[34] I find significant a footnote by a major modern Muslim scholar in a recent Cairo edition of the Ibn Mājah *ḥadīth* collection from which we have quoted. He gives an annotation to: *al-īmān maʿrifah bi-al-qalb wa-qawl bi-*

al-lisān wa-ʿamal bi-al-arkān by glossing the last word as follows (and it is in itself interesting that he feels that a gloss is requisite): *ʿamal bi-al-arkān: ay, al-jawāriḥ, ka-al-ṣalāh wa-al-ṣawm wa-al-zakāh wa-al-ḥajj.*[35]

One may recall that, as we have seen, some of the Western scholars, similarly, have tended—illogically, but with what charitably might perhaps be regarded as substantial if not formal reason—to take *arkān* as the pillars *and* other pious acts.[36]

May we perhaps conclude that the term in this context began by meaning *jawāriḥ*; but say that a situation has over the centuries developed in which no doubt it denotes that, but at the same time and to some extent *connotes* performing the pillars?

PART THREE

Islām in the Indian Context; and Muslim–Hindū Relations

9

The Crystallization of Religious Communities in Mughul India

As the opening sentence here indicates, this essay was composed in 1963. It was written in India and delivered there as a lecture (hence the questions that it poses); it was published half a dozen years later in only slightly revised form as a contribution to the Tehran Festschrift for my friend from Cambridge days, Professor V. Minorsky. Two years later was published a study on Sirhindī of my former McGill student Friedmann, referred to in footnote 11 here, which throws new light on this figure and raises important questions about some of the issues here canvassed.

Exactly four centuries ago, in the year 1563, two men were born of considerable historical significance for India. Both are primarily religious figures. Yet the ramifications of their work also in the political, econômic, and sociological realms are major, until today. One is a Muslim, one a Sikh: Khwājah Bāqī Bi-llāh, born that year in Kābul, died in Delhi 1603; and Arjun, a Panjābī, put to death in Lahore in 1606. Closely associated with the former was another Muslim, one year his junior, Shaykh Aḥmad, also a Panjābī, born 1564 at Sirhind and died there in 1624. These men are recognized as playing a leading role each in the development of his own religious community. The Khwājah Ṣāḥib was a member of the Naqshbandī order (from Central Asia) and Shaykh Aḥmad Sirhindī became his most eminent disciple, so reputed for his outstanding services in Islamic religious revival in the sub-continent that he became known as Mujaddid Alf-i Thānī; that is, the man infusing new life and restoring purity in the Muslim community as it passed the year 1000 in the calendar of its own *hijrī* era. Arjun became the fifth *Guru* of the Sikh community.

Now each of these men has been studied within the context of his own community and its development; and indeed current investigation is under way into each area by men much better qualified than I. My intention here, then, is not to advance new research data; but rather to raise certain questions about the inter-relations of the two developments, Islamic and Sikh, that these men represented and carried forward. It has been customary to treat the two movements separately, as stages in Islamic history and in Sikh history respectively. There may, then, be some value in asking whether they may not be considered together, as constituting or illustrating a single development in *Indian* history: a single development with Islamic and Sikh facets, no doubt, but one in which these may be seen as elements of a broad socio-ideological transformation taking place in India in the sixteenth and especially in the seventeenth centuries. (There would seem to be even certain clues hinting at possible developments of a somewhat similar kind in the Hindū community beginning during Akbar's reign, at Mathura and elsewhere, but I have had no chance to explore these carefully. We shall touch a little on the Hindū developments at the end of this present paper.)

We mention the seventeenth century, because although Bāqī Billāh and Arjun had died, as we have said, by 1603 and 1606 respectively, and Sirhindī by 1624, yet the development that they initiated came to fruition only at the end of that century: in the Muslim case with Awrangzeb, in the Sikh case with Gobind, the tenth and last Guru. These died in 1707 and 1708 respectively. Indeed, if we say that these movements 'came to fruition' in the late seventeenth century, yet they do not stop there: they culminate, one could argue, in the twentieth century, for the history of present-day India has been dominated by this evolution. In fact we may go further and shall be suggesting presently that the processes in which Sirhindī and Arjun were involved, and Awrangzeb and Guru Gobind Singh, and the Muslims and Sikhs, and in 1947 Muslims and Hindūs—that these processes may be seen as part not merely of Indian history but of world history, an instance of what I have come to regard as one of the most consequential developments in man's personal and social life: namely, in the words of my title, the process of crystallization of religious communities, and more specifically, the process that I have elsewhere dubbed 'the reification of religion', a phrase that I have coined to draw attention to this phenomenon.

If I can use the sixteenth–seventeenth century Muslim–Sikh developments to let it be seen what is meant by this process—and better still, if by raising the question in this way some who know the history better than do I, can help me to see where I may have gone astray in my interpretation—then this venture will have been worthwhile.

The transformation of which we speak can be seen perhaps most clearly in the Sikh case. Guru Nānak (1469–1539) is sometimes called 'the founder' of 'the Sikh religion' (or 'of Sikhism'); but no one can see what was historically happening during those two centuries unless he sees that these terms are radically inadequate. I have argued elsewhere[1] that no great religious leader has ever founded a religion (except perhaps Mānī); certainly not Nānak. He was a gentle and intense mystic, a devotee (*bhakta*) who, in spiritually passionate and directly personalist poetry and in a life of humane and humble service, preached sincerity and adoration and the overwhelming reality of God. He attacked religious formalism of all kinds. It was several generations later that his *followers* were religiously formalized, systematized; by organizers such as Arjun and Gobind. From this was crystallized what we call 'followerism' ('Sikh' means 'Disciple').

Nānak held that God is known through righteousness and fervent faith, alone, not through a book or in any conceptual pattern; Arjun compiled a collection of writings so as to constitute a book, a scripture—writings of Nānak along with passages from other saints (including some that we call Hindū, some that we call Muslim, and some that we call Sikh); though of this scripture it was Gobind who finalized the canonization. Nānak refused to call any particular place 'The House of God', asking where is one to find a place where God does *not* dwell. Arjun, at a place thereafter called Amritsar, raised a shrine established by his immediate predecessor Rām Dās into a central temple for the community; and had other temples constructed, for instance at Taran Tāran and Kartārpur. These and Amritsar became centres of pilgrimage —despite Nānak's views on pilgrimage (in a sense, because of them). If a man is great enough to recognize that pilgrimage is not important, then that man's memory is worth making pilgrimage to honour. And so on: Arjun was an organizer, systematizer, formalizer, and he carried out this role very effectively. The movement of which he was the central exponent may perhaps best be measured as a religio-sociological transformation, one that began with Nānak the universalist, who was in a sense *both* a Hindū and a Musalmān, and was congealed by Arjun the separatist, who wrote, 'I am neither Hindū nor Musalmān' (Bhairav) (or again, 'I have broken with the Hindū and the Muslim' [ibid])—and culminated with Guru Gobind Singh the saint who was also a militarist, who organized an army to fight for righteousness, and wrote:[2]

'The Khālṣah shall rule;
Their enemies will be scattered;
Only they that seek refuge will be saved.'

At work here was a process, visible also at other times and places in the religious history of humankind, whereby the attainment of one man in one age who reaches past symbol-systems to that personal and cosmic reality that they are calculated to represent, and teaches that the reality, rather than the symbol, is alone of significance, is made available to other men and later ages by being made available in the form of a symbol-system.

Or, in more social terms: during these two centuries the insight of a visionary who saw humankind, or at least saw his own Indian or Panjābī society, as one brotherhood, without the dividing gulfs of distinct groups, had evolved into the formalism of one who to outsiders has appeared as a communalist who saw sharply separate groups in society, and insisted that the boundary between *his* group and the two others be also sharp. Otherwise, it can be argued, the insight would have been lost, and we might never have heard of Guru Nānak.

Now as I said at the beginning, all this is nothing new. What is to be stressed is that an altogether parallel process, at exactly the same time, was taking place within the Muslim community in India. One must also question any theory that would regard this process as inevitable or natural. Over against some determinists, who would regard all historical development as fixed, one may urge that the basic clue to an understanding of human history is a vivid sense of human freedom; so that no one has really begun to understand what has happened and how things have been what they have been, until he has clearly recognized that they might have been otherwise, and indeed most assuredly would have been otherwise if men had chosen to behave (or to think, or to feel) in a different way.

This is part of what is meant by saying that it is wrong to speak of Nānak as 'the founder of Sikhism'. Nānak had never heard of Sikhism, and would have rejected the idea if he had; just as Jesus Christ did not and could not conceive of 'Christianity', nor Lao Tzu of 'Taoism'. Nānak could well have lived the life he did and preached the message that he preached, with yet nothing for us to call Sikhism emerging in Indian history, if later generations had not produced an Arjun to crystallize his teaching and his followers into a formal structure, and had not produced many thousands of Panjābīs choosing to respond to Arjun's move, and choosing to respond to Nānak's voice in the particular way that Arjun proposed, rather than in some other way. There were, actually, a fair number of Panjābīs who chose to respond in some other way: Sikhs who are of the Mīnā sect, for example; or later, when Guru Gobind Singh completed the work of crystallization that Arjun represents, Sikhs of the Sahajdhārī or Dhīrmalīyā or Rām Rā'īyā sect, or who in protest later founded the Nirankārī movement (nineteenth century). We are in danger of taking the result of the concretizing movement for granted, and thinking that the business of the historian is to trace how the present Sikh community came to its present 'reified' form; forgetting that the true business of the historian is to take nothing for granted, and to uncover how it came about that there is a Sikh community today at all.

One may retort that, after all, all religious communities crystallize in pretty much this fashion; but of course, this is true only of those that do crystallize, and is not true of those that do not. Only, those that do not, do not find their way into history books.

After all, there were other preachers not unlike Nānak, such as his slightly senior contemporary Shaykh Ibrāhīm Farīd (1450–1535), also a Panjābī, whose religious position (as a Ṣūfī) Nānak greatly admired and considerably followed, the works of whose ancestor Farīdu-d-Dīn (Shaykh Farīdu-d-Dīn Ganj-i Shakar) are included in Arjun's *Granth Ṣāhib*; but around whom a subsequent group of disciples did not in fact construct a crystallized community or structured system.

This brings us over to the Muslim side of our question. I have said that the history of Islamic developments in India in the sixteenth and seventeenth centuries seems rather parallel to that of Sikh. Of course, that history is complicated by extensive relationships in the Muslim community in India to Islamic developments over a previous millenium and in other parts of the globe. Nevertheless, here too we distort, I feel, if we lose sight of the fact that the Indian Muslims who constructed the history of their community, even religiously, at this time and place did so as living human beings choosing their way as they went along. This point may be made perhaps forcefully by formulating it as follows. What happened in these centuries in Islamic history in India is usually described as the triumph of orthodoxy; yet this obscures the central significance of what was being enacted. For 'orthodoxy' is a relative term—and in Islamic affairs, also a modern one. There is no word in Arabic or Persian equivalent to this Western notion. If the rigid, structured, crystallized version of Islām as an essentially closed system that we know today had not in fact triumphed, as it might not have done, then that particular system would not today be regarded as 'orthodox'. Modern Muslims are particularly prone to missing this point, feeling that Bāqi Bi-llāh, Sirhindī, and Awrangzeb 'saved' Islām from the disintegration that threatened it in men like Shaykh Ibrāhīm Farīd, Abū-l-Faẕl,

Akbar, Muḥibbu-llāh Jawnpurī, and Dārā Shikoh. If instead these latter had managed, however, to carry the day, so that *their* version of Islamic truth were now prevalent, as might have happened, then most modern Muslims in India would today be feeling as a consequence that (fortunately) the crystallizers, Sirhindī and the rest, whom they would now regard as heretics, threatened the true version of Islām but that this latter was saved—thanks to the effort of its champions, those liberals who would therefore be called 'orthodox'. Both groups would claim that their particular interpretation of Islām is the right one—being 'orthodox' not only in the sense of in fact being historically established now, but 'orthodox' also by being the form (they would believe) that existed in the early centuries (or in the Qur'ān).

Actually, however, this last was in fact a third form. Both interpretations of Islām that were struggling for supremacy in Mughul India, the reified and the Ṣūfī, were in fact new. No doubt, each included as one of its elements an interpretation of past Islamic history and of the Qur'ān that confirmed its particular orientation. The Muslims of that day were busy constructing, and then choosing among, their own original religious positions—constructing them largely out of materials inherited, no doubt, from the past Islamic tradition, but nonetheless constructing them fresh, and choosing among them genuinely, freely. That this was what they were doing is what makes them interesting to the historian. We miss the significance of any century if we do not see its creativity, its genuine freedom.

(If we may take just one item to illustrate the novelty of what is today called Islamic orthodoxy: I have discovered that its central concept, *sharīʿah*, hardly even occurs in Muslim theology for the first six Islamic centuries.[3])

To see Bāqī Bi-llāh and Shaykh Aḥmad Sirhindī at work, then, is to see one particular emergence in Islamic history coming forth, gradually being formulated, championed, fought over, and eventually dominating: ousting rival views and finally persuading not all, but the most effective part, of the community that *this* is what they shall will their religious life to be. One must understand the radical nature of this decision in the life of the community: its profundity; its reverberating consequences, for the people who took it, and for their descendants, and for the Sikhs, and for almost everyone else in India until today. The life of all of us today, mine as well as Indians', is what it is in part because these men acted the way they did, and not otherwise.

Religious history, and indeed all human history, is always like this in process of self-definition—though at some periods with more vitality than at others: Mughul India being one such period.

To appreciate the major change that was eventually effected, one must recall the Islamic situation in that country in early Mughul times. From its first entry, the Islamic movement in India had been characterized by two salient features: political power, and Taṣawwuf. The first devastating conquests, dealing India a blow under which it reeled and which it has never quite forgotten or forgiven, represent the former, which is symbolized by the assertive confidence of the Quṭb Minār. This strand persisted, interwoven into the whole subsequent history of the community. (And indeed, the Pākistān movement in our day may be seen as in a sense the affirmation that Islām cannot exist in the sub-continent without political power.) However, this first phase, especially in its violent aggressiveness, was fairly soon followed by the second, of a totally different order: the Ṣūfī, the form in which the Islamic vision established itself in men's hearts. For some centuries Islām spread at a personal level, in a warmer, and perhaps more lasting, form, through the preaching and the lives of thousands of saints who knew and expressed a profound and universalist theistic humanism. The names, and the messages, of outstanding leaders among these are known and cherished in each part of the country, from Bengāl to Kerala and from Kashmīr to Madrās. Many others are unknown. Yet altogether they added up to a major movement at the deepest human level.

It is to be remarked that simultaneously a development of altogether comparable quality was taking place in India among Hindūs: the Bhakti movement. Some would say not that the two developments were parallel but that they are two facets of one single movement in India during these centuries: called Bhakti in its Hindū form and Ṣūfī in its Islamic. It is difficult to exaggerate the significance of this development in the history of the subcontinent. That Bhakti and Taṣawwuf were interrelated seems clear, though precisely in what ways has yet to be clarified. The relation between the two is a topic still awaiting full exploration.[4] In any case, in both movements the stress was on the individual, not on the group; on the heart and inward attitudes, not on outward institutions; on personal warmth, not impersonal system; on God, not on a structured 'religion'. So far as the Muslim side goes, with which we are here concerned, the orientation was carried far; and it worked for close relations among the various elements that made up Indian society. It had, moreover, repercussions on many aspects of life, far beyond what we usually call the specifically religious. Much attention has been given to the political expression of the movement in the policies of Akbar; but one can see expressions also in almost every facet of life: in language and literature; in music (Tān Sen); in architecture (culminating in the Tāj Maḥall); in painting (the miniatures); in philosophy; and so on. India at the age of Akbar seemed on its way to creating a composite, harmonious, culturally rich society that would have been something quite splendid and also something quite new—new both in Indian history and in Islamic.

As we know, however, before this development had time to work itself out fully, a third phase in Indo–Muslim development was brought into being, worked out by some members of the community (among whom Bāqī Bi-llāh and Sirhindī seem to be crucial) and accepted by a majority of the others, or anyway by the most effective section. That the community chose during the sixteenth and seventeenth centuries to move in this direction, rather than continuing to advance in the Ṣūfī direction in which it had been chiefly moving in the thirteenth, fourteenth, and fifteenth; or rather than elaborating some other, new, phase; this, I am suggesting, is a fact both fascinating and important.

Khwājah Bāqī Bi-llāh was born, as we have said, in Kābul and educated there and at the chief cultural centres of Muslim Central

Asia, especially Samarqand and Bukhārā. He became a member of the Naqshbandī order, and was apparently specifically commissioned to come to India in his mid-thirties, to promote that order there. He did so with vigour, ability, success. Much of the significance of this lies in the fact that this order differed from those typically established in India previously, since most of these had on principle kept clear of affairs of state, feeling that spiritual purity must be kept uncontaminated by worldly snares, particularly politics. The Naqshbandīs introduced a different view, holding that their version of Islām could be established only by the use of the state organization for its implementation. Accordingly, Bāqī Bi-llāh, who seems to have been a person not only of intellectual and cultural prestige and religious dominance but also of political acumen, set himself to collecting and organizing a party of influential Muslim nobles and administrators who could serve to impose a new direction on Mughul policies. Akbar had not carried along with him all his Muslim aristocracy in his own liberalism (we shall return to this point presently); and Bāqī Bi-llāh set out to draw the dissidents together, to encourage and to guide them into what we might call a reactionary bloc. He came first to Lahore and established a close and enduring contact with the emperor's father-in-law, the viceroy Qilich Khān, one of the opponents of Akbar's religious policies; he later moved to Delhi, where he established an especially close link with another Shaykh Farīd, Mīr Murtaẓá Khān, called by a modern Pākistānī writer 'the most religious of the Muslim nobles' (this depends on what one means by 'religious'). This latter took on himself the total financial support of a Khānqāh in Delhi for the Khwājah, and also served as a kind of link-pin in a new activist grouping of nobles, which included presently men like ʿAbdu-r-Raḥīm, commander-in-chief in the Dakkhin, and Khān-i Aʿẓam, Akbar's foster brother. This Shaykh Farīd (under Bāqī Bi-llāh's guidance and encouragement?) became not only the chief rival of Abū-l-Faẕl in ideological matters. (In the *Ruqʿāt*, the author complains that the *Bakhshī al-Mamālik*—that is, Shaykh Farīd—'leads the emperor to follow a completely different path, from what Abul Fazl, with great difficulty and thousands of arguments, persuades him to adopt'.[5]) This Farīd seems to have had something to do with Akbar's eventual estrangement from Abū-l-Faẓl, and certainly with having organized the succession to the throne not for Khusraw, Akbar's grandson whom Akbar favoured, but for a more communalist Muslim: namely, Akbar's son Salīm (Jahāngīr).

It is not quite clear how instrumental Bāqī Bi-llāh may have been in all this; but the less one credits him with direct influence, the more one is left regarding him as formulating theologically the direction in which his society was beginning to move anyway.

In any case, Bāqī Bi-llāh's most striking achievement, perhaps, was his winning over a young and brilliant Panjābī intellectual at court, who was a friend and collaborator of the two brothers Abū-l-Faẓl and Fayẓī: namely, Aḥmad of Sirhind. This young liberal had been writing verses, which I have not seen, under the strident *takhalluṣ* of '*kufrī*'. He also is said to have helped Fayẓī complete his *tafsīr*. This young man, apparently of deeply religious temperament and at this time of highly independent and personalist views, came under the influence of Bāqī Bi-llāh and emerged as an apparently transformed character. He met the Khwājah first in 1599, apparently within two days asked to be admitted as his disciple, although they were virtually of the same age, and after six weeks in the *khānqāh*, sallied forth with a dedicated sense of mission, which inspired him for the remaining quarter-century of his life. The Khwājah himself died fairly soon after the first meeting.

Aḥmad seems to have acquired a firm conviction of the significant role that he had to play in championing 'Islām' in India. In this he was right, for he quickly became the most consequential religious leader in Indo–Muslim development of Mughul times; and with the possible or probable exception of Shāh Walīyullāh 150 years later, the most significant single figure in Indian Islamic history at least until Sir Sayyid Aḥmad Khān. One must admit that whether his influence was direct or indirect is in dispute. In the words of a modern Pākistānī, 'He contributed largely to the swing of the pendulum from Akbar's heterodoxy to Aurangzeb's vigorous ultra-orthodoxy,' [terminology here is twentieth-century, we must remember] 'rather than a return to Babur's and Humayun's policy of *laissez faire*. The rhetoric and appeal of Shaikh Ahmad's letters kindled religious fervour, and resulted in a religious revival' [I personally would call it not a religious revival but a revival of institutionalism and outward form, of the view of Islām-as-a-closed-*system*—and perhaps, as I have suggested, not a 're'-vival at all, but a new development. To me, Shaykh Ibrāhīm Farīd, for instance, Nānak's mentor, is surely equally *religious*, if not much more so] 'which took some time to bear fruit, which completely altered the history of this sub-continent'.[6] Again: 'it would not be far wrong to say that the swing of religious policy from Akbar to Aurangzeb was, in a considerable measure, due to the influence and teaching of Mujaddid Alif Sani'[7] (that is, this man Shaykh Aḥmad Sirhindī).

This influence and these teachings were made effective in his *Maktūbāt*. These are letters that he wrote to key officials at court and in the administration, trying to build up a corps of workers for a cause—a cadre, to use the modern Marxist term; and that were also deliberately published, and fairly widely circulated, building up a new Islamic interpretation among whoever in the community would listen.

The effectiveness of this man's teachings, and especially their direct political influence, have recently been challenged by some of the historians at Aligarh, and by Satīsh Chandar, now at Jaipur. In fact, even the traditional interpretation of Awrangzeb as an institutionally Islamicizing ruler is under attack these days; and perhaps it is no longer as clear as it once seemed that the struggle between Awrangzeb and Dārā Shikoh was really a struggle between conservative and liberal Islamic policies. Yet however much revision may be called for in the classic formulation or in detail, it seems surely incontrovertible that from Akbar to Awrangzeb there was in fact a drift from universalism[8] towards communalism; as there was from Nānak to Gobind, and perhaps also from the Rāmāyana of Tulsī Dās to the Dāsabodha of Rām Dās, the preceptor of Shivajī. And if Sirhindī and his group did not promote this change in the Muslim case, they at least illustrate it symptomatically. We do not yet know enough—at least, I personally do not know enough, and I may not be alone in this—about Indian history, in this major period, in terms of social change, intellectual and artistic development, and the like, to be able to say with confidence what is cause and what is effect, what are the relations among subtle and complex factors, how far political history reflects cultural change, and how far it determined it. Our first task, I am suggesting, is to discern in broad outline what in fact was going on, not merely at the court but in society; and only then can we begin to argue meaningfully about what caused what.

However one may regard the influence of his *Maktūbāt*, after Bāqī Bi-llāh's death in 1603 Sirhindī seems to have been the spearhead of the new and growing movement promoting a rigid, structured, systematic communalism. After Sirhindī's own death in 1624, his son Khwājah Muḥammad Maʿṣūm succeeded him.[9] Again I do not know how much credence should be given to the view, now disputed, that this gentleman managed to get as his personal disciple, and to influence, one of Shāh Jahān's four sons (the one who later became Awrangzeb), in such a way that this prince not only gave his allegiance to the new Islamic tendency towards formalism but also was presently instrumental in effecting a *coup* on its behalf, by staging a successful revolt against the emperor and forestalling the succession of his liberal elder brother, the Ṣūfī heir-apparent, Dārā Shikoh. It is perhaps not as clear as it once seemed that Awrangzeb was acting quite deliberately and explicitly as the champion of a cause, and not merely out of personal ambition. In any case, this cause and its progress are illustrated in a number of other fields as well as the political; which suggests that a broad socio-cultural movement was on foot, and not merely the chance vagaries of political intrigues.

Among these other fields is, for instance, education (evidenced in the founding of the Farangī Maḥall at Lakhnaw in 1698 and its subsequent flourishing; and the establishment of its formalist *Dars-i-Niẓāmī* curriculum as the norm of the Muslim education syllabus which became standard from this time right up to the epoch of the British). The formalizing movement showed itself also in law; as is evidenced in its new systematization in the *Fatāwá-'i-ʿĀlamgīrī*. These far-reaching social expressions were in addition to earlier and more strictly religious emphases: the effective introduction for the first time in India of formal *Ḥadīth* studies by another contemporary of Bāqī Bi-llāh and Sirhindī, namely ʿAbdu-l-Ḥaqq Dihlawī Muḥaddith (1551-1642), and, in metaphysics, Sirhindī's supersession of Ibn al-ʿArabī's *waḥdat al-wujūd* by his new *waḥdat al-shuhūd*. This last may remind us that the political, economic, and sociological consequences of rejecting metaphysical monism can be quite major: to believe in the ultimate unity of the world and the universe is to believe also in the unity of humankind.

Marxists may probably feel that so wide-ranging and radical a change in the social climate as was taking place in India must have had economic causes at its base; and one must certainly listen attentively if they can find these, and show them to have been determinative. Yet at the present stage of my own inquiry, I am left with the impression that the new movement, though it has consequences in all fields including the economic, actually starts in the realm of ideas—and religious ideas at that. If so, it is an example of the crucial role of intellectuals in human history, the decisive quality of their success or failure in handling theoretically the problems with which their society is faced.

Many have dwelt on the consequences of Awrangzeb's victory over Dārā, and have speculated on how different would have been the history of India had the result been the other way. What has less often been noted is that one crucial factor, at least, determining the outcome is that a majority of the Muslim *manṣabdār*, once the issue was clearly drawn, apparently chose to side with Awrangzeb and not with Dārā. There are various reasons for this, no doubt; but one is that by that date, unlike the situation 150 years earlier, the universalist Ṣūfī interpretation of the Islamic order was being adopted by fewer, and the formalist closed-system reified interpretation was being adopted by more, of the effective group in Muslim society. There is a complication here, which I do not yet understand, concerning the choice made by Hindū *manṣabdār*. Tentatively, anyway, it seems fair to say that the history of religion had in the sixteenth and seventeenth centuries moved in this way because, consciously or unconsciously,[10] the actors in that history, the human beings who were making it, chose to think and to feel and to act so and not otherwise.

Over against those who, lately, are questioning the Islamic formalism represented by Awrangzeb's accession, I wonder whether the matter is not somewhat confirmed, or made an all-India phenomenon, by a parallel from the ʿĀdil Shāhī dynasty of Bījāpūr. There, in 1626 Ibrāhīm ʿĀdil Shāh, something of a liberal universalist known apparently to his Hindū subjects as Jagatguru, was succeeded after a rather splendid reign by his son Muḥammad ʿĀdil Shāh, a communalist, who started once again to desecrate temples within the kingdom and to exploit economically, and perhaps deliberately, the Hindū moneyed class.

There remains the question of a relation between the Sikh and the Islamic processes that we have described. Earlier I suggested that the two movements of crystallization seem somewhat parallel; yet the connection was closer than that. For parallels are said not to meet; whereas these two intertwined, at certain points decisively. The two conspicuous moments are the execution of Arjun in Lahore in 1606, by Jahāngīr, on the grounds of his involvement with the movement attempting to put Khusraw on the throne rather than his father; and the execution of Tegh Bahādur in 1675 in Delhi under Awrangzeb. Each of these followed shortly after a major step in a Muslim process of consolidation: the first, on Shaykh Farīd's success in diverting and then suppressing Khusraw's bid for a more Akbar-like reign; the second, on Awrangzeb's similar success in ousting Dārā. These two martyrdoms are of crucial significance in Sikh history, both contributing very basically to the growth of Sikh community self-consciousness, separatism, and militancy. In particular, the attempt forcibly to convert the ninth Guru to an externalized, impersonal Islām[11] clearly made an indelible impression on the martyr's nine-year-old son, Gobind, who reacted slowly but deliberately by eventually organizing the Sikh group into a distinct, formal, symbol-patterned, boundaried community.

In other words, the move to crystallize Islām was more than once decisive in promoting the crystallization of what finally became 'Sikhism'. I find myself speculating to what extent one should see the two movements as two manifestations of a general tendency of the time, and to what extent one should rather see the one (the Sikh) as a pure result of or reaction to the other (the Muslim). Actually both processes were, I think, at work. And it would even be possible to interpret the double process the other way around. Some see the new Muslim communal rigidity as itself a reaction to what its proponents saw as a threat of disintegration, posed by the previous growth of Ṣūfī (and Bhakti) universalism. In this view, Nānak and what he stood for, which is what the Muslim Ṣūfī Shaykh Ibrāhīm Farīd also stood for, constituted precisely the danger that Sirhindī formulated his new ideology to counteract. The very process that put a Muslim writer in a Sikh scripture is just what Sirhindī and his followers were trying to inhibit.

It may perhaps have been noticed above that when Bāqī Bi-llāh arrived in India from Central Asia he found and consolidated certain individuals among the Muslim notables who were unhappy at the extent of Akbar's universalism; and that when his pupil Sirhindī[12] published his letters advocating separatism and formalism, these evoked a response from some members of the community. In other words, the new crystallization development was not totally new. There was something already there to build on; even though the degree to which it later grew strong and prevalent and rigid, and the degree to which it later stressed certain aspects of the Islamic heritage, such as law, to the neglect of others, such as sincerity—*these* were new. Now such an observation of continuity is valid. Like most emergences in human history this movement too was neither totally novel, nor was it a simple reduplication of what had gone before. Rather, it was a new creation yet continuous with, and growing out of, what went before—especially, continuous with and growing out of some elements of what went before to the exclusion of other elements, which tended then to lapse. This is normally how history works. Or shall we say, more accurately, this is how human beings make their history.

The validity of this general truth allows us to tie the sixteenth–seventeenth century phenomena that we have explored, not merely to local Indian developments, but to world history. For I see this process of crystallization and religious development, or more exactly the process that I have called 'reification', as in fact a major pattern in the history of mankind, of which the Mughul instance is one link in a total chain. This process begins, so far as I have been able to discern, in the Middle East—probably first in Īrān—about the sixth to third centuries B.C., and gradually strengthens in the Fertile Crescent about the first, second, and third centuries A.D.; is carried into Europe by the Christian Church, where it lies somewhat dormant until the early modern age, but meanwhile is injected into the Islamic stream in the seventh, eighth, and ninth centuries; which brings it into India from the eleventh, although with full effect only from the seventeenth, as we have been studying; whence it is transmitted also, in the Sikh case at least, into non-Muslim groups there, though the process culminates only in the late nineteenth century when European influence was spreading around the world: I have traced its percolation into Japan, China, and elsewhere in the nineteenth century and find it also invading India again at that time. The Hindū case in India provides a test and illustration of this general thesis. Let us turn to it briefly.

Essentially, this question may be posed: whether in the Hindū case, the process of crystallization, of communalization, of systematization, was virtually absent in the classical, so-called Hindū period of Indian history; that it begins in incipient and rudimentary fashion with the advent of the Islamic movement in the eleventh century; that it takes a further step forward in the Mughul period (beginning perhaps with Rānā Sāngā of Mewār, but gaining force in late Mughul times, as we shall see in a moment); but that it becomes a serious movement only in the nineteenth and especially the twentieth centuries. To make the hypothesis overly bold and overly dramatic, may one ask whether Hinduism was not perhaps born in the nineteenth century.

By this I do not mean, of course, that none of its elements is more than about a hundred years old. When one says that Hinduism was born only in the nineteenth century, and is still in process of crystallizing, one is not being simply absurd. Of course I know that the elements out of which is constituted what we today call Hinduism have existed in most cases for many centuries or indeed millenia. What I mean is that the organizing of those elements into a self-conscious coherent pattern, set over against other comparable patterns or against other aspects of human life—this is a new development, whose recent rise and current progress can be studied. Everyone knows that the parts of the present Hindū complex—philosophic ideas, literary forms, the moral, social, ceremonial, spiritual, architectural and other elements of many different kinds—go back in many cases for hundreds and perhaps thousands of years. My suggestion is that the idea that together these diverse factors cohere to make up a unit, to constitute a particular religion, one systematic formal entity, one member of the series called 'the religions of the world'—this idea, it seems to me, is recent. The coalescence of all the various strands of indigenous culture into one pattern, or presumed pattern, or into one idea, to make up what today is called Hinduism, and especially the coalescence of the varied groups into one great community: these seem to me new.

So far as the Mughul period is concerned, D. S. Sarma, in his *Hinduism through the Ages*[13] summarizes the religious history of the later mediaeval India ('1400 A.D.–1750 A.D.') in six points, of which the first is: 'The various schools of Hinduism hardened into sects'. If this be valid, it would parallel Muslim and Sikh processes that we have noted. It would refer, however, to the separate sects of the Hindū complex, and not yet to a corporate 'Hinduism' as some integrated whole.

In my study *The Meaning and End of Religion*[14] I have considered the emergence into consciousness of the concept and the term (in English) 'Hinduism', noting that the first recorded use of this word is in 1829. I considered a little there the phrase '*Hindu dharma*',[15] used in present-day Hindī for 'the Hindu religion'. I have since found some evidence to suggest that this phrase is first used in the seventeenth century; Bouquet quotes Dāsguptā as suggesting that the term *Hindū* used in a religious sense, 'in connection with a particular religion', is from about that time.[16] The earliest relevant usage that I myself have found is *Hindavī swarajya* from 1645, in a letter of Shivajī. This might mean, Indian independence from foreign rule, rather than Hindū *rāj* in the modern sense. A little later this same champion of the country's indigenous traditions is referred to by his son Sambhājī as *Haindava dharmoddārika*, later in that century.

One would like to see a full study of the term *Hindū*, in both Hindī and Urdū, as used in the literature of the past four or three centuries.

To return to the English term 'Hinduism'. After having been coined, as indicated, early in the nineteenth century, it was used throughout the middle and latter part of that century by Europeans and became standard among Hindūs themselves by the end of the same century, or anyway in the early twentieth. Outsiders, who introduced the term, have always had difficulty in defining it, and even in using it; and the better scholars they have been, the greater the difficulty. The better anyone knows the Indian religious scene, the more complex he recognizes it as being. Originally, however, the term was used in a somewhat glib and even rather contemptuous way by foreigners, perhaps especially missionaries, to lump together everything that they found in the country religiously that was not Islamic. Then, when something called 'Hinduism' was attacked, Indians arose to defend it. Sometimes they arose to reform it also; and the nineteenth-century movements are important for our purposes: Ārya Samāj, Prārthana Samāj, Rāmākrishna Movement, and so on.

English education was also important, which set up in almost everybody's mind the idea that there is a series of entities in the world each called a religion, Christianity, Judaism, Islām, and so on and so forth (the idea that I personally have challenged in my recent book); so that presumably Hindūs also have, or ought to have, one of these. The pressure of this formal idea was intellectually massive. It was supplemented presently by political and even economic formal pressures also. Under these pressures, a system and a community called 'Hinduism' began to take shape, at least in people's minds, over and against those systems and communities already existing as Christian and Muslim.

K. M. Panikkar wrote as follows, to conclude his 1938 lectures, *Hinduism & the Modern World*:[17]

> 'The thesis of this book, as explained at the outset, is to demonstrate that the survival of the Hindus as an effective people is possible only if from being a complex of innumerable social groups, they become a single social organism . . . . The theory of Hindu life so far does not accept the ideal of a Hindu community. But the practice, as we have shown, has changed with measured slowness during the last century, attaining at the present time a rapidity and momentum which could not have been anticipated. The Hindu community, still non-existent in fact has come into existence in idea. The translation of that idea in the realm of practice is the mission of present day Hinduism.'

In his most recent work, *The Foundations of New India*,[18] also, this author shows how in the nineteenth century a process of consolidation of Hinduism, both as a theoretical form and to some degree as a sociological community, was taking place.

I should like to hear critical comments, then, not only on my suggestions about Mughul times, but also about my further suggestion that the advent of the Muslims in 1001 A.D., which introduced into India for the first time the theory and the practice of a large-scale religious closed community, organized, systematic, and formal, with boundaries, began a process of crystallization among the non-Muslim groups in the country; that the Bhakti movement worked against this tendency for some centuries, but that from four and three centuries ago there were marked trends towards partial crystallization once again, even if in fragmentary ways, and that these latter trends were given an enormous new impetus and on a new large scale by the crucial developments of the nineteenth-century European impact—and that still today this process is working itself out.

10

The ʿ*Ulamā*ʾ in Indian Politics

In 1960, while spending a term as visiting professor at the University of London, School of Oriental & African Studies, I participated in a seminar there led by Professor C. H. Philips, director of that School, on 'Politics and Society in India'. Various participants dealt with the role of this or that group in, or the impact of this or that institution (caste, for instance) on, the modern political process. I was invited to contribute a paper on the ʿulamāʾ, *reproduced here. Rather than accepting the notion of 'politics' as given, and dealing with the relation to it of the* ʿulamāʾ *class, I reflected on the recent advent of this Western concept and phenomenon in India and the emergence or hammering out of new relationships as society and its institutions were in process of changing into new shapes. All the papers of that seminar, including mine, were subsequently published under Professor Philips' editorship, and under the same title as the seminar.*

History is development, transition: not merely a sequence of events but a process of becoming. To understand history, is to see the evolution by which something is gradually transformed into something else; by which one situation 'becomes' (the word is so beguilingly simple!) another situation.

Moreover, we are increasingly finding that one of the most challenging aspects of historical studies is the need to see that the concepts in terms of which we analyse a development are themselves part of the flux.

I have been asked to address myself to the question of the ʿ*ulamā*ʾ in Indian politics. It is an excellent question; yet let us not be disarmed by it. In an earlier, more rationalistic day, we might perhaps have begun by defining our terms. Nowadays, more historically, we may see our task as rather that of gaining awareness of the gradual emergence over the years of a situation in India in which these terms come to have meaning, and then the gradual evolution of that meaning. Looking at India today, we note that there is politics in that country, and there is a class of people in Muslim society known as *ʿulamāʾ*. We may well ask what has been the interplay of the two. Yet we must ask at the same time, what are the processes by which these two phenomena have gradually come into being—in their mutual impingement.

Political activity nowadays suggests a conscious participation in a complex procedure that pertains to government but is outside of it. It implies a rather rare and quite special type of rule that either explicitly and deliberately is open to be influenced and even determined by such procedure, or else implicitly is believed to be so. To govern, as either a bureaucrat or an emperor or a tribal chieftain does, is not to be involved in politics; but to influence government, and especially to try to do so, as either an electorate or a protest demonstration may do, is.

The kind of government that allows itself, or the kind of situation in which a government may be forced, to be much influenced by this extraneous activity is something of which the historian takes special note when he sees it. On the whole, he sees it rather seldom as he surveys the broad sweep of human development. That politics exists in India in 1960 in considerable intensity is a significant fact. It is one that has come into being over the course of several decades (with a striking leap in 1947). It has done so through a fascinating process in which the various factors have been many and diverse. The process is the result in part of situations and developments in other parts of the world; conspicuously in Britain, but also from America to Berchtesgarten and Moscow. It is the result in part of non-political matters, from economic and technological change to the writing of books. It is the result in part—and this inevitably is of salient interest though perhaps not of such salient importance—of previous politics in India, on a smaller scale. In the nineteenth century, a few people began to agitate, in what we may designate as an incipiently political fashion, in order that there should be more politics: in order that the government of the country should increasingly be that kind of government to which politics is relevant and where it is effective—ultimately, that there should be independence and democracy; that is, that a fully political situation should obtain. In this particular aspect—it is only one—politics is a dynamic and as it were narcissistic self-unfolding. The success of the movement was self-generating and expansive.

One other among the many factors that played a certain part in the emergence of an increasingly political process in India, one that we may single out for mention for obvious reasons but shall develop only later, is the activity in society of that class of persons known as Muslim *ʿulamāʾ*. By this I mean, not only did these people play a role in politics as a process once politics had emerged, a role that we must investigate; they played a role also, I suggest, in that larger process by which politics in the modern sense came to be.

Before we turn to consider the *ʿulamāʾ* as a phenomenon, however, I would ask to be allowed to make one further general point. The advent of what I have called a political situation—the emergence, that is, of a social complex in which a large number of people consciously participate in determining how they shall be governed—is a significant matter in the history of India, as indeed in the history of any other area. It is a political fact, but has plenty of extra-political consequences (as it had also extra-political causes). The attainment of democracy, whereby society in some degree self-consciously determines its own history and becomes collectively responsible for its own destiny; and also the preceding struggle to attain it, which was already the same thing in part: these are innovations of quite major profundity. Indian men and women have in these decades been entering that new phase of human life—recent for all mankind, though reaching different parts of our planet at somewhat different moments—wherein we are the masters rather than merely the victims of social development. The power to alter our situation that applied science gives us, is of course relevant here also. The fact that as creators of our own destiny we may be turning out to be no wiser than an erstwhile 'providence', and may indeed even use our freedom to commit race suicide, but makes the affair the more poignant.

The advent of political activity as a novel aspect in human life is a deeply significant matter not only in the history of India, but—and we are coming now closer to the topic of our paper—in the history of Islām. For a society to become collectively responsible for its own development—for its own shape and stability and aspiration and achievement—is profoundly significant; not least, religiously.

For some centuries, at least, the Muslim's responsibility to God included many things but not, except in the case of sulṭāns, that of ordering society. To take one example, it is one thing to be a scholar responsible for telling what the books say Islamic law to be; it is another to be a voter responsible for deciding what law a Muslim society in the twentieth century shall choose to enforce on itself. Again, it is one thing to be a society of Muslims juxtaposed to a society of Hindūs or Sikhs in an empire ruled from the top by a Muslim emperor, or a British government, or even a Hindū emperor. It is another thing to be a society of Muslims juxtaposed to a society of Hindūs, in a political situation in which the course of events is determined by the complex of activities in which all these groups may and do, with varying vigour and success, conglomerately participate. And so on. One is not saying here that the new historical situation in which politics was evolving as a central activity was being intellectually grasped in all its immense impact by the *ʿulamāʾ* or by any other class of Muslims. One is merely suggesting that not only is there a role of this group in politics which we may investigate, but also there is a role played by politics in inducing the new situation in which the *ʿulamāʾ*, like everyone else, found themselves; and in which their constituency, the congregations to whom they would preach, have gradually found themselves.

So much, then, for politics, the sheer fact of whose emergence must give us pause. What about the *ʿulamāʾ*? They, too, have emerged. There is a tendency, from which some of us at least have found ourselves suffering, to take this concept for granted; to suppose that there are *ʿulamāʾ* in Islām and that this is somehow 'natural', that they have always been there. Not so. Like everything else on earth, they have come into existence historically; in certain situations, at certain periods, for certain reasons. They constitute a phenomenon the emergence of which is to be investigated, and the course of whose development is if possible to be understood. I am not satisfied that I have come to any adequate understanding here, and I therefore proceed with some caution, and ask you to take these observations as tentative. This much, at least, seems clear: that they emerge in Islamic history in consolidated form a good deal later than is usually supposed, and develop in the Muslim history of India, as a formal and constituted class, a very great deal later—and perhaps even, in certain significant senses, only in the modern period.

It would be startling, and would not even be true, to say that the emergence of the *ʿulamāʾ* as a coherent and organized class took place in the nineteenth century. This much rather is true, and is important even if tautologous: that the existence of a corps of *ʿulamāʾ* in the modern sense is a modern phenomenon. In earlier times the class existed, but in a different form, and with somewhat different functions. The nineteenth-century meaning of the concept is not applicable to any previous century. Or again, the emergence of the corps of *ʿulamāʾ* as a political force, and even as a politically significant force, is a phenomenon of the political, that is the recent, era.

In the general history of Islām beyond India, the emergence of the *ʿulamāʾ* as a class[1] is a phenomenon of the Saljūq period, where the class was created by the state through the *madrasah* system that was set up to produce it. The formation and financing of this class was to provide an institutional basis for an ideological framework that could hold ʿAbbāsī society together and counteract the wide opposition movement whose ideology was Shīʿah. Once the class was organized, however, it developed a momentum and function of its own, and the history of the *ʿulamāʾ* under Muslim emperors is a see-saw of their functioning now as officials and spokesmen of the state, now as the conscious custodians of the conscience of the community and its normative tradition over against the ruler. Therefore there are moments when the *ʿulamāʾ* functioned as a political group, in our sense of deliberately influencing, or trying to influence, government without actually governing.

In the Ottoman empire, especially from Süleyman—that is, from the sixteenth century—the group is formally and carefully organized within and by the state, as an official institution. Otherwise, after the collapse of the ʿAbbāsī empire, over wide areas and periods of governmental instability the *ʿulamāʾ* group developed a new function, which it is very important for us to understand. It is that of carrying Islām in the absence of state support and through the vicissitudes of social upheaval. As armies marched back and forth, and principalities abruptly rose and fell, the social order and especially the moral order existed insofar as they did exist for most of the population not, as in a happier or anyway more stable day, because of the ruler and the state structure but almost despite them—certainly despite the chaos that their warfare and plundering produced. In classical Islamic times it was the pious function of the individual Muslim to be personally obedient to God's specific commands, putting his particular share of Islām into practice; but it was the function of the ruler to see to it that the Islamic system as a whole went forward. Without an empire, on the other hand, the meaning of 'the Islamic system as a whole' seriously shifted, but also the responsibility for its maintenance fell now on the *ʿulamāʾ* class.

If this analysis be valid, the consequences, though subtle, are of the utmost importance. For this meant that Islām for them became the ideal not existentially of an operating social system, but, in essentialist fashion, of an abstracted entity, a pattern of intellectualized norms. In this pattern only a few of the norms could be actually implemented, but the whole disembodied pattern of them could be and was to be reverenced. In this situation one gets the emergence of an *ʿulamāʾ* class whose function in society is that of custodian of a cherished idealized tradition, enshrined as a static essence in their books.[2]

If I do not misread the situation, this may prove to have been the most important religious development in Islām for a thousand years.

This may be kept in mind as background; but in India, Islām had to some degree its own history, or at least its own rhythm of development. The last of the *ʿulamāʾ* 's phases just mentioned crystallizes in India on a significant scale, so far as I have discerned, only after the disintegration of the Mughul empire and in full force only in the nineteenth century. Islām in India was structured somewhat differently from elsewhere. It arrived as a faith and idea whose institutionalization was first that of a state: conquest, dominion, power, social order, were the forms around which primarily it clustered. This continued, of course, and continued important—into the eighteenth century, and as an idea perhaps into the twentieth, as Jinnāḥ found. However, secondly, soon equally important, more intimate, and perhaps more lasting, came Ṣūfī forms. At a personal level the faith was spread in India chiefly by Ṣūfīs, and sustained chiefly by them. That their ideas and sensitivities, perhaps, provided the major content of Indian Islām at least to the seventeenth century is an hypothesis that I cannot altogether verify but that is anyway perhaps hardly extravagant. Certainly on the organizational level through all these centuries it is the Ṣūfī order (*ṭarīqah, silsilah*) that gives Islām its structure (apart from the state).

Many *ʿālim*s were also Ṣūfīs.

And even, curiously, it was in the end Ṣūfīs who called a halt to what eventually seemed the excessively Sufistic trend of Indian Islām.

Although my knowledge of pre-Mughul history is scanty, tentatively I see the evolution of Islām in India as falling, in the premodern period, into three main phases. They can be seen in the relations with Hindūs. The first begins with the violent arrival with the armies of Maḥmūd of Ghaznah and his successors. It is a period of vehement iconoclasm and exclusivism. The second, the Sūfīs' presentation of Islam, on the other hand, which presently gathered strength, won much of India's heart and indeed in later centuries formally converted to the new community many millions of its inhabitants, chiefly no doubt from the lowest castes. I must confess to not understanding, myself, how far Islām and particularly Islamic Sufism of extra-Indian origin influenced the rise and spread of the Hindū *bhakti* movement (eleventh to sixteenth centuries) and *vice versa*; in any case the fact is that relations between the two communities not only improved vastly but even reached a stage where syncretism seemed a possibility. This culminated under the Mughuls, in the sixteenth and seventeenth centuries: at the level of government in the reign and policies of the Emperor Akbar; culturally in such creations as Fatḥpur Sīkrī, miniature painting, and music; ideologically in Dārā Shikoh. The Urdū language might also be instanced. Some Muslims viewed the process as threatening the utter absorption of Islām within Hinduism and its eventual death. A reaction set in; this is the third phase.

The governmental expression of the new development in the reign of Awrangzeb is well known; this is but one aspect of the widespread and multifaceted development that was going on as a deep religious and presumably social transition to an Islām that is *Sunnī*—usually, though I think unjustifiedly, translated 'orthodox'.

This was a broad movement. In considering it, one may supersede any notion that Awrangzeb's policies reflect the whim of one man who chanced to be in power. For Awrangzeb came to the throne instead of Dārā Shikoh in considerable part because a larger portion of the *manṣabdār*s chose to support him; that is, to support neo-classicism rather than liberalism. The movement religiously was led by Naqshbandī Ṣūfīs, of whom the most important is the major theoretician Shaykh Aḥmad Sirhindī (*c*. 1563–1624), who formulated a careful and eventually highly effective rejection of the pantheistic version of Sufism, insisting instead on an interpretation by which it could be, as it then increasingly was, subsumed under an Islām strictly within the bounds of the classical norms, especially the *sharī'ah*. Sirhindī is, I think, the most historically consequential thinker of Indian Islām for these centuries, and so far as I am able at this moment to discern the evolving situation, this new movement, which involved eventually government, economics, art, communal structures and every facet of society, was fundamentally or primarily a religious movement, coming to formulation first in terms of ideas, of which Sirhindī is the chief representative; though my Marxist friends would doubtless argue that the ideas are subsequent or episodic to a primarily economic development. They may be right; one would delight to see their investigation of the case. It may be that my current tendency to see much of man's history as a history of religion is a trifle overdone. In any case, the more I delve into this particular movement in Indian affairs, the more persuaded I am of the depth and breadth of the transition that was taking place.

Another manifestation of the new development is the work of Sirhindī's influential contemporary ʿAbdu-l-Ḥaqq Muḥaddith of Delhi (1551–1642), who as his name implies is remembered for his contribution of *ḥadīth* learning; that is, for an emphasis on re-introducing classical formalism—though despite this he is remembered also as a Ṣūfī hagiographer.

Out of this movement can be seen emerging also systematic or institutionalistic expressions of the new orientation: in the field of law, in the major compilation the *Fatāwá-'i ʿĀlamgīrī*; and in the eighteenth century, in certain systematizations in the field of education, to which we shall return.

It will perhaps be felt that I am being an unconscionably long while in getting around to the topic assigned to me, the role of the *ʿulamāʾ* in Indian politics. I am ready to apologize for this, but also perhaps to defend it on the ground that historically Indian Islām was an unconscionably long while in getting around to producing an institutional *ʿulamāʾ* class to play that role. What I am suggesting is that such a class is, as it were, an eventual product of the transitional movement of the seventeenth and eighteenth centuries that we have just been exploring. The trend back to a conservative Islām at the end of the Mughul period was not the work of an *ʿulamāʾ* class (though individual *ʿālims* who were also Ṣūfī were influential in it). Rather the emergence of such a class was the result, or social deposit, of that trend, a deposit that crystallized out only after the imperial power of Islām had been shattered; in fine, in the nineteenth century. Let us examine this more closely.

The most important thinker in Indian Islām in the eighteenth century was Shāh Walīyullāh of Delhi (1703–1762). If Sirhindī a century and a half earlier had elaborated the intellectual basis on which Awrangzeb's policy rested, Walīyullāh's ideas (which were more powerful than lucid; I must confess that I do not feel that I at all fully understand them) seem to have been those on which has rested any adjustment to the failure of Awrangzeb, or shall we say to the collapse of Mughul power. Walīyullāh was an *ʿālim* Ṣūfī. His formal, institutional status was that of head of the Delhi branch of the Naqshbandī order (from 1719). He was a sensitive observer, not unaware that something quite serious had gone wrong, or was going wrong, with the Muslim position in India. His work was essentially purificationist and revivalist: aiming ideally at a restoration of a refurbished, more disciplined Sufism and a refurbished state power. In this last realm his immediate move was what most of us would call at least disastrous, to use no more pejorative a term: for he invited Aḥmad Shāh Abdālī to invade India, which proved hardly a contribution to the glory of Islām. This is *ʿālim* participation in politics with a vengeance!

The disintegration of the Muslim order in India is virtually the theme of the late eighteenth century and early nineteenth. It is easy to observe in the sphere of government and power: the Marhaṭṭah domination of Delhi, 1782–1803, was flanked by the Sikhs' supersession of Muslim rule in the Panjāb on the one side and by the East India Company's on the other; and in 1799 Tīpū Sulṭān had spectacularly failed in the south to maintain or to regain Muslim might. In the economic sphere the passing of the old order and, under the incipient impact of the results of the industrial revolution, its supersession by a new, have also been reasonably well studied, and the accompanying dislocation and misery are known. In Muslim education, one can trace in Bengal, at least, the crumbling of a school system economically feudal (that is, maintained by land endowments, specifically *muʿāfī* grants, which were gradually, or not so gradually, obliterated). What is not clear to me is what happened to the structure of the Ṣūfī orders. As I have argued all along, these, apart from the state, were the chief institutional form of Islām until this time. This presumably is the period during which they were giving way in this function to the gradual emergence of a structured *ʿulamāʾ* institution; a transition of which one sees the result a little later but of which I do not yet see the process. Of the growth of the latter one gets one or two hints such as the expanding significance of the Farangī Maḥall, Lakhnaw, set up as a typical one-man school in 1698 but developing in the eighteenth century into perhaps India's first nation-wide Sunnī *madrasah* institution; and the spread of its curriculum as a standardized *Dars-i-Niẓāmī*, which came to prevail as dominant formulation for the formation of religious scholars.

However that may be, it was in 1803 again an *ʿālim* Ṣūfī, the eldest son of Walīyullāh, namely Shāh ʿAbdu-l-ʿAziz (1746–1824), who formally, and in the name of Islām, inaugurated a movement to endeavour in overt action to reverse the worldly decline of Islām in India. For when in that year the Marhaṭṭah power in Delhi was overthrown and replaced not by restored Mughul might but by the British, he issued a famous *fatwá* declaring India to be *dār al-ḥarb*. This is the Islamic way of declaring war on behalf of the Islamic community; but the significant fact for our purposes is not only that it was proclaimed (with considerable consequences, as we shall presently see), but also that it was proclaimed not by a ruler but by a religious spokesman acting on his own. This was not yet 'the *ʿulamāʾ*' in Indian politics; but it was the first major step in modern Indian history towards such a situation, as it developed later and directly from this. And in any case it was the closest thing to it of which the opening of the nineteenth-century situation was perhaps capable.

Shāh ʿAbdu-l-ʿAzīz was in the next few years paralleled in his pronouncement by other *ʿālim*s here and there (such as Sharīʿatullāh), so that there was presently in effect an authorization by religious leaders to the members of the Muslim community to act.

If I understand the dynamics correctly, the declaration of *dār al-ḥarb* is not in itself an appeal for action, an eliciting of *jihād* (that comes twenty years later, as we shall see in a moment). It is rather simply a statement that—to use our modern terminology—analyses the situation in new and different terms. For eight hundred years Muslim India had been *dār al-Islām*, which means *inter alia* that the responsibility for its corporate as distinct from individual existence lay with the Muslim ruler. To assert (or shall we say, by 1803 to recognize) that this was no longer so, is to transfer that responsibility elsewhere. But it was not yet clear where else. With whom, with what groups or institutions, the new responsibility lay, was not yet, I think, thought out; nor just what it involved. In what did the responsibility consist? This latter was implied, in terms of the traditional concepts, by the word *ḥarb*, 'war'; and this is not unimportant, but was not yet explicated. As to the question of who would now take over the responsibility for Islām's corporate life, perhaps three sorts of answer were roughly possible: first, the community as a whole; secondly, a corps of *ʿulamā*; thirdly, the intervention of an outside Muslim ruler. In fact the history of the ensuing century shows the development in India perhaps of something of each of these, either in theory or in practice or both. However, before any of these considerations could be well worked out, the whole situation was, of course, immensely complicated by the altogether new and profound matter of the intrusion of the West, as a cultural and social as well as state phenomenon. But this is to anticipate.

The first great development was the Mujāhidīn movement, from the 1820s. Its enemies called it 'Wahhābī', and the term has stuck. I think one should take careful note of this name, particularly as stressing the impression that it made as fundamentally a movement of religious revival and purification. Yet we should drop it in favour of the internal name, which also stresses the Islamic character and includes, not unjustly, an emphasis on martial zeal. It was a mass movement, both funds and personnel being supplied from popular sources, not by rulers. It was inspired, organized, and led by religious dignitaries, *ʿālim*s. The chief of these was Sayyid Aḥmad Barelawī (1786–1831), though he was himself commissioned and inspired by Shāh ʿAbdu-l-ʿAzīz of the *fatwá*, and was accompanied and assisted by the latter's nephew, Ismāʿīl (d. 1831).

Sayyid Aḥmad, as apparently Shāh ʿAbdu-l-ʿAzīz's ablest disciple, had previously been sent by the latter to take part in an operation already on foot, namely a traditional type of resistance to British power by Indian feudal forces, with a Muslim apparently free-lance leader Amīr ʿAlī Khāṇ who was operating with a Marhaṭṭah noble Jaswant Rā'o Holkar. It is significant that in the anti-British orientation an alliance with Hindūs was acceptable; this persists right to 1947. This particular venture failed. Nothing came, either, of an approach to the Sindhiyā of Gwālior's administration, talking of joint anti-British-ness. Thereupon Sayyid Aḥmad, an able organizer, was turned into a popular agitator, to lead a mass movement. He toured North India, stirring up the Muslim populace to take on themselves the re-exalting of the purity and power of Islām, including a *jihād*, enlisting men and raising money. He seems to have organized a considerable army and met with considerable success. For reasons that are not entirely clear, the action when it came was in the Panjāb and Frontier against the Sikhs.* An independent *khilāfat* under Sayyid Aḥmad was set up in Peshawar for a time (1830–1), and there were other successes; but a decisive battle at Bālākot in the Panjāb (1831) brought 'martyrdom' to the leaders and a major setback to the venture. It did not altogether cease: with the major leaders gone, the minor ones divided, the armies dispersed and many lost heart. Nonetheless the movement continued, with headquarters at Sittana in the Sawāt valley, and continued to harass the Sikh state and later the British.

Meanwhile in Bengal peasant uprisings protesting against the heartlessness and hardship of the new order also took the form of Islamic movements led by *ʿālim*s in the name of a purified Islām: the Farā'iẓīyah, from 1804, under a Bengali *mawlawī* called Sharīʿatullāh, who had had his training mostly in Arabia; and the uprisings of 1834, 1841, 1844, and 1846 organized by his son Dūdū Miyāṇ, whose socio-religious activities were co-ordinated with those of the Mujāhidīyah in the North-west, and who seems to have given them more theoretical formulation than his father. On a more circumscribed sphere there was in Bengal and Bihar a more strictly religious reform led by Mawlawī Karāmat ʿAlī of Jānpur, as an outcropping of the Walīyullāhī impetus.

I personally am not quite clear as to how mighty these enterprises were; perhaps about as substantial as was in fact practicable in the then context, for non-state forces. This kind of operation culminated, of course, in 1857—the Mutiny, First War of Liberation, last attempt to restore the Mughuls, or whatever one opts for calling it. A lot of work has once again recently been put into studying this affair; I am not one of those who have gone much into it, but it is perhaps fair enough to generalize that it was complex, and that one of its strands was the Islamic *jihād*. Many *ʿālim*s were involved in this, their activities consisting at times, apparently, in actually fighting, 'sword in hand', but chiefly in organizing, inspiring, and Islamicizing Muslim participation in the struggle. They gave a considerable section of the movement, it would seem, an ideological content and emotional fervour; and, as well, direction.

The uprising, however, as we know, was crushed, with sufficiently decisive power to make it evident that this particular way need not be tried again.

What, then, to do next? What new phase of Islām's Indian evolution could be envisaged as possible or desirable? Some of the *ʿālim*s migrated to Makkah: Ḥājjī Imdādullāh, for instance, who had been one of the prominent leaders in 1857; also the father of the future Abū-l-Kalām Āzād; and others. This was presumably out of sheer discouragement; though I find myself speculating about this, and wondering whether conceivably there was as well some longer-range aspiration in view. Already in 1841 Mawlānā Muḥammad Isḥāq (1778–1846) had gone to Makkah. He was the grandson of Shāh ʿAbdu-l-ʿAzīz and his successor at the Naqshbandī *madrasah* at Delhi, and is said to have been in some ways the brains and even the programmatic organizer of the Walīyullāhī tradition after the failure at Bālākot. He postulated two basic principles for a programme: namely, strict observance of Islamic law, and an alliance with the Ottoman empire. He died in Makkah five years later; but apparently his going was no escapism but a move aimed at exploring the possibility of Ottoman support for his cause.

The next move in India is altogether crucial for our purposes: namely, the setting up in 1867 of a Dāru-l-ʿUlūm at Deoband. That it was founded by a group of *ʿālim*s, chiefly two who were prominent in the 1857 effort, is significant. Equally significant is that, once founded, it flourished: it attracted and sustained support, won the allegiance and services of first-class men, and developed a strong tradition of vitality and quality. In other words, its emergence represents something of fairly widespread significance happening in the Indo–Muslim community. We have already seen something similar happening, a little earlier, with the Farangī Maḥall of Lakhnaw. Deoband was distinctive in that it was considerably more dynamic and deliberate, with a richer and more revivalist tradition behind it (Walīyullāhī) and a clearer, more comprehensive ideal before it: namely, the active rehabilitation of the Indo–Muslim socio-religious situation. It was founded by men who had fought in the 1857 struggle, and who explicitly set out to develop an alternative means towards a similar goal: to produce a corps of *ʿulamāʾ* devoted to the cause of Islām and the freedom of India. The economic aspect is interesting. We remarked above that the traditional Muslim educational system had been tied to feudal patterns in that its financial support was in the form of endowments in land; and we saw that in Bengal the dissolution of those patterns meant the collapse of the educational system. Of the eight principles laid down by the Deoband founders as basic guides for the new Dāru-l-ʿUlūm, the first is that its financial support must be in the form of contributions collected from the people; and it was affirmed that permanent sources of dependable income or governmental support would weaken and divert rather than strengthen the institution. In this fashion, at least, despite the traditional learning, this is an institution of the modern rather than the mediaeval age.

Deoband, then, from the latter part of the nineteenth century, became the chief of a group of institutions that produced that modern phenomenon of Indo–Muslim society, the politically active *ʿulamāʾ*. We need not trace further the role that these played, since this has been ably and informatively done in a recent thesis,[3] and the role of Indian politics in the development of these *ʿulamāʾ* and their corporate function may perhaps be inferred. The career of Abū-l-Kalām Azād should also be studied. If meanwhile here we have been at all successful in asking the right sort of question as to the appearance and significance of this class, it is enough.

11

Aligarh and Religion: A Question

In the early 1950s the editor of the Urdū-language Aligarh Magazine *at the Muslim University in India did me the honour of inviting me to contribute to a special number of that journal to be devoted to Sir Sayyid Aḥmad Khāṇ. I was pre-occupied at the time with the demanding task of bringing into being the new Institute of Islamic Studies at McGill University, and found myself unable to take advantage of the opportunity. Instead, I wrote back propounding a question instead of an article, leaving it to his discretion whether he might wish to publish it. He chose to do so, and it is reproduced here, appearing in English for the first time.*

Not unlike the preceding article here (just above, on the ʿulamāʾ *and Indian politics), it reflects in relation to one particular instance on what was happening to Muslim religious sensibilities and institutions in the novel context that was emerging in India in the nineteenth century and early twentieth.*

It is a signal honour to be invited to make some contribution to this special number of *Aligarh Magazine*. Unfortunately it has not been possible for me in the time available to accede to the editor's kind and gracious request to participate in the venture by writing an article. However, he has been good enough to allow me instead to raise very briefly a question which has been on my mind ever since I first began to study the fascinating and impressive figure of Sir Sayyid, and to speculate on the significance of his movement. The question is not one to which I have found an answer; nor indeed is it one that an outsider perhaps could be in a position to answer. Yet if he is allowed to ask the question, this in itself is sufficient.

My concern is with the development of Islamic thought, and with the religious aspect of the modern history of the Muslim community in India. The first study that I made on this subject a dozen years ago[1] has proven very inadequate at many points and indeed false at several, in its interpretation of events. Fortunately, my understanding has considerably deepened since that time. Yet this one speculation continues to haunt me, indeed more than ever now that I am concerned more with the spiritual than with the politico-economic factors in the processes of religious history.

Sir Sayyid saw the need for modern education in his community, and devoted his energies to seeing to it that this need be met. He also recognized that the community would not be willing (and rightly!) to have modern education, if this meant abandoning Islām. He therefore was careful to provide a college in which both modern secular education and Islamic religious instruction would be simultaneously provided. Yet he also sensed that his own views on religion, his own interpretation of Islām, the endeavours which his own mind was making to synthesize and harmonize his religious tradition with the spirit and knowledge of modernity, were unacceptable to most of his fellow Muslims.

Accordingly, he conceded that in the new College, Islamic instruction should be provided by the recognized—that is, the traditional—religious leaders of the community, in the traditional way. These, of course, were proponents of a traditional interpretation of Islām. He himself felt that this traditional interpretation was in fact an outworn interpretation; that pure Islām in its original pristine form was simpler and more relevant, was less tied to the social decadence of the immediate past. However, he made it clear that he would not force his religious views on the students of the College: the Department of Theology would be quite autonomous and not the source of propaganda for the new views.

Probably it was necessary to make this concession in order to have his English education in the other departments accepted, and in order to have parents send their sons at all. However, is it not possible to question the wisdom of this decision? Or at least, one may speculate about what might have been the result had the concession not been made. How far is it true that the resulting dichotomy of religious-*versus*-secular learning has infected the Aligarh Movement and its attitude to life ever since? The fact that all other studies were in the English language, while the study of Islamics was in Urdū, seems to have had an important psychological effect. Graduates of the College, and of the University since, appear to have adopted an attitude towards the intellectual problems of religion that is special and isolated. The College itself made apparently no attempt to integrate the science, philosophy, modern history, and other matters taught in the College, with the tradition of the *ʿulamā*ʾ. And, since the College did not do so, neither did the students. Indeed, they were induced to feel that to do so was unnecessary.

Not that the Aligarh Movement quite segregated religion from the rest of life. Muslims have never done that; and the recent political history of the sub-continent has illustrated the continued tie between the two. Yet one may ask whether perhaps the situation has resulted in an emotional rather than intellectual attachment to religion, and in an understanding of Islām which is more traditional than contemporary.

Nowadays not a great deal of attention is paid to Sir Sayyid's religious views. Is this because they were not sound, were not interesting, were not very relevant to the problems and the situations confronting modern Indo–Muslims? Or is it simply because they were neglected, in the College which otherwise is a memorial to his vision and his insight? If his *Tafsīr*, for instance, had been studied along with (not instead of!) the other, earlier commentaries; if his interpretation of the Prophet had been examined along with other biographies; would the results have been bad or good? No doubt some would have disagreed; but might this have led to more critical study, to argument and counter-argument, to constructive new theology for the future instead of a return to or maintenance of the old? Would the use of English for religious instruction as well as other instruction have led to more synthesis and integration for the whole world of knowledge, sacred and secular?

The above is in no way meant to suggest that the teaching of religion at Aligarh had in itself been inadequate. It would be absurd for an outsider to criticize Sir Sayyid for his decision or to question the instruction that has in fact been offered. Our concern is not really with the teaching of religion which has been available, but rather the lack of co-ordination between that teaching and the teaching of other things. It may indeed be that the results of the dichotomy have been good. My only real question is to wonder what those results are.

12

Religious Diversity: Muslim–Hindū Relations in India

In May 1976 the University of Minnesota at Minneapolis held a conference on the topic 'Historic Interaction between Hinduism and Islam in South Asia'. I was asked to give the opening address. It is published here perhaps for the first time, being concurrently in press also in India in a volume of the conference proceedings.

This presentation was made after nine years at the Center for the Study of World Religions at Harvard, where I had moved beyond my Islamics concentration to study more carefully than before also Buddhist and Chinese traditions and faith, and especially Hindū, and had studied Sanskrit. I had attained, therefore, a much more serious familiarity with and appreciation for Hindū life and thought than I had had thirty-five years earlier when I first arrived in North India with my Islamics orientation. Alongside the powerful attraction that Hindū outlooks exercised on my mind and spirit, there remained my deep affection for and of course deepening understanding of Islām. In addition, the impact on my mind and spirit had never ceased to be vivid of the culmination of my first half-dozen-year time in Lahore, in the 1947 partitioning of the sub-continent and its accompanying human cataclysm. The gulf between the Islamic and my own Christian, and the collision at that point (and not only then) between the Islamic and the Hindū, were firm in my mind and spirit along with the deep human friendships that at the personal level transcended these gulfs and collisions and continue to do so; friendships among all three. It is obtuse, I have felt, not to recognize both the unitedness and the dividedness of humankind.

Given my concern for the former, I have at times perhaps appeared to some to be less than duly sensitive to the latter. This would be delinquent not only as regards India and its history, but for religious and in fact for human diversity at large. It would be superficial to underestimate the persistent and radical nature of our human differences; or to suppose that one may by-pass these or may subordinate them to some glib generalized thesis. Rather, and this I had come to see as near the heart of comparative religion study, and of human-history study: one must recognize diversity in its full starkness, wrestle with it in its full recalcitrance, and come out with synthesis, if at all, only very clearly on the other side.

The problem confronting the conference, as I saw it, and with which I continue to wrestle, could be stated quite simply—namely, how to understand Hindū–Muslim diversity in India: the fact that some persons and groups in India are, and have been, Muslim, and some, Hindū; and what this implies. By 'understand' I mean something quite major, and quite specific. The academic task is intellectual, and interpretive. It is not primarily a political task; we as comparative religionists (whether Muslim or Hindū or outsider) are not called upon to devise a constitutional framework within which the two groups might live together and operate a state, or an economic system, or a social programme. Our task is not primarily psychological or emotional or moral: to persuade either group or both to be at ease with the other, to live in harmony or at peace, to adopt some worthwhile goal. We have simply to contrive conceptually to apprehend what the situation is; or more historically, what it has been in process of being.

Yet our minds are ill equipped to handle this problem, to rise to this challenge. I see it as one of the more exciting assignments to modern intellectuals. And when I say that it is a theoretical, not a practical, problem, I do not at all mean that an intellectual solution to it would not have practical consequences. Far from it. A great range of modern issues, political, economic, social, educational, legal, and other are distorted by, and solutions to them limp because of, the modern world's incapacity to understand religious diversity—or to understand religion, which amounts to the same thing; or to understand man, which also in significant degree amounts to the same thing. It is characteristic of human beings that we are religiously diverse. My sense of the intellectual task is illustrated in my conviction that if we can move towards understanding our dividedness, this will help us move towards our unitedness.

(i)

In the latter part of this presentation I shall be arguing that the truth of Hindū and of Muslim religious life in India has been and is interdependent in ways not regularly noted. I shall urge two such ways. Over against this, let me begin by emphasizing what may seem an opposite point: namely, that the differences between the two traditions must be taken more seriously, more absolutely, than by Westerners is often done. My threefold thesis is of general applicability, pertaining to religious diversity as a world-wide and history-long human phenomenon, with the Hindū-Muslim situation in India as one specific illustration.

The standard Western view on man and the place of religion in human life—developed gradually since 1648, when the European Wars of Religion finally ended—tends to dominate much modern thinking in this realm, and indeed perceiving. Unconsciously subordinated to it are the particular theories or interpretations that may be advanced, whether of affairs in the West itself or elsewhere on earth. Yet I suggest that it is wrong. It tends to go like this: that religion is not essential or is not ultimate, but is rather some sort of extra tacked on over and above a basic and universal human nature whose central truth lies elsewhere; or that religion is one 'factor' in life or in culture or in society alongside other factors—political, economic, psychological, or whatever; or even is derived from these. Human nature in this view is basically secular; on its mundane base some persons or groups are seen as having for various reasons erected a fancy religious superstructure, or penthouse, of one or another form, so that men and women are perceived as fundamentally 'natural' human beings who have in certain cases a Christian or a Jewish or a Hindū or a Buddhist or a Muslim addendum.

For some years I have been working on a book, to be published presently,[1] that in passing argues that this secularist view of humankind is arbitrary and misleading: that as a matter of empirical observation, as well as of more rational analysis, faith is a constitutive ingredient of what it has meant to be human; that the history of humankind is inadequately understood unless we recognize the Muslim and the Hindū—to take those two examples from India; but also the Christian and the others—not as addenda to being human, but as ways of being human. Men and women, the historian observes (unless his or her prejudices stand in the way of seeing this) have not been human beings first and then Muslim or Hindū (or Christian . . .) in addition, but—normally—have been human *by* being one or other of these.

The great religious traditions of the world have been the salient responses to being human, or the salient attempts to be human. It is through our religious systems that we human beings have most characteristically been, or reached out towards being, what we essentially are. In this respect Western secularism may be seen either as a conspicuous aberration—which it may well come to be recognized as—or more immediately, as one more way of attempting to be human, one pattern alongside the others through which persons or societies historically have endeavoured or are endeavouring to express their basic human reality. It is none too successful an attempt, it begins to appear; and in any case none too helpful if one tries from within it to force into its fixed conceptual categories one's understanding also of the lives of other groups or other ages, of differing pattern. A secularist can no more understand Hindūs or Muslims within the framework of his or her presuppositions than they can understand each other within theirs.

We human beings are not of one given form, on top of which we then construct cultural or religious complexes external to our essential truth. Rather, the essential truth about us is such that it can be expressed or lived only in and through a cultural or religious complex transcending the individual and yet thus far in the world's history still particular, not universal. If the final destiny of humankind historically is to live in terms of a cultural or religious complex common to us all, we have not yet constructed or attained it, even in idea or in theory; the secularists among us perhaps least of all.

My first point, then—and obviously this could and should be developed at great length; but not here—is that religious differences in India, as elsewhere, must be recognized as in some sense ultimate. By that I mean that that diversity deserves, requires, more respect than we have been wont to give it. The three chief groups that have confronted this issue are Hindūs, Muslims, and Westerners; or four, if one divide the West into Christians and secularists—although by now many Christians have been secular in their overall outlook. Among each, there has been a tendency to feel that the problem is intransigent because other people, not oneself, are silly or obtuse or off the track—when they simply are off one's own track. Religious differences express, if anything does, absolutes of the human condition in history. To postulate anything other than the religious as absolute—the political, the economic, the so-called natural as distinct from a so-called supernatural, or whatever—is simply to propound and to adopt some other religious or metaphysical stance.

(ii)

My second point is also historical: namely, that though ultimate, no religious (or for that matter, secular) position is final, in temporal terms. Every religious tradition not merely has a history but *is* a history. Unrelentingly it evolves, however surreptitiously. To be a Muslim, as I have elsewhere defined it, means: to participate at some particular point in the on-going and ever-changing Islamic process; and similarly for being a Christian or Hindū (or secularist). At any given moment the tradition purveys ultimate and absolute validity to personal or community life, and we must not underestimate that. Yet at any given moment also the configuration through which this is done is in process of changing, gradually and usually unwittingly, into some other configuration; and we must never forget that either. The historian of religion reports diversity as a characteristic of human religious and indeed social life that is not secondary, as has often been postulated, subordinable even in theory under something else, but primary; is essential at least in the sense of being a constant, inescapable, and constitutive ingredient. Yet this diversity is not only between one tradition and another, but also between one era and another within a single tradition.

To be a Christian is not the same thing as to be a Jew. Yet to be a Christian in the twentieth century is not the same thing as to be one in the nineteenth, either; let alone, the twelfth or the first. (I mean this not peripherally, not mundanely, but with ultimate theological seriousness: accepting all the metaphysical implications—though of course I shall not here develop these.)

It is this historical dynamic that enables me to propound my second point, of the intertwining of Hindū and Islamic in India, along with and over against their drastic mutual divergence. Each tradition is and throughout has been in constant process of development; and the thesis that I wish to set before you here is that for all their disparateness, the history of each has been what it has been in part, these last thousand years, because of the history of the other. The phrase 'neo-Hinduism' has been coined of late to discriminate from what went before a phase of Hindū religious thought and mood discernible in modern times; but it is an absurd concept insofar as it postulates or implies that what went before was all of a piece, was some fixed entity.

Neo- has been the Hinduism of every century now for the past thirty-five.

'Every religion is a new religion every morning.'[2] This may be more patent for the amorphous Hindū complex than for so systematic and coherent and consolidated a structure as the Islamic. Yet one is a poor historian if one does not see that the Islamic movement too has ever been dynamic, live, creative. 'Every generation of Muslims has made its own decisions', as our late friend Marshall Hodgson has put it. That ought to be a platitude, but alas it is not. The concept *niẓām*, system, has been fashionable in Indo-Muslim vocabulary of late, in speaking of

Islām, but it was not always so: this too has a history, which can be traced, and in fact is relatively recent. Some years ago, also, I published an article[3] reporting an exciting discovery that even the concept *sharīʿah*, seemingly so central to Muslim life, was introduced late in Islamic history (largely after the fall of Baghdād), as part of an important reifying process of thought. Indian Muslims have participated in processes widespread in the Islamic world, transcending India; but the history of Islamic religious life in India has had too its special as well as its generic developments, some of which it has in turn communicated to the rest of the Muslim world outside the sub-continent.

I am speaking of the history of Islām religiously, as I am of Hindū life religiously. It is obvious enough that in the history of music, as well as of economics, and in the history of language and literature, as well as of warfare, there has been mutual interdependence. I am talking specifically, however, of the history of religion: the movement of Islamic faith—God's relation to Muslims, and *vice versa*, if you wish to speak theistically; the history of His Word among them.

The religious life of Hindū India has at times been what it has been, and has become what it has become, in part because of reaction to, influence by, involvement with, Muslim religious life (and of course, more recently, Christian and Western-secular). And *vice versa*, Islamic religious history in India, and even outside, has developed as it has developed in part because of what Hindūs have religiously done, and thought, and been. Religiously, probably the Islamic is both in fact and in theory the world's most cohesive and coherent system; yet in fact, whatever at times the theory, it is not and never has been a closed system.

The most dramatic and best-known example of religious give-and-take—or to use more accurate language, of joint participation in a larger, transcending, development—has doubtless been the mediaeval and still far from adequately explored *bhakti* and *taṣawwuf* movements. I myself have published some investigations[4] on what I have called the crystallization of religious communities in Mughul India, calling attention to parallels between, for instance, the movements formally internal to the Islamic and Sikh traditions respectively represented by Shaykh Aḥmad Sirhindī and Guru Gobind Singh. Let me here suggest a more recent illustration of the mutual involvement that I have in mind.

When in 1947 the sub-continent was divided and Pakistan was set up, the sizeable Muslim community 'left behind' in predominantly Hindū India began a history of its own that has become in part separate from and somewhat, though of course not entirely, independent of the neighbouring history of the Muslim community in Pakistan— and (complicatedly) Bānglā Desh. Its own history, including its religious history, has also been in part dependent on, has been involved with, the religious evolution of the Hindū community in India. Its status as a minority is somewhat precarious. Besides, quite special has been its internal relation to such time-honoured religious questions in the Islamic world as the role of law (*sharīʿah*) in community life, relations to the state, and the like. Now in part the future of the Muslims in India manifestly turns on the treatment accorded to them by the Hindū majority. This in turn depends in part upon the play of two contending forces within the Hindū community, both of age-long standing, and both powerful.

Two strands in the Hindū religious complex, of divergent consequence, are conspicuous: we may call them particularist and universal. The one stresses rigidity of form, especially social form, the closed cohesion of introvert community, separateness, and social distance: it is exemplified in the caste system, and has been cultivated of late by such communalist groups as the Jan Sangh and the Rāshtriya Sevak Sangh. The other emphasis from the Hindū heritage is of liberal humanism: a powerful philosophic and spiritual orientation that stresses tolerance of human diversity, openness of mind and heart, a profound respect for the human spirit, even across social boundaries, and the cosmic validity of all forms of worship. Now both these tendencies in the Hindū community are, as I have said, ancient, deep, and powerful. Both are active today. Which will win out, or how the two will balance or accommodate to or interlink with each other, are questions that may well prove highly consequential not only for the history of India, but perhaps also for the history of the rest of us. In any case, it is clear that what happens in the present-day development of Hindū thought and feeling in this regard will be highly relevant for the evolution of Islamic affairs in India, including religious affairs. The destiny of these two groups is sufficiently intertwined that the internal religious development of the one will in part affect the internal religious development of the other, whether by sympathy or by reaction.

I am proffering this as one rather fascinating example of the generic fact that sometimes what happens in the historical process of one religious tradition is a function of what happens in the historical process of another. The historian discerns this as having occurred in past history and for other communities more often and more crucially than is usually recognized.

(iii)
My third point is more philosophic, although I continue of course to speak as an historian. (The only philosophic problems that are serious are those with which the historian is wittingly or otherwise confronted.) My point may perhaps most bluntly and most poignantly be set forth as follows: I personally am a Christian; yet there is a part of the truth of the Christian Church that in the past only Jews have clearly seen.

Part of the truth of any human reality is with those whom it offends. Religious diversity is part of the ultimate truth about humankind; and that diversity must be recognized and apprehended in all its starkness, and its pathos.

No one has understood any religious position until he or she has understood it both in itself and within the context of all the others. The affirmation has been made that only a Christian can genuinely understand Christianity; only a Muslim, Islām. I would of course have to resign my appointment as a comparativist if I subscribed to this view; yet I understand it, and I should be inclined also to advise anyone to resign who has not felt the force of it, who has not seen its almost-persuasive point. One has not understood Islām if one has not sensed the glory and splendour of the Islamic complex, and its appeal: why it is that outstandingly intelligent persons for century upon century have taken, and take, pride and delight in it and have found and find it lucid and compelling; and—almost—why they have found and find obtuse those who do not agree. To know and to understand Islām means to know a lot of facts but also (in part) to know what it feels like to be a Muslim.

Yet the opposite point has also been made, especially by Westerners in pursuit of objectivity: that only the non-Christian can know and understand Christianity truly. Both positions are right, in part; yet I am propounding here still a third dimension to this: that to understand any human matter, such as a religious tradition and its faith, accurately, one must know not only how it appears to the participant, and how it appears to the objective outside observer, dispassionate and uninvolved, but also how it appears to its opponents, its victims.

Without this comprehensive quality, our understanding will limp of Protestant–Catholic relations in Ireland; or Muslim–Christian in Lebanon; or for that matter race relations in this country [*sc. the U.S.A.*], or the generation gap in Britain, or labour strife in Canada. What a formidable assignment we have taken on, if we aspire to understand Hindū–Muslim divergence in India. How can any mind understand either the Hindū or the Islamic alone; let alone, both together; let alone, each in relation to the other? The answer is simple, of course: it cannot, except superficially. Yet we can be a little less superficial tomorrow than we were yesterday, which is why we have conferences of this sort. I certainly expect to go away from this symposium closer to the truth than I am at the moment, given the quality of those who will be addressing us for these next two days; even though I know that I shall die still a long way from its fullness. Life for the intellectual, however, consists in making progress towards the truth; and also, for the academic community.

This much, however, I have already discerned, and commend to your reflection: that no one has understood either the Islamic or the Hindū movements who, however well he or she may have grasped either separately, has not apprehended the contradictions between them. The incompatibility of the two is part of the truth about each.

Whether one be a Hindū, a Muslim, or a Westerner, and whether one be religious or secular, to fail to understand this is to misunderstand history, to misconstrue religion, and to mistake the human condition.

For I would go further, and say that the clash of Hindū and Muslim is part of the truth about ourselves, each one of us. At stake, *inter multa alia*, is the relation between poetry and prose; science and religion; men and women. The West has made enormous progress lately with its discovery of the relevance, for the interpretation of all religious life, even its own, and indeed all personal life, of the concept 'symbol'—as the Islamic world did centuries ago with its development of the Ṣūfī movement. Yet to understand India (and, I would argue, to understand humankind), one must understand *both* symbolism and iconoclasm. The Indian situation, both over the centuries and today, scintillates as an example of religious or human pluralism, because coming to terms with it inherently means attaining a simultaneous understanding of both pluralism and *tawḥīd*.

Pluralism and *tawḥīd*: Muslim, Hindū, outsider, must come to recognize that both are equally absolute—in India, in the world, and in ourselves.

POSTSCRIPT

[*Having been asked to prepare for delivery at the conference a thirty-minute address, I did so; hence the precise size of the above. First drafts were longer, and inevitably the final form left out much, and over-simplified; yet so would a four-volume study. One section of an earlier, discarded draft is nonetheless added here as an afterword in the light of the conference itself—slightly modified, as will presently appear, in the light of the conference and its activities:*]

Our task is to understand Muslim and Hindū conflict in India; and for that the first step is to understand the Islamic and the Hindū each in its cosmic, transcendentalist, absolutist reference. This is, after all, their primary significance, their *raison d'être*. At the least, our task is not to impose upon them *a priori* an outsider's understanding (modern, secular). That, inherently though surreptitiously, rules out their collision, their incompatibility. Many Western students operate with a concept of religion that forces them, when confronted with religious conflict, to look about for the 'real' (that is, the non-religious) factors that on occasion turn 'mere' religious difference into conflict: into what appears to be religious conflict but for them is 'really' something else. (I myself did this when I was very young.) The interpretations of such observers are then functions of their concept of religion, and of their conception of reality—that is, are functions of their own, usually unconscious, metaphysics—at least as much as of the situation that they are attempting to describe. Western social scientists in particular are in danger of being poor at dealing with such questions.

In affirming that the Islamic and what the West inaptly calls the Hindū are absolutes (neither of them then subsumable under the other, nor can either or both be subsumed under some third position), and in averring that our task is to understand religious conflict in India, I was not forgetting (after all, I am an historian) that our task is also to understand, for other times or places in India, a lack of conflict, and for still others, collaboration. My submission is that we shall understand all three types of situation best if we see the second and third not as instances of a lack of conflict and therefore as something not requiring explanation. For a true historian, every human situation requires explanation, and rewards it: one should everywhere and always be full of wonder at what human beings do and are. Moments of harmony, and of cooperation—and of both there have, thank God, been many—are better understood as transcending differences than as evading them.

One would do well to consider a *mushāʿirah*. And in doing so, one must not fail to appreciate the constructive achievement that is its poetry: fundamentally, a spiritual achievement. Moreover, the historical institution of *mushāʿirah* through which that poetry functions cannot finally be understood by a non-transcendentalist interpretation of humankind.

[Later:] More immediately pertinent, let us consider a musical performance such as the extraordinarily moving evening of song by Ustādh Ḥafīẓ Aḥmad Khāṇ with which this particular conference in Minneapolis ended. The singing, the songs, and the reception by the audience—at moments, the participation of the audience—were instances of Hindū–Muslim relations in India that, along with the massacres of 1947, it was the business of our symposium to appreciate. Among other matters, this occasion, and such music in general, and a *mushāʿirah*, illustrate the inappropriateness of the very concepts 'Hindū–Muslim relations' or '. . . interaction' or the like, for such a case. In a performance like that, and in such music in general, 'Hindū' and 'Muslim' are best thought of not as related, and certainly not as set aside nor indeed even as transcended (it is important to recognize that the occasion cannot be understood as if it were *not* Muslim, or were *not* Hindū); not even perhaps as fused (although that comes closer). Rather, here 'Hindū' and 'Muslim' have become interchangeable terms. Both are still important, both are still absolute; but on a particular occasion *they have become synonyms.*

The two words have not often meant the same thing; but at that particular moment they did. (To achieve this, the meaning of each was intensified, not weakened.)

We said above that to be a Muslim means to participate in the Islamic process in human history; and similarly to be Hindū (or Christian, or whatever). At such moments as that evening of music, these two become historically the same process.

The fact is an accomplishment. And this accomplishment is the act, the spiritual creation, of on the one hand a single person (the singer; but his accompanists, particularly Ṣadāqat Ḥusayn on the *ṭablah*, were also important), and on the other hand of the audience who responded; and in part into it went also the creative spiritual heritage of certain moments and persons and institutions from the past.

This may be carried further. One's theoretical interpretation of the universe is intellectually thin if it does not make room for the fact, and for the marvellous quality of the fact, that human beings can trust each other, can be loyal to each other. Not automatically; but also, not negligibly. Without faith, this would not be possible. (Trust is one of the dimensions of faith.) With faith, which occurs in diverse forms, Indian and other history shows that it is sometimes possible, sometimes impossible. Both conflict and collaboration are aspects of the specifically religious (that is, the essentially human) history of our race.

PART FOUR

Muslim–Christian Relations

13

Some Similarities and Some Differences Between Christianity and Islām

This essay was my first explicitly comparative study—formally correlating (and contrasting) elements of two distinct religious outlooks, and reflecting on the comparisons. It developed systematically, and substantially extended, certain new analogies that I had informally begun to draw in passing in my Islam in Modern History *two years earlier, in my endeavour then to make Islamic patterns intelligible to Christians and those familiar with Christian thinking. I commented also on certain old analogies that, although common, I felt ought not to be drawn since they are in fact misleading. This piece was of some importance for me in laying the groundwork for subsequent comparativist theory. In particular, in line with my general personalist orientation, it shifted the focus of attention from the data of any given religious 'system' to the role of those data in the lives of the persons concerned. Thus the question posed became, not whether or how far a given phenomenon in one religious tradition is itself similar to or different from an apparently comparable one in some other tradition; but rather, whether or how far its effect on a worshipper is similar or different. Certain types of academic study, especially phenomenological, focus on religious objects or symbols, and trace variations and consistencies among recurrent instances of these around the world. Insofar as the Harvard 'school' of comparative religion study has developed a distinctive orientation, it is perhaps by deviating from or supplementing this by attending ultimately to personal involvements or interactions with those objects and symbols (and ideas, and whatever). Similar data may, on inquiry, elicit differing responses in distinctive contexts; and differing data, similar responses. Recognition of this principle has proven fruitful for interpreting not only religious diversity among communities, but also (although this point is not explored in this present essay) the history of any one community; since in that history the same symbols may mean different—even quite different—things in various areas or various social classes or various centuries.*

This study was written for and published in the Festschrift of one of my teachers at Princeton, Professor Philip Hitti.

On the one hand, the most casual observer has always been aware that various religions differ from each other but also in some respects resemble each other. On the other hand, the most sophisticated student can only with difficulty, if at all, designate precisely what the similarities are or even formulate satisfactorily the differences. Usually on careful inquiry matters that seemed at first glance to correspond turn out in fact to diverge in subtle and unexpected ways: the more thoroughly one investigates two systems, the more apparent it becomes that parallels are at best only approximate. Yet at the same time the more familiar one becomes with the totalities, the more persuaded one is that despite differences in detail, which grow and grow, there is also substantial comparability, elusive yet fundamental—which also perhaps grows with increasing understanding. The more assiduously one studies the trees, the more distinct one finds them to be; yet it would be a poor study that, for them, lost sight of the woods.

The question has both practical and academic implications. In the former realm an advance could contribute to the urgent problem of intercommunication among representatives of diverse traditions—something of which our world today stands sorely in need. In the past, adherents of separate faiths have ordinarily not been able to converse fruitfully, for a variety of reasons, one of which has been that it has seldom been clear what the points at issue between them precisely are. If the difference between two systems is total, then dialogue between them is impossible. If on the other hand the difference is partial—as I believe—then dialogue should become feasible once the similarities and the divergences are clarified. If two people know wherein they agree and wherein they differ, then they may intelligibly discuss their respective stands. If, however, each harbours misconceptions about the other's position, and both misconceive what their agreements and divergences actually are, then conversation if it occurs at all proves to be exasperation, or absurdity, or anyway inconsequential. Unfortunately this has largely been the situation historically. Persons of different faith either have not talked together at all, or have talked not with each other so much as past each other.

In the academic realm, I believe that a problem is here raised for the relatively new discipline of comparative religion. It is not directly the task of a pure science actively to engage in practical problems. It is its task, however, to provide the intellectualities with which these may be resolved. In our day man is challenged to foster communication and to construct concord and human fellowships between pairs of religious communities. The ethical worthwhileness of these tasks does not in itself perhaps dictate that a university department should promote them; and indeed they require also a goodwill that it is the responsibility of the religions rather than of any science to foster. Yet the task requires, in addition to goodwill, also new and clarified understanding; and this perhaps the universities, and the universities alone, can pursue and purvey. The decision to build a bridge across a given gulf is the task of the man of affairs, and the building of it is the task of the practical engineer and workman; but the ideas and equations and principles according to which a bridge can be conceived and according to which it will hold up, are the task of the academic engineer and, even before that, of the theoretical physicist. It is my conviction that one of the responsibilities, in our day, of comparative religion studies is that of constructing concepts and intellectual analyses by means of which divergent religious traditions may become mutually intelligible; of constructing statements about religion that will be cogent in at least two traditions simultaneously.

I hold further that the capacity to do this is not merely a goal worth aiming at for ethical reasons, but a criterion of intellectual success whereby the science of comparative religion may gain an experimental testing of its hypotheses. In other words, I suggest that these studies' statements will be valid academically insofar as they approximate to this goal. One assessment of the intellectual validity of a statement about, for instance, the Buddhist religion is whether that statement is meaningful and even persuasive and acceptable both to those who do and to those who do not hold the Buddhist faith. At one level one may aim simply at statements that will prove acceptable both to the academic tradition and to the Buddhist. At a more complex level, which concerns us here, the aim may be the comparative one of a statement about two religions that will be simultaneously cogent to both of them as well as, of course, at the same time cogent to the academic mind whose commitment is solely to intellectual truth.

In the course of my work I have had to consider these matters in particular with regard to Christianity and Islām. The subject is obviously vast, yet I have felt that it would be useful to treat a few at least of its details. Christians, Muslims, and students of comparative religion have all three explicitly or instinctively held that the two traditions, manifestly different, are yet comparable. I would here urge that the comparisons usually drawn at a preliminary level prove at a more advanced level of scrutiny to be less valid than is normally supposed. I would go on to suggest that the similarities, which undoubtedly exist, perhaps lie in rather unexpected areas. While apparently similar elements in the two faiths may on second thoughts diverge, seemingly disparate elements may be examined to see whether on second, or third, or fourth thoughts they turn out to have something unexpected in common.

One of the facile fallacies that students of comparative religion must early learn to outgrow is, I have felt, the supposition that the different religions give differing answers to essentially the same questions. I would hold that rather their distinctiveness lies in considerable part in a tendency to ask different questions. Yet at a still more refined level one must learn to recognize that essentially 'religions' do not exist as reified entities at all; that rather man, in his universalist condition, in the variety of religious traditions asks (varying) questions of the same universe, in relation to the transcendent and evidently unitary reality; or, in more theistic terms, that God, who is not plural, deals with man wherever He may find him as best He can, despite or within the limitations of the variety of religious forms.

Preliminary observations in comparing Christianity and Islām have been that for scripture the one has the Bible, the other the Qur'ān; for founder the one has Jesus Christ, the other Muḥammad; the one has churches, the other mosques; and so on. Such comparisons seem obvious; and yet on closer inquiry the parallels are revealed as not so close, and may indeed prove at best metaphorical and finally even misleading. At least on various occasions I have questioned the validity of any too simple equations in such matters.[1] It has seemed that it might be useful to gather these together in one survey, to extend the inquiry, and to endeavour to point this particular issue perhaps more sharply than has normally been done. The present paper, accordingly, will collate, expand, and reflect.

We may begin with a point that is relatively straightforward, because basically verbal—though one that can be fruitful of misunderstanding nonetheless. This is the phrase 'the will of God'. Christians and Muslims both use this phrase, but refer by it to different concepts. Christians in the most commonly used of all their prayers, taught to them by Christ Himself, say 'Thy will be done', relating this as an aspiration towards seeing mundane affairs accord with a higher pattern, to the 'coming of the Kingdom' of God. It is a deeply meaningful utterance; and 'the will of God' has great moral connotations. To strive to do God's will is man's highest calling—and his greatest failure. The counterpart to this conception in Islām is, as a technical theological term, *riḍā* (*riḍwān*, *marḍī*) (pleasure);[2] but more generally is *amr* (command). One might even venture to set up the correspondence, the will of God is to Christianity as the *sharīʿah* (law) is to Islām. This is gross, but not dangerous since everyone will see the lack of parallel and it is perhaps worth suggesting so that some will also see the partial parallel.

In Islām the will (*mashī'ah, irādah*) of God is not what man should do but what God does do. God's will operates, irresistibly; it would be meaningless to pray that it be done, for it quite certainly will be done, regardless. In fact, it would perhaps be rather silly, if not rather insolent, to speak of man doing God's will. It is not a moral conception, but a determinist one. The Christian counterpart is also sometimes called 'will', ambiguously,[3] but more often the theological problem posed by the relation between God's *amr* and his *mashī'ah* is in Christian circles set in terms of God's foreknowledge (also providence; also predestination; also sovereignty; etc.). For Muslims the will of God is what happens, the command of God is what, in human terms, ought to happen; man can disobey God's command, but cannot contravene His will.

In the most general terms of all one could posit (as has, indeed, been done) that the Muslim equivalent of 'Thy will be done' is (as a verbal noun) *islām*.[4] A *muslim* is by definition one who 'accepts' the charge to have God's ordinances prevail on earth (as they do 'in heaven' as Christians might add), to have His kingdom (politically, the Islamic state) come.

There is even in the historic development of the two religious movements an eventual parallel of ambiguity. The term *islām* began as meaning an active acceptance of (willingness to accept, dedication to) God's *amr*; it came to mean a passive acceptance of, resignation to, His *mashī'ah*.[5] It would be interesting to explore this development and to investigate a possible correlation with the decline of Islamic religion and culture in recent centuries. This may be the theological counterpart of the transition from activism to passivity.

Let us turn to more startling illustrations. The proposition that the Qur'ān is to Islām as the Bible is to Christianity is obviously not absurd. It is widely held, and might be said to be valid as a first degree of approximation. Closer investigation, however, shows it to be an over-simplification. I have suggested that a second degree of approximation, not without its own difficulties yet in a fundamentally religious sense somewhat more valid, is a proposition that the Qur'ān is to Islām as the person of Jesus Christ is to Christianity. Further parallels that I would construct in this series are between Muḥammad and St. Paul (for Roman Catholics, St. Peter?); and between the Ḥadīth and the Bible. My point would be that in the Islamic system the central focus of revelation is the Qur'ān, God's gift to man and the heart of the religion; that Muḥammad is the person who conveyed this message to mankind, who preached it and its implications and organized the community of those who accepted it as normative; that this community gradually built up a body of literature concerning the purveying and implementing and explicating of this message, in the *sunnah nabawīyah*. On reflection it becomes clear that the three elements in this scheme, Qur'ān, Prophet, Ḥadīth, have as their closest counterpart in the Christian scheme Christ, St. Paul (or the twelve Apostles [Arabic sing., *rasūl*] generally, perhaps along with St. Paul), and the Bible (or more specifically, the New Testament).

The Bible is the record of revelation, not revelation itself. The truth of this remark, which has perhaps been more firmly grasped in Christian thought recently than was always the case, is clarified when one reflects on the Muslim misinterpretation of the Gospels apparent in the view that God revealed them to Jesus (*cf.* Qur'ān 57:27). This cannot but be regarded as an error by Christians and by historians of religion, one that has caused some Christians to smile and others to protest. It simply illustrates what would have been the case if the parallel between the Qur'ān and the New Testament or its first four books were what Muslims, and indeed some Christians, have glibly supposed it to be. Actually the parallel between the New Testament—and especially the four Gospels—and the Ḥadīth, is seen to be quite close as soon as one thinks about it. For Muslims to say that Jesus brought the Injīl is as though Christians were to say of Muḥammad that he brought the *Ṣaḥīḥān* or *al-kutub al-sittah*.

Since I have touched on these points elsewhere,[6] I will not stop to elaborate them here, though it is evident that the final implications are major and subtle. For instance, in both traditions salvation is by faith—faith in God and in His revelation. In the Muslim case, faith in 'what Muḥammad brought' is faith not merely in a book but in what that book has to say, and since what the Qur'ān has to say is fundamentally a moral imperative, faith in it means aligning oneself actively with a moral orientation. Hence the law (see next paragraph). Hence also the community, *ummah*, since the law is also social. In the Christian parallel, faith is in God and Christ, which means 'living in Christ' and also (correspondingly) participating in the Church. There is then the further parallel, which I have elsewhere adumbrated,[7] that in Islām the mediator (to use a Christian phrase) between man and God is righteousness. This was true also in the Jewish faith (and even earlier in the Semitic tradition); hence, as St. Paul stresses, Abraham's faith 'was counted to him for righteousness' (Genesis 15:6; Romans 4:3–5). The Christian is wrong, however, if he infers that salvation in Christ is available to sinners but that salvation through a law is not. In Islām, at least, social salvation is through righteousness, but personal salvation is through faith in righteousness,[8] and therefore is available also to sinners.

This leads us on to consider another parallel, which has been obvious and standard, and can clearly not be altogether gainsaid: between the role of theology in Christianity and the role of theology in Islām. Despite the validity, I would suggest that even here there is a danger of over-simplification. Christians, for whom theology has from very early times been central, can suppose that theology and doctrine are central in other faiths also, and indeed sometimes phrase their questions about other men's religions in the words, 'What do they believe?'—even though what people believe is not really the ultimate religious question at all, and often (e.g. ancient Egypt, modern Polynesia) hardly even a primary one. (This is complicated by the confusion of using 'belief' also for the quite different 'faith'.) For certain reasons, of which the Greek influence on early Christian development and the massive Greek element in Western culture generally are the most important, theology has played and continues to play a quite dominant role in

Christianity; intellectual expression of the faith has by many been considered the chief expression. This is simply not the case with Islām. All careful students of Islām recognize the justice of Bergsträsser's statement that the decisive expression of the Islamic faith is the law.[9] So much is this the case that I would argue that in some ways one may suggest that law is to Islām as theology is to Christianity.[10]

Christian students are sometimes startled when they first discover that some major Muslim religious leaders have repudiated theology as an unworthy subject of study, a distraction or human vanity. To complete our equations, we might go on to say that theology (*ʿilm al-kalām*) is to Islām as philosophy of religion is to Christianity: a serious, often brilliant discipline for those who are concerned with it, useful as apologetics, but peripheral to the main development, dispensable, and even suspect.

Similarly with the obvious equation, mosque is to Islām as church is to Christianity. As a first approximation, certainly. But more carefully, the counterpart to the mosque is the chapel. The mosque is a conventicle more than it is an ecclesiastical institution. In the Christian case the basic distinction goes back historically, it would seem, to the distinction in Jewish religious life, incipient at the time of the rise of Christianity, between the cultic worship of the temple and the conventicle-type worship of what became the synagogue. The Christian church has elements of both. Islām, repudiating priesthood, has never known a temple-type cult, and therefore never a temple—except perhaps at al-Ḥaramayn (the term itself is illuminating: except in these two cities, mosques throughout the world are not technically consecrated buildings).

This point can be pursued further. The term 'church' has its meaning as a local church building, the focus of congregational life, only as a derived meaning. The primary meaning is the community of persons, in theory or aspiration the total community of Christians, and even in practice far transcending any local congregation: the Presbyterian Church, the Orthodox Church, and so on. A local 'church' building is a church (and not a chapel) only insofar as it has the formalized sanction of this wider community.

A Christian is a member of a church. A Muslim is not a member of a mosque. In fact, it has been said that there is no counterpart in Islām to the Christian church. In one sense this point is valid; in another, one may argue that in some ways, particularly with regard to the various Protestant 'churches' or denominations, the counterpart in Islām is the Ṣūfī brotherhood. With certain provisos we may suggest the tentative completion of our equation as follows: mosque is to Islām as chapel is to Christianity; *ṭarīqah* (with its *zāwiyah* or the like) is to Islām as church is to Christianity.

If there is any validity in this as a second degree of approximation (and I believe that it has certain sociological as well as theological justification), we must immediately recognize and even insist that this is still gross; further refinements would require a third and fourth approximation.[11] One of the conspicuous difficulties is that a Muslim does not need to be a member of a *ṭarīqah*, even though many are; in some ways, so far as structure is concerned (but obviously not in other ways) the parallel would have to be drawn with an organization such as Y.M.C.A., membership in which is supplementary and optional.

Worth exploring, I would suggest, in quite another realm would be the thought that the idea of *hudá* (guidance) is to Islām somewhat as that of the Holy Spirit is to Christianity. Muslims, not being very interested in theology, as we have remarked, have not much developed a doctrine of God's guidance, particularly His guidance of the Muslim community. In law, however, if not theology, the doctrine of *ijmāʿ* is one illustration of the conviction that God's active (and in some sense redemptive?) dealings with man are not confined to His erstwhile initiative in overt revelation. His mercy and grace in His moves to bring men to obedience and hence communion with Him, though climaxed historically in His sending the Qur'ān, are yet a continuing process.

Certainly the Christian concept of the Spirit has a closer parallel in Islām in the idea of God as *al-Hādī* (the guide) than in any idea associated with the word *rūḥ*.

This brings us on to another parallel which has long intrigued me. Provocative and far from fully congruent, certainly, it is one that it has seemed to me might tentatively be drawn in general between the Trinity in Christian thought and the 'ninety-nine names' of God in Islamic. The similarity is not so much in content as in the form of relationship. I once suggested such an analogy to a liberal Muslim, a scholar of literature with a London doctorate: the intensity of his shock and the swiftness of his repudiation were revealing, but, I felt, not convincing. The Muslim has such a traditional disdain for the Christian doctrine of the Trinity that he cannot easily consider the question as to whether Muslim attempts to deal with the relationship of God to His qualities bear any resemblance to Christian endeavours in this realm. Recently, however, I have found that a protracted and careful discussion of just such resemblances has in fact appeared.[12]

Certainly the splendid phrase 'They are not He nor are they other than He'[13] could be beautifully applied without modification to many modern conceptions of the second and third persons of the Trinity.

Another equation that is deceptively easy to proffer or to hold, but necessary and even easy also to puncture on investigation, is the glib supposition that Islām is to Christianity as Christianity is to Islām. This disregards history, which is far too imperious to be disregarded without cost. It is an immensely significant matter whether one religion precedes or follows another chronologically. Muslims have long been puzzled as well as offended by the fact that Christians reject Muḥammad and Islām with much more vehemence than do Muslims Christ and Christianity. Why can Christians not at least recognize Muḥammad as a genuine prophet, they ask. The real parallel, however, is to the vehemence with which Muslims reject Ghulām Aḥmad and the Qādīyānī Aḥmadīyah movement. It is easy to be patronizing of those whom one supersedes; Christians took the whole Jewish scriptures into their own Bible. It is not at all easy, on the other hand, to be complacent when a subsequent movement arises, *after* one has supposed that the religious question has been finally answered.

There are numerous other areas in which one could explore

questions of this kind, rescrutinizing accepted parallels and suggesting new and subtler ones. I will end with a bold and certainly provocative speculation, one that might offend both Christians and Muslims and elicit ridicule from students of comparative religion, which nonetheless I put forward, not because I necessarily believe it to be valid but because it has seemed interesting and potentially instructive. It raises in a particularly sharp form some of the implications and particularly the difficulties of this kind of work. I would put it in the form of a question: Is there any analogy between the significance for a Christian of the Eucharist and the significance for a Muslim of memorizing the Qur'ān?

On the whole I can well imagine that the answer to this question may probably be 'No'. Yet it is perhaps worth suggesting one or two considerations that could conceivably be advanced in favour of a possible positive answer; and, perhaps even more important, some considerations that suggest that the question perhaps cannot be answered at all. This last possibility is a basically significant point. The reasons that have led me to pose the question at all, even in my own mind, include first of all the analogy that I have already drawn above, and whose force has been vigorously born in upon me in subsequent discourse with both Muslims and Christians: that between the role of Christ and the role of the Qur'ān. These respectively are the points at which the Christian and Muslim find Divinity to have taken the initiative to 'come down' into our mundane world. The Qur'ān, in formal Muslim doctrine pre-existent and uncreated, is for the Muslim the one tangible thing within the natural realm that is supernatural, the point where the eternal has broken through into time. By Qur'ān one means, of course, not the 'ink and paper', but the content of the Qur'ān, its message, its words, ultimately its meaning.[14] The *ḥāfiẓ* (freely, the 'memorizer'; but more literally the 'apprehender') has in some sense appropriated this to himself, has interiorized it in a way that could conceivably suggest to a Christian some analogy with what happens when the Christian in the Communion Service appropriates to himself the body of Christ Who in his case is the mundane expression of God, the supernatural-natural, the embodiment of eternity in time.

At least one must note that the respect that the community has for the Muslim *ḥāfiẓ*, and the significance of the accomplishment for the *ḥāfiẓ* himself, are not simply a recognition of intellectual skill. To memorize the Qur'ān is of quite a different order from memorizing the *Muʿallaqāt*. By this act the Muslim is, as it were, taking the gift of God up off the book and paper in which it is enshrined and incorporating it within himself, so that it becomes for him contemporary and live and inalienably personal.

An interesting point in this matter, however, is not only whether or not the suggestion is valid or ridiculous, but rather the question: How could one possibly know? How is one to find out whether what a Christian experiences in Communion and what a Muslim experiences in *ḥifẓ* are comparable? One may ask Muslims, but they cannot readily tell because they do not know what the Christian Communion service is all about. One may ask Christians, but they do not know the significance of the Muslim rite (may we call it so?). Indeed, both groups are somewhat at a loss even to explain, let us say to a student of comparative religion, what their own experience means to themselves, let alone to assess an alien one. The religious man cannot expound to an outsider what a Communion Service or any such experience really signifies. The student of comparative religion is dealing not only with intangible things but with such profound and subtle and often ineffable intangibles that frequently his position is very precarious indeed. The signifcance of this inherent difficulty has seemed to me sufficiently interesting in itself to justify our raising this question, even though, as I have indicated above, I do not altogether believe that there is perhaps as much in the suggested analogy as seemed to me likely when I first thought of it. In any case I do feel that the question is worth pursuing; a careful investigation of the literature on both sides, illuminated though not superseded by personal discussions with both communities, might finally lead the sensitive and disciplined student of comparative religion to a position where he would be able to give some sort of qualified answer to the question that I have posed. Certainly, at the moment, I myself have not done enough research.

In conclusion, and summary, we may suggest that neither our similarities nor our differences are as great as might appear. My contention would be that all resemblances between elements of distinct religious traditions are analogies rather than likenesses, and that careful comparative studies can be much more fruitful if this is strictly recognized.

Indeed, one may wonder whether faith is not in the end so fundamentally personal a matter that something similar is true even within each tradition, among the persons (or anyway groups) who compose it. If one attempts to consider meaning rather than outward form (and otherwise one is hardly studying religion in a significant sense), then one must proceed with the utmost caution, and must be ready to look for help even in the most unlikely places.

14

Muslim–Christian Interrelations Historically: An Interpretation

The previous piece in this collection offered a comparison of Christian and Islamic outlooks on the world, analytically—in terms of particular elements in each, and their specific meanings for persons living their lives in their light. The present study, written some fifteen or more years later, essays such a comparison from a quite different perspective: the historical. Rather than considering constitutive items one by one, it looks at the two traditions globally, as neighbouring movements in the over-all history of humankind. It argues that in that wider view, the two may be seen as together constituting a larger complex, as distinct but correlated movements interacting in an on-going—and not yet completed!—development.

The implications of seeing things this way are no doubt major. Reasons for not seeing things this way, once it has been pointed out, are arbitrary?—or at least austerely traditional.

This thesis was first presented orally to the American Academy of Religion annual meeting in Chicago in 1974: and in revised form as given here it was published in the Festschrift (1977) for my former colleague at McGill and my predecessor at the Center for the Study of World Religions at Harvard, Professor R. H. L. Slater.

Muslim–Christian 'encounter'? 'relations'? 'interinvolvement'? For the past fourteen centuries a large part of the population of the world has been constituted of two major groups, called Christians and Muslims respectively. The interaction between these two groups has been and continues to be historically significant; also, theologically (on both sides). The purpose of this present essay is to propound a new framework for seeing the history of that relation more truly, understanding it more adequately; or at least, to wrestle with an attempt to forge such a construct; or at the very least, to suggest that the presuppositions with which we have tended in the past to view the mutual impingement are open to improvement.

It is offered in homage to Professor Slater, colleague and friend, as dealing, however inadequately, with issues in which he has been interested; and as touching on matters of which he will recognize the seriousness.

All will doubtless agree that the conceptual categories that we bring to the task determine in some measure our perception of the world. This is so perhaps especially of what has gone on in the historical process. Past and present developments are seen and interpreted within a context constituted by our foundational ideas. The matter is a two-way process, however. If we are intelligent, alert, and open, what we learn, though in part a function of what we presuppose, yet in turn modifies these basic conceptions. To study the history of religion is hardly serious if it does not continually induce a revision of one's deepest categories.

In the case of Islamic–Christian interrelation, one may suggest four basic ways of conceiving the matter:

(i) To say: 'Islām is a Christian heresy' is to formulate the situation in classical-Christian terms (e.g., John of Damascus);

(ii) To say: 'Jesus is an important member of a long line of prophets, beginning with Adam and culminating with Muḥammad' is to formulate it in classical-Islamic terms;

(iii) To say: 'Christianity is one religion, and Islām another' is to formulate it in classical nineteenth-century terms;

(iv) The most fruitful and responsible way to formulate the issue in the light of present-day knowledge and current sophisticated sensibilities, and particularly in terms of world history, the religious history of our race, is a question not yet answered. To it, I address this paper.

I will suggest that a proper elaboration of the fourth stance will include more of both the first and the second, of course in revised form, than the third was either able or willing to do. One may note, in passing, that there have been secular sub-developments of the first formulation; for example, Gibbon's dubbing of the so-called Muslim creed as an eternal truth and a necessary fiction; or modern Western scholarship's analysis of Islām as largely derivative historically. (This last might also include Jewish scholarship showing it as derivative from Judaica.) I will in a moment touch on a modern development of the second. And I will quite supersede the third by suggesting that we may better understand what has happened by discerning the history of the two movements as sub-facets of a transcending complex in which both have participated. But that is to anticipate.

I begin by making three points, which may seem at first irrelevant to the matter at hand; or at least, innocuous. Yet they may serve, by way of detour, to illustrate what is involved, in a neutral and instructive fashion.

The first has to do with Zarathushtra, and the ancient Iranian religious complex surrounding him. It is quite evident, so soon as one reflects on the point, that the role in the religious history of humankind of Zarathushtra and of his milieu is a very different matter from the development of what modern Western scholars, and now even some Pārsīs, called 'Zoroastrianism'. This last is a relatively small fact today and with a relatively narrow history. On the one hand it incorporates a great deal (some of it of much value, certainly of much significance) that does not derive from Zarathushtra. (Why should it?—only a highly particular position believes that the reality of any religion is, ought to be, the teaching of its so-called founder.) On the other hand, and more important for our present purposes, the 'influence' of Zarathushtra and ancient Īrān, if we may use that inadequate word 'influence', has in historical fact been prodigiously operative in religious movements outside the one that self-consciously crystallized around his memory. Notions of cosmic conflict dualism, Heaven and Hell, the Devil, angelology, and much else, which he did not necessarily originate but to which his inspired preaching contributed force, have played a role in Jewish, Christian, Islamic, and other movements, of massive proportions, across half the world. Not merely the impingement of these component ideas and orientations on a substantial phase of, for instance, Christian history, but their almost central significance during that phase, are now well known.

The point here is that modern awareness of the religious history of the world means that in understanding that history we cannot interpret it to ourselves in terms simply of erstwhile categories of thought (specifically, of disparate and independent entities called 'religions') constructed on the basis of radically less knowledge than is ours, both of data and of historical change. The history of several centuries of Christian religious life, we now know, was what it was, in substantial relation to the fact that ancient Iranian religious orientations were what they were. In other words, a true understanding of the religious history of either ancient Īrān or of the later Christian Church requires that each be understood in the context of both. The boundaries, in time and space and conceptually, that we used to erect around given systems, turn out to be postulates of doctrine rather than facts of history.

My first point, then, is that the role of Zarathushtra and ancient Īrān in world religious history radically transcends the history of the explicit Zarathushtrian or Pārsī community. I shall presently suggest that in somewhat comparable ways the roles of both Jesus and Muḥammad in world religious history radically transcend the boundaries of the Christian Church and the Islamic *ummah* respectively.

My second starting point concerns the concept 'Church History', which illustrates another important principle. An earlier position among Christians saw the Church as an entity not merely reified but reified divinely; and therefore an object of historical inquiry. It was envisaged as an idea in the mind of God and as injected as a corporeal reality into human history in the first century A.D. and having a tumultuous but essentially identifiable history since. I do not know how many of my readers will agree that the waning of this theological postulate has been followed by a waning of 'Church History' as a topic, as something distinct from general Western history. In the traditional seminary curriculum, it was a fact worthy of notice that a student could prepare for his (not often in those days, her) Church History examinations, so far as the mediaeval period was concerned, by studying general mediaeval history books, which gave excellent portrayals of Church developments; the seeing of these in context was helpful for their understanding, and such students did well on the exams. When they got into the modern period, however, one could not do that any more. Especially in the United States case I think it is beginning to be widely recognized, at least among younger intellectuals, that what is needed, even in order to understand Christian developments in that land, let alone in order to understand social and human developments, is a history of religion in America. Ecclesiastical history is in this case too narrow to be illuminating; even self-illuminating, we are finding. With the theological postulate gone, I suppose that Ph.D.'s in Church History will cease, within a measurable time, to be given?

Beyond this, however, is the fact that a history of the Church tended to take for granted the Church as a form; whereas the historian—not of the United States in this case, but of the classical Mediterranean world—must deal with the fact that Christians produced a Church, historically, and with the fact that Christian faith has apprehended the world in ways that, *inter alia*, have made a Church for them significant, holy. This is something that no other religious group on earth has done, at least not in quite the same fashion. There was a time when the idea of a Church, even the ideas of the Church, the form, the Sacraments, and all were held to be bequeathed; whereas now we recognize that historically they were constructed. What was bequeathed, if one likes, from Jesus—as, in comparable although not in the same fashion, from the Buddha—was an impetus, around which those who received it and responded to it creatively constructed, and have continued creatively to construct across many lands and across many centuries, a dynamic historical movement. Far from taking either the movement, or the forms in which it has creatively crystallized itself, for granted, the historian must take nothing for granted and must see it as his or her task to study and to interpret the emergence of those particular forms. Students, rather than taking the Church for granted and studying its history, should surely sit there gaping that there is a Christian Church at all, and has been now for twenty centuries. The history of the Christian Church is a sub-facet, albeit a fascinating one, of the history of religion in the Western world.

There is, of course, the further point that until recently Protestant Church histories tended to omit, or at least to underplay, Roman Catholic developments since Trent (of course!), while for Catholics the history of the Church has (equally 'of course') been the history of what others call the Roman Catholic Church. Germane to our particular problem in this essay, also, is the transition—in recent memory—of a history of Protestant–Catholic relations, from a two-entity matter to something more complex but holistic. Would most not agree that a study of this relationship has moved from envisaging two bodies, essentially distinct but in some sort of interaction with each other across a boundary that was nonetheless still felt to separate them, towards a recognition that it has been a history, rather, of the Western Church as some sort of whole with two sub-sectors whose relations with each other were in principle no more important than, nor prior to, the development of both in relation to the rest of the society and the rest of the world?

Some have even been arguing lately, in persuasive Hegelian analysis, that the dialectic of religion and secularism in Western society is itself best seen as an integral development in which neither sector can begin to be understood separately or on its own terms. Several theologians as well as various secular sociologists have been moving towards this kind of view. Certainly an historian of the non-Western world can hardly fail to see Western secularism as a sub-facet of specifically Christian history; indeed, of specifically Western Christian history. It is a whimsy of mine that the first really penetrating history of Western secularism will be written by a *Religionsgeschichtler*. More gently: Where else in a modern Faculty of Arts is one likely to find a good course on the history and understanding of Western secularism, than in a Department of Religion?

The third preliminary issue that I would raise is that of so-called Christian–Jewish relations, in the historical dimension of this issue; or the post-Emancipation concept of a 'Judaeo–Christian' tradition. Most Christians are more familiar with the issues here, than with the comparable ones further East, such as those that might come under a rubric of Christian–Muslim relations. Much, of course, can be said on the Jewish–Christian matter; I wish to draw attention here to only one point, in itself by no means novel. The movement, in world religious history, that begins in Palestine in Old Testament times and moves into modern Western religious life, may be interpreted (so far as over-all schematic pattern is concerned) in any one of three major ways. A choice among these three interpretations is usually made on grounds of religious *a priori* more than of historical analysis. The options are to categorize this large sweep of developments in terms of:

(i) Ancient Israel up to the first century A.D. (or 'C.E.'), continued essentially by the history of the Jews since then; with the Christian movement as an offshoot from this;

(ii) Ancient Israel continued by the Christian Church, with the Jews from the first century A.D. onwards an offshoot or aberration (the orthodox Christian view);

(iii) Ancient Israel, followed by a bifurcation in the first century into two branches, each continuous with what went before but each, also, different from that and from each other.

My suggestion presently will be that the situation is more complex: that once one has taken serious note of the Eastern Church, Semitic-speaking, and especially once one has taken serious note of the Islamic fact, one may think rather of a trifurcation: East, West, and Centre.

This brings us, then, to our topic of consideration: the scope and significance of Christian–Muslim, or Muslim–Christian, relations (part of our problem is illustrated by the fact that something depends on how you state it: Christian–Muslim; or Muslim–

Christian; or again, Islamic–Christian, or Christian–Islamic; and so on).

As those who chance to know my previous writings will recall, I have more than once observed that what used to be thought of as a static and fixed entity called the religion of Islām gives way on careful inquiry to being seen as the on-going process of Islamic history, a divine–human complex in motion; and that even that, on fuller understanding, is recognized as not self-contained but as the Islamic strand in the religious history of humankind. Muslims, in their own way, have long known this last fact. The same, of course, is true in the Christian case. As we have just remarked, it is no longer tenable to interpret the Church as something whose form, whose idea, whose ideas, whose Sacraments, whose existence were bequeathed to it by Christ, were sent down from Heaven. It emerged, rather, as a movement—an enormous movement of the human spirit. It was constructed. Into it have gone components from Greece, from Rome, from Palestine, from the person of Jesus, from that of St. Paul, from paleolithic times (an example of this last is the practice of burial), from Zarathushtrian, from mediaeval Europe, and so on. So far as originality is concerned, on the other hand: there has been originality every morning.

Furthermore, every morning, into both the Islamic and the Christian movements, has gone some measure of transcendence; of grace; a divine component suffusing the human; or sustaining the human, or challenging it, or at least mingling with it. Both these movements, the Christian and the Islamic, have been *movements*: dynamic, ever-changing, reacting with new days, new centuries, new geographic and social and economic and philosophic and human contexts. That is: each of them has participated, every moment, in a larger context far transcending itself. (This context has been divine at one end, mundane, historical, social, at the other.)

The point to which I am working up, via these platitudes, is that each of these two movements has, for fourteen centuries now, participated in a larger context constituted in significant part by the other. For our present purposes, my thesis is that both Christian history and Islamic history are to be understood in significant part as each a sub-sector of a history of human religiousness that is in principle, of course, world-wide and history-long, but for our present purposes must be seen as at least a context of development that we may call Islamo–Christian history.

The Crusades have long been seen as an event in the history of the West, of Christendom. More recently, in striking ways, they have begun to be studied as an episode in Islamic history. No one, however, I will suggest, can in our day be thought to have an adequate grasp of the Crusades, especially as a happening in specifically religious history, unless he has apprehended them—and the Spanish Inquisition, their eventuating culmination—as a crisis emerging in the joint history of the Islamo–Christian complex.

To take another example, less painful. Western historians of thought used to be conscious of Christian scholasticism. They then moved on to a recognition of the 'influence' on that, of Arabic scholasticism; both Muslim and Jewish. (The word 'influence' here is in quotation marks, for I use the term somewhat disparagingly. 'Influence' is a concept derived from astrology, not from either natural science or the study of human history.) A third step is taken, a truer understanding attained, when one moves on from these first and second approximations to a truer historical apprehension. In this, one sees Islamic thought and Jewish and Christian, more or less in that order so far as beginnings go, participating historically in a Mediterranean movement of thought called scholasticism.

Another example is Scripture. Christians have had a Bible; Muslims a Qur'ān. In this case the chronological order is reversed from the scholastic case; those who atomize would say that the 'influence' in this case was the other way round. A better interpretation, I am suggesting, is that, when seen on a world scale, Jews, Christians, and Muslims may all be understood, and understood more tellingly, as participating historically in the religious phenomenon of Scripturalism—initiating their participation in the

Scripture movement at somewhat different stages in its dynamic development, with interesting and important differential results; but the phenomenon of Scripture in no one of the cases can be so fully and accurately understood as when apprehended in all. The concept and form 'written revelation' are historical.

Another example, into which I shall not go here (I have been writing a chapter on it in a book on which I am currently working) is the case of certain motifs in stories of self-denying piety depicting a person's turning his back on the material world to find salvation in a strongly ascetic spirituality. It is possible to demonstrate specific borrowings of popular tales which circulated in only superficially different forms in the various communities. Common throughout, and not only in these tales, is a certain fundamental ascetic orientation with a dualist world-view in which piety consisted in turning away from the mundane in renunciation towards a quite other world of spiritual reality and salvation. This mood of piety, emerging rather late in the history of civilization, was for many centuries remarkably widespread across the Eurasian land mass, and during those centuries Chinese, Indians, Near Easterners, and Europeans largely participated in it, in Buddhist, Hindū, Islamic, Jewish, and Christian ways. This orientation to the world gave way in due course to once again a more monistic, 'this worldly' orientation. Western Europe made this second transition somewhat earlier than did Eastern Europe, though both were Christian; and China earlier than India. Yet eventually all groups have indeed made it. A much more this-worldly chapter in religious history has begun, and we are now in the midst of it, both Muslims and Christians. The history of both our communities participates in that new phase.

Finally, let me touch on a matter near the core of each so-called religion: the idea of God. This idea has been more dominant, more central, in the Islamic case than in the Christian. Yet even the most Christophile or most Christocentric could hardly deny that the idea of God has been decisive for the Church. I should not wish to make the naïve mistake of confusing God with the idea of God. Nonetheless it would be difficult to deny that the idea of God has played a central role both in Islamic and in Christian history; and by this I mean in the spiritual life, the moral action, the community practice, and every other facet of both Muslim and Christian being. The theologian might wish to recognize the justice of this observation by saying that God has mediated Himself to Muslims and Christians through, *inter alia*, their idea of God. I myself will say this in a forthcoming work. Here I wish only to press this point: that the Christian idea of God, to take that instance, in its course over the centuries has been a part of the world history of the idea of God on earth, the historian can now see; Christians receiving from, contributing to, and participating in that total history.

A serious, sensitive study of the idea of God in human history has not yet been written; someday this will be a mighty work. Both Muslim and Western thinkers have tended to take the idea for granted. I say this despite the library of volumes discussing it as a problem. Even our Western irreligious have tended to suppose that the idea of God is 'of course' something that religious people will affect—whereas in the light of a global perspective we now know that this is by no means obvious. The idea of God is one particular religious form. It is one that has had in certain areas and over certain centuries enormous import, and is prodigiously and exquisitely interesting. In any case, it is something Muslims and Christians have shared in common; and the history of neither can be fully or adequately understood in isolation.

In fact, a time is perhaps coming when both Islamic and Christian history will be seen as sub-aspects of what is by all odds one of the world's greatest movements of the human spirit: the theist. Indeed, I hardly see how either a theist or an atheist could disagree with such a thesis.

There is neither space, nor probably need, to develop this argument further. Clearly it could be elaborated in many directions. Conspicuous differences between Christian and Muslim on almost any point could be partly matched by in some fashion comparable differences within the Christian, and within the Muslim, communities. It is turning out to be the case that the comparative history of religion is a requisite perspective for seeing differences between centuries almost as much as between traditions. Let us move, however, to another level.

For some might respond: This is all very well; yet surely you do not dispute the fact that after all, Christians have not been Muslims, and Muslims have not been Christians. Now oddly enough, I do dispute this so-called fact; or rather, I suggest that the historian has a good deal less evidence for this view than the theologian has had conviction. And indeed, I will even suggest that the *modern* theologian maintains the traditional dichotomy more from momentum than from considered theoretical analysis. The *history* of the two movements may indeed be discerned in terms of a transcending historical complex in which both have participated, each in its own fashion. Nonetheless, the historian of *religion* should not, these objectors might hold, stress this historical level so much, to the neglect of the theological, where the dichotomy has surely been acute. My case will end, accordingly, with the contention that theology itself is moving to a point where the convergence is discernible, and may well become inescapable. It hardly behooves a Christian to discriminate too sharply between the historical and the theological level—if it indeed be in history that God acts.

Of course, the theological argument even minimally is more elaborate, subtle, comprehensive than is appropriate or possible here. Two or three volumes, rather, are in order; or two or three generations of sustained reflection, including collaborative reflections between the groups. The historical argument too would of course be massive, if pursued at any length; but in that case I have felt that mere suggestive indications might serve, whereas theology is not so open to mere titillation. Reserving more serious wrestling for other more voluminous occasions, however, let us here call on a few quips from, as it were, the outside to suggest that theologians as well as historians may or must find themselves engaged in new vistas. The quips constitute no argument. They are proffered as suggesting, rather, one or two directions along which an argument might conceivably go; or along which, at least, traditional reasons for not going may perhaps today be challenged.

For clarification, it is perhaps requisite to insist that I myself am not saying, nor even suggesting, that Christian theologians should adopt positions like those adumbrated in these various 'quips'. Some of the positions do not, moreover, represent my own theological views (as the wording, in certain cases, I trust makes clear). What I am saying is that in our day an alert theology ought to be able to give a reasoned judgement on issues such as these considerations raise. Linguistic analysts are asking of theologians much less trenchant questions.

That Christians have not been Muslims, Muslims not Christians, is less clear than one might suppose.

The figure of Christ is not missing in Islām. To be sure, it is presented and treated differently there from in the Christian Church. Yet the presentation and treatment of that figure have differed within Western Christian circles, too; from sect to sect and from century to century. We return here to my trifurcation theme: the branching out, into differentiated substreams, of the movement continuous with what went before in Palestine, and reacting in large part to the person of Jesus—East, West, and Centre. The 'Centre' movement from Palestine continued as the Jews. The other two emerged as the Christian movement. There was a period during which for a time this was in turn divided historically into three areas, roughly comparable in numbers and momentum, and geographically: (from left to right) Latin-speaking, Greek-speaking, and Semitic-speaking. The former two I lump together as having given us the present Church. The Eastern movement used to appear in one chapter in Church History textbooks under the heading 'The Oriental Heresies', a way of dismissing them. Yet of course each of the diverse developments regarded the others as heretical. Historically (and even nowadays theologically?) there is not much point in saying simply that the East was wrong, the West right. Each of the movements developed: dynamically, creatively, constructively. And each in its own way. The West constructed its metaphysical Christologies, which have proven vastly productive; the Semitic world never quite understood these (and the basically Greek categories in which they were articulated), and presently most of the religious movement memorializing Christ but thinking in Semitic languages adopted another metaphysical framework for its religious life which we call Islām. At this point, the Western Church said, they ceased to be Christian. Those who joined the new interpretation and formulation of ultimate truth held, however, that they now understood and honoured Jesus Christ better. Western Christians have never really paused to consider that view.

One might imagine, perhaps, a bold spirit posing some such question as this:

> It is conceivable (theoretically conceivable) that if Jesus came back to earth today, he might perhaps say, 'The Muslims have understood me better than have Christians'?

I leave the reader to ponder that. Worth pondering is, at least, how one would go about answering it. Until a century ago, Western Christians assumed that the Christological formulations of the Western Church were right. We now know that they were historical. (They were attempts to formulate in words—words expressing concepts then available to them or new ones that they could excogitate—what they saw and felt and interiorly knew.) Let me leave my above question aside and go on to ask rather a second and third question, as follows:

What could an objective, secular, historian say on the first question?

Indeed, what can an historian of religion say on it?

Let us consider a possible fourth question. If a choice between 'yes' and 'no' answers about Christians' and Muslims' interpretation of Christ can be made only on priorly articulated positions of faith, on particularist options, does this mean that for a modern man the questions, and especially the positions propounded, and particularly the choice between them, are inadequately conceived? As I argued in my *Questions of Religious Truth* on a comparable question ('Is the Qur'ān the word of God?' [*reproduced below, as the final item in this present collection*]), a strong case can be made that they probably are: the positions are inadequately formulated, and the choice is inadequately conceptualized. In particular, the either/or polarity is undue.

Let us try to answer our question for the historian of religion. And might one speculate whether this would be the answer of a modern sophisticated theologian as well? One possible *religionsgeschichtliche* answer could be imagined perhaps to be: The human person Jesus made an enormous impact on the imagination and spirit of many of those about him; around His memory, inspiration, example, teaching, impact, crystallized a mighty and continuing movement. In the Western Church, He became a symbol: of eternity, of the world, of oneself; of the relation of humankind to ultimacy (of God and man, and of God in man, and of man in God). And it is not even that He became such a symbol, as a full person, for that was not too well known; rather, a few stories about Him, legends, snatches of data—and a living impetus transmitted from generation to generation. At work, the historian of religion would maybe say, was also the continuing openness of men and women to transcendence.

In the Eastern world, the story was in some ways similar, in some ways different. There, too, his memory was cherished, his teaching honoured, his example idealized. A different religious and metaphysical construct was framed, however. Those affected formulated their vision, their experience, their awareness, in diverging ways. Into their articulations went fewer components from Greece and Rome, as one might expect; more from the Palestinian or Semitic heritage. The metaphysical and the humanist elements were less; the idea of God, and of moral imperatives, were emphasized more. After a few centuries a conceptual framework from Arabia, supplied by an Arab preacher named Muḥammad, was adopted. Within that new framework (not fully new; not so new as some have supposed) the populace—hundreds of millions of them—claimed and still claim to be following Jesus, but following him in devotion to God. Now it is true that by this move community between East and West was broken. (It was already precarious.) The Thirty Years' War in northern Europe, and current events in our own day in Northern Ireland, show that

Catholics and Protestants, for instance—each of whom claim to be followers of Christ—do not necessarily constitute a community, either; even though the historian call them both Christians. The recognition of a community of faith beyond differences of doctrinal formulation and other symbol sharing has yet to be achieved.

One possible thesis, then, that a certain type of history-of-religion observation might perhaps proffer, is the following. The subsequent ramifications in world history of the message of Zarathushtra and the religious orientations of ancient Īrān are to be traced outside as well as within the tradition that is explicitly called Zoroastrian or Pārsī. Who is to say that the movement stemming from Jesus (and before) is not to be traced as much outside the explicitly Christian Church as within?

The other way round, also. Western historians tend to hold that Islām as a religion began in the seventh century A.D. in Arabia. Muslims affirm that Islām started on the day of creation, if not before; that Abraham was a Muslim, Jesus was a Muslim. Not to understand (and even: not to accept?) these affirmations is not to understand Islām.

And in some sense, not to understand them is not to understand either Abraham or Jesus.

At the very least, not to understand and to accept them is not to understand Arabic. (And some historians would say: to suppose that Islām began in the seventh century is not to understand the fifth and the sixth centuries, in the Near East.)

Traditional Muslim theologians perhaps were inclined, like traditional Christian ones, to exclude outsiders; but a modern liberal Islamic thinker would doubtless agree, as the Ṣūfīs have classically done, that Christians, at their best, have been *muslim* in the true meaning of the term, devoting themselves to God in faith.

It would seem to me perhaps rewarding if those of us who are concerned—whether historically or theologically or in any other serious fashion—with these matters (or indeed with religious interrelations generally) would think out what our position would be, confronted with a thesis such as the following. For such a thesis could, not implausibly, be championed.

Christians throughout their history have been *muslim* (in the literal meaning of that term; they have consecrated themselves to God's will and truth) as best they have been able to discern how to be so; in the highest sense to which in the best light of their intellect and conscience they could rise. Muslims throughout theirs have been *Christian* (in the literal meaning of that; they have been followers and reverers of Christ) as best they have been able to discern how to be so; in the highest sense to which in the best light of *their* intellect and conscience they could rise. And if it be retorted that Muslims have not been Christian in the *true* sense of that word, or that Christians have not been *muslim* in the true sense of that, then a possible riposte might in turn be that also relatively few Christians have been Christian in the true sense, or Muslims muslim.

Less pointedly, the argument might be developed in terms of accepted goals, thus; and is in this form perhaps worth pondering. In the modern world many are not so sure, any longer, that the true meaning of following Christ actually or optimally or transcendently is explicitly known, nor the true meaning of committing oneself to God's will, yet both meanings are well worth our striving to find out; both are well worth our remaining or becoming involved in the process of loyally pursuing. In such process we must expect in part to differ, both from other members of our own group and from members of other groups. Yet we may and should respect their striving, their discerning, their process; and expect them to respect ours. This applies both to individuals and to groups. In the modern world, we are jointly involved in the quest for truth and righteousness; and in our groping response to all divine initiatives to illumine these.

This much, at least, in conclusion, is perhaps manifest: that a modern historiography, and even a modern theology, if either is to be at all sophisticated, must approach the question of Muslim–Christian relations in terms of a single complex of which the two parts are different, but not discrete; they are to be understood as elements of a dynamic whole.

The history of what have been called Muslim–Christian relations has never been written, nor so far even conceived, except by those who consciously or unconsciously have thought of themselves as outside one or other of these groups, or outside both of them; and this thinking has coloured their perception of what has gone on. A different—and I would submit, a truer—perception and formulation of that history will be the work of someone who sees him- or herself as within the total complex, and can present it therefore so. For every participant in that history has in fact been within the total complex; and his or her history has been what it has been in substantial part because of this transcending fact.

A history of Catholic–Protestant relations can be written by a thinker who is primarily a Catholic or a Protestant less adequately than by one who is first of all a Christian and who sees the interrelations of these two groups as a development within the total history of the Christian Church (or even, some might contend, by an outsider who sees them not as absolutely two but as two divergent yet interconnected facets of that one Church, evolving in a society of which one is oneself a member?). Just so, the historiography of the Islamic–Christian encounter will be moved to a new level when we have learned to see it as the intertwining destiny of human beings whose relation to God has for now fourteen centuries taken these two classes of forms.

The religious history of the world is the history of *us.* Some of us have been Muslims, some Christians. Our common history has been what it has been, in significant part because of this fact. Yet it is a common history for all that; and cannot be properly understood otherwise.

And if that be true of the past fourteen centuries, how much more so of the coming fourteen.

15

Muslim and Christian: Faith Convergence, Belief Divergence

My discovery that the verb āmana *in the Qur'ān is mistranslated by 'believe' (and its correlate noun,* īmān, *as 'belief') was exciting; its implications, drastic. I waited eight years before publishing the discovery, and before presenting it to a Muslim audience (above, pp. 110–134 of this collection). Waiting gave me the chance to work out carefully what had at first been a counterpart hunch, only, and on inquiry soon showed itself highly probable, yet only gradually became fully provable: namely, that in the Bible, also, the category of 'believing' was mistakenly read in by modern misunderstanding. In the interpreting of Christian life also, as of Islamic, belief, it turned out, had only recently usurped faith as the central motif. The thesis with regard to the Bible was set forth and documented with some precision in the Richard Lectures at the University of Virginia (published as my* Belief and History, *1976). The ramifications of these discoveries were major: for understanding the history and nature of religion on our planet (my* Faith and Belief, *1979); for theology, Christian and generic (*Towards a World Theology, *1981); and as I suggest in this presentation here, for interpreting Christian–Muslim relations in reference to God. The two communities diverge in belief, converge in faith: this I do not here argue, so much as elucidate.*

The investigation leading to the new understanding involved a study of the history, in the Western world, of the concept of believing. Some of this, especially for the English-language concept, I set forth in the second of my two Iqbal Memorial Lectures at the University of the Punjab, Lahore, in 1974. This followed immediately on my presentation, in the first of those lectures, of the thesis about faith and belief in the Qur'ān—the thesis already given, above, in this collection. Excerpts from the second exposition are given here; chiefly I here reproduce those parts of the argument that draw theological inferences from the new awareness. Originally, as shows through here also in the wording at places, I linked this closely with my analysis of the Qur'ān material. In this present collection, I have taken the liberty of separating the two, since the Qur'ān study takes its place naturally among expositions of other central Islamic concepts, whereas this inquiry fits decidedly with other essays on Muslim–Christian relations. Besides, in this case, the situation is on a comprehensive scale, for the whole book, what in that case in Lahore was true explicitly for my wrestling with the faith/belief question: namely, that the inquiry of an outside intellectual into the meaning of Islamic religious life is integral with his inquiry into the meaning of human life generically, his own included. An advance in comparative-religion consciousness, if true and deep, is an advance in self-consciousness, both personal and corporate.

It is modern Western civilization that has conspicuously held belief to be a basic religious category: has held believing to be what religious people characteristically do. In challenging this notion, therefore—in contending that the significant issue is decidedly not belief, but faith, which is drastically different—I am criticizing my own culture, which I feel in this matter as in some others has misled itself and mis-led others. In suggesting two days ago[1] that the concept 'believing' does not occur in the Qur'ān, and that it is a mistranslation in modern English to render any Qur'ān term so, I admitted that most English versions of the Qur'ān do in fact use the word. The reason is that it has become deeply embedded in modern English thought, in the religious field; and it is certainly going to be extremely difficult to extricate ourselves from the resultant confusion. I personally am hoping that the Qur'ān case and the Islamic instance generally may help us in the West to recognize the true situation in these matters more clearly. I trust that you will agree with me that the spiritual crisis of the modern world is such that we must learn from each other, and help each other, in attempting to cope with it.

Not that Christians should need to look outside their own tradition to realize their recent aberration. For them also, faith has been the crucial issue. This was true originally; and it was true for the classical and the mediaeval Church, and for the Reformation. It is only in modern times that Christendom has tended to lose sight of this; as we shall see.

I discern three reasons why 'believing' has come to be thought of—in my view, wrongly—as central to religious faith in modern Western thought. One, you Muslims share with us: namely, the contemporary situation of the world; including especially religious pluralism, but including also the powerful thrust of scientific thought and the powerful array of competing ideologies. The second matter is the special, and indeed rather peculiar, position of theology in Christian life. In the Islamic complex, it is the *sharīʿah* that holds pride of place: I think that you have never given to *kalām* the same prominence that you have given to *fiqh*, nor that Christians have given to theology. This has to do in part with the massive influence of Greek thought on the Christian Church, for good and ill.

These two issues have received much notice from Western thinkers. My third matter is one to which little attention has been paid: namely the history of the word 'believe' in the English language. (There is a comparable, although perhaps less decisive, history of counterpart concepts in other Western languages; but I shall leave them aside.) I intend to concentrate on this language matter in this present lecture. So far as I know, I am the first person to give this issue the importance and attention and interpretation that I feel that it must have, and to which my recent studies have astonishingly led me. It is my conviction that the word and concept 'believe' have radically changed their meaning over the centuries; to the enormous confusion of modern religious thought.

No one language in Christian life has played the role that Arabic has in Islamic life; and a history of Christian concepts of faith would involve a whole series of languages, notably Hebrew, Greek, Latin, plus at the very least German, French, and English. Obviously, in this lecture it would be neither appropriate nor feasible even to touch on these. Personally I have become convinced that it is possible, and requisite, to do with the Bible, both Old and New Testaments, the kind of thing that I attempted before you this week with the Qur'ān. Some day I plan to publish an argument that it is a mistranslation to render anything in the Bible by the modern words 'belief' or 'believe'—although the suggestion will certainly stir up controversy. This would not directly interest most of you, however. What I have chosen to do instead, and what I hope may prove of interest, is to show how the classical situation has shifted in modern times so that the notion of faith has become watered down and distorted into the notion of believing.

I begin, then, where two other presentations, if I were to give them, would leave off: namely, with the position that the Bible, like the Qu'rān, and the early Christian Church, like the classical Muslim community, set forth a particular view of the world and then designated within it the decisive quality of faith—as an orientation and commitment of the person, conceived and articulated in terms of that over-all view. I am not here concerned with whether their total understanding and interpretation of the universe were right or wrong; all that I am saying is that, given that particular vision, they defined within it, and in terms of it, both faith and infidelity, both acceptance and non-acceptance.

By the way, I may remark in passing that it is no small achievement to generate a world-view, a comprehensive conceptual system, which gives order to man's perception of the universe and within which man's destiny may be discerned and discussed. Nonetheless it is that destiny, and not that world-view, that is and always has been crucial.

It can be shown, for instance—I think, beyond question—that the Latin term *credo* did not mean 'I believe' until at least the eighteenth century, and probably the nineteenth. Spokesmen for the Christian Church held that God is, that he has acted in Christ, and so on; and they then expounded the act of faith, as they called it, in terms of a personal engagement, a recognition or encounter, a pledging of allegiance, in relation to these matters. There was a time when the declaration of faith in God, *credo*, meant, and was heard as meaning: Given the reality of God, as a fact of the universe, I hereby proclaim that I align my life accordingly; I hereby give to Him my heart and soul. It has come to mean, with belief as now the issue, rather something of this sort: Given the uncertainty about God, as a fact of modern life, a particular person proclaims that the idea of God is part of the furniture of his mind. The difference is drastic.

It could be illustrated, I suppose, if you will allow me this liberty, by returning to our material of the last lecture. Would the difference not be dramatic, even shocking, between the classical *shahādah* on the one hand, and on the other hand a modern formula that instead might run something like:

aẓunnu an lā ilāha illā-llāh, wa-aẓunna anna Muḥammadan rasūlu-llāh.

Or in Urdū: the difference between

Khudā par īmān lātā hūṇ

and:

Sochtā hūṇ kih Khudā hay.

Let us look then, at the process by which 'believe', in English, has come to mean *ẓanna*, *sochnā*.

Things change. By now, most of us have become accustomed to the fact that all here on earth is in transition. The continents drift back and forth across the oceans, their mountain ranges—which look so solid and firm—in fact rising and falling. The Great Bear did not point to a Pole Star in the northern sky for the classical Greeks as it does for us. Social institutions, although not always in such rapid flux as at present, have, we now know, constantly been being transformed.

Languages, too, have histories; and words change their meanings with the centuries, some more than others. 'Manufactured' used to mean 'made by hand'; and 'villain' was once simply 'rustic'. And so on. Most such changes are merely quaint and of passing interest: they matter little. A major shift in the meaning of the English word 'believe', however, not only has, I find, occurred over the centuries, as can be demonstrated, but also has proven of massive consequence and fateful significance, I shall argue—so deeply embedded is the term in Christian usage, and so central has it remained, until today.

Let us begin with etymology. Literally, and originally, 'to believe' means 'to hold dear'; virtually, to love. This fact—and it is a hard, brute, fact—provides the force and substance of my entire thesis. Let me emphasize it, reiterate it. Let me ask you to remember it, throughout the remainder of this lecture and even, if you will allow me to plead, throughout the remainder of your life. Literally, and originally, 'to believe' means 'to hold dear'.

This is what its German equivalent *belieben* still means today. *Die beliebteste Zigarette* in an advertisement signifies quite simply the favourite among cigarettes; the most popular cigarette; the most prized. Similarly the adjective *lieb* is 'dear, beloved' (*mein lieber Freund* is 'my dear friend'). *Die Liebe* is the ordinary German noun for 'love'; and *lieben* is the verb 'to love' (*ich liebe dich*: 'I love you'). *Belieben*, then, is to treat as *lieb*, to consider lovely, to like, to wish for, to choose. This root survives in English in the modern-archaic 'lief', as in Tennyson's poem *Morte d'Arthur*: 'As thou art lief and dear'—that is, beloved, *maḥbūb*. One finds it, too, in quaint phrases such as: 'I would as lief die as betray my honour'.

This same root shows in Latin, as in *libet*, 'it pleases'; in the Latin phrase used in English, *ad lib.* (for *ad libitum*): 'as one likes; at pleasure'; and in the noun *libido*, 'pleasure', projected into modern usage by the Freudians. *Libet* and *libido* are also found, although less commonly, in the forms *lubet* and *lubido*.

[*This lecture proceeded with brief remarks on other etymological cognates, Sanskrit, Old High German, Old English, illustratively, and then proffered examples of usage from Middle English and early modern. This material has since been enlarged through more elaborate investigations, including a close study of Biblical usage somewhat paralleling the Qur'ān inquiry just presented, and the results have been or are being published in two books:* Belief and History, *Charlottesville: University Press of Virginia, 1976, chapters 2 and 3, and* Faith and Belief, *Princeton: Princeton University Press, 1979, chapters 5 and 6. We give here only two brief extracts from the remainder of the original lecture, exemplifying the treatment. The first refers to an anonymous mediaeval preacher.*]

The earliest recorded use, according to the Oxford English Dictionary, of the word 'belief' is in a homily from the late twelfth century, where it is averred that Christian men should not set their hearts, we might say, on worldly goods. The phrasing is '. . . should not set their belief' on them. There is no suggestion here that Christians should regard the material world as unreal, illusory; should not believe in it, in that modern sense. On the contrary, it is implied that the mundane is concrete enough, but is not worth esteeming, should not become beloved. One is certainly expected to give it intellectual recognition, but should not give it one's allegiance, nor award to it one's reliance—and thus, one's soul. The question is not about what exists: rather, about what is to be one's attitude and orientation to what exists. (This is exactly as we saw in the Qur'ān case.)

It is assumed here that both God and the world exist. At issue is, which gets one's allegiance.

Two contrasts are set up in this passage. First, one should set one's heart, one's *bileafe*, not on temporal possessions 'but on God alone'. Secondly, the Christian, who holds not the world dear but God, is contrasted in the next sentence, in fact the next word, with the *zitsere*, which means: the covetous, the greedy, and this is followed by the phrase: 'who sets his mind on his goods'. The person who does this is said to be the devil's child. Thus the opposite of 'believing in God' here is not not believing; it is thinking about, thinking highly of, material possessions and therefore being the child of the devil.

Now this is illuminating, if we consider it carefully. The preacher says that a Christian should set his heart on God, and that the person who sets his heart on things of this world is a child of the devil. This being so, we today would say that that preacher believed in the devil. In our modern sense of the word, undoubtedly he did believe in the devil; but in his sense of the word it would be an insult and a libel to say this of him. He recognized the existence of the devil, right enough; but the whole point of his homily was that one should, partly for that very reason, *belieb*—that is: hold dear, love, give one's heart to—God alone. If he heard you speak of believing in both God and the devil simultaneously, he would think that you were mad—schizophrenic. To him, God and the devil were obviously both there: but you have to choose between them in your behaviour. The question of interest was: to which do you give your allegiance.

The situation here is once again like the Islamic instance at which we looked last time. What we would call believing in God, and what we would call believing in the devil, are both presupposed, *both* in the case of a good Christian whose commitment is to the Divine, and in that of the covetous man whose heart is set on this world. Belief in the modern sense of the term is simply not at issue. In this sermon the word *bileafe* serves to designate what we call faith, and what he in effect called loving, cherishing, holding dear.

Now a further refinement is instructive. When that mediaeval preacher says that the covetous or greedy man is a child of the devil, we can understand him perfectly well, and even be said to agree with him—even if we ourselves do not believe in a devil. This is quite curious, if you reflect upon it. In this instance we readily enough, and cheerfully enough, recognize his intellectual framework, his theoretical pre-suppositions; and we are ready enough cheerfully to move quickly beyond them, and in a sense to dismiss them, in order to deal with the substantive point that he was making. We do not allow the fact that our conceptual system is different from his, to stand in the way of our sensing and coping with his position. On the other side of these matters, on the other hand, most moderns are unwilling or unable to do as much with the mediaeval notion of positive faith. They can see that faith went beyond, and still goes beyond, belief; but insist that nonetheless it included it, and somehow must include it.

A belief in the devil is not necessary to a recognition of greed as devilish. Yet a belief in God is thought to be required for a recognition of faith as divine.

I trust that that is not too poetic for you.

[*Our second excerpt here begins with the final portion of a presentation of the late mediaeval Church reformer Wycliffe, whose use of the term elsewhere was discussed, and then the lecture proceeded, and concluded, as follows:*]

Again, from Wycliffe, here is a passage where the notion is clearly one of obedience, along with what in modern terms would be called disbelief at the theoretical level. It describes a situation where one follows, and patterns one's behaviour upon, here under force, what one explicitly rejects with one's mind. 'They made us beleue', he writes, 'a false law'. Obviously no one can compel us to believe, in the twentieth-century sense of the word, what we deem to be a false proposition; this would be meaningless. We can be compelled to serve, however, to act in terms of, what we regard as a wrong injunction.

In the same fashion Wycliffe used 'belief' for 'obeying' when in his translation of the New Testament into English he rendered Acts 26:19 ('I was not disobedient to the heavenly vision') as: 'I was not unbileefful unto heuenly visioun'—that is, I did not fail to act out in practice what I saw to be God's will for me.[2]

The two versions of Wycliffe's translation into English of the Bible illustrate, however, a shift that was beginning to take place. In the earlier one he uses *bilefe*, but in the later this is replaced at many points by the new word 'faith', which was then just beginning to come into use as the English form of Latin *fides*, through the French. The transition is described in the *Oxford Dictionary* as follows:

'*Belief* was the earlier word for what is now commonly called *faith*. The latter originally meant in Eng[lish] (as in O[ld] French) ''loyalty to a person to whom one is bound by promise or duty, or to one's promise or duty itself,'' as in ''to keep faith, to break faith,'' and the derivatives *faithful*, *faithless*, in which there is no reference to ''belief''; i.e. ''faith'' was [equal to] fidelity, fealty. But the word *faith* being, through O[ld] F[rench] *fei*, *feith*, the etymological representative of the L[atin] *fides*, it began in the 14th C[entury] to be used to translate the latter, and in course of time almost superseded ''belief,'' esp. in theological language, leaving ''belief'' in great measure to the merely intellectual process or state in sense 2 [*sc.* below]. Thus ''belief in God'' no longer means as much as ''faith in God'' ' (and there then follows a reference to a nineteenth-century quotation). (*Oxford English Dictionary*, s.v.)

These developments can continue to be traced; we do not have the time to follow much further. Let me simply say that by 1611 this transition was virtually complete, so that in the King James version of the Bible of that year the word 'faith' occurs 233 times, the world 'belief', once.

That is, for the noun. There is, however, no verb in English connected with 'faith', as there is in Greek or Arabic. Therefore the translators kept 'believe' as a verb, meaning what it had meant before: to love, to hold dear, to cherish; and conceptually, to recognize. In a sense, my thesis today is simply that the time has come to complete the transition also with the verb. In the three and a half centuries since the Authorized Version, the word 'faith' has not altogether lost its original religious meaning, but the words 'believe' and 'belief' have. I am therefore suggesting that we drop 'belief/believe' as religious terms since they no longer refer to anything of spiritual importance. We have to rediscover what 'faith' means, and then to begin to talk about that; and as a verb, to discover what to have faith (to be faithful) means, and what to commit oneself means; to rediscover what 'believe' used to mean, in the Middle Ages, and as recently as 1611 in the English Bible.

It is fascinating to trace the further developments of the meaning of this verb, and to watch it making the transition from the older sense of having faith to the present-day sense of holding an opinion: from *īmān lānā* to *sochnā*. To trace this, however, would require a book, on which I am working, and not simply one lecture. In very brief summary let me say that the changes can be seen to have taken place most significantly, I find, in the seventeenth and early eighteenth centuries, with shifts in meaning of religious writing on the whole following a century or so behind the shifts in extra-ecclesiastical usage (the distinction between religious and secular is not so clear early on as it later became). Hobbes, Locke, and Hume are among the illuminating representatives of usage, and for the nineteenth century John Stuart Mill and John Henry Newman; though I have more work to do on all this.

There are at least three transitions that can be observed as gradually occurring: one towards the impersonal, and two towards the non-committal. The first has had to do with the object of the verb. That object begins by almost always being a person; it ends by almost always being a proposition. This signifies a shift from an interpersonal relation to a theoretical judgement: from an action of the self, in relation to other selves, to a condition of the mind. In between the two came an intermediate stage. Between believing a person (in the sense of trusting him, having faith in him) (I-Thou), and believing a proposition (in the sense of agreeing with its ideas intellectually) (eighteenth and nineteenth centuries), came a phase of believing a particular person's statement (in the sense of trusting that person to be honest and telling the truth) (seventeenth and eighteenth centuries). This still persists among some Roman Catholics.

The distinction between believing a person, and believing a proposition (the former in the sense of entrusting oneself to him, little or much) survived into the early years of this present century, in a differentiation between 'believing in' and 'believing that'. Indeed there are to be found a few apologists among whom this still, but rather ineffectively, survives.

The second transition that can be documented has been one in the form of the verb. It signifies a shift from existential to descriptive: from 'I believe' to 'he believes' or 'they believe'—the first involving self-engagement, commitment, the last simply reporting a fact. In Shakespeare, for instance, 'believe' can be shown to be one of his favourite verbs—the incidence of occurrence is statistically very high; and yet I find that the great majority of these are in the first person singular. Less common is the second person imperative: 'believe me', in the sense to 'trust me'; while it turns out that third-person usage is surprisingly rare.

The third transition that can be detected has been from believing what is true (like the Arabic word *taṣdīq*, which involves adding something to a true statement, by way of recognizing and acting upon it), towards utter neutrality, so that one may believe equally what is true, what is false, and what is uncertain. (*Āmana* is seldom used in relation to what is *bāṭil*; and there was a time when 'believe' was not, also.) On this last point, I have even come up with evidence strongly suggesting that this transition has continued in motion right into our own day, with momentum, so that in the middle and latter part of the twentieth century there is material to indicate that the words 'belief', 'believe' now carry for many speakers and writers, and probably for all in certain contexts, an implicit though perhaps unconscious preference for designating the holding of an opinion that is in fact false; or at the very least, dubious. Let us consider the three propositions:

(i) he recognizes that A is B;
(ii) he is of the opinion that A is B;
(iii) he imagines that A is B.

In the first case, the wording shows that he is right; in the last, that he is wrong; in the middle case, no stand is taken. Now I have discovered a tendency in English usage over the centuries for the word 'believe' to shift from number (i), where it began (once it got diverted from persons to propositions), through number (ii), before, during, and after the eighteenth century, towards number (iii), incipiently at the present time.

One of the differences between secular and religious people nowadays in the English-speaking world is that the word 'believe' means different things to each. Religious persons have participated in all these developments undoubtedly less than have secular persons. Yet unquestionably they have participated; and certainly have been influenced by them. Let me reiterate the three trends. The object of faith used to be a person (God and Christ in the Christian case: Muslims must remember that in Christian understanding God is personal); the object of believing has come to be an idea, a theory. Secondly, the act of faith used to be a decision, the taking of a step, of cosmic self-commitment; the state of believing has come to be a descriptive, if not passive, condition. Thirdly, the mood of faith used to involve one's relation to absolutes, to realities of surpassing grandeur and surety; the mood of believing involves one's relation to uncertainties, to matters of explicitly questionable validity.

The statement 'I believe in God' used to mean: 'God is there; and I hereby give my heart and soul to Him. He gave me existence; and I offer my life to be judged by Him, trusting His mercy'. Today the statement 'I believe in God' can be understood as meaning: 'Since there is a serious question as to whether God is there or not, I hereby declare that my opinion is in favour. I judge Him existent'. And insofar as a moral commitment or life behaviour is involved, it would add 'and I trust my judgement'.

It is sometimes said these days that faith in God, in the sense of surrender, trust, engagement, requires a prior belief in God. Might we not be inclined to turn this upside-down: without faith, it is impious to believe? Might one almost wonder whether someone would be willing to go beyond this and to say dramatically: if one does not have faith, belief is blasphemous; if one does have faith, belief is unimportant?

Actually, I myself would not be willing. It is dramatic, and suggestive; but I fear that it is not quite true. Beliefs are important; especially for those of us who are intellectuals, whose commitment is to the life of the mind, to the use of reason, to intellectual understanding of the world, including its religious life, including even faith.

Where, then, have we arrived, in the course of these two evenings? I have suggested three things: that for the classical Islamic outlook, and for the classical Christian outlook, the crucial question was that of faith; and that in modern Western culture, attention has been shifting from that to the quite different question of belief. I personally hold that the ultimate, and urgent, and decisive, human question still is faith, in the sense of a total, personal, positive relationship to *al-Ḥaqq*; and that in comparison with this all other issues are secondary. Nonetheless, the recent Western emphasis on belief, although it may be misplaced, and dislocative, yet is hardly either fortuitous or silly. We have traced the shift of attention from faith to belief (in English, from 'believing' in the classical sense to 'believing' in the modern sense); but we have not yet explained it. I suggest, in conclusion, that an explanation emerges from the very matter that we have uncovered: namely, that classically, religious beliefs used to be not emphasized but presupposed.

The religious crisis of the modern world has arisen in that presuppositions, which had been virtually unconscious, or at least had been accepted as manifest and stable, were raised to the level of consciousness. Or perhaps we should speak not of levels, up or down, but of horizontal distance from the perceiving self; should speak not of raising ideas or patterns of ideas to consciousness, nor even, maybe better, of lowering them to such a level, but rather of objectifying them and removing them to a distance: the transforming transition in the realm of religion from consciousness to self-consciousness.

The Islamic and the Christian world-views used to be the conceptual frameworks, the intellectual systems, patterns, within which thinking was carried on, and within which faith and infidelity were conceived and articulated. These coherent systems of ideas had been not something at which men looked, but through which they looked—at the world, at themselves, at their neighbours. Or, changing the metaphor, and speaking of Western Christendom, may we not assert the following: that what had been taken for granted, and had formed the basis for the superstructure on which our particular drama was mounted, was brought out into the open, for critical intellectual scrutiny, and therefore could no longer serve as presuppositional base on which our faith, and our whole religious and indeed social life, could rest. When that happened, we unwittingly shifted our categories. (And that 'unwittingly' is crucial.) We diverted our attention from the meaningful question of faith (the question of what one does, given the symbol-system) to the modern question of belief (the question of whether to have that particular symbol-system or not).

For a time we took the two questions to be synonymous. This meant that many ostensibly religious men urged that it was important to say 'yes' to the belief question; and many critically thinking men, that it was important to say 'no' to the faith question. Both were wrong. The confusing of the two questions was our undoing—substantially before, but conspicuously since, even religious men have been finding that when it comes down to it they do not, in fact, believe the erstwhile presuppositions. Fortunately, however—though it may prove painful—the synonymity can no longer be maintained. I would suggest that, rather, a sophisticated modern position is to recognize the presuppositions as, classically, presuppositions, now seen to have been obtaining on earth in a great variety of forms, and to recognize, modernly, the symbol-systems as symbol-systems—with the significant question having always been, as it is still today, what one does within the symbol-system of one's choice, what responses one makes in terms of it.

It has always been significant, what symbol-system one chose; and will continue to be. Yet the central religious question has always been not that, but another; the final religious category, as the Qur'ān well illustrates, and as the Church once proclaimed, is the category of faith, of response.

From this angle, might one not conclude by suggesting that the significant question for today, or at least for tomorrow, has become new. Not, for others, what do men believe; but rather, with what symbol-system do they choose to operate, and, given it, what does each do within it. And for ourselves: not what do we, or shall we, believe; but rather, with what symbol-system shall we operate, and now that we self-consciously know that it is that, so that we cannot naïvely presuppose it nor perhaps, for some, believe it, what does it mean to have faith in terms of a symbol-system that *qua* system is anthropogenic, and historical, although the life lived in terms of it may be, as it was designed that it should be, theocentric, and eternal.

Many of you may not wish to go so far; especially, for one's own beliefs. At the least, I suggest that this offers a significant key for an interpretation of other men's faith: the faith of those whose beliefs may differ from one's own. Let me close on that note, developing for a brief moment, for your criticism, a proposal concerning the faith of Muslims and Christians—whose beliefs, we know well, diverge, but whose faith, I suggest, may nonetheless be seen to converge more than one might imagine if one focussed on beliefs rather than on faith.

But first, let me return to the point where we began: with a reference to Iqbāl. It would be presumptuous of me to claim that he would have been interested in these considerations; although his concept of *mu'min* in his poetry has encouraged me along these lines. This much, however, I can affirm: that he did much to introduce me to Jalālu-d-Dīn Rūmī, by whom and by other Persian Ṣūfīs I have been profoundly influenced. The mystics, including Iqbāl though he was chary of the name, have taught me that all mundane forms can be pointers to the divine, and despite their diversity have served men as the channel through which their own encounter with the divine is mediated; that there are diverse forms for faith. Alas, I am no poet, but a plodding intellectual; yet perhaps the poet and the Ṣūfī would tolerate, even if not applaud, an intellectual's attempt to see beliefs also, conceptual systems, not as faith but as mediators of faith, forms and systems in terms of which our forefathers found their way to God—and indeed, more boldly, as forms and systems in terms of which God, Truth, *al-Ḥaqq*, found His way to the lives of men in divers communities. Belief has not been faith. But God has been able, and willing, to use beliefs—of more than one sort; but reasonable, sincere—as a matrix for men's faith, men's life in Himself.

I close, then, on a theological note, if you will allow me. In classical *kalām* the question was discussed as to whether one should say, *Ana mu'min, in shā' Allāh*, or whether it is proper to affirm, rather: *Ana mu'min, ḥaqqan* – 'I am a man of faith, if

God will', or: 'I am a man of faith, in truth'. On the one hand, the person who hopes that he has faith, but knows only that it is God who decides, and it is His grace, with human presumption ruled out. On the other hand, the one who proclaims in joy that he has indeed made his commitments, and he knows that God's mercy has received him. Like most theological problems, this one fascinates me. Not being an 'either/or' sort of person, I prefer to try to appreciate the issue; and I tell my students that their understanding of Islamic religious life will be rich only if they can feel the force, can feel deeply the mighty force, of both positions. Maybe you will wonder if I am taking too great advantage of my not having to choose.

However that may be, I have a novel solution to the problem (and its close Christian counterpart) to propose to this gathering as my final conclusion to these lectures. It is this: that I choose to affirm:

Ana mu'min, in shā' Allāh
Naḥnu mu'minūn, ḥaqqan.

So far as concerns my own personal case, I prefer diffidence and leave the issue in God's hands; but so far as concerns our two communities, Muslim and Christian, I affirm with conviction that corporately we both have faith. The systems in which we conceptualize our relation to God, formalize it, moralize it, differ; but that relation itself, I make bold to say, obtains in both cases, and is sure.

Our beliefs differ, and that is important. Yet it is not ultimately important; it is not what God Himself is finally interested in. The cosmic issue is faith. And faith, I submit, we both have. *Ana mu'minun in shā'a-llāhu*; *naḥnu mu'minūna ḥaqqan.* I am a man of faith, I hope that God will grant; we are people of faith, in very truth.

16

Is the Qur'ān the Word of God?

The concluding item in our collection presents the first of three addresses that together constituted my Taylor Lectures at Yale Divinity School for 1963. This was my first public appearance in the field of theology (as distinct from Islamics or comparative religion). I took the opportunity to ask the Christian audience to address seriously an Islamics question. My own answers, together with further questions with which a theologian comparatively aware must nowadays wrestle, were developed in the subsequent two talks; the three, with an additional lecture that was a critique of the then-faddish 'death-of-God' movement, were published as my Questions of Religious Truth, *1967. As usual, I did not publish this piece until I had tried it out also on a Muslim audience, which I had had an opportunity to do in India the following year. The response of both groups, surprised though each was by the unexpected exposition, encouraged me.*

One might speak rather of three constituencies: the Christian and the Islamic, as represented by the two respective audiences for this address, and (although usually I take this one tacitly for granted) the academic. I as an intellectual in the modern world have always as my primary obligation and final commitment my loyalty to truth—subject to test at the hands of my fellow intellectuals, who constitute, of course, the primary audience of every thesis proceeding out of a university. I have developed the view, however, and articulated it elsewhere at some length, that the arguments of a student of religion or of a particular religious or indeed any human community, should in principle be persuasive to other intellectuals, not only, but in addition also to intelligent and alert members of the group or groups about which he and she writes. This is especially important when the theses advanced are radical. (Also vice versa*: once this principle is absorbed, intellectual discoveries become indeed radical.)*

It seems perhaps appropriate that this volume should close with a question; and indeed, with a question on a matter of ultimate seriousness.

That God speaks, or has spoken, to man has long been a joyous proclamation or quiet assumption of religious faith; more recently, however, it has seemed less clear what such a conviction might mean. I propose that we can illuminate this matter by asking, Is the Qur'ān the word of God? This query, I suggest, is worth discussing, is a question that will repay thoughtful consideration for a moment.

By this I do not mean simply that a possible answer to it may be of some significance. Later on we shall spend a certain amount of time formulating some parts of an answer. I shall be presenting for reflection some arguments that may induce perhaps favourable consideration of that particular sort of reply. And I shall be propounding that in any case, any serviceable answer must be rather complex and subtle. Before we reach that stage, however, and whatever one may think of the particular road along which I shall suggest that an answer may be found, the question itself is interesting, and the types of answer that it usually gets. There is reward in pondering some of the matters that such a question involves in the modern world.

First of all, we must observe an arresting fact: that in the past, there have normally been two answers to this question—namely, 'yes', and 'no'. Each of these answers has tended to be clear and straightforward. Some people have given one, some people the other; but whichever it was, it has been given with confident assurance, and even with force. Indeed, for over thirteen centuries now, much of mankind has been divided, quite sharply, into two groups, between whom the boundary has been clear and at times the gulf deep: those who have held that the Qur'ān is the word of God, and those who have held that it is not. Now this, I submit, is a remarkably curious situation, once one pauses to reflect on it.

Let us elaborate a little on how curious it is.

The question, after all, is not a minor one. If a problem were peripheral to men's serious concerns, then there would be no harm, and little cause for comment, if it went unresolved even for centuries, as this one has. But this question—and others, of course, not unlike it; but this one will suffice to illustrate for us the issues that are involved—this question is manifestly a radically important one. Those who have answered it 'yes' have taken the answer passionately. They have been willing to die for it; and what is perhaps more important, if one remarks that people may be stirred to die for many roseate causes, they have been willing to live for it too, to order their lives in accord with it, day after day, year in, year out, generation after generation, patterning their behaviour and controlling their choices and selecting their goals, and to persist, firmly but quietly—against both opposition and distraction, against both attack and indifference—in taking it seriously.[1]

The other group, whose answer has been 'no', have in one sense shown no corresponding passion or fanfare. Yet their persistence has been hardly less steady; and the seriousness of their rejection, not really less. Their conviction has been just as firmly held that the answer is not only 'no', but is obviously 'no'—so obviously 'no' that the matter is not worth bothering about. The West's very indifference to the question is a measure of the profundity of its assurance. Westerners allowed centuries to pass without going around busily asking themselves whether the Qur'ān is the word of God, not because they did not have the time or were unconcerned, not because they thought that such issues did not matter (what could matter more?), but because at heart they took for granted that they knew very well what the answer was.

One may guess that this is still true today for many modern men and women.

Britain at the turn of this century was fairly persuaded that the Indian rope trick was a fake; but it was not totally sure, and was interested in finding out: eager to explore and willing to be convinced. On the Qur'ān, on the other hand, the 'no' as well as the 'yes' group has been certain of its position at a very deep level indeed.

The question, then, is not a minor one. Nor are the groups that have answered it this way or that. It is no small band of eccentrics that holds this book to be God's word; nor is the idea a passing fashion among some volatile crowd. Those who have held it are to be numbered in the many hundreds of millions. And as we have already remarked, it has continued to be held over wide parts of the world for century after changing century. Civilizations are not easy to construct, or to sustain; yet great civilizations have been raised on the basis of this conviction. Major cultures have sprung from it, winning the allegiance and inspiring the loyalty and shaping the dreams and eliciting the poetry of ages proud to bow before its manifest grandeur and, to them, limpid truth. A thousand years ago the world looked differently from how it looks today; partly, at that time Europe was an under-developed area, while the Islamic empires, of whose splendour a caricature has been preserved for our children in the Arabian Nights, were the centre of scientific achievement, of economic might, of military prowess, of artistic creativity—empires built and manned by those who not incidentally but centrally said 'yes' to the question that we are considering. On their 'yes' they built and held all their achievements.

Equally impressive, however, have been those who have said 'no'. They, too, are not negligible. They, too, are to be numbered in the hundreds or thousands of millions. They, too, have constructed great civilizations, have made great cultures dynamic. The outsider distorts his world if he fails to recognize what has been accomplished on earth by those inspired by the positive response. The Muslim distorts *his*, if he fails to appreciate the possibilities evidently open and beckoning to those who say 'no'.

By this one is not suggesting that the matter is irrelevant. Far from it. To be rejected almost out of hand is any thesis that religious matters are inconsequential in human history; much modern knowledge can be devoted to championing the opposite. The word of God is or ought to be humankind's crucial concern. And even the secular historian must reckon much more profoundly than has been his recent wont with man's religiousness and its massive expressions. Islamic history cannot begin to be understood if one fails to see it in its fundamentally Islamic quality. That is trite; but one may go on to say, perhaps a little more provocatively, that European history cannot really be understood either unless its underlying 'no' to the Islamic question is taken into account. At certain points this is obvious—Charles Martel at the battle of Poitiers; the Crusades; Lepanto; the siege of Vienna; and so on—but it is true also at many others. The only reason an historian can write the history of Europe without tracing throughout the fact of its resounding or tacit 'no' to our question is the simple reason that he takes that 'no' so utterly for granted, and presumes so unconsciously that his readers will take it for granted also. Few will dispute the contention that the history not only of the Muslim world but of Christendom would have been seriously different from what it has been, had our question been answered differently, on either side.

The two groups, then, have been numerous; prodigiously numerous. And they have been great; of monumental influence. They have also (and here we approach the heart of our problem) been intelligent. At least, they have included intelligent men and women; highly intelligent. There have been stupid and petty persons, no doubt, on both sides, and human history would have been different without them. Yet among those who said 'yes' to our question, and among those who said 'no' to it, there have been those of keen, indeed of superlative, intelligence. Each answer has been sustained by persons brilliant, wise, informed, careful, honest, critical, and sincere. It is sometimes said that people simply accept the religious beliefs with which they are brought up. Yet even if this were true of ninety-nine percent of a community, it would be in a sense quite defensible and hardly worth comment if the other one percent, the leaders whom the followers accept, are independent thinkers. And no historian can argue that it is true of a hundred percent—nor can any preacher, or parent, who know well enough that it is not so easy as such a scoffer suggests, to induce people to accept a truth that you not only have heard but have personally seen. There are blind believers, and there are blind non-believers; but both are logically, and actually, secondary to those whose 'yes', and to those whose 'no', to our question is reasoned and sincere.

Perhaps what I have been saying will sound platitudinous. We all know that people differ on religious questions, so why the fuss? This brings us to a further matter: that we human beings have not only given two opposite answers to this question, but we have also come to accept such a fact without disquiet. This is curious. The radical divergence might well make both groups more restless with their own answers than either has often thought it necessary to be. At the very least, there is an intellectual challenge: how is one to rationalize the divergence, to conceptualize it, to interpret it intelligibly? (We leave aside for the moment the theological and the moral implications; this intellectual problem sufficing us, just now.) Are our minds to be content to accept lying down the total divergence, unreconciled, on a major issue?

This acceptance, as a matter of fact, is a little more complicated than might appear. It does exist, on both sides. Yet on both sides, it appears on inquiry, there are certain tendencies towards qualifying it. This is not surprising, since to accept the dichotomy on the intellectual level, fully, is to set for oneself a quite serious theoretical problem; and it is easier, certainly more comfortable, to suppress or to evade such problems than to solve them. This can be done among the negative group, the non-Muslims, by not recognizing the intelligence to be found on the other side. If one does not know, or does not appreciate, this, then it becomes possible to dismiss the other position as 'superstition'—that is, as ideas that are held without any grounding in reason, and that are not a serious option for the enlightened.

This stand has, in fact, often been taken, either openly or surreptitiously, consciously and disdainfully or subtly and unawares.

On the Muslim side something similar occurs. There there is also a further, rather subtler rejection. Some Muslims seriously believe that the prophethood of Muḥammad—that is, the belief that the Qur'ān comes from God—is so rational and straightforward as to be self-evident; so that anyone who rejects it is obtuse or perverse, or both. This idea underlies a good deal of the bitter Muslim reaction to the Western academic study of Islamics. Another Muslim stand questions not the intelligence but the moral integrity of the 'no' group. It supposes that the non-Muslim recognizes the theoretical validity of the Qur'ān's being from God but that he nonetheless, for reasons best known to himself (or to God), chooses not to 'submit' to it, not to live in accord with its message. I have actually met Muslims who believe this; and who felt that this view paid the Christian the compliment of presuming that he was not so stupid or so spiritually insensitive or so discourteous as to be blind to the Qur'ān's authenticity, and accepted him as a strange character who chose not to live up to the vision that had been vouchsafed him. I sometimes wonder if this attitude, conscious or unconscious, on the part of Muslims is perhaps more widespread than one imagines.

However that may be, and however many persons there may be on either side who have not recognized the situation in its true starkness, my own position, quite firmly, is that one must accept, what is empirically the case, both intelligence and sincerity on both sides. A hidden disdain for the other party is a psychologically perhaps satisfying but morally reprehensible and intellectually untenable refuge. Our problem rests on facts, and must be dealt with as such. To the question, Is the Qur'ān the word of God? some persons, intelligent and sincere, say 'yes', and some, also intelligent, also sincere, say 'no'.

If we explore this matter somewhat further, an additional refinement becomes necessary—one of great importance. For in actual practice, though the answers have indeed been given, the question has not really been asked. By this I mean that the question, though it logically precedes the answers, historically follows them. It is presupposed, but not formulated. And indeed is not a religious Weltanschauung largely a matter of presuppositions? The professional task of academic comparative religionists is to intellectualize, if possible, what is going on in the religious life of the great communities of mankind. Our business is precisely to bring into the open in theoretical formulation the positions that persons of faith inwardly take, and particularly to bring into the open the questions to which their religious positions are the answer. In most cases, of course, this is a very much more exacting and subtle affair than in the present one. Sometimes it takes years of patient exploration, and great depths of sensitive understanding, to discern what those questions are. Yet even in the present case, where the question is quite straightforward and obvious, nonetheless in practice it has hardly ever been asked. This fact too can be illuminating.

In the Muslim world, you will not find, or would not have found for centuries gone by, a lecture announced for theologians carrying as its title the question with which we have begun this lecture. Nor do I know of any book in the Muslim world with this title. Muslims do not publicly ask, Is the Qur'ān the word of God. There are many books, and no doubt there have been many lectures, in which the answer (the affirmative answer) has been given. But there are not books, and have not been lectures, in which the question was asked; precisely because the answer was given, was known, was accepted. Perhaps it was not firmly accepted, and had to be argued, or explained, buttressed or confirmed. Hence the books. Hence the long debates among the theological schools, the long explanations and discriminations, the interpretations of meaning, the ferreting out of subtleties, the long history of theological discussion and conflict. Yet the whole discussion and debate, with all its ramifications, comes under the heading of answer, not under the heading of question.

Similarly in the West. Without looking into the matter, one may guess that it was probably novel that a lecture by a Christian minister in a Christian theological setting should bear the title, 'Is the Qur'ān the word of God?' as is the case with this lecture of mine. Again, the reason is the same: the question has not been asked, because the answer has been constant. One may suppose that anyone who undertook to go through previous Taylor Lecture series at Yale would find the answer 'no' to our question given many, many times; and certainly in other theological seminaries, and other activities of Christendom over the centuries, the answer 'no' has been reiterated endlessly. We said at the beginning that we would ask that this question be considered seriously; in asking this, it appears, one is asking not only something perhaps novel, but even something searching, something radical. Indeed, one of the profound movements of our time, of which the leaders of the Church are restlessly and uncomfortably aware, is that the Church, inchoately but disturbingly, is beginning to ask this kind of question, not rhetorically, but genuinely. It is beginning to ask it because it is beginning to feel, inchoately but disturbingly, that the long-standing answers may not be adequate; or at least that they are not self-evident.

The Muslim world, also, is moving into what may possibly become a profound crisis, too; in that it also is just beginning to ask this question, instead of being content only with answering it. Young people in Lahore and Cairo, labour leaders in Jakarta and Istanbul, are beginning to ask their religious thinkers, and beginning to ask themselves, 'Is the Qur'ān the word of God?' Answering this question has been the business of the Muslim world for over thirteen centuries. Asking it is a different matter altogether, haunting and ominous.

In fact, the question, Is the Qur'ān the word of God? insofar as it is a genuine question, is a threat—both to Christian and to Muslim theology, simultaneously and for the same reason.

A Christian theologian who asks it would be probably at least a heretic, if that category of thought were still in use. A Muslim who asked it publicly today might quite possibly be killed.

Before we explore this explosive matter, however—the dynamics of modernity; the transformation through which we are living, or on which at least we are embarked—there remains one major point about the past positions, the answers. Each side has tended to think of the other as prejudiced. If one removes the pejorative flavour of that accusation, there is a certain validity on both sides, in the technical sense that each position is in fact a 'pre-judgement', a coming to the problem with one's mind already made up. Muslims do not read the Qur'ān and conclude that it is divine; rather, they believe it to be divine, and then they read it. This makes a great deal of difference, and I urge upon Christian or secular students of the Qur'ān that if they wish to understand it as a religious document, they must approach it in this spirit. If an outsider picks up the book and goes through it even asking himself, What is there here that has led Muslims to suppose this from God? he will miss the reverberating impact. If, on the other hand, he picks up the book and asks himself, What would these sentences convey to me if I believed them to be God's word? then he can much more effectively understand what has been happening these many centuries in the Muslim world.

It is not only Christian theologians or missionaries, however, whose answer has been a taken-for-granted 'no'. The Western academic scholar, too, has not studied the Qur'ān, asking himself whether this be divine or human. He has presumed before he started that it was human, and he has studied it in that light. Some of the more sensitive outside scholars have remembered, as they studied, that *Muslims* believe this to be God's word; others have done not even that, one would judge from their writing; but virtually none of them, quite manifestly, has ever asked himself, Is God speaking to *me* in these words? I said just now that I doubt whether Christian ministers have in the past lectured to ministers under a title, 'Is the Qur'ān the word of God?' I am quite confident that no academic scholar in the West has ever lectured on this theme. For one may be sure that the question has never occurred to him to be needing asking. If you scrutinize the scholarly studies of such Western students of the Qur'ān as Jeffery, Richard Bell, Blachère, von Kremer, and the others, you will realize that such a possibility never once entered their minds. They did not conclude that the Qur'ān is the word of Muḥammad; they started with that view, which was never for a moment challenged. One of them, even, has formulated it in so many words (unwittingly, of course: he was simply dealing with the question of whether the text now available is historically reliable). He wrote: 'We hold the Ḳor'ān to be as surely Moḥammad's word, as the Moḥammadans hold it to be the word of God'.[2]

Both the 'yes' and the 'no' positions, then, are pre-convictions.

Secondly—and this is major—both positions work. Each has found a pragmatic justification. Those who adopt either position, and follow it through consistently, find their reward. Perhaps there is in the end no more cogent argument for any religious position, Christian or other, than that those who adopt it find that it authenticates itself. 'Our fathers have lived by it over the centuries, and it has proven itself to them; we have tried it ourselves, and we find that it is true.' Those who have held the Qur'ān to be the word of God have, by holding this, found that God does in fact speak to them through it. They have ordered their lives in accord with it, and have found that that pattern rewards them by bringing them into the divine presence. The Book promises to those who submit to its letter and spirit, guidance and boldness and inner peace and endurance in this world, and felicity in the next. We have no evidence on affairs in the next world, but so far as this world is concerned the promise, to those who believe, has in fact been redeemed. Islamic history, and the godliness of my personal Muslim friends, corroborate the Muslim's affirmative answer.

Equally striking, the outsider's negative answer is also self-authenticating. Western scholars, such as those that I have mentioned, and many others, approach the Qur'ān quite heedless of a possibility that it might be God's word; persuaded that its source was mundane, they look for that source in the psychology of Muḥammad, in the environment in which he lived, in the historical tradition that he inherited, in the socio-economic-cultural milieu of his hearers. They look for it, and they find it. They find it, because quite evidently it is there. Muslims may protest all they like that such scholars are dishonest; the fact is that they are human, and like all scholars they may and do make mistakes, and like all scholars they admit it, and yet essentially they have been motivated by intellectual integrity, by scientific method, by disinterested, disciplined inquiry. Where their hypotheses have failed to explain the facts, they have changed the hypotheses, or at least the next generation has. Not only does the method work; it has proven enormously fruitful. Western scholarship on the Qur'ān has uncovered a mass of material otherwise quite lost; has reconstructed an historical picture, has traced developments, has established interpretations, that are unassailable.

Those who hold the Qur'ān to be the word of God, have found that this conviction leads them to a knowledge of God. Those who hold it to be the word of Muḥammad, have found that this conviction leads them to a knowledge of Muḥammad. Each regards the other as blind. From what I have said, you will perhaps discern that in this matter I feel that in fact each is right.

So much for the past. In a schematically simplified way I have delineated the situation that has arisen over the centuries as men and women have adopted one or the other of two essentially dogmatic and contradictory answers to our question. I have hinted that at the present time in this matter, as in every other in which humankind is involved, change is beginning to be discernible. And for the future, I am prepared to speculate that something quite new in this realm both will and should develop—new not only in content but in form.

As we have remarked, in the past there have been essentially two answers to our question: namely, 'yes', and 'no'. These answers have been both personal, and social; but even in the personal case, they have tended to be not individualist, but in groups. A whole community has given one answer, and a whole community the other. The two groups have then lived in isolation from each other, in basic ignorance of each other. And such contact as there has been between the two has more often than not been conflict—suppressed, in rivalry and disdain, or overt, in war. From now on, one may devoutly hope that the violence at least, and presently the conflict and even the disdain, have been or may be left behind. And the isolation and ignorance are in process of departing, from both sides. Civilizations in the past lived insouciant of each other; this is no longer so, and clearly, for the future, we shall be living in 'one world'. We have become aware of each other, quite vividly; and are gradually becoming aware of each other at a cultural and even a theological level, so that our lives from now on are to be lived in a global society in which all of us are intermingling participants.

So far as our particular problem goes, this means that the days are surely over when we can be content with a situation in which some of us, either glibly or emphatically, give one, and others of us give another, of two stridently different answers to what has appeared to both of us to be a relatively straightforward, and certainly an important, question. At least, I for one am simply intellectually restless at so conspicuously irrational a dichotomy. As an intellectual, I feel challenged by the theoretical incoherence; I feel driven to strive for an answer that, if it has not yet attained universal validity, will at least have transcended the evident limitations of the dichotomized past.

Of course, another possible reaction to the discomfort of an intolerable contradiction is not on the intellectual level but on a practical: to seek a solution not by finding a new answer intellectually that will do justice to the facts of the present polarity, but by striving to create a new situation, in which the dichotomy will have been replaced by a uniformity. On the Muslim side, this moral response takes the form of missions. The Islamic has been one of the three or four[2a] great missionary movements on our planet. Throughout Islamic history there have been those unwilling to accept a world divided into those that answered 'yes' and those that answered 'no', who therefore set out to convert the others, so that all would say 'yes'. In the other direction, a counterpart is a possible debunking mission, aimed at discouraging any 'yes' answer. We may note that in the past this debunking has been common both to Western secularists and to Christians, the latter having taken for granted that to affirm Christ as the word of God 'of course' involves saying 'no' to the Qur'ān's being the word of God too.

We shall return to this point later; at the moment I would simply remark that it does not seem likely that the intellectual problem will be solved for us in this missionary way—in either direction: by changing the status quo so radically that the question will no longer arise.

I do not know how many will share my sense of an intellectualist imperative to construct a theoretical answer more comprehensive, coherent, and unifying than the traditional ones. Quite apart from that, anyway, there are certain contemporary historical considerations to which one must attend. These indicate that—whether we like it or not—new types of answer, new analyses of the question, are in fact being engendered. These considerations are directly related to the point that we have just made: that the isolation of the two groups is giving way to an intermingling, and the ignorance of each for the other is giving way to awareness.

I have argued that each of the two groups' answers does, in fact, work. This is true on its own premises, and within the confines of its own group. One may rephrase the situation more accurately, by saying that each *has* worked, for its own group, so long as the isolation of that group from the other has been maintained. Now that that isolation is disappearing, however, both the pragmatic and the theoretical justification of each answer is proving inadequate.

Let us take the 'no' answer first, as it has been worked out carefully by Western orientalist scholarship. That answer, we have said, has shown itself capable of accounting for all the facts about the Qur'ān—except the facts of the religious life of the Muslim community, the life that has developed since, among those who have said 'yes' to our question. Western scholarship on the Qur'ān has taken the Qur'ān as a seventh-century-Arabian document; and, as such, has analysed and explained it roundly. It has not much considered it, however, and has not much explained it, as an eighth- and a twelfth- and a twentieth-century document, as a continuingly contemporary and timeless book on which the faith of men of faith has been continuingly fed. It has studied it as a literary document, and has brilliantly understood it as a literary document. It has done little to understand it, or even to try to understand it, as a religious document: living, life-giving, the point at which the eternal not only is thought to, but for a devout Muslim actually does, break through into time, lifting him out of his historical environment and introducing him, not only in theory but in exuberant practice, to transcendence. How the Qur'ān came to be what it is, is one question, to which the Western sceptic has addressed himself. How the Qur'ān came to do what it has done, for believing Muslims across the centuries since, is another: the actual life-giving source of the religious life of the continuing community.

As this latter is becoming more known, as contact has grown with living Muslims as men of faith, as knowledge and insight have increased not only into the outward facts of Islamic history but into the inward life of those who have lived within that history as servants of a living and speaking God; so the awareness has come that the traditional Western answer explains only some of the phenomena. It is true insofar as it goes, but it has become increasingly evident that it does not go far enough.

We said above that scientific inquiry stands ever ready to modify its hypothesis; and as a matter of fact, the non-Muslim West has just begun to soften, even to withdraw, its 'no'. In a recent article, the professor of Arabic at Harvard, Sir Hamilton Gibb, doyen of Western Islamicists, explicitly states in passing: 'For myself, I unhesitatingly accept the term "Revelation" (in Arabic *tanzīl*, "sending down" or *waḥy*, "inner communication") as the description of Muḥammad's personal experience, although Islam, like the other monotheistic religions, is faced with the necessity of reinterpreting the no longer tenable mediaeval concepts of "revelation" '.[3]

Similarly, a Christian theologian like Kenneth Cragg, leading theorist of Protestant missions to Muslims, no longer responds to the Qur'ān by rejecting it theologically.[4] And it seems clear that the next generation of scholars, without accepting the traditional Muslim answer, will go beyond the traditional non-Muslim one. What answer they will give is not yet evident, not even to them; so that it is not too fanciful to suggest that the non-Muslim observer of Islām is for the first time engaged in asking the question that we are discussing. He is in the midst of a search, and will soon be increasingly self-consciously in the midst of a search, for a new type of answer: neither a simple 'yes' nor a simple 'no' but some *tertium quid*, more subtle, more complex, tentative, yet to be hammered out.

Similar considerations pertain for the Muslim world, for the group that has traditionally answered a straightforward 'yes'. This answer, too, has worked; it has proved richly rewarding, fruitful, creative. It has justified itself. Yet it too has worked within its own premises, and has justified itself within a community isolated in large part from others. Just as the 'no' answer has served satisfactorily to explain the Qur'ān itself, but not to explain the facts to which the 'yes' answer has given rise, so in reverse the 'yes' answer of the Muslims has served to cope with the Qu'rān itself, but it does not cope with the facts to which the 'no' answer has given rise. The Muslims' affirmative answer, or the elaborations of it that the community has developed, have been able to handle the matters that have arisen within the community. But in our day it has been proving itself incapable of handling the new historical data that Western scholarship on the Qur'ān, for example, has been not only uncovering but making available also to Muslims. The knowledge, the reconstructions, that sceptical historical criticism from abroad has purveyed, makes the traditional 'yes' answer, in its traditional form, inadequate.

Until now, the situation has been rather desperately complicated by political overtones: Western scholarship has been resisted, or decried, by Muslims as a tool of Western imperialism, as something deliberately calculated to undermine Muslims' faith; malicious, hopefully irrelevant. Yet even those who do not feel that Western imperialism is a horse too dead to be worth flogging any more, are not immune from a new emergence. For this non-Muslim scholarship is being taken up these days not only by the infidel West, but by Hindūs in India and Buddhists in Japan, and to some degree even by the new generation of Muslims themselves. Isolationism is going; in principle, it is gone. Like the rest of us, Muslims from now on are going to have to live their lives, even their religious lives, as participant members of a world community.

The historical facts that give sense to the proposition that the

Qur'ān is a mundane product, can no more be gainsaid by Muslims than can, by outside observers, the religious facts that give sense to the proposition that it is a divine word, a power of God unto salvation for those that believe.

One symbol of the end of isolation is the new collaborative academic centres that are being set up, in which Western scholars and Muslims work together toward understanding, so that every remark about Islām by a Westerner is consciously made in the presence of Muslims, and every remark about Islām by a Muslim is explicitly made in the presence of those who cannot give a simple 'yes' to our question.

And although much of the Muslim world is on the defensive against what seems to it the attacks and threats of outside theories, nonetheless the best minds and most honest spirits in that community are themselves sincerely searching for a new answer to our question, one that will do equal justice to the transcendent element in their tradition, and yet will at the same time be meaningful and persuasive to those whose horizon is global and whose historical understanding is realistic. As a modernist Pākistānī has shown in a revealing study,[5] the answers of acute minds in classical Islamic terms themselves to our question were not so simplistic as more recent conceptions would suggest. A Muslim friend told me once that his wife was startled to learn (from him) that the Qur'ān did not 'come down' to Muḥammad from heaven as a bound volume; another Muslim friend once told me that, for him, the Qur'ān was the word of God to Muḥammad just as *The Messiah* was 'revealed' to Handel who said of it that the heavens were opened to him and he heard this music and wrote it down.

In other words, the Muslim world also is beginning to be in search of an answer to our question more subtle, more realistic, more historical, more complex than the traditional 'yes or no'.

Significant in this new situation, where both traditional groups are setting out in search of a larger answer, is the fantastically potential novelty that, in the process, both groups are beginning to deliberate on each other's books.

Perhaps because I believe seriously in the unity of knowledge, and believe seriously in the unity of mankind, I rather imagine that the only answer to our question that will satisfy the non-Muslim and the only answer that will satisfy the Muslim will in coming years be identical. I am not unaware that this is a radical position, crucial for Christian theology and also for Islamic. That it is radical does not disturb me, since I am deeply persuaded that in the twentieth and twenty-first centuries the religious history of humankind will be taking a major new turn. We shall not go here into that rather elaborate and problematic matter. Yet that Christian theology must, and I think will, ponder this question, and hammer out some answer for itself, is both an illustration and a measure of the newness of not only Christian life, but of Muslim life as well. I cannot see how in principle any answer to our question can be truly adequate for a Christian unless it were also and simultaneously truly adequate for a Muslim; and yet if that be true, how profoundly novel the religious history of both our groups has become!

I do not mean that Christians and Muslims will cease to be different; but I do suggest that intellectually their understandings must converge, even if morally they choose to respond differently. Reactions to the universe, the existential religious response, may presumably continue to be a personal or group adventure. Theory, on the other hand, it is the business of those of us who are intellectuals to universalize.

I have elsewhere elaborated the thesis that the task of comparative religion is that of constructing statements that will be true in more than one tradition simultaneously. Even if one does not wish to follow me here, nonetheless the minimum fact that from now on Christian theologians will be professionally at work on a central issue of Islamic theology (and perhaps presently also *vice-versa*) will make it not only true, but vivid, that a new age in man's religious development is being ushered in.

(In passing, one may also let drop the suggestion that the dawning of this new age is relevant to the otherwise vexed question of the future of Christian missions. Also, of Muslim missions.)

We live, then, in a world where for all men a question such as that with which we began is becoming an open question, to which the answer is not known but has to be discovered; and where the question itself is no longer simple, but has to be understood.[6] One may at a minimum suggest that we do not yet know fully all the ways in which God has spoken, and speaks, to man.

Notes

NOTES TO CHAPTER ONE: ISLAMIC HISTORY AS A CONCEPT

1. Northrop Frye, *The Educated Imagination*, Toronto: Canadian Broadcasting Corporation, 1963 (The Massey Lectures, Second series), p. 24; Bloomington: Indiana University Press, 1964, p. 64.
2. The sort of thing that I had in mind when I composed this sentence has since been spelled out in detail in a brilliant article of Daniel Pipes, ' "This World is Political!!": the Islamic Revival of the Seventies', *Orbis: a Journal of World Affairs*, 24 (1980): 9–41.
3. This quotation is from one of my own (unpublished) lectures in General Education at Harvard.

NOTES TO CHAPTER TWO: THE SHAHĀDAH AS SYMBOLIC REPRESENTATION OF MUSLIM FAITH

1. [These three are what the West calls 'religious' movements. Since writing this, I have come to speak rather of five world missionary enterprises on our planet to date: the three here mentioned plus, more recently, the Marxist and the Western-secular. All five have been zealous to make converts around the world, and have succeeded on a considerable scale.]
2. [This idea, just touched on here, was many years later carefully elaborated in my Iqbal Lectures (below, pp. 110–134 and 265–281 of this collection), and more generically in my most recent large comparative study, *Faith and Belief*. I came to feel that the point is indeed 'basic in all religious life', of massive importance.]

NOTES TO CHAPTER THREE: THE HISTORICAL DEVELOPMENT IN ISLĀM OF THE CONCEPT OF ISLĀM AS AN HISTORICAL DEVELOPMENT

1. 'Is Islām the Name of a Religion?', delivered at Princeton University, January 1957. 'Should the Great Religions Have Names?', delivered at the University of Tehran and the American University at Cairo, February 1958. [These and this present study were subsequently developed into a

book, recently re-issued in a new edition in paperback: *The Meaning and End of Religion*, New York: Macmillan, 1963; New American Library, 1965; San Francisco: Harper & Row, and London: S.P.C.K., 1978.]

2. R. Brunschvig, 'Perspectives', in G. E. von Grunebaum, ed., *Unity and Variety in Muslim Civilization*, Chicago: University of Chicago Press, 1955, pp. 47 and 61; citing A. J. Wensinck from the article ṢALĀT, *Handwörterbuch des Islam*, Leiden: Brill, 1941 [actually, this article appeared first in 1925 in the first edn. of *The Encyclopaedia of Islam*].
3. In my studies noted in note 1 above.
4. Most notably Helmer Ringgren, *Islam, 'aslama, and Muslim*, Horae Soederblomianae (Travaux publiés par la société Nathan Söderblom), II, Uppsala, 1949 (Lund: C. W. J. Gleerup). See also the abstract of an as yet unpublished paper, D. H. Baneth, 'The original meaning of *islām* as a religious term; a renewal of a mediaeval interpretation' in *Proceedings of the Twenty-Third International Congress of Orientalists, Cambridge . . . 1954,* Denis Sinor, ed., London: Royal Asiatic Society, n.d. [*ca.* 1956?], pp. 305 f. Professor Baneth was kind enough to let me see the manuscript of the whole. James Robson, ' "Islām" as a Term', *The Muslim World*, 44 (1954): 101–109, adds nothing to Ringgren for the classical period. David Künstlinger, ' "Islām", "Muslim", "aslama" im Ḳurān', in *Rocznik Orjentalistyczny* 11 (1935): 128–137, should also be consulted.
5. [*A doctoral student at Harvard has since undertaken this study under my direction and the completed dissertation has now been published: Jane I. Smith*, An historical and semantic study of the term 'Islām' as seen in a sequence of Qur'ān commentaries, *Missoula, Montana: published by Scholars Press for Harvard Theological Review, 1975 (Harvard Dissertations in Religion, 1)*].
6. My study is based on the admirable concordance of Muḥammad Fu'ād ʿAbd al-Bāqī, *al-Muʿjam al-mufahras li-alfāẓ al-Qur'ān al-karīm*, Cairo: Dār al-Kutub al-Miṣrīyah, 1364 [*ca.* 1945]. [*For fuller discussion see my studies noted at note 1 above, especially chapter IV of the published work.*]
7. E.g., *wa-kafarū baʿda islāmihim,* 9:74.
8. I have also entered on cards all titles from that index in which the following terms appear: *islāmī*, *muslim*, *īmān*, *īmānī*, *mu'min*, *dīn*, *dīnī*, *adyān*, *diyānah*, *millah*, and in certain senses (those relating to religion) *niẓām*. Except for *islām* I have not yet studied the collections systematically.
9. I have no figure for how many of the approximately 25,000 titles in Brockelmann's index, from which this list is constructed, are of works before 1300 *hijrī*. A rough guess might put the number at 15,000 to 20,000.
10. Cf. above, note 8.

11. That is, 84 to 56.
12. In the Brockelmann index, for the present century *islām* occurs 52 times (our list B), *imān* four times. The entries in B not from Brockelmann are not here considered since they were compiled *ad hoc*.
13. It is interesting to reflect on how much more prominent a role in such a situation as modern Pakistan is played by the concept of *islām* than by the concept of *imān*. Might one suggest that perhaps a fundamental fallacy of the 'Islamic state' advocated was the assumption that Islām can be considered without giving attention to the question of *imān*?
14. Ibn Rajab al-Ḥanbalī, *Ghurbat al-islām*, ed. Aḥmad al-Sharbāṣī, Cairo: Dār al-Kitāb al-ʿArabi, 1373/1954, pp. 27–28.
15. Cf. below, note 20.
16. The work may be spurious (so Horovitz in *EI*, first edition, s.v. WĀḲIDĪ); that at least the title is not original is evident from his other titles as given in *Fihrist* s.v. or in Brockelmann.
17. Cf. S II 128/4b_2 with S II 119, last line.
18. Note 1 above.
19. In modern Bayrūtī dialect this has reached a point where *jīrunā islām* is colloquial for 'the people next door are Muslims'.
20. Three of the works require special mention. Muḥammad Kurd ʿAlī, in his prefatory remarks (p. 10) in his Damascus edition (1365/1946) of our A 11, Ẓahīr al-Dīn al-Bayhaqī's *Ta'rīkh ḥukamā' al-islām*, states that this title is recent, the original being *Tatimmat ṣiwān al-ḥikmah*. With regard to A 13 (sixth/twelfth century), al-Balawī's use of the title *Ādāb al-islām*, the wording of the Brockelmann citation implies that the phrase as well as the work itself is rather from the pen of the third/ninth century writer Abū ʿUbayd. The word *islām* here as a literary term is contrasted with *jāhilīyah*; Christian writers in the period after the Prophet would presumably be hospitably included. One may compare the fact that, apparently, the term *islāmī* is first used (Lane, s.v.) in literary rather than religious or even historical discussions in the same sense. With regard to A 15: Al Shayzarī's *Jamharat al-islām* is included here, although it is debatable whether this entry should rather (or also?) go with the group *ahl al-islām*, *millat al-islām*, already noted; see above, our text at note 15.
21. See A. K. S. Lambton, 'Quis Custodiet Custodes: Some Reflections on the Persian Theory of Government, I' in *Studia Islamica* 5 (1956): 129.
22. Since writing the above sentence, I am happy to find that apparently my prediction is indeed to be proven wrong; for my colleague Dr. Fazlu-r-Rahman is undertaking to write such a history. [*Since this study was first published, that history has appeared: Fazlur Rahman*, Islam, *London: Widenfeld & Nicolson, and New York: Holt, Rinehart and Winston, 1966, E. O. James, gen. ed., History of Religion Series.*]

23. Cf. my *Islam in Modern History*, Princeton: Princeton University Press, 1957 [1977], pp. 8–9, note 5, and in general Chapter I there [*and, subsequently my solution to the problem in* The Meaning and End of Religion, *my work cited in note 1 above*].
24. Brockelmann, S III 320, speaks of Hanotaux's article as in *Ta'rīḫ* II 382/95, and Muḥammad ʿAbduh's reply as 395/411. In the edition of Rashīd Riḍā, *Ta'rīkh al-ustādh al-imām* accessible to me—namely, the second, Cairo: al-Manār, 1344—the former is vol. 2, pp. 401–414, and the six answers of ʿAbduh are given pp. 415–468. The Hanotaux article is cited there as translated by Muḥammad Masʿūd (Bey), then one of the editors of *al-Mu'ayyad*, and published therein 1317 (= 1899–1900) as *Qad aṣbaḥnā al-yawm izā' al-islām wa-al-mas'alah al-islāmīyah*. The French original was phrased: *Face à face de l'Islam et la question musulmane*.
25. The title of the first Arabic edition (Cairo: al-Maṭbaʿah al-ʿUthmānīyah, 1316/ca. 1898) was *Taṭbīq al-diyānah al-islāmīyah ʿalá nawāmīs al-madanīyah* (Brockelmann, *loc. cit.*).
26. Worth investigating, perhaps, is the question as to why Wajdī translated the French 'Islam' by the Arabic *al-diyānah al-islāmīyah* in 1898 and by *islām* in 1904 (cf. preceding note).
27. Brockelmann, S III 184.
28. Cf. below, note 30.
29. Of entries 3 to 27 in list B, covering the modern period until 1910—twenty-five titles in all—four are by Christians (B 3, 23, 24, 25), at least three are translations (B 5, 9, 19), and five or six are addressed to or are answers to non-Mulims (B 4 [presented to a Stockholm congress—see its preface; it is presumably then also a translation], 14?, 15, 20, 21 [first written in Oxford and presented to an Orientalist conference in Algiers, according to the preface of the 2nd edn., p. 18; presumably then also a translation], 26). A more thorough study may show that still more should be included in this last group. For instance, Brockelmann characterizes the author of B 10, 11 as a great defender of Islām against Christian culture (S II 763); is the editor of B 6 perhaps a non-Muslim?—and so on.
30. The resultant outlook on Islām I have analysed in Chapter 3 ('The Arabs') of my recent *Islam in Modern History* (above, note 23). The present study has led me to wonder whether the process that resulted in that orientation is maybe to be looked for in the writings of the period here under consideration, as perhaps an important turning point. I would also wonder whether I should perhaps refine some of the interpretations. To take one example: the wide effectiveness is recognized of Jurjī Zaydān's *Ta'rīkh al-tamaddun al-islāmī*, 5 vols., Cairo: Maṭbaʿat al-Hilāl, 1902–1906, in popularizing among Arab Muslims their sense of past

cultural glory. One may ask whether the title of his book did not introduce into modern Arabic thought the concept 'Islamic civilization' as such. (I have not searched out whether al-Afghānī had used precisely this concept.) In my study I referred, of course, to this work (p. 54; cf. p. 94, note 2); but I treated Zaydān as almost peripheral to the modern Arab Muslim's developing religious consciousness, because of his not being a Muslim. As a result of my present investigation, however, I am forced to ask whether conceivably his not being a Muslim is not in itself of significance: whether rather than being peripheral, his contribution specificially as a non-Muslim may not be of prime consequence. For my argument went on to show that the modern Muslim's concept of Islām, exemplified in the case of Wajdī, comes close to the concept of a non-believer. Perhaps the non-Muslim has (unwittingly) played a more central role in the modern disintegration of Muslim religious thinking than we have recognized.

31. Brockelmann, S III 276.

NOTES TO CHAPTER FOUR: ISLAMIC LAW: ITS 'SOURCES' (*UṢŪL AL-FIQH*) AND *IJTIHĀD*

1. I use the term 'will' in English because in English (with its non-Muslim culture) no other word, I believe, conveys the meaning as adequately. In Islamic usage, however, the literal Arabic equivalent of 'will' is not here appropriate. Cf. below, pp. 237 f. of the present collection.
2. This is, in practice, though often not explicitly, the situation of certain individuals in all modern Muslim countries, who take their own stand on Islām independently of whatever the *ʿulamāʾ* may say. In a sense the Turkish nation as a group might also be said to fall within this category. Their *ijtihād* consists not only in a modification of the traditional *fiqh*, but in a rejection of it as a whole system, and an interpretation that what God requires of human society, at least for today, is a social order of a new kind—one in which the pursuit of justice is not dictated by a deduced logic from a *fiqh* system but by an induced and constructive deliberation from the facts as seen by a sensitive (viz. *mu'min*) conscience.

NOTES TO CHAPTER FIVE: ISLAMIC LAW: *SHARĪʿAH* AND *SHARʿ*

1. H. A. R. Gibb, *Mohammedanism: an historical survey*, London: Oxford University Press, 1949, p. 106.

2. G. Bergsträsser, *Grundzüge des islamischen Rechts*, bearbeitet und herausgegeben von Joseph Schacht, Berlin & Leipzig: de Gruyter, 1935, p. 1. Later in this present essay, it will become not without significance perhaps that actually Bergsträsser here is designating by *das Recht* not *al-sharīʿah*, but *al-fiqh*. *Fiqh* is originally a *maṣdar*, the subject of its verb being man (not God)—a point, we shall later see, of some consequence.
3. For example, in my *Islam in Modern History* (above, our chap. 3 here, note 23), especially Chapter I.
4. I here deliberately omit from consideration not only *fiqh* writing, another field altogether, but also *falsafah* and the thinking of other groups.
5. Text in the Ḥaydarābād edition: Dā'irat al-Maʿārif al-Niẓāmīyah, 1321 h. Cf. A. J. Wensinck, *The Muslim Creed: its genesis and historical development*, Cambridge: Cambridge University Press, 1932, Chapter VI.
6. My method, in this instance, has been to look up the originals of the relevant references in Albert N. Nader, *Le Système philosophique des Muʿtazila (premiers penseurs de l'Islam)*, Beyrouth: Lettres Orientales, 1956, especially I: I: iv: 4 (pp. 93–95) and II: II: ii (pp. 294–309), where this author attributes a concept of law to them.
7. Text in the Ḥaydarābād edition: Dā'irat al-Maʿārif al-Niẓāmīyah, 1321 h. Cf. Wensinck, *op. cit.*, chapter VII.
8. Texts as follows: *Maqālāt al-islāmīyīn*, ed. H. Ritter, 2 vols. Istanbul: Maṭbaʿat al-Dawlah, 1929–1930; *Risālah fī istiḥsān al-khawḍ*, Ḥaydarābād: Dā'irat al-Maʿārif al-Niẓāmīyah, 1323 h. These two were used for basic work; they were later supplemented in part, especially regarding indexes, etc., with *Kitāb al-lumaʿ*, ed. Richard J. McCarthy, Beyrouth: Imprimerie Catholique, 1953, and *Kitāb al-ibānah ʿan uṣūl al-diyānah*, Ḥaydarābād: Dā'irat al-Maʿārif al-Niẓāmīyah, 1321 h. For this last, cf. Walter C. Klein, trans., . . . *al-Ashʿarī's . . . Ibānah*, New Haven: American Oriental Society, 1940.
9. Text in the Ḥaydarābād edition: Dā'irat al-Maʿārif al-Niẓāmīyah, 1321 h.
10. Ibn Baṭṭah al-ʿUkbarī, *Kitāb al-sharḥ wa-al-ibānah ʿalá uṣūl al-sunnah wa-al-diyānah*, in Henri Laoust, *La Profession de foi d'Ibn Baṭṭa*. Damas: Institut Français de Damas, 1958.
11. Richard J. McCarthy, ed., Beyrouth: Imprimerie Catholique, 1957. Because of his apparently full *fihris al-iṣṭilāḥāt wa-al-kalimāt*, pp. 408–438, I have contented myself with those passages to which this index refers under *sharīʿah* and *sharīʿat Mūsá*, without checking the remainder of the text for this term.
12. *Risālat al-iʿtiqādāt al-imāmīyah*, by Abū Jaʿfar Muḥammad ibn ʿAlī ibn Bābawayh al-Qummī. Translated as Asaf A. A. Fyzee, *A Shīʿite Creed*, London: Oxford University Press, 1942, Islamic Research Association Series, no. 9.

13. Text in the Istanbul edition; Maṭbaʿat al-Dawlah, 1346/1928.
14. *El-Irchad*, par Imam el-Harameïn, éd. et trad. par J.-D. Luciani, Paris: Imprimerie Nationale (Librairie Ernest Leroux), 1938.
15. Abū Ḥāmid al-Ghazzālī, *Iḥyā' ʿulūm al-dīn*, Bk. 2, Sect. 1. I have used the Cairo edition of the Lajnat Nashr al-Thaqāfah al-Islāmiyah, Aḥmad Ibrāhīm al-Sarāwī, ed., 16 vols., 1356–1357.
16. Text used: edition of Muṣṭafá al-Qubbānī al-Dimashqī, Cairo: al-Maṭbaʿah al-Adabīyah, n.d.
17. I have used the text in the Shākir edition of Taftāzānī, see below, my note 20 here.
18. I have used the Badrān edition, Cairo, of *Kitāb al-milal wa-al-niḥal*. The same writer's *Nihāyat al-iqdām* is considered separately in Part II of this present essay, below (at note 49 ff.).
19. ʿAlī ibn Ḥanẓalah ibn Abī Sālim al-Wadāʿī, *Kitāb simṭ al-ḥaqā'iq*, ed. ʿAbbās al-ʿAzzāwī, Damas: Institut Français de Damas, 1953. The inclusion of this writer on Ismāʿīlī beliefs demonstrates the somewhat haphazard way in which I originally went about collecting writings for this study. (To be frank, my first method was to examine such works as were on a given day on the *kalām* shelves of the library of the School of Oriental and African Studies, London, and not borrowed or misplaced.) In a preliminary survey of this kind, there is perhaps some value in this sort of 'random sampling', as the statisticians call it. I subsequently supplemented this selection, however, by reference to likely works cited on the topic of law in such standard studies of *kalām* as Wensinck, Gardet and Qanawātī, etc.
20. Maḥmūd Shākir, ed., *Kitāb sharḥ . . . Saʿd al-Dīn al-Taftāzānī ʿalá al-ʿAqā'id al-Nasafīyah . . . li . . . Najm al-Dīn ʿUmar al-Nasafī*, Cairo, 1331/1913.
21. Ritter edn., pp. 290–297.
22. Thirty-one articles in Klein, *op. cit.*, pp. 31–35; but McCarthy, in *Kitāb al-lumaʿ*, edn. cited, Appendix IV, pp. 233–254, with his sixty-three, is more discriminating.
23. The earliest case that I have discovered where the root appears in the wording of one of the topics for discussion is al-Ghazzālī's *al-Iqtiṣād fī-al-iʿtiqād*, where, of the fifty-three headings (listed pp. *a-b-j*, edn. cit.), the term *sharīʿah* does not appear, but *sharʿ* (we shall consider these varying forms presently) occurs in two: *al-daʿwah al-sādisah* of *al-quṭb al-thālith*, edn. cited, p. 85, and *al-bāb al-thānī* of *al-quṭb al-rābiʿ*, p. 94. Cf. our note 32 below.
24. Ritter edn., vol. I, *alif* to *ṭā*; vol. II, *kāf-ṭā'* to *lām-bā'*. The list itself, its wordings derived from the text, seems to be constructed modernly by the editor? Cf. our note 32 below.

25. *Ibid.*, Table of Contents, re p. 40.
26. *Ibid.*, re pp. 60–61; cf. re pp. 329–333.
27. *Ibid.*, re pp. 191 ff.
28. *Ibid.*, pp. 158–163.
29. *Ibid.*, pp. 175–176.
30. *Ibid.*, pp. 203–206.
31. *Ibid.*, pp. 225–226.
32. Even the word *sharᶜiyah* in the heading for a section (*ibid.*, pp. 474–477) in Ritter's Table of Contents (vol. II, p. *lām-alif*) would seem to be the modern editor's? In the text, this term is not found.
33. Fayẕī ('Fyzee'), *op. cit.*, p. 93. The English is from Fayẕī's translation, except that where I have given 'they are *aṣḥāb al-sharā'iᶜ*, namely . . . ,' he writes: '. . . they are the masters of the religious paths (*aṣḥābu' sh-sharā'iᶜ*), namely . . .'.
34. See our preceding note, just above.
35. The text of the Arabic is, as I have indicated, not available to me, but no other passage in the English seems to be a translation of *sharīᶜah* or its plural, or of *sharᶜ* or a corresponding adjective.
36. Laoust, *op. cit.*
37. *Ibid.*, Arabic, p. 3; cf. French trans., p. 5.
38. According to the apparently careful index.
39. *Ibid.*, Arabic, p. 35; cf. trans., p. 60.
40. Put together from Shākir, *edn. cit.*, pp. 493–494.
41. al-Ghazzālī, *op. cit.*, vol. I, p. 158.
42. The fact that this begins with this particular writer is to be correlated, no doubt, with Wensinck's reference on him and his period, to 'the increasingly intellectualist and systematizing tendencies that show themselves in several forms of the creed from al-Baghdādī's time onward' (Wensinck, *op. cit.*, p. 270).
43. Cf. below, our note 45 here.
44. This is a tendency that in general terms I have discerned and formulated in my exposition of a general theory: *The Meaning and End of Religion*, (1963) (*above, note 1 to Chap. 3 of this collection*).
45. It is instructive to compare Nādir, himself an Arab, in various versions. In French, he speaks of 'la volonté de Dieu' and 'la Loi qu'elle ordonne' (*op. cit.*, [our note 6 above], his p. 94). In his earlier Arabic version of his book, *Falsafat al-Muᶜtazilah*, vol. I (Alexandria: Dār Nashr al-Thaqāfah, 1950), pp. 97–98 (the Arabic, however, although published earlier, is itself a translation of a French thesis, written in Paris under Western guidance; the author is not a Muslim) he gives *al-irādah* and *al-sharīᶜah* for these, and uses both *sharīᶜah* and *sharᶜ* in this section. The original Arabic (Muslim) writer that he cites, however, Abū Hudhayl, does not

use this concept, but *amr*, *ḥukm*, and *khabar* in the passage instanced. More telling: in his chapter entitled 'L'Homme et la loi', Nādir actually quotes al-Jāḥiẓ, and Thumāmah via al-Khayyāṭ, as saying 'On ne peut pas être soumis à Dieu si l'on ne connaît pas sa loi', 'Ceux qui ont connu Dieu et sa Loi', 'Ceux qui n'ont pas connu Dieu ni sa Loi' (French, pp. 296, 297; in Nādir's Arabic, II: 108–109, he uses the term *sharīʿah*), whereas the original Arabic here, if one looks up his references, is rather: *al-ʿilm bi-mā nahá ʿanh*, and *al-ʿārifūn bi-mā umirū bihi wa-nuhaw ʿanh*, and so on. (His references for al-Jāḥiẓ and al-Khayyāṭ here are somewhat inaccurate; they should read al-Khayyāṭ pp. 86, 95 respectively, rather than Nādir's 87 [his French, p. 296 note 5, p. 297 note 1].) In similar vein, one may note also Wensinck, who speaks for instance of the orthodox' thinking of God's imposing on man 'either a different law or no law at all' (*op. cit.*, p. 261), with reference to al-Baghdādī, p. 213, line 10, whereas if one looks up this reference one finds that it actually reads: *qāla aṣḥābunā: jā'iz min Allāh taʿālá an ya'mura bi-kull mā warada amruhu bih; wa-law nahá ʿammā amara bihi, jāz—wa-ka-dhālik, law amara bi-mā nahá ʿanhu, jāz.*

The differences are subtle, but germane to our later argument; and at a religious level, crucial.

46. It would be moving from the realm of objective, empirical observation to that of interpretation to say that *sharʿ* is *never* found as a concrete noun. For certain passages may be seen as ambiguous, and there are doubtless borderline cases. I can report, however, that with only three exceptions, which are considered at some length [at our pp. 105 f., 107 f.,] below, I never found *sharʿ* particularized (as was often, indeed normally, the case with *sharīʿah*) by the addition of any qualification—such as *al-sharʿ al-islāmī*, or *sharʿunā*, or *al-sharʿ* αλ-Μυηαμμαδ1, or *hādhā al-sharʿ*. The exceptions are all from al-Shahrastānī's *Nihāyah* (cf. our note 49 below).
47. *Encyclopaedia of Islam* [first edn.], s.v. SHARĪʿA.
48. Cf. our note 45 above; there are countless other instances.
49. Ed. and trans. Alfred Guillaume, London: Oxford University Press, 1934. The English title-page reads: *The Summa Philosophiae of al-Shahrastānī: Kitāb Nihāyatu 'l-iqdām fī ʿilmi 'l-kalām.*
50. *Op. cit.*, Arabic, pp. 370–371.
51. W. D. Ross, *The Right and the Good*, Oxford: Clarendon, 1930, p. 22.
52. Gibb, *op. cit.*, p. 111.
53. See my article, 'Law and Ijtihad in Islam: . . .' (1960) [reprinted above in this present collection, pp. 78–86].
54. Guillaume, *op. cit.*, p. 119, translating the Arabic, p. 370, lines 9–10 (*maʿná al-ḥasan mā warada al-sharʿ bi-al-thanā' ʿalá fāʿilihi*).

55. Keats was inspired by his contemplating of a Greek work of art to remind us that this view is un-classical. [He concludes his *Ode on a Grecian Urn* with the well-known lines:

    Beauty is truth—Truth Beauty,—that is all
    Ye know on Earth, and all ye need to know.]

56. Even for Muslims, if an outsider may be allowed to express an opinion, there has been a danger of a subtle form of idolatry in confusing the two, as the Ṣūfis have observed.
57. Guillaume, *op. cit.*, Arabic, p. 389, lines 2, 3; English trans. p. 124.
58. *Ibid.*, Arabic, p. 501, line 1; English trans., p. 158.
59. In the two preceding notes.
60. Those whose knowledge of Arabic is more meticulous than mine will know whether such construction forces too far the usage of an objective genitive following a *maṣdar*. W. Wright, Arabic Grammar, Cambridge: Cambridge University Press, 1933, vol. 2, p. 61, para. 28, would allow this 'occasionally'. Such a genitive is rare; but since any use of *sharᶜ* with a genitive is rare, this fact might be adduced to support my interpretation, as well as to undermine it. One way of elucidating the point is to ask whether one would conceptualize (and linguistically express) *sharᶜ Adam* and *sharᶜ Muḥammad* together as *sharᶜuhumā* or as *al-sharᶜān*. I know of no dual or plural for *sharᶜ*, in any *kalām* writer. In any case, no doubt we have here, whatever the grammar, a case illustrating the transition that eventually did take place from absolute to particular.
61. Arabic, p. 389, lines 1–3.
62. Arabic, p. 500, line 15, to p. 501, line 3.
63. The more conscious one is of God, or of His imperatives (*aḥkām*), the less one is conscious of, or concerned with, law (*sharīᶜah*). This remark may be seen either as a religious judgement, or as a statistical, empirical, report.
64. Neither Bergsträsser nor Gibb has said just this (cf. our notes 1–2 above); but it is sometimes said.

NOTES TO CHAPTER SIX: FAITH, IN THE QUR'ĀN; AND ITS RELATION TO BELIEF

1. [Mohammad Iqbal, *Six Lectures on the Reconstruction of Religious Thought in Islam*, Lahore: Kapur, 1930; reprinted later as Sir Mohammad Iqbal, *The Reconstruction of Religious Thought in Islam*, London: Oxford University Press, 1934, and again Lahore: Ashraf, 1944.]
2. [This has since been completed, and has been published under the title *Faith and Belief*, Princeton: Princeton University Press, 1979. Chapter 3 of that work incorporates a modified version of this lecture.]

3. [From my *Meaning and End of Religion*, 1963 edition, p. 112; paperback reprint (1964), p. 103; (1978), p. 112.]
4. [The reference here was to my book *The Faith of Other Men*, and specifically to the Islamics chapter, which is given above in this present collection, pp. 26–37.]
5. The chief references for this group are as follows: 2: 46, 230, 249/12: 42/17: 102 (but cf. 17: 101)/18: 53/24: 12/37: 87/38: 24/41: 48/69: 20/72: 12/75: 25, 28/83: 4. In these instances, one could argue that a concept 'believing' does indeed appear; it is not, however, a religious category, is not commended, is quite casual and of no particular importance. It is not something that Muslims characteristically do, or are supposed to do.

NOTES TO CHAPTER SEVEN: FAITH, IN LATER ISLAMIC HISTORY; THE MEANING OF *TAṢDĪQ*

1. *A Commentary on the Creed of Islam: Saʿd al-Dīn al-Taftāzānī on the creed of Najm al-Dīn al-Nasafī, translated with introduction and notes* by Earl Edgar Elder, New York: Columbia University Press, and London: Oxford University Press, 1950 (Austin P. Evans, ed., Records of Civilization: Sources and Studies, #43).
2. The present study is not primarily an historical one; neither by intent nor otherwise, except incidentally. It does not investigate development (which was intricate), nor concern itself with the earliest phases of that development. Rather, being concerned to elucidate simply the meaning of one term (*taṣdīq*) which gradually became standard in *īmān* discussions, it deals primarily with usage at a relatively mature phase of classical and even mediaeval development. The first to posit the equation of *al-īmān huwa al-taṣdīq* was perhaps the Murji' thinker Bishr al-Marīsī. (See Abū al-Ḥasan al-Ashʿarī, *Kitāb maqālāt al-islāmīyīn*, ed. Hellmut Ritter [*Die dogmatischen Lehren der Anhänger des Islam: Bibliotheca Islamica*, I] Istanbul/Leipzig 1929–1930, I:140. Cf. below, our note 26.) It was taken up by al-Ashʿarī himself (*Kitāb al-lumaʿ*, ed. and trans. by Richard J. McCarthy, [Beyrouth: Imprimerie Catholique, 1953], Arabic, p. 75; English trans., p. 104). Historically there was a pre-Ashʿarī stage when *maʿrifah*, rather than *taṣdīq*, was canvassed as the role of the heart (if any: whether along with or over against *iqrār* and *ʿamal*) in *īmān*, but this gained but little lasting favour. (Cf. below, at our notes 43 ff.) Once *taṣdīq* was accepted as the heart's role, it prevailed and remained virtually unchallenged until Ibn Taymīyah, who, using the conception of *ʿamal al-qalb* or *aʿmāl qalbīyah* (as distinct from external *aʿmāl*), insisted that *taṣdīq*, which at best is one of these acts, is not sufficient in itself to constitute

īmān. I have accumulated some evidence to suggest, but have not weighed or sifted it enough yet to prove, that by *taṣdīq* Ibn Taymīyah may exceptionally tend to understand merely or primarily an intellectual judgement (along the lines that, on the basis of other texts than his, I am otherwise criticizing in this present paper), and that therefore he finds it an inadequate interpretation of *īmān*, even *bi-al-qalb*. Faith is not merely or even primarily belief, he would then be saying; but I here claim that the earlier writers were also saying this, inasmuch as to them, including those who were content with the *īmān*-equals-*taṣdīq* formula, the latter term can be seen to have signified a good deal more than that. (See Ibn Taymīyah, *al-Īmān*, Damascus: al-Maktab al-Islāmī, 1381, 1961, *passim* and esp. pp. 259–260.)

If my general interpretation of *taṣdīq* be validated, an historical study of its use might then follow. If the suggested view of Ibn Taymīyah be correct (and I have found no other *kalām* writer to agree with him), then so far as an historical dimension of our problem is concerned, it could mean that the development would perhaps be that *taṣdīq* meant what I am here suggesting, in the minds of most writers (with varying degrees, of course, of sensitivity and insight) for perhaps some five centuries over the classical period, from roughly the third century on, but that the meaning then began to give way, at least in certain circles (perhaps those most influenced by, or reacting against, *falsafah*?), to one closer to the logicians', and/or to its presently accepted sense. I am doubtful about this, however; for against it is that Taftāzānī, who is later than Ibn Taymīyah, and even Kastalī, who is much later, are much more personalist.

Historical presentations of the processes of *īmān* discussions, especially in their formal and especially in their early aspects, have, of course, been done, most notably by Wensinck, Izutsu, Gardet and Qanawātī; and one looks forward to a comprehensive new study of *kalām* promised by Wolfson. [This last work has now appeared: Harry Austryn Wolfson, *The Philosophy of the Kalam*, Cambridge, Mass., and London: Harvard University Press, 1976 ([Wolfson], Structure and Growth of Philosophic Systems from Plato to Spinoza, IV)].

3. Harry A. Wolfson, 'The terms *taṣawwur* and *taṣdīq* in Arabic philosophy and their Greek, Latin and Hebrew equivalents', *The Moslem World*, 33(1943):114–128.
4. As his title suggests, the writers that Wolfson's article investigates are chiefly the *falāsifah* (al-Fārābī, Ibn Sīnā, Ibn Rushd), but he includes also Ghazzālī's study of these (*Maqāṣid al-falāsifah*) and Shahrastānī's treatment of them (in *al-Milal wa-al-niḥal*).
5. The latter conceptual tradition, the academic, within which this present submission is done, might manage to apprehend the classical Islamic form

of faith without managing to comprehend the classical Islamic substance of faith. Faith is precisely that element in religious life that makes the difference between insider and outsider. [In the years since writing the above, and especially with my generic study *Faith and Belief*, I have come to perceive that the 'form of faith', as I tend to use that phrase, makes the difference between insider and outsider, while 'substance of faith', if one were to use those terms (of which I myself would today be chary), may, for persons of faith of whatever form, converge. Cf. also Chapter 15 below in this present collection.]

6. The term *al-imān* in Arabic is ambiguously generic or specific (human or Islamic; 'faith' or 'the faith'). The ambiguity was resolved (did not appear) in a convergence by those who thought or felt that human faith normatively (ultimately; truly; divinely) is what outsiders would call faith in its Islamic form. This has been the standard Muslim position.
7. I am currently at work on a comparative study of faith concepts which includes an investigation of the Latin term *credo* and the English term *believe*. [Later: This study has now been completed: *Faith and Belief* (1979); additional material on the historical shifts in meaning of *believe* was meanwhile published in my *Belief and History*, Charlottesville: University Press of Virginia, 1977.]
8. *Ṣaḥīḥ al-Bukhārī*, 'Kitāb al-īmān'. In the edition *bi-Sharḥ al-Kirmānī* (Cairo: al-Maṭbaʿah al-Bahīyah al-Miṣrīyah), ʿAbd al-Raḥmān Muḥammad, ed., 2nd edn., 1358/1939, it is Bāb 47, vol. 1, p. 194. In the Muḥammad Fu'ād ʿAbd al-Bāqī edition (Cairo: Dār Iḥyā' al-Kutub al-ʿArabīyah, 1368/1949), it is Bāb 1, p. 2, *ḥadīth* #5.
9. It could perhaps be argued that the other types of answer—that faith is *iqrār* and/or *ʿamal*—are, like the *ḥadīth* just quoted, synthetic rather than analytic statements about Islamic faith: that they indicate what having faith means (entails) in human life rather than what the word 'faith' means at the conceptual level.
10. Sometimes *s-q-m* is coupled over against *ṣ-ḥ-ḥ* as an opposite. One instance that I have happened upon is in Rāzī, *Tafsīr*, 3:19—*aḥwāl al-khalq fī-al-ḥusn wa-al-qubḥ, wa-al-ghinā wa-al-fuqr, wa-al-ṣiḥḥah wa-al-suqm, wa* . . . : *Mafātīḥ al-ghayb*, vol. 2, Istanbul: al-Maṭbaʿah al-ʿĀmirah, 1307 [1889–1890], p. 626.
11. On the matter of the classical Islamic view of the morality of truth and lies, it is perhaps not inappropriate to quote here something that I had occasion to write elsewhere in commenting on a passage of the *Nihāyat al-iqdām* of al-Shahrastānī, who 'contends that a false sentence is not intrinsically better or worse, morally, than a true one. Some truths, he says, are not very pretty. There are some who would agree with this, holding that it is not lies themselves, but the telling of lies, that is wrong. Our author

goes further: for him, the telling of lies, even, is not intrinsically moral or immoral. What is wrong, hellishly so, is for *me* to tell a lie—or for you to do so. And the reason for this is that God has created us and commanded us not to lie.' [This quotation is from my *sharīʿah* article, reproduced above in this present collection, on pp. 104–105.]

12. And what eternity is all about, too, in a sense. The reality of the objective world, although it is prior to our personal orientation to that reality, in the end will vanish; but the way that persons have responded to that reality is of a transcending significance which, to use poetic imagery, will survive, will cosmically outlast the world. The mundane world is independent of man and is not to be subordinated to his and her whimsies. Yet ultimately, in this vision, man if he and she relate themsleves truly to reality is greater than the world.
13. Ibn Mukarram ibn Manẓūr, *Lisān al-ʿArab*, 15 vols., Bayrūt: Dār Ṣādir/Dār Bayrūt, 1374–1376/1955–1956, vol. 10, p. 193. Muḥibb al-Dīn Muḥammad Murtaḍá, *Sharḥ al-Qāmūs al-musammá Tāj al-ʿarūs*, 10 vols., Cairo: al-Maṭbaʿah al-Khayrīyah, 1304 [*ca.* 1886] ff., vol. 6, p. 403. The latter part of this paragraph is a paraphrase from the *Tāj al-ʿarūs* entry, s.v. *ṣ-d-q*. (The wife-beating phrasing is my modern counterpart to the Zayd illustration actually used; and similarly for the book-giving.)
14. *al-ṣidq muṭābaqat al-qawli al-ḍamīra wa-al-mukhbara ʿanhu maʿan. Tāj al-ʿarūs*, p. 404, lines 5, 6.
15. I say 'trilateral' because in a statement three things are involved: the person who makes the statement, the statement itself, and the facts that it purports to describe. In a game, cheating similarly involves three things: the cheater, his or her action, and the rules of the game. I leave aside for the moment a question (in the end, perhaps exceedingly important) as to whether we should in fact include a fourth element in the complex: the person spoken to, the other player. The common view that the truth of a statement is a function of the relation between it and the overt facts may be termed a bilateral theory. A relationship cannot be unilateral.
16. Wilfred Cantwell Smith, 'A Human View of Truth', to be published also presently in *Proceedings* of the University of Birmingham 1970 Conference on the Philosophy of Religion. [These Proceedings have since been published, as John Hick, ed., *Truth and Dialogue: the relationship between* [sic] *world religions*, London: Sheldon, (P. R. Baelz, gen. ed., Studies in Philosophy and Religion [vol. 2]), and *Truth and Dialogue in World Religions: conflicting truth-claims,* Philadelphia: Westminster, both 1974.]
17. This highly important phrase is often cited; for instance, *Tāj al-ʿarūs*, p. 405, lines -2, -1, from the *Ṣiḥāḥ*, in explication of *ṣiddīq* as *dāʾim al-taṣdīq* (below, our note 21); and also by *Lisān alʿArab*, p. 193, col. 2,

lines -6 ff. Cf. also the passage from al-Ṭabarī cited at our note 45 below.

18. *Tāj al-ʿarūs*, p. 406, line 1.
19. *Lisān al-ʿArab*, p. 193, col. 2, line -3.
20. More strictly, *ṣiddīqah* (our note 25 below) as *dhāt taṣdīq: Lisān al-ʿArab*, p. 193, col. 2, lines -2, -1; and also *Tāj al-ʿarūs*, p. 406, line 2.
21. *Lisān al-ʿArab*, p. 193, col. 2, lines -6, -5; and *Tāj al-ʿarūs*, p. 405, line -2, citing *al-Ṣiḥāḥ*.
22. *Tāj al-ʿarūs*, p. 405, line -3.
23. *ibid.*, line -1.
24. Same ref. as for our note 20 above.
25. Mary is termed *ṣiddīqah* in Qur'ān 5:75; see our note 20 above.
26. This begins from the very first time, apparently, that this explication of *īmān* is introduced into the discussions, by Bishr al-Marīsī: *aṣḥāb Bishr al-Marīsī yaqūlūna inna al-īmān huwa al-taṣdīq, li-anna al-īmān fī-al-lughah huwa al-taṣdīq, wa-mā laysa bi-taṣdīq fa-laysa bi-īmān*—Ashʿarī, *Maqālāt*, I: 140. The point is repeated by, for instance, al-Māturīdī and continues with virtually all subsequent *kalām* discussions of the matter. See Abū Manṣūr al-Māturīdī, *Kitāb al-tawḥīd*, ed. Fatḥ Khulayf, Bayrūt: Dār al-Mashriq, n.d., p. 375, line 7; cf. p. 377, line 11.
27. The 'over against' here is my own; but there is explicit support for it in the sources. In *kalām*, some of the writers included the special logicians' use of *taṣdīq* in their interpretation of *īmān* as being *taṣdīq* (e.g. Taftāzānī, *Sharḥ al-ʿAqā'id al-Nasafīyah*, Cairo: Dār Iḥyā' al-Kutub al-ʿArabīyah [ʿĪsá al-Bābī al-Ḥalabī] n.d. [1335?], p. 125, lines 5–6); but others had reservations, or explicitly rejected this. For instance, Aḥmad Mūsá al-Khayālī contrasts *al-taṣdīq al-manṭiqī* with that *fī bāb al-īmān*; and 'Iṣām al-Dīn al-Isfarā'īnī contrasts *al-taṣdīq al-madhkūr fī awā'il kutub al-mīzān* with *al-taṣdīq fī kutub al-kalām*. Al-Isfarā'īnī also writes: *wa-la yakhfá ʿalayka al-farq bayna al-īmān wa-al-taṣdīq alladhī yubḥathu ʿanhu fī kutub al-mīzān*. (References for these three: on the margin of the Cairo edition of the Taftāzānī work just cited, p. 125, lines 24–25 [viz. lines 7–8 of his section], 30–31, 2–3.) Cf. also Muṣliḥ al-Dīn Muṣṭafá al-Kastalī, on the margin of the Istanbul: Yūsuf Ḍiyā edition of the same work, 1326 [1910], p. 152, lines -6 ff.
28. 119 times; and other forms of the verb (not counting, of course, the preposition *bayna*, but including *bayyannā*) a further 138 times.
29. On 'moral' rather than 'legal' as the better, more accurate, translation of *sharʿī*, and the better attribution to the Islamic outlook generally, cf. my *sharīʿah* article above, pp. 87–109.
30. Wilfred Cantwell Smith, *Islam in Modern History*, 1957 [1977], p. 17 (italics in the original).
31. [This article, and conspicuously this paragraph, were written at a time when I was still under the impression, widespread in the modern West,

that the recent Christian emphasis on 'believing' as a religious category has been standard in the Church, at least since the impact of Greek intellectuality on Christian thinking—rather than being virtually a modern aberration, as I have since discovered. Even the phrase 'leap of faith' originally meant, perhaps, not the leap from uncertainty into a decision to believe (without sufficient evidence), so much as the leap from mere intellectual theorizing into committed practice? See my remarks above (pp. 110 f.) introducing these articles in this present collection.]

32. *differunt secundum perfectum et imperfectum opinio, fides et scientia*: St. Thomas Aquinas, *Summa Theologiæ*, Prima Secundae, qu. 67, art. 3. *Fides est . . . supra opinionem et infra scientiam*: Hugo of St. Victor, *De Sacramentis*, lib. I, pars X, cap. 2. [Since writing this, however, I have come to see that *scientia* here means something more than mundane human knowing. Cf. note 31 above.]
33. The passage in full reads: *wa-al-īmān wājib ijmālan fī mā ʿulima ijmālan wa tafṣīlan fī mā ʿulima tafṣīlan*. In the Cairo edition, p. 129, lines 4–5; in the Istanbul edition, p. 157, lines 11–12. On the pointing of the finite verb, cf. our next note, and note 63 below.
34. *al-taṣdīq ʿibārah ʿan rabṭ al-qalb ʿalá mā ʿulima* (or: *mā ʿalima*, sc., *al-qalbu*) *min akhbār al-mukhbir*. This definition is attributed to *baʿḍ al-mashāyikh* by Taftāzānī, Cairo, p. 129, lines 18–19. On the reading *ʿulima*, here and elsewhere, cf. our note 63 below.
35. *huwa idhʿān li mā ʿulima wa-inqiyād lahu wa . . .* al-Kastalī, p. 152, lines 11–12. *Huwa* here refers to *al-taṣdīq*, which *al-īmān* has just been said to be. The passage is cited more fully in our note 51 below.
36. Qur'ān 2:146 and 6:20: *alladhīna ātaynāhumu-l-kitāba yaʿrifūnahu kamā yaʿrifūna abnā'ahum.*
37. Qur'ān 27:14: *wa-jaḥadū bihā wa-stayqanat-hā anfusuhum ẓulman wa-ʿulūwan.*
38. Qur'ān 9:74: *wa-kafarū baʿda islāmihim.*
39. Once man is confronted with the truth from God, he and she are to choose whether to accept or to reject. *Al-ḥaqqu min rabbikum fa-man shā'a fa-l-yu'min wa-man shā'a fa-l-yakfur*: Qur'ān 18:29.
40. al-Kastalī, p. 152, lines 16–17.
41. Strictly, the differences between *taṣdīq* in *kalām* and *taṣdīq* in logic, although major, are of a different order from those obtaining between the former and modern Western understandings. See the references given above in our note 27. The contrast there tends to be in terms of knowledge: although the logicians themselves speak of *taṣdīq* as one of the divisions of *ʿilm*, the *mutakallimūn* interpret the logicians' *taṣdīq* as having to do with believing rather than knowing, while their own concept of *taṣdīq*, they say, excludes opinions, ignorance, and hearsay. 'Logical

taṣdīq includes mere belief': *al-taṣdīq al-manṭiqī yaʿummu al-ẓannī* (al-Khayālī, p. 125, line 25 [8]). *al-taṣdīq al-mīzānī yaʿummu al-ẓunūn* (al-Isfarā'īnī, p. 125, line 32). *al-taṣdīq fī kutub al-kalām qism li-al-ʿilm al-mufassar bi-mā lā yaḥtamilu al-ẓann wa-al-jahl wa-al-taqlīd, bi-khilāf kutub al-mīzān* (id., p. 125, line 31). Al-Kastalī, despite remarks of this kind and over against his strong preceding emphasis on the truthfulness involved in *taṣdīq* (our note 40, above), does cautiously admit that this latter term may occasionally get used in its sense of sincerely acting upon one's convicions even in cases where those convictions may be invalid: *huwa amr zā'id ʿalá-al-ʿilm, bal rubbamā yataʿallaqu bi-al-maẓnūn wa-al-muʿtaqad ayḍan wa-li-hādhā yubná al-ʿamal ʿalayhimā*; but he adds, *wa-ammā māhīyatuhu mā hiya* ('nonetheless, its nature is what it is') (*op. cit.*, p. 152, lines 16–21).

42. Taftāzānī, Cairo, p. 129, lines 16–17. The passage is given in Arabic more fully below, our note 53. *Iʿtiqād*, in this and other passages, has in *kalām* thought its more or less literal meaning of 'binding oneself' to an idea, not merely holding it passively. For a distinction, even in modern Arabic, between it and *ra'y*, 'belief', 'opinion' see Aḥmad Amīn, '*al-ra'y wa-al-iʿtiqād*', in his *Fayḍ al-khāṭir*, vol. I, pp. 1–3. (The original of this article appeared in the journal *al-Risālah*, Cairo, Oct. 16, 1933.)
43. Taftāzānī, Cairo, p. 129, lines 13–16: . . . *anna baʿḍ al-qadarīyah dhahaba ilá anna al-īmān huwa al-maʿrifah wa-aṭbaqa ʿulamā'unā ʿalá fisādihi li-anna ahl al-kitāb kāna yaʿrifūna nubūwat Muḥammad ṣallá Allāh ʿalayhi wa-sallam ka-mā ya-ʿrifūna abnā'ahum maʿa al-qaṭʿ bi-kufrihim li-ʿadam al-taṣdīq wa-li-anna min al-kuffār man kāna yaʿrifū al-ḥaqq yaqīnan wa-i[nna-m]ā kāna yunkiru ʿinādan wa-istikbāran.*

    In the Istanbul edition, this passage is found. p. 158, lines 8 ff.; it reads *Allāh taʿālá*, and supplies the reading *inna-mā*, which is obscured in my copy of the Cairo text.
44. Kastalī, p. 152, lines 6 ff.: *anna al-taṣdīq laysa ʿibārah ʿan al-ʿilm bi-ṣidq al-khabar aw al-mukhbir, was-illā, lazima an yakūna kullu ʿālim bi-ṣidq al-nabī ʿalayhi al-salām mu'minan bihi, wa-laysa ka-dhālik. Fa-inna kathīran min al-kuffār kānū ʿālimīn bi-ṣidqihi ʿalayhi al-salām, kamā dalla ʿalayhi qawluhu taʿālá.*
45. Abū Jaʿfar Muḥammad ibn Jarīr al-Ṭabarī, *Jāmiʿ al-bayān fī tafsīr al-Qur'ān*, ad 49: 14. I have used the edition of 1323–1329 [1905–1912], Cairo: al-Maṭbaʿah al-Kubrá al-Amīrīyah, vol. 26, p. 89. In this passage, and the one cited at our next note, also those at notes 17, 18 above, *taṣdīq* has to do especially with *ʿamal*, acting. In the threefold formula serving as a definition of faith or as a framework for its discussion, with which we began, and in most of the *kalām* treatments, the general question at issue was subdivided into heart, tongue, and outer action—and the term *taṣdīq*

was associated with the first of these (*al-taṣdīq bi-al-qalb*, or *taṣdīqun bi-al-qalb*). It is worth noting, however, that at times in the discussions this term was associated rather (or also) with the second or third: with tongue (e.g., Bishr—Ritter, *op. cit.*, I:140) or with outward action. An example of *taṣdīq bi-al-ʿamal* in a definition of faith is provided by Zamakhsharī: *fa-in-qulta, mā al-īmān al-ṣaḥīḥ, qultu, an yaʿtaqida al-ḥaqq, wa-yuʿarriba (yuʿriba) ʿanhu bi-lisānihi, wa-yuṣaddiqahu bi-ʿamalih. Fa-man akhalla bi-al-iʿtiqād, wa-in shahida wa-ʿamala, fa-huwa munāfiq; wa-man akhalla bi-al-shahādah, fa-huwa kāfir; wa-man akhalla bi-al-ʿamal, fa-huwa fāsiq.* (Notice also the use of *kāfir* here as clearly not 'unbeliever'—to that, *munāfiq* here comes closer—but as the believer (knower) who repudiates the implications of what he sees. The *shahādah* here (a verbal noun, *maṣdar*) is the public engagement to participate. *Al-Qur'ān maʿ tafsīrih al-Kashshāf ʿan ḥaqā'iq al-tanzīl, li-al-imām al-ʿallāmah Abī Qāsim Jār Allāh Maḥmūd ibn ʿUmar al-Zamakhsharī al-Khwārizmī*—[English title-page:] *The Qoran; with the commentary of . . . al-Zamakhsharī* . . . ed. by W. Nassau Lees . . . and Mawlawis Khadim *H*osain and ʿAbd al-*H*aiy, Calcutta: printed and published by W. Nassau Lees, 1856, vol. I, p. 22, lines 8–10.

46. More fully: *laysa al-īmān bi-al-taḥallī wa-lā bi-al-tamannī wa-lākinna mā waqara* . . . . This statement is frequently atttributed to al-Ḥasan al-Baṣrī, but is cited as an *ḥadīth* from the Prophet by Abū Manṣūr ʿAbd al-Qāhir ibn Ṭāhir al-Baghdādī, *Kitāb uṣūl al-dīn*, Istanbul: Maṭbaʿat al-Dawlah, 1346/1928, pp. 250–251.
47. al-Baghdādī, *op. cit.*, p. 248, line 2.
48. Taftāzānī, Cairo, p. 125, lines 3 ff.: *wa-laysa* [sic] *ḥaqīqat al-taṣdīq an yaqaʿa fī-al-qalb nisbat al-ṣidq ilá al-khabar aw al-mukhbir min ghayr idhʿān wa-qubūl. bal, huwa idhʿān wa-qubūl li-dhālik, bi-ḥaythu yaqaʿu ʿalayhi ism al-taslīm, ʿalá mā ṣaraḥa* [*or: ṣarraḥa*] *bi-hi al-imām al-Ghazzālī. wa-bi-al-jumlah huwa al-maʿná alladhī yuʿabbaru ʿanhu bi-al-fārisīyah bi-kirawīdan*. The last point is repeated later, at p. 130, line 4.
49. Taftāzānī, Cairo, p. 128, lines 15–16. [Cf. the 'leap of faith' idea, above, our note 31.]
50. Cf. our note 44, above.
51. Kastalī, p. 152, lines 6, 11–16: [*inna*] *al-taṣdīq laysa ʿibārah ʿan al-ʿilm bi-ṣidq al-khabar aw al-mukhbir . . . bal, huwa idhʿān li-mā ʿulima wa-inqiyād la-hu wa-sukūn al-nafs ʿalayhi wa-iṭmi'nānuhā bi-hi wa-qubūluhā bi-dhālik, bi-tark al-jaḥd wa-al-ʿinād, wa-binā' al-aʿmāl ʿalayhi.*
52. Cf. our note 42, above.
53. Taftāzānī, Cairo, p. 129, lines 16–17.
54. E.g.: *kānū āmanū fī-al-jumlah; thumma ya'tī farḍun baʿda farḍ, fa-kānū yu'minūna bi-kulli farḍ khaṣṣ*—Taftāzānī, Cairo, p. 129, lines 1–2.

55. E.g.: *al-taṣdīq bi-hā* (*sc.*, *bi-al-aḥkām*) (*ibid.*, line 17). It may be noted that I am taking *ḥukm, aḥkām* here and usually as imperatives, signifying the command of one in authority (*viz.*, God). This interpretation is supported by the constant parallels with *farḍ*, *awāmir wa-nawāhin*, etc., as well as by the contexts and by the general Islamic orientation (and by the way that I have heard the word used in colloquial parlance in the Muslim world). The prevailing sense of incumbent duties that permeates the Muslim consciousness—and, more formally, the central significance of *sharʿ*, *sharīʿah*—are to be recalled here. Gardet tends rather toward 'état juridique' (Louis Gardet, *Dieu et la destinée de l'homme*, Paris: Vrin, 1967, p. 381).
56. E.g.: *taṣdīq ḥukm al-nabī.*
57. E.g.: *al-mu'min bi-Allāh huwa al-muṣaddiq li-Allāh fī khabarih, wa-kadhālik al-mu'min bi-al-nabī muṣaddiq la-hu fī khabarih*—al-Baghdādī, pp. 247–248.
58. al-Taftāzānī, Cairo, p. 131, line 2.
59. Also in the first part of the Baghdādī passage just quoted (in our note 57, just above).
60. Najm al-Dīn Abū Ḥafṣ ʿUmar al-Nasafī, *ʿAqīdah*, in William Cureton, ed., *Pillar of the Creed of the Sunnites* . . . London: Society for the Publication of Oriental Texts, 1843, appendix. Rather than simply *jā'a*, the reading *jā'a bihi* appears in both the Cairo and the Istanbul editions of the Taftāzānī *Sharḥ*. Cairo, p. 126, lines 3–4; Istanbul, p. 153, lines 8–9. The text without *bi-hi* is given in the latter at the very end of the book, however. *Bi-hi* is not generally used in the formulae from earlier centuries.
61. With *bi-hi*: cf. preceding note.
62. al-Taftāzānī, Cairo, p. 126, lines 4–5.
63. Three readings are possible:

    ʿulima . . . majī'uhu
    ʿallama . . . majī'ahu
    ʿalima . . . majī'ahu

    I have chosen the first for my transliteration and my translation. In the second, which is rather forced, the subject of the verb is the Prophet. In the third, the subject is the understood subject of *al-taṣdīq*. Such a reading of *ʿalima*, with *al-muṣaddiq* as the understood subject, is a possibility for each of the cases considered above (cf. our notes 33, 34, 35 and elsewhere) where I have read *ʿulima*. It does not, in any case, affect the sense or modify our argument.
64. It might be possible to submit that, especially with the second and except with the third pointing of *ʿalima* (cf. preceding note), a given man's *īmān* could be envisaged as a *taṣdīq* by him of what other people know to be

true. This, however, would constitute a kind of *taqlīd*, with all the ensuing problems as to whether that amounts to *īmān* or not. And in any case the force then of *ḍarūrah* would, in such an interpretation, be awkward, to say the least. So too would be *ijmālan*. And why was this clause introduced into the explications at all, if not to make the point that our own argument here is endeavouring to elucidate.

65. al-Taftāzānī, Cairo, p. 126, line 5. The Istanbul edition, p. 153, line 12, reads *yanḥaṭṭu*, presumably then *darajatahu*: 'it is not less in rank'.

NOTES TO CHAPTER EIGHT: FAITH, IN LATER ISLAMIC HISTORY; THE MEANING OF *ARKĀN*

1. [This present paper appeared before the *taṣdīq* study (our preceding chapter, just above) was published. A reference to it as forthcoming was given here.]
2. Both this phrasing of the formula and this characterization of its prevalence are taken from the highly representative seventh/fourteenth-century thinker Taftāzānī, although he himself does not hold the triple view and goes on to show at some length how Najm al-Dīn ʿUmar al-Nasafī, on whom he is commenting, argues to refute the third phrase as a part of faith. He presents this unacceptable position, however, as *madhhab jumhūr al-mutakallimīn wa-al-muḥaddithīn wa-al-fuqahā'*. *Sharḥ . . . Saʿd al-Dīn al-Taftāzānī ʿalá al-ʿAqā'id al-Nasafīyah*, Cairo: Dār Iḥyā' al-Kutub al-ʿArabīyah ('Īsá al-Bābī al-Ḥalabī), n.d. [*sc.* 1335/1916], p. 128. In the 1326 [1908] Istanbul edition, Yūsuf Ḍiyā, ed., the triple formula occurs at p. 156 and the *jumhūr* . . . phrase at p. 155.

   The earliest instance that I happen so far to have come across with the triple rhyme is in the fourth/tenth-century Ḥanbalī writer Ibn Baṭṭah (died 387/997). His wording, with an unusual order for the first two parts, is: *qawl bi-al-lisān, wa-taṣdīq bi-al-janān, wa-ʿamal bi-al-arkān*. I take this from his *Kitāb al-sharḥ wa-al-ibānah ʿalá uṣūl al-sunnah wa-al-diyānah* in the edition of the text by Henri Laoust, Damas: Institut Français de Damas, 1958, pp. 47–48 (French title: *La profession de foi d'Ibn Baṭṭa*). In a footnote appended to his translation of this passage, Laoust says: 'Cette définition de la foi est exactement celle que l'on trouve chez Abū Ḥātim ar-Rāzī (*Ṭabaqāt*, I, 286) et Abū Bakr al-Āǧurrī (*Kitāb aš-šarīʿa*, 119–132)' (p. 78, fn. 1). Abū Ḥātim (see Laoust, *ibid.*, 'Introduction', pp. xvi–xvii) was from the preceding century, and 'fut l'un des premiers et des plus grands disciples d'Ibn Ḥanbal'; his follower Abū Bakr was a generation earlier than Ibn Baṭṭah (cf. *ibid.*, pp. xli–xlii). To the actual wording of these two writers, however, I have not had access. In the Ibn Baṭṭah text the definition is strictly not of faith as such. More precisely, the author has just designated that which God enjoins on mankind, through His prophets and His books, as faith in God; the meaning of which, he says, is *taṣdīq* of what is revealed. The formula here cited is then presented as a definition of that *taṣdīq*.

From the third/ninth century a triple formula, but with only two clauses rhyming, I find in the *ḥadīth* collections of Ibn Mājah, as follows: *al-īmān maʿrifah bi-al-qalb, wa-qawl bi-al-lisān, wa-ʿamal bi-al-arkān*—*Sunan*, ed. Muḥammad Fu'ād ʿAbd al-Bāqī, Cairo: Dār Iḥyā' al-Kutub al-ʿArabīyah (ʿĪsá al-Bābī al-Ḥalabī), 1372/1952, vol. I, p. 26, lines 1–2—'Muqaddimah', *Bāb* 9, #65. This is the earliest use of *arkān* in this connection that has thus far come to my notice.

3. 'Faith is knowing with the heart, confessing with the tongue and performing *the chief works*' (emphasis mine)—A. J. Wensinck, *The Muslim Creed*, Cambridge: Cambridge University Press, 1932, p. 267. This is article 24 of a treatise that he calls Fiḳh Akbar III, and dates 'possibly from the beginning of the eleventh century A.D. . . . the so-called Fiḳh Akbar of al-Shāfiʿī' (p. 264). One presumes that my italicized words translate *al-arkān*, and indeed the formula as a whole would seem to suggest probably the same wording as Ibn Mājah's given above (in our preceding reference) (except reading *iqrār* rather than *qawl*)? I have not, however, been able to see the original Arabic of this passage (Wensinck renders it from a Cairo manuscript, unpublished, of which I have not succeeded in procuring a photocopy). In each of the many instances where Wensinck's English translations use the word 'limbs', I have been able to check the originals and have found *jawāriḥ*. An example: when he cites Jahm ibn Ṣafwān as speaking of 'works performed with the limbs', p. 132, the original Arabic is *al-ʿamal bi-al-jawāriḥ*, in al-Ashʿarī, *Maqālāt al-islāmīyīn*, ed. H. Ritter, Istanbul: Maṭbaʿat al-Dawlah, 2 vols., 1929–1930, vol. 1, p. 132, line 8.
4. Laoust, in his translation of the formula of Ibn Baṭṭah cited above (our ref. 2), renders the phrase as 'et mettre en pratique les devoirs fondamentaux de l'Islâm (*arkān*)' (p. 78) with a footnote, which we shall consider later, in which he amplifies (contradicts?) this translation by remarking: 'Par *arkān*, on devra comprendre tous les devoirs d'obligation (*farā'iḍ*)'. Laoust, *op. cit.*, p. 78, fn. 1.
5. '. . . the "doing" of the cardinal duties'—Toshihiko Izutsu, *The Concept of Belief in Islamic Theology: a semantic analysis of* îmân *and* islâm, Tokyo: Keio University; Yokohama: Yurindo, 1965, p. 142, citing the Cairo, 1948, edition of al-Shahrastānī, *al-Milal wa-al-Niḥal*, p. 138 (or 139?).

6. '[T]he performance of the prime duties of religion'—Arthur Jeffery, ed., *A Reader on Islam: passages from standard Arabic writings illustrative of the beliefs and practices of Muslims*, 's-Gravenhage: Mouton, 1962, p. 379. The Arabic original of this reads: *al-aʿmāl bi-al-arkān*; Sayf al-Ḥaqq wa-al-Dīn Abū al-Muʿīn al-Nasafī, *Kitāb Baḥr al-Kalām fī ʿIlm al-Tawḥīd*, ed. ʿAbd al-Qādir . . . al-Kurdī al-Sanandjī, ʿIlmīyah Press of Kurdistān, 1329/1911, p. 6. At other places Jeffery uses the English word 'members'; e.g., in his *Islam: Muḥammad and his Religion*, New York: Liberal Arts Press, 1958, p. 159, *tris*, but here it turns out that the Arabic original reads *al-jawāriḥ*, *jawāriḥuhu*, and *bi-jawāriḥihi*; Abū Bakr ibn al-Ṭayyib al-Bāqillānī, *al-Inṣāf fī mā yajibu iʿtiqāduhu wa-lā yajūzu al-jahl bi-hi*, ed. Muḥammad Zāhid ibn al-Ḥasan al-Kawtharī, 2nd ed., [Cairo:] Mu'assasat al-Khānjī, 1382/1963, p. 55 (Jeffery cites this text from a 1950 edition). Two paragraphs later Bāqillānī changes his wording in a highly interesting fashion to which we shall be giving close attention presently; Jeffery, *op. cit.*, p. 160, *tris*, continues to translate with the word 'members'.
7. I have found in Gardet no clear instance of a straightforward translation into French of *arkān* in our formula; nor even any direct reference to an instance of the formula clearly including this particular word. The phrase *œuvres des membres* is cited repeatedly in Louis Gardet, *Dieu et la destinée de l'homme*, Paris: Vrin, 1967, e.g., pp. 356, 361, 364, as standard; but it could correspond to an original Arabic *jawāriḥ*. In the earlier work, Louis Gardet et M.-M. Anawati, *Introduction à la théologie musulmane*, Paris: Vrin, 1948, on the other hand, there is mention of *œuvres prescrites*: e.g., p. 333, 334. In the former case, p. 333, this phrase is explicated as if by the pillars: '. . . confession verbale (*shahâda*) et œuvres prescrites. Ces dernières doivent s'entendre avant tout des œuvres obligatoires: prières rituelles, jeûne du Ramadân, aumône légale, pélerinage à la Mecque,—et secondairement des œuvres surérogatoires'. In the latter case, p. 334, it is for these authors 'l'accomplissement "par les membres" des œuvres prescrites'. The references that they give (p. 333, fn. 5, and p. 334, fn. 1) are to an edition of Bājūrī (Cairo, 1352/1934; see Gardet and Anawati, *op. cit.*, p. 13), other than the one, *Sharḥ al-Bayjūrī ʿalá al-Jawharah* (*sc.* of Lāqānī), ed. Ḥusayn ʿAbd al-Raḥīm Makkī, Cairo, 1374/1954, to which alone I have had access, and in which, within the sector on *īmān*-and-*islām*, pp. 38-44, I do not find the phrase *ʿamal bi-al-arkān* nor . . . *bi-al-jawāriḥ*, nor indeed the terms *jawāriḥ* or *arkān* except the latter in the phrase *al-arkān al-khamsah* which Bayjūrī uses in commenting on Lāqānī's use of the *ḥajj*, *ṣalāh*, etc. as illustrations (*mithāl*) of the action (*ʿamal*) that goes with faith. In other words, I have not succeeded in uncovering an Arabic wording directly

underlying the French. It seems probable that the interpretation is general.

On the other hand, in his recent article IMĀN, in the latest volume of the new *Encyclopaedia of Islam*, Gardet diverges a trifle from Laoust (cf. *supra*, ref. 2) and goes further than he in translating *ʿamal bi-al-arkān* as 'to fulfil the pillars of Islam' (English ed., III, 1171, column 2, section 4). Further, in speaking of the view of those who 'saw "works" as an integral part of faith, even as faith itself' he affirms: 'By *ʿamal* (and its plural *aʿmāl*) should be understood the "pillars of Islam" (including the profession of faith), and with them the works prescribed by the Ḳur'ān' (*loc. cit.*, column 1, section 3)—but again without reference to an actual text, and without indication of the force of his conjunctive phrase 'and with them'.

8. See, e.g., *Lisān al-ʿArab*, Beirut: Dār Ṣādir/Dār Bayrūt, 15 vols., 1374–1376/1955–1956, s.v., vol. 13, pp. 185 f.; or *Tāj al-ʿArūs*, Cairo: al-Maṭbaʿah al-Khayrīyah, 10 vols., 1304 ff., vol. 9, pp. 219 f. Cf. E. W. Lane, *Arabic–English Lexicon*, London and Edinburgh: Williams and Norgate, 1863–1893, s.v., vol. 2, pp. 1148 f.
9. Both *Lisān al-ʿArab*, *edn. cit.*, p. 186, lines 1–2, and *Tāj al-ʿArūs*, *edn. cit.*, p. 219, line 29, give *jawāriḥ* as one meaning of the *arkān* of a person; more or less in passing.
10. *Al-īmān huwa al-taṣdīq* is the standard wording for the generic statement, unamplified; but in the triple formula with the *bi-* complements it is rather *taṣdīqun bi-al-qalb* (not *al-taṣdīqu . . .*), *iqrārun bi-al-lisān* (not *al-iqrāru . . .*), and *ʿamalun . . . .* Similarly—in Ibn Mājah, for instance, ref. 2 above—it is *maʿrifatun bi-al-qalb*. Exceptions, where the definite article does occur, are the Abū al-Muʿīn al-Nasafī quotation given above, ref. 6, and the Ghazzālī one below, ref. 27; but this usage is relatively rare.
11. Since writing the above, however, I have come across in Baghdādī a clause *ʿamala bi-al-kabā'ir*, performing major sins, with which *bi-al-arkān* in the sense of the pillars would be formally quite parallel—Abū Manṣūr ʿAbd al-Qādir . . . al-Baghdādī, *Kitāb al-Milal wa-al-Niḥal*, ed. [Albert] Naṣrī Nādir, Beirut: Dār al-Mashriq, 1970, p. 77, line 10. One might, therefore, be tempted to withdraw this argument; were it not that the same construction with *bi-* occurs also when the noun is a concrete noun, not a *maṣdar*, as in *al-aʿmāl bi-al-arkān*.
12. To illustrate the outward acts that go with faith, Lāqānī in his *Jawharah* does indeed proffer as examples (*mithāl hādhā*—that is, *mithāl al-ʿamal*) the pilgrimage, etc., citing the other four pillars (though he does not call them that); and Bayjūrī comments that the *shahādah* is omitted from mention in this enumeration because it has figured previously in the discussion as a separate item. Cf. ref. 7 above, with the remark on the

phrase *al-arkān al-khamsah* which there occurs—Bayjūrī, *op. cit.*, pp. 42 f., esp. p. 43, line 14 of the commentary.

13. Quoted (as from his *Sharḥ al-Arbaʿīn al-Nawawīyah*) by Mullā Ḥusayn ibn Iskandar al-Ḥanafī in his commentary on the *Waṣiyat al-imām al-aʿẓam Abī Ḥanīfah* entitled *al-Jawharah al-munīfah*, p. 78 of the second Ḥaydarabad: Dā'irat al-Maʿārif al-Niẓāmīyah edition, 1367/1948, in the collection *al-Rasā'il al-sabʿah fī al-ʿaqā'id*.
14. Gardet, *Destinée*, p. 356.
15. In the course of his exegesis of Qur'ān 3:19 (*Inna al-dīna ʿinda-llāhi-l-islām*), he writes: *al-islām wa-al-īmān ʿindanā wa-ʿinda al-Muʿtazilah bi-maʿnan wāḥid, ghayr anna ʿindahum anna fiʿl al-wājibāt min afʿāl' al-jawāriḥ min al-īmān . . . wa-ʿindanā anna afʿāl al-wājibāt min afʿāl al-qulūb—allatī hiya al-taṣdīq—min al-īmān; fa-ammā afʿāl al-jawāriḥ, fa-laysat min al-īmān, wa-in kānat wājibah*—Abū Jaʿfar Muḥammad ibn al-Ḥasan al-Ṭūsī, *al-Tibyān fī tafsīr al-Qur'ān*, ed. Aḥmad Shawqī al-Amīn and Aḥmad Ḥabīb Quṣayr, 10 vols., various places and publishers, 1376–1383/1957–1963; vol. 2, Najaf: Maktabat al-Amīn, 1376/1957, pp. 418 f.
16. For example, Baghdādī quotes this *ḥadīth* immediately following upon the word *al-arkān* concluding the triple-formula definition of faith in another *ḥadīth*. Abū Manṣūr ʿAbd al-Qāhir . . . al-Baghdādī, *Kitāb uṣūl al-dīn*, vol. I, Istanbul: Maṭbaʿat al-Dawlah, 1346/1928, p. 251, lines 8–10. It would seem difficult to reject the notion here that in Baghdādī's mind *imāṭat al-adhá ʿan al-ṭarīq* is one instance of an *ʿamal bi-al-arkān*.
17. An interesting example of how a classical Muslim mind worked on these matters is afforded again by Bāqillānī, from whose discussion on the import of works for faith we can see what sort of works he had in mind. Following a paragraph in which to designate these works he has used *ʿamal bi-al-arkān*, he turns to consider the case of a person who has *taṣdīq* but not works; and he mentions in illustration of these latter three, indeed, of the five 'pillars' but then gives as further instance a quite different item: *ṣalāh, aw ṣiyām, aw zakāh, aw qirā'ah fī mawḍaʿ tajibu fīhi al-qirā'ah, aw ghayr dhālik min al-wājibāt*. Next, he discusses the case of a person whose works are fine, but whose *taṣdīq* is faulty on one single point; and to illustrate this he chooses one of two prohibitions—rather than any positive obligation, pillar or not; *op. cit.* (our ref. 6 above), p. 50, lines 12–13, 14 ff.
18. Baghdādī indicates as the position held by some (namely, the majority of *aṣḥāb al-ḥadīth*): *inna al-īmān jamīʿ al-ṭāʿāt farḍihā wa-naflihā* (or, still more emphatically: *farḍuhā wa-nafluhā*?), and then elaborates that there are within this then three types: a minimal, which is an (inactive?) knowledge of God by which one is saved from *kufr* and from permanence

in Hell; a second level, which consists in performing the ordained duties and avoiding major sins (*adā' al-farā'iḍ wa-ijtināb al-kabā'ir*) and by which one is saved from being *fāsiq* and from entering Hell; and the highest sort, which is performing *all* good works and avoiding *all* sins (*wa-huwa adā' al-farā'iḍ wa-al-nawāfil maʿa ijtināb al-dhunūb kullihā*); *op. cit.*, p. 249. A question just does not arise of a division or level or type of faith for those who perform the five pillars but no more—an issue that would presumably have come into discussion if *al-arkān* designated those pillars.

19. For example, among the Muʿtazilah, Abū al-Hudhayl (*sc.* al-ʿAllāf) and ʿAbd al-Jabbār ibn Aḥmad; see the latter's *Sharḥ al-uṣūl al-khamsah*, ed. ʿAbd al-Karīm ʿUthmān, Cairo: Maktabat Wahbah, 1384/1965, p. 707, lines 16–19 (cf. also second paragraph of p. 708).
20. For example, from among the same group, Abū ʿAlī (*sc.* al-Jubbā'ī) and (his son) Abū Hāshim. See ʿAbd al-Jabbār, *op. cit.*, p. 707 (and first paragraph of p. 708).
21. Cf. the phrases with *ijtināb* in the Baghdādī reference above (our ref. 18). Similarly Taftāzānī, *op. cit.* (our ref. 2 above), rebuts the thesis that *ʿamal bi-al-arkān* is part of faith, by citing *inter alia* the Qur'ān's acknowledging the faith of those who have sinned—and whose sin is unrelated to the pillars (*ṭā'ifatān min al-mu'minīn iqtatalū*), and by speaking generally of a person's having *taṣdīq* whether he *atá bi-al-ṭāʿāt aw irtakaba al-maʿāṣī*, *op. cit.*, Cairo edn., p. 128; Istanbul edn., pp. 156, 157, again with no special reference to the pillars and equal attention to the performance of sin.
22. For instance, see al-Ghazzālī, in the passage cited below, at our ref. 27.
23. Cf. our ref. 2 above. Ibn Mājah (third/ninth century) is the one early occurrence of the term *al-arkān* in the discussions of *īmān* that I have met; along with his contemporary Abū Ḥātim al-Rāzī, if Laoust's reference may be followed. It becomes a little more current in the following century; perhaps dominant (but not yet exclusive) in the fifth/eleventh; and as we have said, established by the seventh/fourteenth.
24. *Bi-fatḥ al-jīm* (unfortunately, I have misplaced my reference for this).
25. An example is the *ḥadīth* quoted by Ibn Mājah; *supra*, ref. 2.
26. *Op. cit.*, p. 49, lines 2, 4, 5 (*jawāriḥ*), 18, 20 (*arkān*); p. 50, line 2 (*arkān*). In the last three cases the three matters (*qalb, lisān, arkān*) are juxtaposed.
27. *Rubʿ* 1, Book 2, *Faṣl* 4, *Baḥth* 3. I have used the 1356/1937–1938 Cairo edition (16 volumes) of the Lajnat Nashr al-Thaqāfah al-Islāmīyah; this passage appears at vol. 1, pp. 205 ff. (pp. 13 ff. of the second *juz'*). In passing, one may remark that the late Nabīh Fāris, in his English translation of this book, not only translated *al-arkān* as 'the pillars [of Islam]',

but goes out of his way then to add '[according to the pillars of Islam]' parenthetically to other occurrences, in this passage, of *aʿmāl*, not only where this term occurs unspecified but even once where my edition of the Arabic has *bi-al-jawāriḥ*—Nabih Amin Faris, trans., *The Foundations of the Articles of Faith, being a translation with notes of the Kitāb Qawāʿid al-ʿAqā'id of Al-Ghazzālī's 'Iḥyā' ʿUlūm al-Dīn'*, Lahore: Ashraf, 1963, p. 105, lines 13–14, 22; p. 106, line 3.

28. *Op. cit.*, *edn. cit.*, p. 206, line 4.
29. *Loc. cit.*, lines 5–11.
30. Bāqillānī, *op. cit.*, p. 49, line 2 from bottom, and p. 50, line 2.
31. And Jeffery so translates it; above, ref. 6 (*ad fin.*). This is the only instance that I have noticed in the literature where a modern Western scholar translates so. In this context, this rendering is indeed 'inescapable'.
32. One awaits the article RUKN in the new edition of the *Encyclopaedia of Islam*.
33. As is well known, in the famous opening *ḥadīth* in the *Ṣaḥīḥ* of al-Bukhārī, no designation is given. It runs, simply, *al-islām ʿalá khams*.
34. An example is provided by Lāqānī's poem; cf. above, our ref. 12.
35. The edition by the impressive scholar to whom we all owe so much, Muḥammad Fu'ād ʿAbd al-Bāqī, of the *Sunan* of Ibn Mājah, *op. cit.* above, our ref. 2.
36. Cf. Laoust, Gardet, and Gardet & Qanawātī, as quoted above, our refs. 4, 7.

NOTES TO CHAPTER NINE: THE CRYSTALLIZATION OF RELIGIOUS COMMUNITIES IN MUGHUL INDIA

1. *The Meaning and End of Religion* [above, our chapter 3 here, note 1].
2. More strictly, 'is reputed to have written'. The passage that follows in our text is uncanonical, and although attributed to the tenth Guru, is now said to have emerged among his followers when the Khālṣah was set up. Both the Panjābī original and the translation I owe to Sikh friends; it is a well-known 'litany', but I do not have a written source. The two preceding quotations are from the Guru Granth Ṣāḥib, Bhairav Rāga (Rāg Bhirao). An alternative English rendering will be found in *Sri Guru Granth Sahib (English version), translated and annotated by* Gopal Singh, Delhi, Jullundur City, Ambala Cant.: Gur Das Kampur & Sons, 4 voll., 1960–1962, p. 1084.
3. [The reference here was to my *sharīʿah* article, given above, pp. 87–109.]
4. The careful study of R. C. Zaehner, *Hindu and Muslim Mysticism*, London: Athlone Press, 1960, is not the last word on the subject.

5. S. M. Ikram, *History of Muslim Civilisation in India and Pakistan*, S. A. Rashid, ed., Lahore: Star Book Depot, n.d. [*sc.* 1962], p. 251. [An abridged version of this work, ed. Ainslie T. Embree, appeared as S. M. Ikram, *Muslim Civilization in India*, New York and London: Columbia Univerity Press, 1964.]
6. *Ibid.*, p. 267. [The original has the misprint 'rehetorical'.]
7. *Ibid.*, p. 270.
8. That Akbar was a universalist is a perhaps controversial contention; but at least he represented and was influenced by a universalizing tendency.
9. Perhaps not immediately; but in any case soon, when his elder brother Khwājah Muḥammad Saʿid (perhaps his successor) died.
10. The notion of 'unconscious freedom' may seem strange to some; but freedom is a much more subtle matter than it is sometimes credited with being.
11. The execution of Tegh Bahādur, done while the emperor apparently was away from Delhi, was accompanied by what was perhaps the Islamic 'formality' of offering conversion as an alternative; but the interpretation of this as an attempted forcible conversion was made vivid by the subsequent Sikh community.
12. The linking together of the two men, Bāqī Bi-llāh and Sirhindī, should not be taken as suggesting that the ideas of both were by any means identical, or even closely similar. Differences were substantial; and the actual contact between the two men was, as we have indicated above, limited. Our thesis is rather that both were significant contributors to the same general movement, towards a formal systematization of what presently came to be called Islām. An unpublished doctoral thesis submitted recently to McGill University, to which I have not had access, apparently argues that in his own lifetime Sirhindī was known not as a conservative, certainly not as 'orthodox', but as a radical, not as a champion of *sharīʿah* but as an overly pretentious Ṣūfī. While awaiting the publication of this thesis, I am left wondering whether in any case it might not be seen as corroborating rather than refuting my interpretation, which would see Sirhindī as an innovator whose ideas came to be thought of as 'orthodox' only much later when they had eventually prevailed. It may turn out that Shāh Walīyullāh in the eighteenth century, who synthesized Bāqī Bi-llāh and Sirhindī, as well as much else, is the catalyst of the new movement conceptually; though it would still seem that Bāqī Bi-llāh and especially Sirhindī were major protagonists. [This thesis has now been published, and those interested in the topics raised here should undoubtedly consult and ponder its presentations: Yohanan Friedmann, *Shaykh Aḥmad Sirhindī: an outline of his thought and a study of his image in the eyes of posterity*, Montreal and London: McGill–Queen's Press, 1971.]

13. Bombay: Bharatiya Vidya Bhavan, 1961, p. 277.
14. *op. cit.*, our ref. 1 above.
15. *Ibid.*, pp. 63–66; with references, pp. 256–259.
16. *Ibid.*, ref. 56, p. 259. I have since discovered, in private conversation with Dr. Bouquet, that Dāsguptā had given him the information also in private conversation.
17. Allahabad and London: Kitabistan, 1938, pp. 110 f.
18. London: Allen & Unwin, 1963.

NOTES TO CHAPTER TEN: THE ‘*ULAMĀ*’ IN INDIAN POLITICS

1. Before this period, *ʿulamāʾ* (and perhaps even ‘the’ *ʿulamāʾ*?) are found as a species, but hardly yet as a class.
2. Some work that I am doing in another area of study [*subsequently published: above, pp. 87–109*] suggests that perhaps their *ʿilm* was at first of *aḥkām* rather than of a conceptualized *sharīʿah*. This matter is extremely complex, and more factors than are here noted went into the ossification (to use a modern Muslim's term) of the *sharīʿah*. Even before the political disintegration, the process of fighting against discontent (‘heresies’) contributed. We are here attempting to uncover one facet of a development, without claiming that it is the sole face.
3. Subsequently published as Ziya-ul-Hasan Faruqi, *The Deoband School and the Demand for Pakistan*, Bombay etc.: Asia Publishing House, 1963.

NOTES TO CHAPTER ELEVEN: ALIGARH AND RELIGION: A QUESTION

1. *Modern Islām in India* (1943).

NOTES TO CHAPTER TWELVE: RELIGIOUS DIVERSITY: MUSLIM–HINDŪ RELATIONS IN INDIA

1. *Faith and Belief* (1979).
2. A remark that I myself launched before I learned to drop the phrase ‘a religion’.
3. [*Above, pp. 87–109 in this collection.*]
4. [*Above, pp. 177–196 in this collection.*].

NOTES TO CHAPTER THIRTEEN: SOME SIMILARITIES AND SOME DIFFERENCES BETWEEN CHRISTIANITY AND ISLĀM

1. See my *Islam in Modern History* (1957) [1977], especially Chapter 1, notes 11, 13, 14, 27 and 28; pp. 16–18, 30 f.
2. *Ibid.*, note 11; p. 16.
3. Accordingly, the same phrasing 'Thy will be done' is sometimes used by Christians as an expression of resignation, or of a desired resignation. This is when it is used not as a prayer, with reference to a future or in dedication to coming action; but after an event. An instance is when a mother has seen her child die, and cries, or is admonished to cry, 'Thy will be done'; that is, 'May I accept the fact that Thy will has been done', on the theory in this case that whatever happens is *ipso facto* God's will. The problem of attempting to reconcile this interpretation with the belief that God wills what is good has exercised many a theologian, and many such a mother. The same problem is found in Islām. Indeed, an intellectual if not a moral counterpart to it is also found in other determinist world-views, such as Marxist, or some scientific secular, ones.
4. 'The word "*Islam*" itself may be literally interpreted, "*Thy will be done*" '—the Honorable John T. Wood, Congressman from Idaho, in the House of Representatives on February 25, 1952; the *Congressional Record*, 48:28 (but *lege* 98:28), as quoted in *The Muslim Sunrise*, 24/4 (Fourth Quarter, 1952): 18. I do not know Mr. Wood's source.
5. Smith, *op. cit.*, last sentence of note 11, pp. 16–17.
6. *Ibid.*, p. 17, note 13.
7. e.g., *ibid.*, p. 17.
8. *Ibid.*, p. 19.
9. E.g., H. A. R. Gibb, *Mohammedanism*, London: Oxford University Press, 1949, p. 106.
10. Smith, *op. cit.*, pp. 19–21.
11. Taking 'Church' not as one particular denomination but in its widest, deepest sense as the whole body of Christians, a divine-human complex, holy, catholic, then of course *ummah* is to Islām as Church is to Christianity. This is true but not complete; since, as is well known, *ummah* is to Islām also as society, state, are to Christianity. It would be interesting to explore too the connotations of *jamāʿah* in this connection.
12. H. A. Wolfson, 'The Muslim Attributes and the Christian Trinity', *Harvard Theological Review* 49 (1956): 1–18.
13. *Lā huwa wa-lā ghayruh—Sharḥ . . . al-Taftāzānī ʿalá al-ʿAqāʾid al-Nasafīyah*, Cairo: Dār Iḥyāʾ al-Kutub al-ʿArabīyah (ʿĪsá al-Bābī al-Ḥalabī), n.d. (*sc.* 1335 h./1916), p. 70

14. It is the Word (*kalām*) of God; it is not He nor is it other than He. 'We do not say that the words and letters are pre-existent, eternal . . . . The [uncreated] Qur'ān, which is the Word of God Transcendent, "written in our copies, . . . apprehended (memorized) in our minds/hearts, . . . recited with our tongues, . . . heard with our ears" . . . is nonetheless not something circumstantial that happens in those copies, hearts/minds, tongues, ears; rather, it is a pre-existent eternal Idea subsisting in the very being of God (*huwa maʿnan qadīm qā'im bi-dhāt Allāh*)'—Taftāzānī, *op. cit.*, pp. 82–83.

NOTES TO CHAPTER FIFTEEN: MUSLIM AND CHRISTIAN: FAITH CONVERGENCE, BELIEF DIVERGENCE

1. [*sc.*, in the first of these two Iqbāl lectures; above in this collection, pp. 110–134.]
2. [The translation within parentheses is that of the King James Version, retained also in the modern Revised Standard Version. With this Biblical verse it is illuminating to compare *taṣdīq* in Qur'ān 37:105: 'Thou hast already fulfilled the vision' (*qad ṣaddaqta al-ru'yā*).]

NOTES TO CHAPTER SIXTEEN: IS THE QUR'ĀN THE WORD OF GOD?

1. Christians are in danger of missing the full force of the Muslim position on this matter, by supposing that the analogy with the Qur'ān is the Bible. Rather, the parallel is to the Christian doctrine that Jesus Christ is the Word of God. Throughout this present discussion, this point should be borne vividly in mind: that the Muslim attitude to the Qur'ān is like the Christian attitude to Christ. [Cf. above, pp. 238 f.].
2. William Muir, *The Life of Moḥammad from Original Sources*, T. H. Weir, ed., Edinburgh: John Grant, 1912, p. xxviii, quoting without precise reference 'Von Hammer', presumably Joseph von Hammer-Purgstall.

2a. [Or five. Cf. note 1 to chap. 2, p. 301 above.]

3. Hamilton A. R. Gibb, 'Pre-Islamic Monotheism in Arabia', *Harvard Theological Review* 55 (1962): 269.
4. See, for instance, his *The Call of the Minaret*, New York: Oxford University Press, 1956, and *Sandals at the Mosque*, London: S.C.M., and New York: Oxford University Press, 1959.
5. F. Rahman, *Prophecy in Islam: philosophy and orthodoxy*, London and New York: Allen & Unwin, 1958.

6. It is perhaps unnecessary to add (I hope the point has been manifestly implicit throughout) that this whole discussion may presumably be transposed, whether on to parallel Hindū or Buddhist issues, or back into internal Christian terms. A consideration of the Western/Muslim divergence over the Qur'ān is applicable at least in principle to a secular/Christian divergence over Christian positions. To suppose that there is, or even ideally should be, a generic 'yes' or 'no' answer to such questions as whether Christ is the Word, or the Son, the incarnate revelation, of God, must surely be superseded. The question remains as important, as destiny-determining, as ever it was; but the answer is not so simple, is no longer impersonal.

Provenance

The various chapters of this book are being published here for the first time, or have appeared previously, as follows. An asterisk indicates those to whom acknowledgement and thanks are hereby expressed for permission to reprint.

1. Never before published.
2. 'Muslims', chapter 4 of Wilfred Cantwell Smith, *The Faith of Other Men*, Toronto: Canadian Broadcasting Corporation, 1962; New York: New American Library, 1963; New York, San Francisco, etc.: *Harper & Row (Harper Torchbooks), 1972.
3. In *Bernard Lewis and P. M. Holt, edd., *Historians of the Middle East*, London, New York, etc.: Oxford University Press, 1962 (*School of Oriental and African Studies, University of London: Historical Writing on the Peoples of Asia [4]), pp. [484]–502.
4. 'Law and Ijtihad in Islam', in *International Islamic Colloquium Papers*, Lahore: Panjab University Press, 1960, pp. 111–114.
5. 'The Concept of Shariʿa among some Mutakallimun', in *George Makdisi, ed., *Arabic and Islamic Studies in Honor of Hamilton A. R. Gibb*, Leiden: *Brill, 1965, pp. [581]–602.
6. This and chapter 15 below: 'Faith and Belief. [I:] Some considerations from the Islamic instance. II: Some considerations from the Christian instance.' *Al-Hikmat: a research journal of the *Department of Philosophy, University of the Punjab*, Lahore 6 (1975–1976): [1]–20, [21]–43. This chapter, and part of 15 below, were used in modified form also in my *Faith and Belief*, Princeton: *Princeton University Press, 1979.
7. Never before published. Its publication has for some time been announced as forthcoming in Parviz Morewedge, ed., *Islamic Philosophical Theology*, Albany: State University of New York Press; but this volume's appearance seems to have become problematic.
8. '*Arkān*', in *Donald P. Little, ed., *Essays on Islamic Civilization: presented to Niyazi Berkes*, Leiden: *Brill, 1976, pp. [303]–316.
9. In Mojtaba Minovi, Iraj Afshar, edd., *Yād-Nāme-ye Īrāini* [sic]*-ye Minorsky*, Tehran: Tehran University, 1969, pp. 197–220 (of the Latin script section).
10. 'The ʿUlamā' in Indian Politics', in C. H. Philips, ed., *Politics and Society in India*, London: Allen & Unwin, 1963, pp. 39–51. (*School of Oriental and African Studies, University of London.)

11. Not previously published in English; the Urdū version, entitled 'Ek Sawāl', in *ʿAlīgaṛh Maygazīn*, Aligarh, 1955, pp. 81–83.
12. Not previously published. Arrangements are currently under way for its possible appearance as a chapter in a volume to be edited by ʿĀbidullāh Ghāzi, to be published probably in New Delhi.
13. 'Some Similarities and Differences between Christianity and Islam: an essay in comparative religion', in James Kritzeck and *R. Bayly Winder, edd., *The World of Islam: studies in honour of Philip K. Hitti*, London: Macmillan, and New York: St. Martin's Press, 1959, pp. 47–59. (Copyright by *Department of Oriental Studies, Princeton University.) (A paragraph added a couple of years later is published here for the first time. The original volume [1959] is being republished, New York: Arno, 1980.)
14. 'Interpreting Religious Interrelations: an historian's view of Christian and Muslim', in **SR: Studies in Religion/Sciences religieuses*, 6/5 (1976–1977): [515]–526.
15. See item 5 above.
16. Chapter 2 of Wilfred Cantwell Smith, *Questions of Religious Truth*, New York: *Scribners, and London: Gollancz, 1967.

Publications of Wilfred Cantwell Smith

BOOKS

Modern Islām in India: A Social Analysis. Lahore, Minerva, 1943.
Revised edition: London, V. Gollancz, '1946' (*sc.* 1947).
Reissued: Lahore, Sh. M. Ashraf, 1963, 1969; New York, Russell & Russell, 1972; and pirated edition, Lahore, Ripon, 1947 (with a spurious chapter 'Towards Pakistan' by an unknown other hand).

Pakistan as an Islamic State. Lahore, Sh. M. Ashraf, '1951' (*sc.* 1954).

Islam in Modern History. Princeton, Princeton University Press, 1957.
Reissued: London, Oxford University Press, 1958; New York, New American Library (Mentor Books), 1959; London, New English Library (Mentor Books), 1965; Princeton and London, Princeton University Press (Princeton Paperback), 1977.
Taped for Recording for the Blind, Inc., Washington, 1973.
Translated into: Arabic (pirated, 1960; authorized, 1975), Swedish (1961), French (1962), Indonesian (1962–1964), German (1963), and Japanese (1974).
Portions translated into: Urdu (1958–1959, 1960) and Arabic (1960).

The Faith of Other Men. Toronto, Canadian Broadcasting Corporation, 1962.
Enlarged edition: New York, New American Library, 1963.
Reissued: New York, New American Library (Mentor Books), 1965; London, New English Library (Mentor Books), 1965; New York and London, Harper & Row (Torchbook), 1972.
Translated into: Swedish (1965).
Part II ('The Christian in a Religiously Plural World') reprinted in *Religious Diversity* (infra) in slightly abridged form; also in John Hick and Brian Hebblethwaite, edd., *Christianity and Other Religions*, [London:] Collins (Fount Paperbacks), 1980, pp. 87–107.

The Meaning and End of Religion: A New Approach to the Religious Traditions of Mankind. New York, Macmillan, 1963.
Reissued: New York, New American Library (Mentor Books), 1964; London, New English Library (Mentor Books), 1965; San Francisco, Harper & Row, and London: S.P.C.K., 1978.

Modernisation of a Traditional Society. Bombay, Calcutta, etc., Asia Publishing House, 1965.
Chap. 1, reprinted in slightly abridged form in *Religious Diversity* (infra).

Questions of Religious Truth. New York, Charles Scribner's Sons; and London, V. Gollancz Ltd., 1967.

Translated into: Japanese (1971).
Second chapter ('Is the Qur'an the Word of God?') reprinted in slightly abridged form in *Religious Diversity* (infra).

Religious Diversity. Willard G. Oxtoby, ed. New York and London, Harper & Row, 1976.

Belief and History. Charlottesville: University Press of Virginia, 1977.

Faith and Belief. Princeton: Princeton University Press, 1979.

Towards a World Theology. London, Macmillan, and Philadelphia, Westminster, 1981

ARTICLES ON RELIGION GENERALLY

'The Comparative Study of Religion: Reflections on the Possibility and Purpose of a Religious Science.' In: *McGill University, Faculty of Divinity, Inaugural Lectures* (Montreal, McGill University, 1950), pp. 39–60.

'The Christian and the Religions of Asia.' In: *Changing Asia: Report of the Twenty-Eighth Annual Couchiching Conference: A Joint Project of the Canadian Institute on Public Affairs and the Canadian Broadcasting Corporation* (Toronto, Canadian Institute on Public Affairs, 1959), pp. 9–16.
Reprinted: *Occasional Papers*, Department of Missionary Studies, International Missionary Council (World Council of Churches), London, no. 5 (April, 1960); also as 'Christianity's Third Great Challenge', *The Christian Century* 77:17 (April 27, 1960) 505–508; also, abridged, *The Beacon*, London, 39 (1962), 337–340.

'Comparative Religion: Whither—and Why?' In: Mircea Eliade and Joseph M. Kitagawa, eds., *The History of Religions: Essays in Methodology* (Chicago, The University of Chicago Press, 1959), pp. 31–58.
Reprinted in abridged form in *Religious Diversity* (supra).
Translated into: Urdu (1962), Japanese (1962), and German (1963).

'Mankind's Religiously Divided History Approaches Self-Consciousness'. *Harvard Divinity Bulletin* 29:1 (1964), pp. 1–17.
Reprinted in slightly abridged form in *Religious Diversity* (supra).
Translated into: German (1967).

'Secularism: The Problem Posed'. *Seminar*, New Delhi, 67 (1965), pp. 10–12.

'Religious Atheism? Early Buddhist and Recent American'. *Milla wa-Milla*, Melbourne, 6 (1966), pp. 5–30.
Reprinted: John Bowman, ed., *Comparative Religion: The Charles Strong Trust Lectures 1961–70* (Leiden, E. J. Brill, 1972), pp. 53–81.

'The Mission of the Church and the Future of Missions.' In: George Johnston and Wolfgang Roth, eds., *The Church in the Modern World: Essays in Honour of James Sutherland Thomson* (Toronto, The Ryerson Press, 1967), pp. 154–170.

' "Traditional Religions and Modern Culture." ' In: *Proceedings of the XIth International Congress of the International Association for the History of Religions*, vol. 1, The Impact of Modern Culture on Traditional Religions (Leiden, E. J. Brill, 1968), pp. 55–72.
Reprinted in slightly abridged form in *Religious Diversity* (supra).

'Secularity and the History of Religion.' In: Albert Schlitzer, ed., *The Spirit and Power of Christian Secularity* (Notre Dame and London, University of Notre Dame Press, 1969), pp. 33–58. Discussion follows, pp. 59–70.

'University Studies of Religion in a Global Context.' In: *Study of Religion in Indian Universities: A Report of the Consultation Held in Bangalore in September, 1967* ([Bangalore], Bangalore Press, n.d. [1970]), pp. 74–87.

'Participation: The Changing Christian Role in Other Cultures,' *Occasional Bulletin*, Missionary Research Library, New York, 20:4 (1969) 1–13.
Reprinted: *Religion and Society*, Bangalore, 17:1 (1970) 56–74; in abridged form in Gerald H. Anderson and Thomas F. Stransky, eds., *Mission Trends No. 2* (New York, Paulist Press, and Grand Rapids, Eerdmans, 1975), pp. 218–229; and in *Religious Diversity* (supra).

'The Study of Religion and the Study of the Bible,' *Journal of the American Academy of Religion* 39 (1971) 131–140.
Reprinted with minor alterations in *Religious Diversity* (supra).

'A Human View of Truth,' *SR: Studies in Religion/Sciences religieuses* 1 (1971) 6–24.
Reprinted: John Hick, ed., *Truth and Dialogue: The Relationship between World Religions* (London, Sheldon Press, 1974); *Truth and Dialogue in World Religions: Conflicting Truth-Claims* (Philadelphia, Westminster Press, 1974), pp. 20–44, with a new addendum, 'Conflicting Truth-Claims: A Rejoinder,' *ibid.*, pp. 156–162.

'Programme Notes for a Mitigated Cacophony' (a review article on R. C. Zaehner, *Concordant Discord*, 1970), *The Journal of Religion* 53 (1973) 377–381.

'On "Dialogue and Faith": A Rejoinder' [to Eric J. Sharpe, 'Dialogue and Faith,' in the same issue], *Religion* 3 (1973) 106–114.

' "The Finger That Points to the Moon": Reply to Per Kværne' [Kværne, ' "Comparative Religion: Whither—and Why?" A Reply to Wilfred Cantwell Smith,' in the same issue], *Temenos*, Helsinki, 9 (1973) 169–172.

'World Religions' (in the section, 'What's in Store for '74? Looking Ahead in Various Areas of Contemporary Life'), *The Christian Century*, 91:1 (1974) 16.

'Religion as Symbolism,' introduction to Propaedia, part 8, 'Religion,' *Encyclopaedia Britannica*, 15th ed. (Chicago, Encyclopaedia Britannica, 1974), vol. 1, pp. 498–500.

'Methodology and the Study of Religion: Some Misgivings.' In: Robert D. Baird, ed., *Methodological Issues in Religious Studies* (Chico, Calif., New Horizons

Press, 1975), pp. 1–25 ('Discussion,' pp. 25–30). 'Is the Comparative Study of Religion Possible? Panel Discussion,' with Jacob Neusner, Hans H. Penner, ibid., pp. 95–109. 'Rejoinder,' pp. 123–124.

'An Historian of Faith Reflects on What We are Doing Here.' In: Donald G. Dawe and John B. Carman, edd., *Christian Faith in a Religiously Plural World* (Maryknoll, New York: Orbis, 1978), pp. 139–148.

'Divisiveness and Unity.' In: Gremillion, Joseph, ed., *Food/Energy and the Major Faiths* (Maryknoll, New York: Orbis, 1978), pp. 71–85.

ARTICLES ON EDUCATION, WEST/EAST STUDIES, AND CULTURE CONCERN GENERALLY

'Achievement Tests in History,' *Education*, Lucknow, 24:1 (1945) 57–62.

'Objective Test in History,' *Education*, Lucknow, 24:2 (1945) 53–60.
Reprinted: *The Punjab Educational Journal*, Lahore, 29 (1944) 309–313, 336–345.

'The Place of Oriental Studies in a Western University,' *Diogenes* no. 16 (1956) 104–111.
Translated into: French (1956), German (1957), and Spanish (1958).

'The YMCA and the Present,' *Bulletin*, National Council of Young Men's Christian Associations of Canada, Toronto, 34:4 (June, 1960) 3–5.

'Non-Western Studies: The Religious Approach.' In: *A Report on an Invitational Conference on the Study of Religion in the State University, Held October 23–25, 1964 at Indiana University Medical Center* (New Haven, The Society for Religion in Higher Education, [1965]), pp. 50–62. Comments and discussion follow, pp. 62–67.

'Objectivity and the Humane Sciences: A New Proposal', *Transactions of the Royal Society of Canada* (Ottawa, Royal Society of Canada, 1975), 4/12 (1974), pp. 81–102.
Reprinted in abridged form in *Religious Diversity* (supra).
Reprinted in: Claude Fortier et al., *Symposium on the Frontiers and Limitations of Knowledge/Colloque sur les frontières et limites du savoir* (Ottawa, Royal Society of Canada, 1975), pp. 81–102.

The Role of Asian Studies in the American University. The plenary address of the New York State Conference for Asian Studies, Colgate University, October 10–12, 1975. [Hamilton, N.Y.]: Colgate University, [1976]. (Pamphlet.)

'The University.' Review article of: Murray Ross, *The University: The Anatomy of Academe*, New York, 1976, in *Dalhousie Review*, 57 (1977–78): 540–549.

'Thinking about Persons.' *Humanitas*, 15 (1979): 147–152.

ARTICLES ON ISLAMIC SUBJECTS

'The Mughal Empire and the Middle Class: A Hypothesis', *Islamic Culture*, Hyderabad, 18 (1944), pp. 349–363.

'Lower-Class Uprisings in the Mughal Empire', *Islamic Culture*, Hyderabad, 20 (1946), pp. 21–40.

'The Muslim World.' In: *One Family* (Toronto, Missionary Society of the Church of England in Canada, 2 vols. 1947–1948), vol. 2, pp. 27–32.

'Hyderabad: Muslim Tragedy', *Middle East Journal*, 4 (1950), pp. 27–51.

'The Muslims and the West', *Foreign Policy Bulletin*, New York, 31:2 (October, 1951), pp. 5–7.

'Islam Confronted by Western Secularism, (A): Revolutionary Reaction.' In: Dorothea Seelye Franck, ed., *Islam in the Modern World: A Series of Addresses Presented at the Fifth Annual Conference on Middle East Affairs, Sponsored by the Middle East Institute* (Washington, Middle East Institute, 1951), pp. 19–30.
Translated into: Arabic (1953).

'Modern Turkey—Islamic Reformation?' *Islamic Culture*, Hyderabad, 25:1 (1952), pp. 155–186.
Reprinted in abridged form, with comments: *Die Welt des Islams*, n.F. 3 (1954), pp. 269–273.
Translated into: Turkish (1953).

'Pakistan', *Collier's Encyclopedia*, 1953.

'The Institute of Islamic Studies [McGill University],' *The Islamic Literature*, Lahore, 5 (1953), pp. 173–176.

'The Importance of Muhammad' (review article), *The Canadian Forum* (September, 1954), pp. 135–136.

'The Intellectuals in the Modern Development of the Islamic World.' In: Sydney Nettleton Fisher, ed., *Social Forces in the Middle East* (Ithaca, Cornell University Press, 1955), pp. 190–204.

'Propaganda (Muslim)', *Twentieth Century Encyclopaedia of Religious Knowledge* (Grand Rapids, Baker, 2 vols., 1955), II, pp. 767–768.

'Ahmadiyyah', *Encyclopaedia of Islam*, new edition (Leiden and London, E. J. Brill, 1956).
Translated into: French (1956).

'Amir Ali, Sayyid', *Encyclopaedia of Islam*, new edition (Leiden and London, E. J. Brill, 1956).
Translated into: French (1956).

'The Christian and the Near East Crisis,' *The British Weekly*, London, 138, no. 3658 (December 20, 1956), p. 5.
Also published in: *The Presbyterian Record*, Toronto, 82:1 (January, 1957), pp. 16–17.

The Muslim World (pamphlet, Current Affairs for the Canadian Forces series, vol. 10, no. 4). Ottawa, Bureau of Current Affairs, Department of National Defense, 1956), 26 pp.
Translated into: French (1956).

'Islam in the Modern World', *Current History*, 32 (1957), pp. 321–325.
Reprinted: *Enterprise*, Karachi, January 4, 1958; *Morning News*, Karachi, April 12, 1959.

'Independence Day in Indonesia', *The McGill News*, Montreal, Winter, 1957, pp. 23–24.

'Aga Khan III', *Encyclopedia Americana* (1958).

'Law and Ijtihad in Islam: Some Considerations on Their Relation to Each Other and to Ultimate and Immediate Problems', *Dawn*, Karachi, January 5, 1958.
Reprinted: *Pakistan Quarterly*, Karachi, 8 (1958), pp. 29–31, 63; also in *International Islamic Colloquium Papers: December 29, 1957—January 8, 1958* (Lahore, Panjab University Press, 1960), pp. 111–114.
Translated into: Urdu (1958), Arabic (1960).

'Some Similarities and Differences between Christianity and Islam: An Essay in Comparative Religion.' In: James Kritzeck and R. Bayly Winder, eds., *The World of Islam: Studies in Honour of Philip K. Hitti* (London, Macmillan; and New York, St. Martin's Press, 1959), pp. 47–59.
Translated into: Urdu (1964).

'India, Religion and Philosophy: Islam', *Encyclopedia Americana* (1960).
Reprinted: W. Norman Brown, ed., *India, Pakistan, Ceylon*, revised edition (Philadelphia, University of Pennsylvania Press; London, Oxford University Press [1964]), pp. 104–107.

'Modern Muslim Historical Writing in English.' In: C. H. Philips, ed., *Historians of India, Pakistan and Ceylon* (Historical Writing on the Peoples of Asia, 1) (London, Oxford University Press, 1961), pp. 319–331.

'The Comparative Study of Religion in General and the Study of Islam as a Religion in Particular.' In: *Colloque sur la sociologie musulmane: Actes, 11–14 septembre 1961* (Correspondance d'Orient, 5) (Bruxelles, Publications du Centre pour l'étude des problèmes du monde musulman contemporain [1962]), pp. 217–231.

'Iblis', *Encyclopaedia Britannica* (1962).

'The Historical Development in Islam of the Concept of Islam as an Historical Development.' In: Bernard Lewis and P. M. Holt, eds., *Historians of the Middle East* (Historical Writing on the Peoples of Asia, 4) (London, Oxford University Press, 1962), pp. 484–502.

'The 'Ulamā' in Indian Politics.' In: C. H. Philips, ed., *Politics and Society in India* (London, George Allen & Unwin Ltd., 1963), pp. 39–51.

'Druze', *Encyclopaedia Britannica* (1963).

'Koran (Qur'ān)', *Encyclopaedia Britannica* (1964).

'The Concept of Shariʿa among Some Mutakallimun.' In: George Makdisi, ed., *Arabic and Islamic Studies in Honor of Hamilton A. R. Gibb* (Leiden, E. J. Brill, 1965), pp. 581–602.

'The Islamic Near East: Intellectual Role of Librarianship,' *Library Quarterly* 35 (1965) 283–294. Discussion follows, pp. 294–297.
Reprinted: Tsuen-Hsuin Tsien and Howard W. Winger, edd., *Area Studies and the Library* (Chicago & London, The University of Chicago Press, 1966), pp. 81–92 (92–95).

'The Crystallization of Religious Communities in Mughul India.' In: Mojtaba Minovi and Iraj Afshar, eds., *Yād-Nāme-ye-Īrāini*[sic]*-ye Minorsky* (Ganjine-ye Taḥqiqāt-e Īrāni, no. 57; Publications of Tehran University, no. 1241) (Tehran, Intishārāt Dāneshgāh, 1969), pp. 197–220.

'The End is Near' [annotated translation from Urdū of Ṣiddīq Ḥasan Khān, reputed author, *Iqtirāb al-Sāʿah*]. Published anonymously in: Aziz Ahmad and G. E. von Grunebaum, eds., *Muslim Self-Statement in India and Pakistan 1857–1968* (Wiesbaden, Otto Harrassowitz, 1970), pp. 85–89.

Orientalism and Truth: A Public Lecture in Honor of T. Cuyler Young, Horatio Whitridge Garrett Professor of Persian Language and History, Chairman of the Department of Oriental Studies. Princeton, Program in Near Eastern Studies, Princeton University, 1969. 16 pp. (Pamphlet.)

'Arkān.' In: David P. Little, ed., *Essays on Islamic Civilization Presented to Niyazi Berkes*, Leiden: E. J. Brill, 1976. pp [303]–316.
Translated into: Turkish (1977).

'Faith and Belief (some considerations from the Islamic instance)' and 'Faith and Belief (some considerations from the Christian instance)'. *Al-Hikmat: A Research Journal of the Department of Philosophy*, University of the Punjab, Lahore, 6: 1–20, 21–43, '1975' [sc. 1976].

'Interpreting religious interrelations: An Historian's View of Christian and Muslim.' In: *SR: Studies in Religion/Sciences religieuses*, 6 (1976–77): 515–526.

'Tauḥīd and the Integration of Personality.' *Studies in Islam*: Quarterly Journal of the Indian Institute of Islamic Studies, New Delhi, 16 (1979): 127–128. (Discussion, pp. 128–129.)

PUBLICATIONS IN TRANSLATION

Arabic

('Islam Confronted by Western Secularism: Revolutionary Reaction', 1951) 'Al-Islām yuwājih al-ʿilmānīyah al-gharbīyah', trans. Iṣḥāq Mūsá al-Ḥusaynī with notes by ʿAli ʿAbd al-Wāḥid Wāfi. In: Philip K. Hitti, et al., *Al-Islām fī naẓar al-Gharb* (Bayrūt, Dār Bayrūt, 1953), pp. 38–59.

(*Islam in Modern History*, 1957, partial translation) 'Al-Islām wa al-taṭawwur', 'Al-Islām fī al-taʾrīkh al-ḥadīth.' In: Niqūlā Ziyādah, ed., *Dirāsāt Islāmiyah* (Bayrūt, Dār al-Andalus, 1960), pp. 295–402.

(*Islam in Modern History*, 1957, pirated edition, abridged) *Al-Islām fī al-taʾrīkh al-ḥadīth* (Kutub siyāsīyah, 163). Cairo, n.d. [1960].

(*Islam in Modern History*, 1957, authorized translation) *Al-Islām fī al-taʾrīkh al-ḥadīth*, trans. and with a foreword by Dr. M. Kāmil Ḥusayn. Bayrūt, al-Muʾassasah al-ʿArabīyah li-al-baḥth wa-al-nashr, 1975.

French

('The Place of Oriental Studies in a Western University,' 1956) 'Le Rôle de l'université dans un monde à civilisations multiples,' *Diogène*, Paris, 16 (1956) 3–13. Traduit par Nicole Laming.

('Ahmadiyyah,' 1956) 'Ahmadiyyah', *Encyclopédie de l'Islam*, nouvelle édition, Leiden and Paris, E. J. Brill, 1956.

('Amir Ali, Sayyid,' 1956) 'Amir Ali, Sayyid,' *Encyclopédie de l'Islam*, nouvelle édition, Leiden and Paris, E. J. Brill, 1956.

(*The Muslim World*, 1956) *Le monde musulman* (brochure, in the series Actualités, revue destinée aux forces canadiennes, vol. 10, no. 4). Ottawa, Bureau des actualités, Ministère de la Défense nationale, 1956, 26 pp.

(*Islam in Modern History*, 1957) *L'Islam dans le monde moderne*, préface et traduction de A. Guimbretière. Paris, Payot, 1962.

German

('The Place of Oriental Studies in a Western University,' 1956) 'Die Orientwissenschaft an einer Universität des Westens,' *Diogenes*, Köln-Marienburg, 16 (1957) 522–530.

(*Islam in Modern History*, 1957) *Der Islam in der Gegenwart*, übertragen von Hermann Stiehl. Frankfurt und Hamburg, Fischer Bücherei, 1963.

('Comparative Religion: Whither—and Why?' 1959) 'Vergleichende Religionswissenschaft: wohin—warum?' übersetzt von Dr. Elizabeth Schmitz-Mayr-Harting. In: Mircea Eliade und Joseph M. Kitagawa, hrsg., *Grundfragen der Religionswissenschaft: Acht Studien* (Salzburg, Otto Müller Verlag, 1963), pp. 75–105, 239–256.

('Mankind's Religiously Divided History Approaches Self-Consciousness,' 1964) 'Das erwachende Selbstbewusstsein von der geschichtlichen Vielfalt der

Religionen,' von Hans-Joachim Klimkeit ins Deutsche übertragen. In: Rudolf Thomas, hrsg., *Religion und Religionen: Festschrift für Gustav Mensching zu seinem 65. Geburtstag* (Bonn, Ludwig Rohrscheid Verlag, 1967), pp. 190–208.

Indonesian

(*Islam in Modern History*, 1957) *Islam dalam sedjarah modern*, diterdjemahkan oleh Abusalamah. Djakarta, Bhratara, 2 vols., 1962–64.

Japanese

('Comparative Religion: Whither—and Why?' 1959) 'Korekara no hikaku-shūkyōgaku no arikata.' In: M. Eriāde, J. M. Kitagawa, hen., *Shūkyōgaku nyumon*, Kishimoto Hideo, kanyaku (Tokyo, Tōkyō daigaku-shuppankai, 1962), pp. 47–84. Reprinted 1966.

'Shoshūkyō no kyōryoku wa kanōka—Jinrui kyōdōtai e rekishi-teki shimei-kan o' ['Is inter-religious co-operation possible? The problem of world community in historical perspective'], *Yomiuri Shimbun*, Tokyo, January 9, 1966, p. 11. (Published only in Japanese.)

(*Questions of Religious Truth*, 1967) *Shūkyō no shinri*, Kasai Minoru, yaku. Tokyo, Riso Sha, 1971. (Shūkyō shisōsen sho, 10).

(*Islam in Modern History*, 1957) *Gendai ni okeru isuramu*, Nakamura Kojiro, yaku. Tokyo, Kinokuniya, 1974.

Spanish

('The Place of Oriental Studies in a Western University,' 1956) 'La Función de la universidad en el complejo cultural de nuestro mundo,' *Diógenes*, Buenos Aires, 3 (1958) 3–12.

Swedish

(*Islam in Modern History*, 1957) *Islam i modern tid*, förord av H. S. Nyberg, till svenska av Ulla Carlsted. Stockholm, Natur och Kultur, 1961.

(*The Faith of Other Men*, 1963) *Människor av annan tro*, till svenska av Axel Ljungberg och Alf Ahlberg. Stockholm, Natur och Kultur, 1965.

Turkish

('Modern Turkey—Islamic Reformation?' 1952) 'Modern Türkiye dini bir reforma mi gidiyor?' *İlâhiyat Fakültesi Dergisi*, Ankara, 2 (1953) 7–20.

('Arkān,' 1976) '*Erkân*,' cev. Mehmet Dağ. *İslâm İlimleri Enstitüsü Dergisi*, Ankara, 3 (1977): 301–314.

Urdu

'Ek Sawāl' ['A Question'], Alīgaṛh Maygazīn, Aligarh, 1955, pp. 81–83. (Published only in Urdu.)

(*Islam in Modern History*, 1957, partial translation) 'Islām in māḍarn hisṭarī: Ek bāb kā tarjamah,' Mutarjim: Ẕiyā'u-l-Ḥasan Fārūqī, *Burhān*, Delhi, 14 (1958) 285–300, 349–364; 15 (1959) 45–58.

(*Islam in Modern History*, 1957, partial paraphrase) 'Pākistān kī Islāmī riyāsat, parofaysar Ismith kī naẓar men,' paraphrase by ʿAbdu-r-Raḥmān ʿAbd, *Chirāgh-i-Rāh* (Naẓarīyah'-i Pākistān nambar), Karachi, 12:12 (December, 1960) 277–290. 'Istidrāk,' (Khurshīd Aḥmad), pp. 290–294. 'Muẕākirah: Pākistān awr Islāmī naẓarīyah—Ḍākṭar Wilfarayḍ Kaynṭwal Ismith' ['Discussion: Pakistan and Islamic theory']. (Response to, and elaboration of, pp. 277–294; published only in Urdu.) pp. 363–366.

('Comparative Religion: Whither—and Why?' 1959) 'Maẕhab kā taqābulī muṭāliʿah: Kiyūṇ awr kis ṭaraḥ,' mutarjamah'-i jināb Sayyid Mubārizu-d-Dīn Ṣāḥib Rafʿat awr Ḍākṭar Abū Naṣr Muḥammad Ṣāḥib Khālidī, *Burhān*, Delhi, 49 (1962) 197–216, 262–281, 348–355.

('Some Similarities and Differences between Christianity and Islam,' 1959) 'Islām awr Masīḥiyat—Kuchh farq, kuchh yaksāniyāṇ: Ek taqābulī muṭālīʿah'-i maẕāhib.' In: *Dunyā-e Islām*, tarjamah'-i Sayyid Hāshimī Farīdābādī (Lahore, Maqbūl Akayḍamī, 1964), pp. 73–94.

Selective Index

Note: The list of entries in this index does not aim at completeness. On the one hand, there is no entry such as "Qur'an", for instance, nor even "Christian", since these occur too frequently for an index to them to be useful. On the other hand, of the several hundred authors and terms from the bibliographic lists in Chapter 7, none is entered here unless it be included as occurring also elsewhere. On the whole, also, geographic names, often incidental, are not listed.

abadī, 23
ʿAbbāsī dynasty, 201, 202
Abdālī, Aḥmad Shāh, 206
ʿAbduh, Muḥammad, 61, 72, 73
ʿAbdu-l-ʿAzīz, Shāh, 74, 207, 209, 210
ʿAbdu-l-Ḥaqq Muḥaddith, Dihlawī, 190, 205
ʿAbdu-r-Raḥīm Khān, Mīrzā, Khān-i Khānān, 186
Abraham, Ibrāhīm, 93, 108, 240, 262
Abū Ḥanīfah, 90, 91, 92
Abū-l-Faẕl Allāmī, Shaykh, 182, 186f.
Abū-l-Kalām Āzād, 210, 212
Adam, 36, 57, 106, 107, 108
adhān, 4f., 12, 16, 18, 31
ad libitum, 270
ʿAdil Shāhī dynasty, 191
Aḥmad Barelawī, Sayyid, 208f.
Aḥmad Khāṇ, Sir Sayyid, 187, 213–216
Aḥmad Khāṇ, Ustādh Ḥafīẓ, 229
Aḥmad Shāh Abdālī, 206
Aḥmad Sirhindī, Shaykh, *see* Sirhindī
Aḥmadīyah Movement, 243
Akbar, Mughul emperor, 178, 183, 185, 186f., 188, 191, 192, 204
Aligarh Muslim University, 135, 188, 213–216
ʿalima, 80, 121, 129, 131, 153, 154. See also *ʿilm*, *ʿulamāʾ*. Cf. *ʿarafa*
ʿamal, 137, 154, 156, 164, 166, 167, 169, 170, 171, 173. Cf. *ʿamala*, 91
āmana, 122, 159, 265, 276. See also *īmān*
āmīn, amen, 124
Amīr ʿAlī Khāṇ, 209
amr, 84, 91, 101, 157, 237, 238. Cf. *ḥukm*; commands (of God)
Anawati, *see* Qanawātī
angelology, 249
Apostle, Muḥammad as, *see* prophethood of Muḥammad
ʿaqada, 121. *ʿaqīdah*, *ʿaqāʾid*, 65, 66, 69, 76, 90, 91, 94, 121, [136f.], 158. See also *iʿtiqād*
ʿaql, 70, 91, 98f., 101, 106
ʿarafa, 121, 153, [154], [155]. *maʿrifah*, 153, 172. Cf. *ʿalima*
Aristotle, 9
Arjun, Guru, 177, 178, 179f., 181, 182, 191
arkān, chap. 8 (163–178), and 3, 52, 66, 69, 73, 75, 116, 137
art, in relation to faith; Islamic art, 7–9, 10, 11, 17, 21f., 31. Cf. calligraphy
Ārya Samāj, 195
asceticism, 256
Ashʿarī, Abū al-Ḥasan ʿAlī al-, 90, 91, 92f., 96
usmāʾ al-husná, al- the names of God, 243
Averroes, 29
Avicenna, 29, 243
Awrangzeb ʿĀlamgīr, Mughul emperor, 178, 182, 187f., 189, 190, 191, 204, [205], 206
Āzād, Abū-l-Kalām, 210, 212

azalī, 23
Azhar, *al-Jāmiʿal-*, 51, 74, 78

Bābur, Mughul emperor, 188
Baghdādī, Abū Manṣūr ʿAbd al-Qāhir al-, 90, 95, 96, 156
Bālākoṭ, battle of, 209, 210
Bāqī Bi-llāh, Khwājah, 177, 178, 182, 183, 185–187, 189, 190, 192
Bāqillānī, Abū Bakr Muḥammad ibn al-Ṭayyib, 90, 96, 171, 172
Barelawī, Sayyid Aḥmad, 208f.
bāṭil, 145, 276
Beethoven, Ludwig von, 8
belieben, 270
belief, believe, as concepts, *passim*; esp. chapp. 6, 15 (110–134, 265–281). Distinction between 'believing in' and 'believing that', 275
Bell, Richard, 291
Bergsträsser, Gotthelf, 241
Berkes, Niyazi, 163
bhakta, 179
Bhakti movement, 184f., 192, 196, 204, 223
Bible, 121, [139], 237–239, (quoted, 240), 243, 253, 255f., 265, 268, 270, (quoted, 273), 274
Billy the Kid, 24
Blachère, Régis, 291
Bouquet, Alan Coates, 195
Brockelmann, Carl, 47f., 49, 50, 54, 64–76
Byzantium, Byzantine empire, 19, 56

calligraphy, Arabic, 22, 29, 30, 31. Cf. art, Islamic
Calvin, John, 130
caste, caste system, 197, 204, 224
commands (of God), 46, 80, 81, 237. Cf. *amr*, *ḥukm*, etc.; cf. *also* will of God
Communion Service, Eucharist, 244f.
Cragg, Kenneth, 296
credo, 32, 140, 268f. "Creed" of Muslims, see *shahādah*
Crusades, 255, 286
crystallization of religious movements, chap. 9 (177–196), and 203, 206, 223. *See also* reification; systematization

dār al-ḥarb, 207f.
dār al-islām, 208
dār al-ʿulūm, see Dāru-l-ʿUlūm
Dārā Shikoh, 183, 188, 189, 190, 191, 204
dars-i-Niẓāmī, 189, 207
Dāru-l-ʿUlūm, Deoband, 211[f.]
Dāsguptā, Surendranāth, 195
de Boer, T. J., 61
Deoband, 211, 212
Devil, 131, 249, 271–273
δοξα, 130
dualism, 249, 256
Dūdū Miyāṉ, Muḥsin al-Dīn Aḥmad, 209
dunyā, 23

East India Company, 206
Elder, Earl Edgar, 99, [135]
'επιστημη, 130
Eucharist, *see* Communion service

faith, *passim*; esp. chapp. 6, 7, 8 (110–173) and 15 (265–281). See also *īmān*
falsafah, 61, 63, 74, 76, 138, [139]
Farā'iẕīyah movement, 209
farḍ, *farā'iḍ*, 53, 64, 69, 157, 159, 168
Farangī Maḥall, 189, 207, 211
Farīd, Shaykh Ibrāhīm, 182, 188, 192
Farīd, Shaykh, Mīr Murtaẕá Khāṉ, 186f., 191
Farīdu-d-Dīn Ganj-i-Shakar, 182, 191
Fatāwá-i ʿĀlamgīrī, 190, 205
Fatḥpur Sīkrī, 204
fatwá, 207, 209. Cf. *fatāwá*
"Fayẕī": Abū al-Fayḍ ibn Shaykh Mubārak al-Mahdawī, 187
Fayẕī, Āṣaf ʿAlī Aṣghar, 93
Fazlu-r-Raḥmān, [298]
fides, 273f. *See also* faith
fiqh, chap. 4 (78–86), and 18, 88, 153, 172, 267. See also *sharīʿah*, etc.
Friedmann, Yohanan, 177
Frye, Northrop, 7f.

Gardet, Louis, 165, 167
Genet, Jean, 24
ghalaṭ, 146
Ghaznah, Maḥmūd of, 203
Ghazzālī, Abū Ḥāmid Muḥammad al-, 51, 52, 54, 56, 57, 64, 70, 90, 94, 96, 157, 170f.
Ghulām Aḥmad, Qādiyānī, 243
Gibb, Sir Hamilton A. R., 87, 88, 103, 296
Gibbon, Edward, 249
giravīdan, 123, 157
γνωσις, 130
Gobind Singh, Guru, 178, 179f., 181, 188, 191, 224
Granth Ṣāḥib, [179], 182
Guillaume, Alfred, 100, 103, 104, 106, 107
Guru Arjun, Guru Nānak, etc.; *see under* Arjun, Nānak, etc.

ḥadd, 65, 158
hādī, 242
ḥadīth, 52, 66, 83, 91, 141, 168, 172, 190, 205, 239
ḥāfiẓ, *ḥifẓ*, 244f.
Ḥafīẓ Aḥmad Khāṇ, Ustādh, 229
ḥākim, 80, 81. Cf. *ḥukm*
Handel, George Frederick, 298
ḥaqq, 74, 101, 126, 130, 131, 140, 142f., 278, 280f., *ḥuqūq*, 61, 67, 68, 71, 74. *ḥaqīqah*, *ḥaqā'iq*, 66, 68, 69, 74, 101. *ḥaqqaqa*, 150. *taḥqīq*, 73, 75, 156. *taḥaqqaqa*, 108
Ḥaramayn, al-, 241. Imām al-Ḥaramayn, *see* Juwaynī
ḥarb, 60, 66, 72, 207, 208
Heaven & Hell, 22f., 25, 116, 163, 249, 252
Hegel, Georg Wilhelm Friedrich, 252
ḥifẓ, ḥāfiẓ, 244f.
Himalaya mountains, 30
Hindūs, *passim*, esp. Part III (175–230)
ḥisbah, 55, 60f., 66
Hitti, Philip, 234
Hobbes, Thomas, 275
Hodgson, G. D. Marshall, 14, 222
Holkar, Jaswant Rā'o, 209
hudá, 242
ḥukm, *aḥkām*, 53, 64, 66, 68, 73, 74, 80, 81, 83, 91, 99, 101, 106, 107, 108, 157, 159. Cf. al-Ḥākim, 80, 81. See also *amr*, commands, etc.
Hūlāgū, Mongol ruler, 13
Humāyūṇ, Mughul emperor, 188
Hume, David, 275

Ibn ʿAbd al-Wahhāb, Muḥammad, [53]-54, 69, 70
Ibn al-ʿArabī, Muḥyī al-Dīn, 51, 52, 66, 190
Ibn Bābawayh al-Qummī, 90, 93, 96
Ibn Baṭṭah al-ʿUkbarī, 90, 93, 96
Ibn Ḥajar al-Haythamī, 167
Ibn al-Ḥanzalah ibn Abī Salīm al-Wadāʿī, 91, 96
Ibn Mājah, Abū ʿAbd Allah Muḥammad ibn Yazīd, 172
Ibn Rushd, *see* Averroes
Ibn Sīnā, *see* Avicenna
Ibn Taymīyah, 51, 54, 55, 56, 60, 61, 66, 67
Ibrāhīm the prophet, 108. *See also* Abraham
Ibrāhīm, ʿAdil Shāh, 191
Ibrāhīm Farīd, Shaykh, 182, 188, 192
iconoclasm, 203, 227
ijmāʿ, 79, 242
ijtihād, chap. 4 (78–86), 87
Īl-Khānī dynasty, 57
ʿilm, 70, 72, 80, 101, 130, 241. See also *ʿalima*, *ʿulamā'*.
Imām al-Ḥaramayn, *see* Juwaynī, al-
īmān, chapp. 6, 7, 8 (110–173), and 43, 47, 50, 52, 53, 54, 55, 66, 67, 68, 69, 70, 265, 269, 275. See also *mu'min*. *al-īmān al-ijmālī*, *al-īmān al-tafṣīlī*, 161
Imdādullāh, Ḥajjī, 210
Injīl, 239
Inquisition, the Spanish, 255
in shā'a Allāh (istithnā'), 280f.
International Congress of Orientalists, 87
Iqbāl, Sir Muḥammad, 111, 112f., 265, 280

iqrār, 137, 164, 167, [171]
irādah, 238. Cf. *mashī'ah*, *riḍā*, etc.
ʿIṣām al-Dīn, *see* Isfarā'īnī
Isfarā'īnī, Ibrāhīm ibn Muḥammad ibn ʿArabshāh ʿIsām al-Dīn, 91, [96]
Isḥāq, Mawlānā Muḥammad, 210
islām as a term, chap. 3 (41–77), 238. Cf. *muslim*
Ismāʿīl Shahīd, Shāh, 209
iʿtiqād, 51, 65, 68, 90. *iʿtaqada*, 121. Cf. *ʿaqīdah*, s.v. *ʿaqada*
Izutsu, Toshihiko, 165

jaḥada, 123
Jahāngīr, Mughul emperor, 187, 191
Jalālu-d-Dīn Rūmī, 280
James, St. (quoted), 33
Jan Sangh, 224
janān, 137, 170f.
Jaswant Rā'o Holkar, 209
jawāriḥ, 165–173
jazm, 158
Jeffery, Arthur, 165, 291
jihād, 208, 209, 210. Cf. *mujāhidīn*
Jinnāḥ, Muḥammad ʿAlī, 203
John of Damascus, St., 248
Juwaynī, Imām al-Ḥaramayn, al-, 90, 95, 96, 97

kadhiba, *kādhib*, 131, 144, 145, 146, 147
kafara, *kāfir*, *kufr*, 94, 122, 126, 131, 154, 155, 161
kalām, 52, 70, chap. 5 (88–109), 116, 121, chapp. 7, 8 (135–173), 241, 267, 280. *See also* theology
Karāmat ʿAlī Jānpurī, 210
Kastalī, Muṣliḥ al-Dīn Muṣṭafá al-, 155, 158
khalīfah, *khulafā'*, 57, 74. Cf. *khilāfat*, 209
Khān-i Aʿẓam, Mīrzā ʿAzīz Kokā, 186
Khārijī movement, 153, 164, 167
khaṭa', 145. Cf. *akhṭa'a*, 83
Khayālī, Aḥmad ibn Mūsá, al-, 91, [96]
khilāfat, 209. Cf. *khalīfah*
Khusraw Khān Sulṭān, 187, 191
Kingdom of God, 18
kufr, see *kafara*
Kufrī (*takhallus*), 187
Kutub al-sittah, al-, 239

lā ikrāha fī al-dīn, 84f.
Lao Tzu, 181
Laoust, Henri, 165
law, Islamic law, moral law, *see sharīʿah*
Lepanto, battle of, 286
libet, *libido*, 270
lieben, *die Liebe*, 270
Locke, John, 275
λογος, λογικος, 102

Macbeth, 7f.
madrasah, 201, 207, 210. Cf. also De'oband, Farangī Maḥall, etc.
muḥbūb, 270
Mahdī, Muḥsin, 136
Maḥmūd of Ghaznah, 203
Majūs, 94
Mānī, as founder of religion, 179
marḍī, 84, 237. Cf. *riḍā*. *See also* will of God
Marhaṭṭah, 206, 207, 209
maʿrifah, 153, 172. Cf. *ʿarafa*
Martel, Charles, 286
Marxist, 23
maṣdar, verbal noun, 43, 47, [51], 79, 87f., 98, 99, 102, 107, 108, 122, 124, 139, 238
mashī'ah, 19, 238. *See also* will of God
mashrūʿ, 107, 108. Cf. *sharaʿa*
Maʿṣūm, Khwājah Muḥammad, 189
McCarthy, Richard J., 92
mediator, between God and man, 240
Micah the prophet, 36
Middle East Studies Association of North America, 3
Mill, John Stuart, 275
Minorsky, Vladimir, 177
missions, missionary movements, 19, 31, 195, 294, 296, 299
Moses, Mūsá, 93, 108
mosque, 4, 16, 27f., 29, 241, 242
mu'adhdhin, 31. Cf. *adhān*
muʿāfī, 206. Cf. feudal financial patters, 211

Muʿallaqāt, al-, 245
mubīn, 123, 152, 153
muezzin, *see mu'adhdhin*
Mughul, 15, chap. 9 (177–196), 203–207, 210, 223
Muḥammad the Prophet, *passim*. Cf. prophethood of Muḥammad
Muḥammad ʿAbduh, 61, 72, 73
Muḥammad ʿĀdil Shāh, 191
Muḥibbullāh Jawnpurī, 183
mujaddid, 61, 76. Mujaddid Alf-i Thānī, 177, 188; cf. Sirhindī
Mujāhidīn, Mujāhidīyah, 208, 210. Cf. *jihād*
mujtahid, 80, 81, 82, 84. Cf. *ijtihād*
mu'min, 47, 123, 126, 155, 164, 280f. God as *mu'min*, 156. See also *īmān*
munāfiq, 154
Murtaẓá Khān, *see* Farīd, Shaykh
Mūsá, Moses, 93, 108
mushāʿirah, 228f.
mushrik, 65, 124–126. Cf. *shirk*
muslim as a term, 47, 238, 262f.
mutakallimūn, chap. 5 (88–109), 123, 154. See also *kalām*
Muʿtazilah, 80, 90, 99, 167, 168
Mutiny, the Indian, 1857, 210, [211]
mystics, *see* Ṣūfī

Naqshbandī, 177, 186, 204, 206, 210
Nānak, Guru, 179f., 181, 182, 188, 192
Nasafī, Najm al-Dīn ʿUmar al-, 90, [91], 94, 96, [135], 157, 159
naskh, 94, 108
nawāfil, 168
Newman, John Henry, 275
niẓām, 222. Cf. crystallization, reification, systematization
Noah, 93, 108
'No Parking' sign, 127f.
νους, 98
nubūwah, 52, 70. Cf. prophethood of Muḥammad; also *risālah*, s.v. *rasūl*

Ottoman empire, 15, 202, 211

Panikkar, K. M., 196
Pārsī, *see* Zarathushtrian
Partition of India, 1947, 178, [198], 217, 224, 229
Paul, St., 37, 239, 240, 254
Peter, St., 37, 239
phenomenology, 233
Philips, C. H., 197
Plato, Platonic, 43, 78
Poitiers, battle of, 286
Prārthana Samāj, 195
prophethood of Muḥammad, 28, 32, 33, 35–37, 92, 94, 147, 155, 215, 243, 248, 269, 287f. Cf. *nubūwah*

Qadarī, school of thought, 155
Qādiyān, Qādiyānī movement, 243
Qanawātī, G.-C. (or M.-M.), 165
Qilich Khān, 186
qiyās, 79
Quṭb Minār, 184

Rām Dās, Sikh Guru, 180
Rām Dās, Marhaṭṭah poet, 188
Rāmakrishna movement, 195
Rānā Sāngā of Mewār, 193
Rashtriya Sevak Sangh, 224
rasūl, *risālah*, 94, 239, 269. Cf. prophethood of Muḥammad
reification of religion, systematization, 27, 45, 97, 101, 179, 193. Cf. crystallization; *niẓām*
revelation, *passim*; esp., chap. 16 (282–301). See also *tanzīl*, *waḥy*, Handel
riḍā, *riḍwān*, 19, 237. Cf. *marḍī*. *See also* will of God
r-k-n-, 165. Cf. *arkān*
Ross, Sir W. David, 102
rūḥ, 70, 242
rukn, 165. Cf. *arkān*
Rūmī, Jalālu-d-Dīn, 280

Sabbath, Jewish, 11f., 23
ṣadaqa, *ṣidq* [131], 142, 143f., 146–148, 156. *ṣaddaqa*, see *taṣdīq*
Ṣadāqat Ḥusayn, 229
ṣaddaqa, 140, 142. Cf. *taṣdīq*

Ṣafawī dynasty, 15, 54, 57
ṣaḥḥa, *ṣaḥīḥ*, 63, 75, 142, 144f.
Ṣaḥīḥān, al-, 239
Salīm, Mughul prince, Jahāngīr, 187, 191
Saljuq, 56, 201
salvation by faith, 240
Sambhājī, Marhaṭṭah prince, 195
Sarma, D. S., 194
Sanjar, Sulṭān, 57
Satīsh Chandar, 188
satyam, 142f.
Schacht, Joseph, 89
science, 9, 20f., [72]
scholasticism, 255
secularism, secularist, secularization, 15, 23, 24, 57, 63, 111, 138, [140], 214f., 219, 220, 221, 223, 227, 228, 252f., 260
Seljüq, *see* Saljuq
Shāfiʿī, Muḥammad ibn Idrīs al-, 13
shahādah, chap. 2 (26–37), and 90, 94, 126, 164, 167, 168, 171, 249, 269
Shāh Jahān, Mughul emperor, 189
Shahrastānī, Abū al-Fatḥ Muḥammad ibn ʿAbd al-Karīm, 90, 95, 96, 98, 100–108
Shakespeare, William, 8, 276
sharʿ, *sharaʿa*, 52, 66, 85, chap. 5 (87–109)
sharāʾiʿ, 52, 53, 64, 66, 68, 70, 71, 72, 73, 93, 108
sharīʿah, Islamic law, moral law, 5, 16, 29, 36, 37, 65, 73, chapp. 4–5 (78–109), [153], 183, 204, 211, 223, 224, 237, 240, 261, 267. Cf. *tashrīʿ*, 74
Sharīʿatullāh, Mawlānā Ḥajjī, 207, 209
Shīʿah, Shīʿī, 139, 201
shirk, 29, 124. Cf. *mushrik*
Shivajī, Marhaṭṭah leader, 188, 195
ṣidq, 140, 144, 145, 146, 147f., 150, 156, 159. Cf. *ṣadaqa*, *taṣdīq*
Sikhs, chap. 9 (177–196), 224
silsilah, 203. Cf. Ṣūfī
Sindhiyā of Gwalior, 209
Sirhindī, Shaykh Aḥmad, chap. 9 (177–196), 204–206, 224
Siyālkūtī, al-, 91, [96]
Slater, Robert Henry Lawson, 247, 248
sochnā, 269, 275
Ṣūfī, 13, 16, 18, 22, 30, 34, [35], 55, 139, [151], 152, 182, 183, 184f., 189, 190, 192, 203, 204, 205, 206, 207, 227, 242, 262, 280. See also *taṣawwuf*
Süleyman the Magnificent, 54, 202
sunnah, *sunnī*, passim. *al-sunnah al-nabawīyah*, *sunnat al-nabī*, 13, 239
symbol (as a concept), 227
system, systematization (of religion), 45. See also *niẓām*

Ṭabarī, Muḥammad ibn Jarīr al-, 20, 53, 64, 156
tafsīr, 18, 47, 187, 215
Taftāzānī, Saʿd al-Dīn Masʿūd ibn ʿUmar al-, 91, 96, 99, 123, 135f., 155, 157, 160, 162
taḥqīq, see *ḥaqq*
Tāj Maḥall, 185
taklīf, 91, 99, 101
Tan Sen, Mughul musician, 185
tanzīl, [244], 296, [298]. Cf. revelation
ṭarīqah, 203, 242. Cf. Ṣūfī
taṣawwuf, 184f., 223. Cf. Ṣūfī
taṣdīq, chap. 7 (135–161), and 116, 163–168, 276
tashrīʿ, 74. Cf. *sharīʿah* etc.
taslīm, *taslīm kardan*, 43, 51, 60
tataghayyaru al-aḥkām . . . , 81
tawḥīd, 5, 227. Cf. oneness of God, 33–35 *et passim*
Tegh Bahādūr, Guru, 191
Tennyson, Alfred Lord, 270
theology, theologians, Islamic theology, 22, 29, 42, 87, 110, 114, 119, 135f., 152, 153, 156, 160, 183, 187, 214, 215, 237, 240f., 242, 256–259, 263, 265, 289–299. See also *kalām*
Thirty Years' War, Wars of Religion, 219, 261
Tīpū Sulṭān, 206
Trent, Council of, 252
Tulsī Dās, 188
Ṭūsī, Abū Jaʿfar Muḥammad ibn al-Ḥasan al-, 168

ʿulamāʾ, *ʿālim*, 80, 83, 84, chap. 10 (197–212), 213, 215. See also *ʿalima*
Umawī, Banū Umayyah, 13
ummah, community, *passim*
University of the Panjab (*since the 1960's*, '. . . Punjab'), 78, 111, 112, 265
uṣūl, *uṣūl al-fiqh*, 52, 69, 70, chap. 4 (78–86)

verbal noun, *see maṣdar*
verus, *veritus*, 142f.
von Kremer, Alfred, 291

waḍat al-shuhūd, . . . *al-wujūd*, 190
Wahhābī movement, 53, 208. Cf. Ibn ʿAbd al-Wahhāb
waḥy, 296. Cf. revelation
wajaba, *wājib*, 72, 91, 101, 103, 104
Walīyullāh, Shāh, 187, 206, 207, 210, 211
Wensinck, Arent Jan, 89, 165
will of God, 18, 19, 34, 80, 153, 237f., 263, 273. Cf. *irādah*, *riḍā*, *mashīʾah*, etc.; also *amr*, *ḥukm*, etc., *and* commands
Wolfson, Harry Austryn, 136, 137f., 141, 150
world history of religion, 20, 27, 178, 193, 220, 247, 248, 250, 254, 255, 269
World of Islam Festival, London, 1976, 8
Wycliffe, John, 273

Young Men's Christian Association, 242

ẓanna, *ẓann* 122, 128–131, 269
Zarathushtra, Zarathushtrian, 94, 249f., 254, 262
zāwiyah, 242